OFFICE MANAGEMENT AND SECRETARIAL PRACTICE

OFFICE MANAGEMENT
AND
SECRETARIAL PRACTICE

By

Dr. Y. P. Singh
B. Singh
G. S. Gandhi

GYAN

Office Management and Secretarial Practice

ISBN : 978-81-212-0112-4

First Published 1987, reprint 2013 in India by
Gyan Publishing House
23, Main Ansari Road, Daryaganj,
New Delhi - 110002
Phones : 23282060, 23261060
Fax : (011) 23285914
E-mail: books@gyanbooks.com
website: gyanbooks.com

Printed at : Sagar Color Scan, New Delhi.

PREFACE

No Business Organisation worth the name can run without an efficient 'office.' Similarly, no Company can fulfil the legal obligations without an efficient 'Company Secretary.' And, no Boss can shoulder the responsibilities of Office without an efficient loyal right-hand, the 'Private Secretary'. All these have the tremendous importance in the modern world of Commerce.

For quite some time, it was greatly felt that there should be the availability of one Book, in condensed form, to cater to the requirements of B. Com. students and those who have taken up vocational courses. Though a number of books may be available on the subjects like Office Management and/or Company Secretarial Practice, yet the dearth of one book covering all the above subjects in one was certainly felt in the field of vocational studies, Many students take up Secretarial Course along with B. Com. and they have to face a lot of problems in getting suitable books. In light of this, the present book has been written.

The Book is divided into two parts—Office Management and Secretarial Practice. The portion of Secretarial Practice covers the Company Secretarial Practice as well as Private Secretarial Practice. The most simple and easily understandable language has been used so as to give a quick grasp to the average student. At the end of each Chapter, the exercise questions have been given, most of them from the past examination/s of the University as well as the Board of Technical Education. Thus, an attempt has been made to make the Book compact and more useful for the students.

We are quite sure that the readers would like the Book and,

continue to send us their valuable suggestions for its further improvement.

We thank all our friends including Mr. B.R. Jain, a leading pactising as Chartered Accountant, and Ms. Sangeeta Mahendru, B. Com., for giving us valuable suggestions and assistance in completing the job.

Delhi
1st Sep. 1987

—AUTHORS

CONTENTS

Part-I : Office Management

Part-II : Secretarial Practice

PART I

OFFICE MANAGEMENT

1

THE MODERN OFFICE AND ITS DEPARTMENTS

Meaning

When you ask someone 'Where are you going to' and he/she replies, "I am going to Office", the idea comes to your mind that an 'office' must be some room or part of a building where some persons would be sitting on chairs, with heaps of papers, files or folders on their tables and they must be dealing with papers or doing the clerical work like writing or typing etc. With this image about an office, to a layman, the office is a place where the clerical or paper work is performed.

The dictionary meaning of the term 'Office' is as under :

"An Office is a place where business is transacted or professional services are available."

Hence, we may say that an *Office is a place* where the clerks or *babus* work or where the clerical or paper work is done.

Old Concept

The above definition of 'office' is what we call as old or Traditional Concept of Office because from the time immemorial the office has been called as *the place or a room or a part of building where the paper or clerical work is performed.*

Modern Concept

However, in the present day world, the meaning of an office

has changed considerably. Because of the complexities and diversification of business activities, the scope of office has also widened and now-a-days we do not confine the office work or clerical work or paper work to a particular room or part of a building, rather we perform the office work anywhere and it is performed by anyone anytime. A business executive does the clerical or paper work himself by sitting in his hotel room while on business tour. A salesman is doing the paper or clerical work by standing on the roadside when he is taking an order from a shopkeeper. Similarly, a foreman may perform clerical or paper work in the factory when he writes on a slip of paper about his requirements of men and material etc. Hence, we should not limit our definition of office to a particular place or room but we should say that *office is a function* and not a place. Whoso ever does it or wherever it is done, we are not concerned with but if it is a paper work or clerical work, we say that it is an office work. Edward Rouche has rightly said—

"It is mistake to regard an office as a specific place instead we are forced to conclude that an office exists any where, that certain kinds of work are performed."

In view of the foregoing facts, we may say that 'OFFICE IS WHAT AN OFFICE DOES'. The meaning of it is that an OFFICE is known by its functions. However, an ideal definition of 'OFFICE' may be given as under :

"OFFICE is the organ or an integral part of a business organisation where the information is received or collected analysed or processed, recorded and communicated to all concerned."

Objectives or purposes

Now-a-days almost all Business Organisations have got an office. There is Income-tax Office, Sales-tax Office, Charatered Accountant's Office, Advocate's Office, Export House Office and also the offices of traders, manufacturing organisations and so on. What for and why ? The simple answer to this question is that every organisation is having an office for the purpose of doing some office work or paper work or clerical work and for doing allied works. As such, the following may be the various objectives or purposes of an office :

1. To give and to take any information useful in business. An office is called the 'information centre' from where all sorts of informations can be taken or given.

2. To preserve all sorts of information and records. Since 'records' refer to all sorts of papers or letters or documents required for reference any time in future, these are retained with the organisation for some time and it is the office which keeps them safe and in proper order by way of filing and indexing.
3. To direct and co-ordinate the activities of various departments or sections of a business organisation.
4. To plan the policies of business and ensure their implementation.
5. To maintain accounts and prepare other financial data useful for the organisation.
6. To give assistance to management in carrying out the policies or details of work in order to fulfil the organisational objectives.

From the above points, it may be observed that an office is the important organ of a business organisation where all sorts of information is received or collected, analysed, processed and communicated to all concerned for achieving the goals of the organisation. That is why, an office is called the 'information centre', a 'memory centre' or 'the hub of all business activities'. It is like the mainspring in a watch. Just as a watch cannot run without the mainspring, similarly no business can run without an efficient office. Hence, the importance of office is increasing day by day and it is now felt the efficiency of an organisation depends upon its efficient office.

Functions of an Office

We know that an office performs certain paper or clerical work. If we go into detail, we shall come to know that an office performs so many things. The entire functions of an office may *be broadly classified under two heads* :

(i) Basic or Primary Functions.
(ii) Secondary or Subsidiary Functions.

The Primary or Basic Functions of an office are those works which are primarily to be done by an office and without them there is no existence of office, whereas the secondary or subsidiary functions are those which are of assisting nature. The secondary functions of an office are also called '*Office services*'.

FUNCTIONS OF AN OFFICE

PRIMARY OR BASIC

1. Receiving or collecting information.
2. Recording information.
3. Analysing/Processing information.
4. Communication of information.
5. Protection of Business Assets.

SECONDARY OR SUBSIDIARY

1. Handling the mail—inward and outward.
2. Typing & duplicating.
3. Filing & Indexing.
4. Accounts and finance.
5. Handling telephone, telex etc.
6. Stationery & supplies.
7. Developing Procedures & Methods.
8. Public Relations.
9. Other routine administrative matters like— Selection, training, placement and remuneration of personnel ; providing best possible working environment ; planning, organising and controlling work etc.

(Chart showing various functions of an office)

The above functions of an office may be explained in the following paragraphs:

Primary or Basic Functions

1. **Receiving or collecting information** : The 'information' may be anything or a piece of advice or news that may be utilised anytime by anyone. It may be in regard to price of goods, terms of payment, terms of delivery, accounts balances etc. Whatever information is desired, the same is collected or received by the office. The office is called an 'information centre'.

2. **Recording information** :—Whatever information is received or collected at the office, the same is retained or preserved for utilizing it any time in future. An office does this work by arranging all letters, documents or papers in some order and keeps them in files or folders. For early location of any paper or document out of the bulk, an index is prepared by the office so that any paper required anytime may be easily available to anyone.

3. **Analysing or processing information** : Whatever information is available at the office, the same is like a raw-material or it is in the crude form. Out of that, whatever is relevant or useful at a particular time, the same is taken out to serve the purpose. This we call as analysing or processing of information for the work performed by the office.

4. **Communication of information** : By communication, we mean the passing on of informations or ideas or opinions from one person to another. The office performs this function by way of writing letters, using telephone, telex or using any other media of communication.

5. **Protection of Busniess Assets** : Business assets are certain things which are owned by a business in the form of men, materials, machinery, money and methods (popularly called five Ms). It is the basic function of an office to keep proper records of all these business assets and to ensure their proper upkeeping and maintenance. so that all these are ready to serve the purpose of business.

Secondary or Subsidiary Functions

1. **Handling the Mail** : It is the office where all information is received through letters. The term 'Mail' is used to denote the letters which are received by an Organisation and the copies of letters which are sent out, which we may call as "inward mail' and 'outward mail'. The office handles both of them. If any letter is received, the same is acknowledged, opened, scrutinized and action is taken upon by office. If a letter is sent out, the office drafts it, types it, prepares the envelope and posts it.

2. **Typing and duplicating** : Typing is the process of reproducing the written matter in a legible and attractive manner. Duplicating is the process of taking multiple copies of a single letter or document. Both these activities are performed by the the office.

3. **Filing and Indexing** : 'Filing' is the system of record-keeping and 'Indexing' is anything that indicates or points out. Both of them are used by an office for preserving the records of papers or documents etc. so that any paper required at a particular time may be easily located without wasting much of time.

4. **Accounts and Finance** : A systematic recording of business transactions is what we call as accounts keeping or accounting. Finance involves both cash and bank transactions. The office has to prepare and maintain all the books of accounts like cash book, ledgers etc. and also to keep records and keeping a control over the banking transactions.

5. **Handling Telephone, Telex etc.** These are the means or media of communication of information. Telephone is used for verbal communication and the telex is meant for written messages. Both these machines are handled by the office for receiving and giving information.

6. **Stationery and Supplies** 'Stationery' consists of all articles like pen, pencil, pins, clips, papers, carbons, envelopes and printed forms etc. which are used for assisting the paper or office work. The office has to arrange to purchase them, store them and distribute them to workers in the Organisation.

7. **Procedures and Methods** : 'Procedure' consists of various series of steps taken to complete a particular work, whereas a 'Method' denotes the way or manner in which the work is performed. The office develops them and ensures proper follow-up of all procedures and methods which are framed by the organisation.

8. **Public Relations** : It is the work of keeping liaison or close contact with others especially the outside agencies or bodies. The office does this work through correspondence or telephone, telex etc.

9. **Other Routine Administrative Matters** : The office performs and undertakes all the routine administrative matters like selecting the persons, giving them proper training and placing them at proper posts and also preparing and distributing their salaries and maintaining the entire records about their leave, medical aid and other benefits etc. The office makes all arrangements for providing best possible working environment in the Organisation by proper lighting, maintenance and cleanliness of premises, interior decoration, providing proper furniture and taking all security measures etc. The office helps the management in carrying out their functions of

planning, organising, directing and controlling the activities of the organisation.

From the above, it is clear that an office performs the multifarious functions for a Business Organisation and, that is why, we say that an office is the organ or an integral part of a business organisation.

IMPORTANCE OF OFFICE

We have already discussed that an office is an important organ of a Business Organisation. However, the importance of an office may be adjudged from the following :

"No business worth the name can exist without an efficient office."

According to *Prof. Dicksee*—

"The office is to a business what the mainspring is to a watch."

Just as a watch cannot run without the mainspring of its wheel, similarly, no business can run without the office. The office has also been compared with the "Brain in a Human Body." Just as the brain in a human body is like a store house of all informations of whatever we observe or hear, similarly the office is a 'Memory Centre' of all business information. Someone has also said that "Office is the hub of all business activities" or "the nerve centre of all business activities" which means that the office is like the main pivotal point around which the wheel rotates. Just as a wheel cannot rotate without a hub, similarly no business activity can be carried on without the office. Such is the importance of an office.

Looking at the various functions performed by an office, we can adjudge its importance from two angles as given below :

OFFICE

Clearing House of business information.	Warehouse of business assets. (5Ms)
1. Receiving or collecting information.	1. Men.
2. Recording information.	2. Materials.

3. Analysing/processing information.	3. Machinery.
4. Communicating information.	4. Money.
	5. Methods.

From the above chart, it may be observed that an office is like a Clearing House. The 'Clearing House' is a banking term and it denotes a place where the representatives of various banks get together at some common place and exchange the cheques drawn on each other and settle the accounts by making book entries. Like a 'Clearing House', the office is also the place where the information is exchanged. The warehouse is a place where the goods are stored and kept safe for sometime. Similarly, the office also keeps safe the assets of a business by keeping a proper record of them as well as by up-keeping or maintaining them.

Due to such great importance of an office to the business, the office is called an 'information centre', a 'service centre' an 'administrative or control centre', a 'co-ordinator' and an 'intermediary.' If we say that an office is the centre of all business activities, we shall not be at fault.

Principal Departments of a Modern Office

In a bigger Organisation, the office work may be divided into various departments or sections so that the work may by performed easily and efficiently. Each Department or Section performs specialised work. The following list shows the names of principal departments of a modern office :

1. Correspondence Section.
2. Typing & Duplicating Section.
3. Mailing Section.
4. Filing Section.
5. General Office.

Now, we shall discuss about the respective sections in the following paragraphs.

Correspondence Section : Correspondence is one of the means of written communication in an Organisation. This section deals with writing and drafting of letters which may be sent to outsiders or to persons within the Organisation.

There may be two systems of dealing with the correspondence ;

(*i*) Centralised Correspondence ; &
(*ii*) Decentralised or Departmental Correspondence.

Centralised Correspondence : When all the correspondence relating to the various functional departments of an Organisation is handled at one place or in one section, we call it centralised correspondence system. In such a system, 'the persons specialised in drafting and writing letters perform the duties of making correspondence on behalf of all the departments of a business organisation. No other department is generally authorised to write letters under such a system. There are certain ***advantages*** of such a system : (i) The drafting of letters is done by the specialists and, hence, the efficiency is increased : (ii) It is useful to management as the co-ordination between different functional departments can be easily maintained. The management gets uptodate knowledge of all the departments at one place. (iii) The uniformity and standardisation may be easily maintained if the correspondence is centralised because the same style of writing may be adopted and a certain level of standard may be maintained in respeet of the machines, stationery and other equipments. However, there are certain *disadvantages* also. These are : (i) The letters requiring technical details cannot be effectively written as the specialists may not be having complete knowledge about the technical aspects ; (ii) The delays might take place because of the rush of work ; (iii) There may be communication gap with the concerned functional department because they might not be having the records of correspondence made on their behalf. (iv) Secrecy cannot be maintained as information goes in other hands.

Decentralised or Departmental Correspondence : When each functional department of a business organisation e.g. production, purchases, sales etc. write their own letters themselves, we may call it decentralised or departmental system of correspondence. There are some advantages of this system, like (i) The letters requiring technical details may be drafted efficiently : (ii) The work may be done without delay ; and (iii) Secrecy may be maintained because the information remains within the department itself. However, the disadvantages of this system are : (i) The correspondence may not be systematic and efficient and (ii) Uniformity in correspondence cannot be maintained.

However, in a modern Organisation, both the above systems may be adopted simultaneously. The routine correspondence may be handed over to the centralised correspondence section and the specialised letters may be drafted by the concerned department itself.

Typing & Duplicating Section :

We have discussed the details of a typewriter and the typing process in the Chapter 'OFFICE MACHINES AND EQUIPMENTS'. Similarly, we have discussed about the duplicating in the same chapter.

So far as typing is concerned, it is the process of reproducing the written matter in an attractive fashion. Also, it is one ot the important services rendered by an office. For efficient working, the typing work may be performed according to the following two systems :

(*i*) Centralised Typing or Typing Pool ;
(*ii*) Decentralised or Departmental Typing.

Centralised Typing Pool : When the entire typing work of an Organisation is performed at one place called the 'Typing Pool', we may call it centralised system of typing. The 'Typing Pool' is a separate room where a few typists are seated and entrusted with the entire work of typing of all the functional departments of the Organisation. There are certain *advantages* of the Typing Pool : (i) The efficiency is increased as the typists are always doing the same type of work again and again ; (ii) The work load is distributed amongst a number of typists because, in the typing pool, there may be a number of persons doing the job of typing ; (iii) The supervision and control becomes easy & efficient because the Incharge of this particular department is an expert and he may guide to all the typists very well ; (iv) It helps in reducing the noise in an office because a separate room is provided to all the typists pooled together and the noise of clicking of typewriters does not go outside the room which ultimately does not disturb other employees of office ; & (iv) The work may be easily carried on non-stop despite the absence of one or two typists on a particular day. However, there are *disadvantages* of Centralised Typing or Typing Pool. These may be—(i) The work may be delayed as much time may be wasted in sending the matter to the typing pool and getting back the typed matter ; (ii) The typists do not generally show so much loyalty, attention and concentration because they always feel that it is the work of other department. (iii) The secrecy cannot be maintained as the information passes through many hands ; (iv) There are difficulties in typing the technical details because the typists might not be familiar with all the technical aspects of each and every functional department ; and (v) This system might encourage unhealthy practices amongst the typists. They may become lethargic thinking that there are others also to perform the work.

Departmental Typing : When the typing work pertaining to a particular functional department is performed within the department itself by its own typist on the typewriter of the same department, we may call it departmental typing. With such an arrangement, there may be some *advantages*, such as, (i) The work is performed without delay within the department itself : (ii) The secrecy may be maintained because the papers do not pass through many hands ; (iii) The work may be done with devotion and loyalty due to the sense of belonging inculcated in the typist/s ; (iv) There may not be any difficulty in getting to know about the technical details, if any ; However, the *disadvantages* of this system are : (i) The uniformity of work and standardisation of machines and equipments may not be maintained ; (ii) The workload cannot be shared or distributed because all the work has to be completed within the department itself and there would be no one to help, and (iii) The problem of noise due to the clicking of typewriter may be there and it might disturb the other employees in the department.

However, in a modern office, both the systems may be adopted. For routine typing work, a 'Typing Pool' may be created and for the executives separate typists may be provided to attend to the confidential or urgent works. The problem of noise may also be solved.

So far as *duplicating work* is concerned, it is generally centralised almost in all the offices because the work is such that it can be viably and efficiently performed at a centralised section. The other details about duplicating have been given by us in the Chapter 'Office Machines and Equipments'.

Mailing Section

The details about the 'mail' have already been discussed by us separately, giving the description about the inward and outward mail respectively. However, the main functions of the Mailing Department are to receive, record, sort out and disposing of the inward letters, properly recording and despatching the outgoing letters. All these works may be performed collectively within one department or the respective functional departments may be asked to handle all the works themselves. Or, both the systems may be used in one Organisation, depending upon the requirements of work.

Centralised Mail-handling : When all the incoming and outgoing letters are handled within one department or section on behalf of all the functional departments of a business organisation, we call it 'Centralised Mail-handling'. In this system, all the letters, at first hand, are received at one place. Afterwards, these are opened, sorted out and recorded then and distributed to the respective departments for disposal. Similarly, all the departments prepare their letters and send them to the centralised mail department, where envelopes may be prepared, postage stamps affixed, recording may be done and ultimately all the letters are put into the mail box.

Such a system has got several *advantages* : (i) It saves a lot of labour, cost and time because there is no duplication of work and the necessary stationery required for the purpose may be purchased in wholesale at one place ; (ii) It leads to effective supervision and control of work because all the work is performed under the guidance of an expert ; (iii) It results in uniformity and standardisation of work ; and (iv) The work may be expedited because the required force of persons is readily available to perfom the work. However, the *disadvantages* of this system are : (i) There is unnecessary wastage of time and energies in getting and sending letters to and from the concerned departments ; (ii) The secrecy cannot be maintained as the letters have to pass through many hands.

Departmental Mail-handling : Under this system all the respective departments perform the work of handling mail within the department itself using their own staff and equipments. Such a system is workable only at such places where the number of letters pertaining to a particular department is large. However, this system has got the *advantages* like : (i) No delay in doing the work ; (ii) Maintenance of secrecy ; (iii) No unnecessary duplication of work, etc. But the drawbacks are that uniformity cannot be maintained and separate establishments are required to be maintained for the purpose. At the same time, economics cannot be effected because the stationery etc. required for the purpose is not purchased in wholesale as a lot.

However, in practical life, we find that the bigger Organisations always resort to Centralised Mail-handling because of its varied advantages.

General Office

We know that an Office has to perform a number of functions for a business organisation, like handling mail, typing, duplicating, and accounting etc. Some of these activities are centralised, whereas the others are performed within the respective department. To the former, we call as 'Centralisation of Office Services' and the latter as 'Decentralisation of Office Services'.

The 'General Office' is that unit of a business organisation which performs such works that have not been centralised or decentralised. It is rather the 'Control Centre' of all the activities of an Organisation. That is why, we may call it 'General Administration Office' or G.A.D. (General Administration Department). In Government Offices, the G.A.D. unit takes care of the building, furniture, security and safety arrangements of the whole Organisation. All the general and the miscellaneous works are performed by General Office. Earlier, we have discussed about the specialised departments of office. Whatever the other works are remaining, the same are performed at the General Office. The General Office takes care of all the departments or units of the whole Organisation by having a system of feedback from the other units. The controlling statements are sent by respective units, on the basis of which general administration is carried on.

CENTRALISATION AND DECENTRALISATION OF OFFICE SERVICES

Meaning of Centralisation :

"Centralisation of office services means physical concentration of common office services in one department known as General Office, under the supervision and control of a person known as Office Manager."

From the above definition, we can understand that while the office work or office services are concentrated at one centre, we call it Centralisation of office services. As we know, office work is the paper work or clerical work and the special features of office work are that, it is not the main function of a Business Organisation, but part of the main function and also that it is not homogeneous in nature. If there is a trading concern, its main functions are, buying the goods and selling them at the best available price. If it is a Manufacturing Organisation, its main functions may be purchase, production and sales. Hence, we may say that the 'office work, is not the main function in itself, But to perform and complete the main function, certain paper or clerical work is to be performed like writing a letter, receiving a letter, typing, accounting etc. This part of work is what we call as 'office work.'

A Business Organisation may be divided into various sections or departments, in order to complete the objectives, on the basis of functions, process, customers, geographical location etc. These sections or departments work as independent units and specialise in their own work. Each of such unit has to perform certain paper or clerical or office work in order to complete its work. For example, the purchase department has to make purchase of goods on behalf of the Organisation. For this purpose, letters are written to various manufacturers or dealers and quotations are called for. Orders are placed, payments are made, etc. Like this, every unit or section of a Business Organisation has to perfom certain work which we call office work or paper work. When the office work on behalf of all such units or sections or departments is performed at one place called the 'General Office,' we call it centralisation of office services.

According to *Geoffrey Whitehead*—

"Centralisation is a system where control is exercised from the centre on the activities of all departments and branches. Detailed instructions on methods and procedures to be followed are issued from Head Office and a system of 'reporting back's is instituted to keep Head Office informed of development.

The meaning of the term 'Centralisation of office services' would be more clear from the following chart :—

Business Organisation

Purchases Department	Production Department	Sales Department
Office work	Office work	Office work
	General Office	

Types of Centralisation

There are two types of 'Centralisation of office services' as under :-

(i) Physical Centralisation.
(ii) Functional Centralisation.

In '*Physical Centralisation*' the entire office work, right from receiving a letter, opening, recording, scrutinizing to drafting, typing and despatch of a letter-all activities are undertaken at the General Office. Whatever the paper or clerical work is to be performed, the same is done at the General Office.

The '*Functional*' centralisation of office services is one where only a few *common office services* like typing, mailing, telephone, telex etc, are centralised at one place and rest of the office work is performed at the respective units or sections of the Organisation. In bigger organisations, functional centralisation, is very common and the same is done in order to have specialisation, better efficiency, reduction of noise etc. For example, a Typing Pool is created where all typists and the typewriters are kept in one room so that there is no disturbance to other persons in the organisation. However, for Functional Centralisation of office services, it is necessary that the same functions should be common to all units or sections. For example, inward mail. Since every department or section or unity has to receive letters, the function of inward mail can be easily centralised.

Advantages of Centralisation

When the office work is centralised, the following benefits are derived :—

1. **Economy**—Since the entire work of office is performed at one place, the articles for office use are purchased in bulk or in wholesale, which results in saving office cost. The things may be purchased at a lesser cost.

2. **Specialisation**—The workers in the General Office are continuously doing the same type of work again and again. Hence they get specialisation in work. If, for example, a typist is doing only typing throughout the time, he/she gets specialised knowledge in the typing job. The specialisation results in better quality of work and greater output.

3. **Equal Sharing of Work**—In Centralisation, it is possible to share the burden of office work equally amongst all persons

because, in General Office, there are more persons to perform the office work.

4. **No Duplication of Work** : When the entire work is performed at one place only, there is no chance of doing the same work again. For example, there is a letter pertaining to two sections or departments. In General Office, there will be only one letter of reply for both of them. Otherwise, in decentralisation two letters of reply might be sent one each by respective section.

5. **Standardisation of Methods and Equipment** : By 'standardisation' we mean using the same type of machines or equipment in all sections of units of one organisation. In General Office, it is easy to maintain the standardisation. If, for example, typewriters are to be purchased, all typewriters of 'Remington' may be purchased for the General Office. In decentralisation, each section or unit might purchase a different make of the typewriter.

6. **Better Superivision and Control** : As the Office Manager in the General Office is specialised person and well-expert in office work, he can very well control and supervise the office work performed by other subordinates in the office. The sectional Incharges, in decentralisation, may not be expert in office work. As such, they cannot control and supervise the office work so efficiently.

7. **Greater Flexibility** : In General Office, it happens that in case the work increases little more or decreases little-bit, there is no effect of it because there is a team of office workers in General Office to perform the work. No material change in men, materials, machinery, equipments etc is required. As such, the flexibility is more in centralisation.

8. **Better Flow of Work** : By 'Flow of work, we mean the speed with which the office work pases on from one desk to another, When the work is divided into various series of steps and each series of work is performed by a separate person, then it is necessary that the work should move fast from one person to another so chain of work might be completed without any problem. This that the entire flow of work is much better in centralisation because the office manager divides and distributes the work in such a manner that there is no hindrance and maximum efficiency is attained.

Disadvantages of Centralisation

There are certain drawbacks of centralisation of office services :

1. **Delay in Work** : When the office work is performed at central or general office, there is a movement of work from res-

pective department to General Office and vice-versa which wastes much of the time and, as such, the work is delayed.

2. **Lack of Secrecy** : The work cannot be kept confidential in centralisation as it has to pass on many hands from respective section to General Office and vice-versa. This is the main drawback of centralisation of office services. On the other hand, when the work is performed in respective section or department, secrecy can be maintained.

3. **No Departmental Loyalty** : Since the persons working in General Office feel that the work is of other department, they do not have the sense of belonging. They always feel that it is others' work and the result that they do not take utmost care while performing the work. This may result in many mistake and delays also.

4. **Bureaucracy and Other Malpractices** : The General Office workers always try to dictate their own terms because they know that other departments or sections have to depend upon them for getting the office work done. It might result in Bureaucracy and authoritarianism like malpractices in the Organisation.

However, the above drawbacks of centralisation may be overcome by the decentralisation of office services which has been explained in the following paragraphs.

Decentralisation of Office Services

By Decentralisation to office services, we mean that each section or functional department has its own staff, machines and equipment to perform the office work and the entire office work is performed within each section or department itself.

It is just reverse to centralisation of office services. Under it, each section or department has to perform the entire work itslf and the sectional incharge is entrusted with sufficient authority or power to appoint men and purchase any machine or equipment but it is the responsibility of department Incharge to ensure that all office work is performed well and within the Department itself.

Advantage of Decentraisation

1. **No Delay** : When the office work is performed within the department itself, no dealy takes place. Much time is saved which is otherwise wasted in giving and taking work from the general office.

2. **Secrecy** : The work of confidential nature may be easily

performed without it being known to others because the work secrey remains confined within the four walls of a particular department or section. There are lesser chances of information being leaked out.

3. **More Output** : The output of work is more in decentralisation because there is no wastage of time in passing on work to others and getting it back. Hence, much time may be saved and more work can be performed in the organisation.

4. **Departmental Loyalty** : The worker of particular section or department knows that his/her existence is linked with prosperity of his/her own department. As such, he puts his whole-hearted attention to work and devotes more time in attending to the departmental work.

Disadvantages of Decentralisation :

In a way, whatever are the points of advantages of centralisation, the same may be the points of disadvantages of decentralisation. However, the following points of drawbacks may be noted :

1. There is an *increase in office cost* because the question of bulk purchases of items does not arise in decentralisation. Every section has to purchase separately the things required by it.
2. There is a *difficulty in equally sharing the workload* of office work as the number of persons in respective department is limited.
3. *Specialisation in office work* cannot take place as the person working in respective department has to perform all types of work himself. There is no one to help him. He cannot become master of office work, rather he may be jack of all trades.
4. The *supervision and control of office work becomes difficult* as the sectional incharge is not so expert in office work as Office Manager in Gerneral Office.
5. There is a *lack of flexibility*, as there cannot be anyone to help the worker of each section. Whatever work comes to him, he has only to do that.
6. There is *under-utilisation of machines and equipments* as the scope of work in each section is very limited. The machines and equipments cannot be fully utilised because of lack of work at departmentallevel.

Whether Centralisation or Decentralisation ?

Many times, the question is asked whether we should select, 'Centralisation' or 'Decentralisation' of office services ? We know now that there are certain advantages and disadvantages in both the systems. In smaller organisations, there is no question of 'decentralisation' of office services as there are no sections or departments. However, in a bigger Organisation, either there can be centralisation or decentralisation or both. The relative advantages and disadvantages are compared to decide about it. However, in an ideal organisation, both may be adopted. Certain specialised services may always be centralised, like typing, duplicating and Mailing etc. Rest of the other services may easily be performed in the respective section or department. By doing so, it would solve all the problems or drawbacks of any one system.

Common Office Services which may be Centralised (i.e. Functional Centralisation) The following office services are common to all departments or sections of an Organisation and the same may easily be centralised.

1. Handling Mail.
2. Communication services e.g. telephone, telex, telegram etc.
3. Typing and Duplicating.
4. Filing and Indexing.
5. Stationery and other supplies.
6. Reception.
7. Office Maintenance and Cleanliness.
8. Employment and Training of clerical staff.
9. Routine Correspondence.
10. Attendance, leave, salary etc., of personnel working in the Organisation.

DECENTRALISATION VERSUS DEPARTMENTATION :

Many times the above two terms are confused and these are treated to be one and the same. Actually speaking, the 'Departmentation' is simply the process of dividing and distributing the work in an Organisation. The departmentation may be done on the basis of products, process, functions, type of customers or geographical location etc. However, departmentation is simply a process of dividing the work on any basis. 'Decentralisation' is a bigger term and includes in itself not only the work but is also concerned with the authority and responsibility of doing the work. In decentralisation, the sectional incharge is not only given to perform a particular work but he is also authorised to do anything like appointing requisite staff and purchasing machines or equipments etc. He is responsible for all the work. If anything goes wrong, he is answerable for that. Hence, we may say that 'Decentralisation' includess 'Departmentation'.

There is another basic difference between these two terms. Since 'Decentralisation' is more concerned with the delegation of authority and responsibility, it is said that the Decentralisation and 'Departmentation' go reverse to each other. Where there is more 'decentralisation' the departmentation is less and vice-versa. For example the Managing Director of a Concern has got more authority and responsibility. He can do anything in the interest of the Organisation. He has wide powers or authority, but there is very less of departmentation at his level. He has to look after every thing of the Organisation. As we move to lower hierarchy of Organisation, we find that there are so many departments and the respective departmental incharge has got very less authority, as compared to the Managing Director. So we say that the more the departmentation, the lesser is the authority or, in other words, there is less decentralisation. As such, the two terms go reverse to each other.

Is the Office Work Unproductive ?

Many times, the question is asked whether the office work is productive or may it be treated as unproductive ? As we know, the office work is a paper or clerical work and it is different from producing the actual goods or services. Many people think that since the office is not physically producing anything which may be seen or touched, the office work is unproductive. But it is not correct to say so because the office work is like a raw-material for business and the entire purchases, sales, production etc. are carried on with the assistance of office work. If the office does not furnish information or keeps records, it would be difficult to do any business. Hence, the office work enables any unit to produce goods or services. It would therefore be difficult to call the office work as unproductive. After all, it renders essential services for productive purposes.

QUESTIONS

1. What is an Office ? Explain the functions performed by a modern office.
2. "The office is to a business, what the mainspring is to watch". In light of this statement, explain the importance of office to a modern business organisation.
3. Explain the importance of modern office.

   (*B. Com. Pass, Delhi, 1986*)
4. What are the functions of an 'Office' ? Discuss the importance of office in modern business organisation.

   (*B. Com. Pass, Delhi, 1985*)
5. (a) What is an 'Office' ? Discuss the functions of 'Office' ?

   (b) State the qualities that make a good office manager ?

   (*B. Com. Pass, Delhi, 1984*)
6. What are the advantages and disadvantages of centralisation of office services ? (*B. Com. Pass, Delhi, 1981*)
7. Explain the nature of relationship of office with functional departments like sales, purchase and accounts departments.

   (*B. Com. Pass, Delhi, 1981*)
8. What do you mean by centralisation of office services ?

   What are its advantages? Discuss the services in which centralisation is more desirable ? (*B.T.E., Delhi, 1987*)
9. Describe the main departments of a modern office.

   (*B.T.E. Delhi, 1984*)

2

ORGANISATION AND MANAGEMENT OF OFFICE

Meaning

'Organisation' is the process through which the total work is determined, divided and distributed amongst different people who are entrusted with the authority and responsibility to achieve the goals. It is one of the important functions of management and involves mainly the arrangement of men, material, machinery and equipment and utilising all of them in such a way that the objectives are accomplished. For this purpose, the total activities are determined and the various persons are assigned the jobs on the basis of principles of division of labour and specialisation. For getting the work done, the persons are delegated authority but with responsibility. Authority cannot go without responsibility because the same may otherwise be misused. Nobody is prepared to assume the responsibility unless and until the authority is delegated. Hence, both of them go together.

As we know, the office work is the paper or clerical work and may include handling mail, typing, accounts, filing and indexing etc. All these works may be performed in the office. For this purpose, it is necessary that all the activities of varied nature must be organised in such a way that the office work is accomplished without much of the problems and with efficiency. As such, we may say that the office organisation is the process of determining the activities to be done, grouping and regrouping the entire office activities, allocating the different jobs to different persons and delegating the authority or power to them with responsibility. In organising the office, the organiser shall have to determine the total activities to be performed by the office and then divide or distribute them to different persons e.g., typing work to a typist or typists, accounts work to an accountant or accountants, cash work to a cashier or cashiers and so on. After allocation of duties to different persons, the authority shall have to be delegated appropriately with responsibility and, thus, ensure that the entire office work is performed efficiently-quantitatively and qualitatively.

Steps or Elements

From the idea about 'Organisation' given herein above, we may come to know that in the process of organisation, the following steps are generally taken :

(i) **Determining the Activities** : First of all, the total amount of work, to be performed, is determined in volume and in value and thereafter the same is divided or distributed. Since one man cannot perform all the works alone, it is necessary to find out the total work and then arrange for the number of person(s) so as to cope with the work.

(ii) **Grouping and assigning jobs** : The work is divided into suitable groups depending upon the nature of work. The groups or sections are created e.g. Accounts Section, Typing Section, Filing Section etc. After creating them, the different persons are assigned the jobs to be performed by them on the basis of their qualifications and talent specialisation.

(iii) **Allocation of duties** : The duty sheet of each and every office worker is prepared, giving specifically the nature and volume of work together with the time schedule Each office employee is expected to occomplish the work as per the duty list.

(iv) **Delegating Authority with Responsibility** : 'Authority' implies the power entrusted with a person for the purpose of getting the work done. The term 'Responsibility' assumes the accountability expected of a person for the work to be accomplished. The authority is the maximum at the top level of management and the responsibility is also linked with it. For example, the chairman of a business organisation has got all the powers to spend money or appoint or dismiss any person but, at the same time, he is also answerable to others if something goes wrong in the organisation. In the process of organisation, one of the persons is appointed as the sectional incharge and he or she is delegated the authority also but he or she is answerable if anything goes wrong in his or her section.

Thus, through the process of organisation, it is possible to avoid delay or duplication of work, ensure optimum utilisation of resources and facilitating co-ordination for the purpose of achieving the organisational goals. It can, therefore, be said that organisation is the real task force which makes the performance of work possible.

Principles of Organisation

While organising the office work, the following important guidelines may be observed :

(i) **Unity of Objectives** : Whatever may be the number of sections or departments in an office, the uppermost common objective is to accomplish the paper or clerical work of different nature. All of them should have the same objective and not the different ones. The entire work has to be geared up for achieving the common objective.

(ii) **Efficiency** : This principle states that the work of office should be arranged and carried on in such way that maximum quantity of quality work is performed very smoothly. For attaining efficiency, it is necessary that the right person should be allotted for the right type of job. For example, if someone is a good typist, the typing work should preferly be allotted to him.

(iii) **Division of Work** : Whenever a number of persons have to perform the work, it is necessary that the work should be divided and distributed amongst all of them in such a way that each one of them gets the day's full work. It must not happen that someone is overloaded with the work and the other has no work to perform at all. Hence, equitable distribution of office work must be done.

(iv) **Span of Supervision** : There is a limit to which the supervision may be done easily and effectively. For example, one person may easily supervise 5 or 6 persons working under him, beyond that the supervision may not be effective or result-oriented. While organising the office work, this principle should always be kept in mind.

(v) **Scalar Chain of Authority** : In every enterprise, there is a set structure of position of various authorities like the top-level boss, medium level management and the workers. The authority always runs from the top level to the lower level of management. It is the highest at the top level and goes on reducing as we move down to the lower hierarchy. The line of authority at the various levels should be clear-cut and well-defined so that the work may be carried on smoothly.

(vi) **Parity of Authority with Responsibility** : This principle states that the authority always goes alongwith the responsibility. If only authority is delegated without fixing up the responsibility, it may be misused. On the other hand, if any responsibility is thrust without giving the authority, it will not work as nobody would assume any responsibility without getting sufficient authority.

(vii) **Unity of Command** : This has a meaning that each subordinate should be responsible to his/her immediate boss and that all the bosses or officers incharge should have the same common objective about the enterprise. Each and every person in the enterprise should be responsible to one and one immediate boss only and not to several others, otherwise there will be a chaos and conflict in the organisation.

(viii) **Proper Balance** : There should be a optimal balance in allocation of the work. It should not happen that there are more persons in a section where the work is less and there is no person where the work is much more. In the absence of balance of work, the objectives may not be accomplished.

(ix) **Flexibility** : Flexibility is the power of adjusting to the changed position quickly without making any material change. Similarly, in the office organisation, the structure should be formed in such a way that it may adapt to any change in the volume of work in the office. If the work increases or decreases a little bit, nobody should sit idle or require a material change. If there is a flexibility in the organisation, it may easily adapt itself to the future expansion.

(x) **Continuity of operations** : The organisational structure should be formed in such a way that there is no hindrance to the work and that the work may be continuously performed whether someone comes or goes out. For this purpose if some one is absent, the next person is allowed to officiate or work in his/her place at office.

Organisational Structure

It is the collective name given to the various authorities or positions created in an enterprise. Since the process of organisation involves division of work and co-ordinating the efforts of various persons in such a way that the common objectives are achieved, it is necessary that there should be a clear-cut and well-defined structure. The following are the main types of organisational structure :

(i) **Line organisation** : Under this form of organisational structure, there is a clear line of authority. The authority flows vertically from top to bottom. The topmost boss is vested with the highest authority and as soon as we come below the strueture, the authority goes on reducing e.g., the chairman, general manager, branch manager and so on. It is the oldest and most simple form of organisational structure and may easily be understood by all concerned because the clear-cut line of demarcation is visible between the various scales of status. It facilitates prompt decision-making and also ensures proper discipline and harmony in the enterprise because everyone knows his or her authority and responsibility. However, the line organisation suffers from the disadvantage that it does not take into account the specialisation and that its success depends mainly upon the individual holding the post.

(ii) **Line and staff organisation** : Under this type of structure, there is a vertical line of authority from top to bottom but at each level of management, the services of specialised persons as staff officers are availed of. The staff renders specialised services such as legal advice, financial planning, personnel matters etc. Thus, it is a combination of the line as well as staff organisation systems. This structure has got all the advantages of the line as well as other advantages of specialised services at the proper levels of management.

The following Chart gives the clear idea about the Line and Staff organisation :

Chairman & Mg. Director

General Manager I General Manager II

General Manager I			General Manager II	
AGM (Production)	AGM (Purchase)	AGM (Marketing)	AGM (Personnel Manager) Law Officer	AGM (Finance) Chartered Accountant Cost Acctt. Co. Secretary

In the above chart, you will observe that at the top level, there is the chairman and managing director (the highest authority). Below him in the line, are two General Managers, I and II. Under first general Manager, there are three Assistant General Managers whereas under the second General Manager, there are two Assistant General Managers. This represents line organisation. However, for assisting the AGM (Personnel), there are two staff officers viz.

the Personnel Manager as well as the Law Officer. Similarly, for assisting the AGM (Finance), there is the Chartered Accountant, Cost Accountant and the Company Secretary (all staff). It shows the line and staff organisation relationship.

(iii) **Functional Organisation** : When on the basis of specialised functions like production, purchases, sales, administration the departments are created, we may call it the 'Functional. Organisation'. All the activities of similar nature are grouped in one and all aspects of any one activity are taken up at the same place. The functional departments are created and the same are headed by the experts in the specialised field of activity. The functional organisation has got various advantages like specialisation, standardisation, efficiency, avoiding duplication, effective supervision etc. However, this type of structure suffers from the disadvantages of complications. confusions, officialdom and higher costs etc.

(iv) **Committee Organisation** : Whenever a few persons are collectively entrusted with a particular work to be performed by all of them collectively, we may call it a committee organisation. It is not a different form as such but under the existing set up, certain specialised works are separately allotted to a committee formed for the special purpose like sports committee, finance committee etc. These committees may be *ad hoc* (i.e. constituted for the specific purpose) or standing (i.e. having the permanent members). Such type of organisations have got many advantages like pooled knowledge or collective decisions, co-ordinated efforts, participation and effective communication but there are chances of difference of opinion, delay in decision-making, expensiveness, vested interests etc.

Factors influencing Organisational Structure :

Of the line, Line and staff, functional or committee organisational structures, which one should be ideal for a particular enterprise, it will depend upon the following factors :

(i) **Nature and volume of business** : What type of product is dealt with ? Whether the business is carried at a small-scale or large-scale ? Both these points would determine, to a large extent, as to which type of structure is chosen. If there is a variety of products dealt in and the business is carried on a large-scale, the functional organisation would be the most suitable. On the other hand, if the business is medium or small scale, the line organisation may be the most suitable.

(ii) **Geographibal location** : If the business is limited to the local place, the functional organisation may be more suitable. Where the business is spread over to far off places, the line or committee organisation may be more beneficial.

(iii) **Degree of supervision and the staff** : Where the number of staff members is large and the supervision is effectively required, the line organisation would be found more suitable or the committee type organisation would serve the purpose. Where more specialisation is required, functional type of organisation may be opted for.

(iv) **Continuity and permanence** : Where the business is continuous, regular and of the permanent nature, a complex organisation will not serve the purpose. Instead the line of management should be clear-cut and well-defined. On the other hand, if the business is of fluctuating nature, the *ad hoc* committee type of organisation may also serve the purpose.

(v) **Degree of mechanisation** : In the enterprises where mechanisation is more, the degree of supervision may be less and a simple type of organisation may serve the purpose. On the other hand, where the mechanisation is not perverse, an effective manual supervision may be required and the complex organisation may suit the requirements.

(vi) **Management Policies** : The organisational structure always depends upon the policies adopted by management of an enterprise. If the management requires more participation of workers, the authorities may be kept limited in number. Where more controls are required, the number of supervisors will have to be increased.

However, it is not necessary that at all times, only one type of organisational structure will be found more suitable. It is subject to change based on the cirumstances. The dynamic and challenging management adopts the more flexible structure and may switch over to any type as per the needs of the hour.

However, the organisation structure may be shown or represented with the help of organisation charts or manuals.

Organisation Charts

An organisation chart is a graphic representation of various positions or authorities in the Organisation by drawing formal lines of authority and accountability of various levels in the management hierarchy. It also shows the relationships between the members of the organisation as well as the different sections or departments of the office. At a glance, one can easily understand the entire organisational set-up and the functions performed at the different levels of management hierarchy. The chart drawn on page 27 showing the line and staff organisation may be a good example.

There are various *advantages* of the organisation chart : (i) It shows a bird's eye-view of the clear-cut and well-defined lines of authority and accountability. The topmost Authority is shown first and thereafter the subordinates working under that authority. (ii) It is helpful to management as the management can immediately locate the effects, if any, in the entire set-up ; (iii) It helps the workers in knowing their position and guides them for their day-to-day working as they may approach the appropriate authority for any of their problems or issues. Overall, the organisation charts are important tools in deciding the organisational structure of any business enterprise.

However, the *drawbacks* of the charts are ; (i) These are expensive and time-consuming ; (ii) These are unable to show any changes effected in the set-up ; (iii) These do not show the informal relationship between the various positions. Still, the organisation chart is the blue-print of the hierarchy of the levels of management.

Organisation or Procedure or Office Manual

It is generally a printed booklet containing the procedural instructions to be followed by the members of an organisation for their day-to-day routine. It is an authoritative guide to the Organisation as such. It is rather a source of information for the employees or workers for better performanee of their working. In every big enterprise, the procedure manual is readily available in the form of a printed bound book and the same may be used as a guide to complete the routine works in accordance with the policies framed by the management. Generally, the Office Manual contains the name and address of Organisation, nature of business, major objectives, structure or set-up of the Organisation, administrative policies, job descriptions, rules and regulations, routine procedures and the working facilities vis-a-vis the authority or power vested with various levels and their accountability, etc. The manual differs from organisation to organisation and its volume or size depends upon the information given by the management. For preparing the Manual, generally, a committee or committees are formed by the departmental heads of executives of the enterprise who draw an outline draft of the same well within the framework of policies set-up by the top management. After compilation and editing the information, a final draft is prepared and got printed at the central level. The requisite number of copies are obtained and one copy is handed over to each departmental head for keeping the same under separate lock and key.

An Organisation Manual is prepared with manifold objectives in view—procedural instructions for adhering to by the staff, information source for the unknown and tool for the successful implementation of policies of management.

The Office Manual has many *uses* : (i) It avoids delays duplication and wastage of work : (ii) It obviates the necessity to explain the rules or procedures to staff ; (iii) It brings in uniformity and standardisation throughout the Organisation ; (iv) It works as an authoritative source of information ; and (v) Helps the management in controlling over the state of affairs and punishing the erring staff.

However, the *drawbacks* are : (i) It is expensive to prepare and print the manual and the smaller organisations cannot afford to have it ; (ii) There is no scope for flexibility and creative action on the part of staff ; (iii) The additions and alterations become difficult and cumbersome.

Delegation of Authority and fixing Responsibility :

For the purpose of getting the work done through people in an Organisation, an important administrative process is the delegation of authority or power by the central authority to the various lower levels of management hierarchy. Since one man alone cannot complete the huge works, it is the practice that the work is distributed to the various officers and they are vested with certain powers so that they can take work from their subordinates. Certain norms are fixed up and accordingly the authority is shared or entrusted at different levels of management. The authority may be in respect of incurring expenses or giving sanctions or in connection with taking decisions on administrative matters. The process through which powers are vested with various managers or officers of an enterprise, may be called the 'delegation of authority'.

It may not be out of place to mention here that the authority does not go alone but it is always accompanied with the responsibility. The idea behind it is that the authority may be appropriately used and not misused. No one assumes the responsibility without appropriate entrustment of authority and, at the same time, no one can properly use the authority unless and until the responsibility is thwarted upon him. Similary, the degree of responsibility varies with the quantum of authority. More authority, more responsibility—lesser authority, lesser responsibility. The scalar principle of authority also states that the authority flows from top level to the lower level and is the maximum with the topmost authority or management and goes on reducing as soon as we come down to the lower levels of hierarchy.

The delegation of authority is of greater *importance* in an Organisation because it (i) enables the managers to take work from people working in the field, (ii) makes it possible to divide and distribute work between different persons ; (iii) enables quick decision-making at all the levels and avoid delays ; (iv) relieves the top-management of the monotony of routing works so that they may concentrate more on making fruitful policies for expansion and development ; and (v) fosters healthy relations between various executives.

However, in the process of delegation of authority, the division of work is done, duties are assigned, powers are vested and the accountability or responsibility is fixed up after taking into account the following *principles* of delegatian of authority :—

(i) Assignment of duty is made in terms of objective or results expected to be achieved.

(ii) Authority co-exists with the responsibility.

(iii) Responsibility cannot be delegated but it is made on obligation with the authority.

(iv) Accountability or Responsibility is unitary i,e. the person holding the authority is alone accountable for the results. Though a manager may delegate the authority vested in him to his subordinates, yet he alone will be accountable if something goes wrong.

However, delegation of authority is an important tool in the hands of management for getting the things done through subordinates. Still, it is exposed to a number of risks and dangers both for the superior and the subordinate as there are so many weaknesses of the delegation of authority, like—misuse of authority, desire of authority, desire of dominance, lack of confidence, lack of ability and controlling capacity on the part of superiors as well as reluctance to assume responsibility on the part of subordinates.

DIFFERENCE BETWEEN ORGANISATION, ADMINISTRATION AND MANAGEMENT

As we know, the term 'Organisation' is used to denote the process involving determination of activities, assignment and allocation of jobs to different persons, delegating authority and fixing the responsibility. All this is done for accomplishment of cnterprise goals. Under the organisation, we have to arrange men, materials, machinery and equipment etc., and put them to use so that the results are achieved successfully. The various components of organisation are division of work, assignment of duties to subordinates, delegation of authority and fixing up the responsibility. It is one of the important fuuctions of management.

The term 'Administration' is concerned with the execution of policies or programmes laid down by the management of an enterprise, It is a specialised activity which ensures putting the wheel into action or is concerned with the implementation of policies in order to achieve the goals. Based on the policy framework of the management, the administration organises the men, material, machinery, methods and equipments in such a way that the goals are achieved. Thus, administration decides the organisation but it concentrates mainly on the practical aspect of things.

'Management' is a wide term used to denote a function or process of getting the things done through other people. It involves many important functions like planning, organising, staffing, directing, motivating and controlling. The managcment through its own policies ensures achievement of goals. It may take the help of administration or the organisation. Organisation is a part of management.

As the above three terms are used synonymously or many times confused, it is necessary that a clear-cut relation or difference between them be established so that these may be used appropriately. Actually speaking, the three terms are distinct from each other. Management is the widest term whereas 'Organisation' is a smaller term and forms part of management. Administration' is that part of management which is concerned with thc execution or putting into practice the policies framed by the management and that the 'Administration' decides the organisation. However, it is difficult to distinguish clearly the terms 'Administration' and the 'Management' because, in many Organisations, the Managing Director alongwith the Board of Directors forms the policies and is also responsible for the execution or implementation of those policies. It is really difficult to say whether the administration executes the policies or the Management implements the policies. Both of them may do the same work. In the real sense, the term 'Administration' is mostly used in government circle and the term Management' is used in business circle. As such, in practical life. both these terms may be used to denote synonymous sense.

OFFICE MANAGEMENT

Generally speaking, the term 'Office Management' is used to denote the management of office operations. If we analyse both the words separately, the 'office' refers to an information centre where the information is received, collected, analysed or processed and communicated to others. Similary, the term 'Management' refers to the process of getting the things done through other people. Thus, the meaning of 'Office Management' may be taken as a process of getting the work of information done through the personnel working in the office. It may also be called the information management' or the 'administrative management' because the office management is largely concerned with the management of information or undertaking the administrative works for the business enterprise. As we know that the office work is not the main function of a business enterprise but others like purchase, production, sales etc., rather each of such work involves paper clerical work, that is why the office management has a different conception than the business management. *J.C. Denyer* in his book 'Office Management', has stated as under :-

"Office Management is part of the wider aspect of business management, but in so far as it is the controlling element, it is a very important part."

Further, while explaining the meaning of 'Office Management' *J.C. Denyer* has maintained that the word 'manage' means 'to guide' and to have under command or control and refers to the managing a horse. There is in fact something in common between the management of an office and that of a horse. When managing a horse one has to control its direction and keep the load as light as possible. In the same way, an office manager has to keep up the direction of office work and make the office work as light as possible for the office personnel.

William H. Leffingwell has defined the modern office management as a 'work simplification'.

Keeping in the view the above definitions as given by various Authorities on office management, it may be said that office management is the process through which the paper work gets performed from office personnel in such a way that it serves the purpose of a best information centre. In the modan days, the office management has become a separate subject of study and a branch of management science. In the subject of office managent, we have to study, briefly the planning of office accommodation, its lay-out, working environment and handling the various office services like mailing typing, duplicating, filing, indexing etc. In view of this, we may define 'Office Management' as a science and an art which deals with the arrangement of men, material and equipments etc., and controlling the various office services in such a way that the information of business is made available without delay. In other words, we may say that the office management is concerned with planning, organising, staffiing, dissecting and controlling of various office activities in order to accomplish the objectives of business information.

Characteristics or Salient Features

From the definition of office management given in the foregoing paragraphs, we may derive at the following characteristics or special features of office management :-

1. It is the *pr ocess* i.e. a number of steps are taken e.g. planning the work, lacation, accommodation, lay-out, arranging men, machinery and equipments and then controlling over the same.
2. It is concerned with *getting the things done through people* i.e. office personnel.
3. The very purpose of office menagement is handling business information i.e. receiving or collecting the same, analysing or processing, recording and communication of information useful for business.
4. It is a *science as well as an art* because it is based on certain set rules or procedures which are applied for practical purposes.

Elements

The fundamental things which are included in the office management are as under :-

(*i*) **Men or Personnel** : The very purpose of office management is getting things done through people i.e. the various office activities like mailing, typing, duplicating, filing etc. are performed by the persons, skilled and unskilled, who are duly selected, properly placed, trained and controlled for the purpose of accomplishment of goals. Without persons, office management cannot cannot be done. Some of these persons are specialists e.g. accountants, typists etc., whereas the others are of the general category e.g. the clerks and also the unskilled persons e.g. the peons or messengers etc.

(*ii*) **Machinery and Equipments** : For performance of the office work, a number of machines and equipments are required e.g., typewriter, duplicating machine, accounting machines, addressing machines, stationery articles, printed forms etc. In the most modern office, we find that the most sophisticated machines and equipments like computers, word-processors etc. are used for accurate and efficient working. Without them it may not be possible to handle the office activities.

(*iii*) **Methods** : The word 'method' is used to denote the manner in whieh the work is actually accomplished. A letter may be written by hand or typewritten. The postage stamps may be affixed manually or with the help of a franking machine. It is the method which decides the way to action. The entire office routine or procedures are accomplished by following the methods developed by office manager,

(*iv*) **Working Environment** : Since the office work is the paper or clerical work and is concerned with the application of brain, it is necessary that the best possible physical concitions of work are provided. Interior decoration, furnishings, furniture, sanitation, good lighting, safety and security measures to reduce the noise etc; are included in the working environment, without providing the best working conditions, the office work cannot be accomplished. The office manager has to ensure that the working environment is provided for getting the office work done.

(*v*) **Information** : The main objective of office is to collect and provided information to the management, staff and the outsiders without much wastage of time. As such, the office management has the sole criteria as to how best the information is made available, and used for the purpose of decison-making.

THE OFFICE MANAGER

The office manager is a person who does planning, organising, staffing, directing and controlling of the various office activities performed to accomplish the objectives of a business enterprise. He or she is the Office incharge and under whose guidance the office personnel perform the various office duties. The office manager is vested with authority and he or she is also responsible for all that is done at the office.

In the most modern days, the job of office manager has become much more challenging and dynamic, because of the changing pattern of society as a whole. The modern office is not the same type of office as used to be in the good old days when the 'Babu' (the popular nomenclature for clerk) used to sit in the room filled with heaps of papers and files and work till late evening. The changing pattern of office is such that most of the paper or clerical work is performed with the help of sophisticated machines like the computers and/or word-processors. The methods of letter-writing, mail-handling filing, indexing etc., have changed considerably and the communication systems have been modernised. Many new systems have been developed like the management information system, systems analysis, data processing etc. The time has become the most valuable factor for all sorts of business and the efficiency is required to handle the modern situation. Most of the manual devices have been replaced by the machines. Hence, the main job of the modern office manager is confined to planning the resources and organising them in an efficient manner so that with great speed the information is obtained or analysed or passed on to others. The onus of the modern office manager lies in meeting the challenges by developing fast and sound system of management information, reducing the amount of unnecessary paper work, developing the form information, handling the automated office, motivating the clerical staff properly and finding out the new methods of working in order to cope over the fast pace of progress.

Qualifications & Qualities :

In order to meet the challenges thwarted upon the modern office manager, it is essential that the office manager should be well competent and highly qualified. Besides that, he or she must possess the requisite personality traits. We shall discuss them in the following paragraphs :

(i) **Sound educational background** : In the modern days, it is essential that the office manager should be a graduate or post-graduate with the sound knowledge of commerce, accounts, administration and/or management. Education imparts knowledge and gives awareness of the worldly things.

(ii) **Professional Qualifications and/or Training** : Only the education will not serve the purpose. The office manager should have completed professional courses like secretarial practice, office management, business administration etc. He should be well trained in office procedures, management information systems, data processing etc. With this, he or she may adopt the tricks of trade.

(iii) **Knowledge of correspondence and accounts** : For an office manager, it is necessasy that he or she should be perfect at drafting letters, reports etc., as the work involves it heavily. At the same time, the office manager may have to manage the books of account of business for which he or she should have complete knowledge and expertise.

(iv) **Knowledge of office procedures and routine** : The various aspects of office routine e.g. mailing, filing, indexing etc., must be well-known to the office manager. Unless one knows them, it is difficult to take work from the subordinates. The office manager has to be a good guide to office staff.

(v) **Knowing use of office machines & equipments** : Most of the offices in the modern days are equipped with latest machines and equipments and those are costly as well as sophisticated. Though specialised operators are available to work on these machines, yet the basic operations of these machines and equipments must be known to the office manager so that the controlling function may be discharged without much of the problem.

(vi) **Personality Traits or Qualities** : As an office manager, one should possess certain personal qualities like punctuality, regularity, honesty, devotion to duty, discipline, sense of responsibility, leadership qualities, ability to delegate authority, tactfulness and the capacity to supervise and manage the affairs of office. The office manager should be able to command respect and win over others.

Functions of an Office Manager :

The functions to be performed by an office manager will largely depend upon the size and volume of business which is required to be undertaken and the system of information adopted by the enterprise. Basically, the office manager is required to handle all aspects of office work right from planning the office accommodation, its layout, providing congenial working conditions including the machines and equipments to recruitment, placement and training of office personnel, motivating them to work and controlling the work. On the one hand, he is responsive to the higher management of the enterprise whereas, on the other hand, he has to take work from his subordinates and use the tact for getting the work done. It has really become a challenging job in the modern days and only the tactful and competent persons can hold this assignment. Though there is no water-tight compartment in which we may keep the functions of the office manager because of the fast changing pattern of business needs, yet the important functions are summarised below :—

(i) **Management Functions :** The primary functions of management e.g., planning, organising, directing and controlling etc., have to be performed by the office manager. In planning, the office manager has to decide in advance what is to be done and how the work is to be done. As per the policy framework of top management, the office manager has to prepare the plans, programmes, budgets etc. In organising, the office manager has to divide and distribute the entire office work amongst persons, allocate the jobs, delegate authority and fix up the responsibility. For this purpose, suitable number of sections or departments may be created in the office like the cash, accounts, typing & duplicating, filing & indexing sections and so on. The specialised persons may be entrusted with the job and the manager may ask them the progress from time to time. In directing, the office manager has to motivate office personnel to do the right type of work for the office by way of appreciating their work, giving them incentives or punishing them for the mistakes. For the purpose of controlling, the office manager has to assess their performance from time to time by fixing the standards and evaluate the actual work. All these are management functions which are performed by the office manager.

(ii) **Office location, accommodation and lay-out** : The office manager has to select the site for office by taking into account the various fact, decide the office premises and the lay-out so that the office work may be performed efficiently without wastage of time and man-hours. Effecting the changes in the organisational set-up of office is also a part of the job of office manager.

(iii) **Providing Working Environment** : The office manager has to ensure that proper and adequate physical conditions are provided at the place of working. It may include colouring of walls, furnishings, lighting arrangements, maintaining temperature by way of coolers or air-conditioners and the ventilators, arrangements for sanitation and cleanliness, provision for toilets, water-coolers, canteen etc., providing safety and security to office and taking measures for reducing the internal and external noise. All human-beings are governed by their whims and desires. As such, they can work efficiently under good atmospheric conditions.

(iv) **Arranging modern machines and equipments** : In order to cope with the fast increasing needs of information in business, the office manager has to make arrangement for the requisite machines and equipments and train the staff to work on them so that the work is performed accurately, quickly and protected from frauds etc.

(v) **Arranging Forms, Stationery and other supplies** : The office work cannot be performed without printed forms or other stationery items like paper, pin, pencils, pen etc. All these are arranged beforehand and issued to staff for use. For properly controlling these items, the office manager has to assess the requirements and then arrange for their centralised purchase, storage and controlling consumption etc.

(vi) **Handling Personnel Matters** : For the members of staff working under the office manager, he or she has to keep uptodate records about their leave, salaries and other matters. The pay-rolls are prepared and salaries are distributed to the staff. Overtime is controlled. All these matters are to be looked after by the office manager. Proper and timely training of staff is arranged for.

(vii) **Developing office procedures and methods** : For an efficient working and rendering efficient services, the office manager has to develop the new methods and short-cut procedures and apply them in the day-to-day working. For this purpose, time and motion studies may be conducted or valuable suggestions may be invited from the staff and those may be implemented in the best interest of all. It is the duty of the office manager to ensure that all the office services are rendered efficiently.

(viii) **Co-ordination** : In a big office, the office manager has also to co-ordinate the efforts or works of different sections in such a way that there is no duplication or wastage and the office expenditure remains well within limit. For this purpose, he may arrange meetings, progress reports or work-sheets etc.

(ix) **Maintaining good human relations** : One of the functions of office manager is to maintain good relations between workers, superiors, subordinates and the outside public. When cordial relations are maintained, each and every person co-operates and works happily towards achieving the goals.

Thus, the office manager has to ensure that the office operations are carried out smoothly and efficiently under his/her stewardship.

Role of Office Manager :

Keeping in view the various functions performed by the office manager, we may say that the office manager has to play a major role in office operations. Let us not forget that the office work is a service to the business organisation and anything performed by the office manager is well reflected in business. If office work is performed efficiently and uptodate information is quickly equipped, the business may finalise profitable deals and earn huge profits. On the other hand, an inefficient office might lead to loss for the business. Much depends upon the office manager.

The role of office manager may be adjudged from the following :—

(i) As a Guide : The office manager acts as a good guide to office workers in the sense that he shows the right direction to them so that their output is concrete and they work to achieve the goal. In the absence of right type of guidance, the workers may work with trial and error basis which might result into wastage and extravagance.

(ii) As an Administrator : As an administrator, the office manager ensures that whatever polices or programs are framed, the same are duly executed or put into practice. As such, there is the practical importance of the office manager.

(iii) As a Leader : A leader is the person who takes his followers and shows them the right way. Similarly, the office manager leads the office personnel, and makes them to strive for better results. He is a pro in carrying out the office operations. The subordinotes follow him.

(iv) As a Co-ordinator : As a liasion officer, the office manager co-ordinates the efforts of various departments or sections so that the entire staff works as a good team. This way, the office manager helps in avoiding duplication, delay, wastages and extravagance. At the same time, it ushers in uniformity and standardisation throughout the organisation.

Thus, from the functions and multiple role of office manager we may derive the conclusion that the office manager is a very important person in the business world. His services are valuable for the business enterprise as a whole.

Training of Office Manager

'Training' is the process of imparting or developing a specialised skill for practical application by the person who is trained. That is, training is given to a person for apprising him of the new atmosphere and moulding his attitude in such a way that he becomes useful in practical life. Likewise, the training is imparted to the Office Managers also so that they become proficient and efficient in managing the affairs of office. Two types of training is generally given :—

(i) **Induction Training** : Under this type of training, the courses are arranged in the training centres or colleges in such a way that the new person becomes familiar with the routine and atmosphere of work. The classes are conducted in a phased programme in such a way that the trainee gets refreshed and gets familiar with the basic infrastructure.

(ii) **On the job Training** : It involves the practical aspect of the job. The trainee has to gain knowledge by actually working on the desk. Every big Organisation has a system of recriting management trainess who are qualified persons but they are not fully familiar with the actual office working. During a stipulated period of time these people are imparted intensive training and made fit for the job.

Both the above types of tranining is useful for Office Managers because with the former they gain perfect theoretical knowledge of office routine and, through the latter, they get used to practical working. The training enables the office managers in knowing the different tricks of trade, latest developments in the field had also given them an opportunity open discussion with the experts for satisfying themselves fully.

RELATIONSHIP OF OFFICE WITH OTHER FUNCTIONAL DEPARTMENT

We know it very well that the office work, which is mainly the papes work or clerical work, is not the *main* function of a Business Organisation because the business activities may involve production, purchase and sale of goods or services. But, for performance of these business activities, the office work is a pre-requisite e.g. writing a letter for getting or giving information in connection with production, purchase or sale, As such, office is a separate segment other than the Functional Departments like Praduction Department, Purchase Department, Sales Department etc. *The Functional Department may be defined as a separate department or section which undertakes a specialised activity of business.* There may be any number of functional departments in a Business Organisation depending upon the nature and volume of business activities.

The Office, being 'Information Centre' and the 'Hub of all the business activities', has a direct and the definite relationship with other functional departments of the Business Organisation because the General Office receives or collects information for the Functional Departments, keeps a record of information and communicates information for and on behalf of them. Similarly, the Functional Departments provide work for the office rather create the paper or clerical work. The Office prepares policies, plans. methods, procedures and protects business assets i.e. men, materials, machinery, methods and money. Ultimately, the success in achieving the goals of business lies in the efficient working of 'Office' because the office can co-ordinate the activities of various Functional Departments in such a way that the goals are achieved.

Office and Production Department

The Production Department performs the activities of purchasing the raw-materials and converting them into semifinished and finished goods by using the machines and technology. It involves a lot of paper work like correspondence, typing, accounte, finance etc. The Production Department has to keep a continuous touch with the Sales Department for maintaining the level of production. The information is given and taken through the Office only. The wrong or delayed information might hold-up the production work. Most of the leading Industries of the world base their operations on the papcr-work. About the Ford Company of U.S.A., it is said that they use one ton of paper for every ton of motor-cars produced and they are the pioneers in the line of business throughout the world. As such, we may say that the office is closely associated with the Production Department, rather both of them are interdependent.

Office and Purchase Department

The functions of Purchase Department involve purchasing goods and materials for the business organisation, either for processing and for sale to customers, Most of the success of any business lies in economical purchases—right goods at the lowest price. Favourable terms for purchase and availing credit are to be negotiated, All this requires advance information from all possible corners and the same may be made available by the Office. Accounts and Finance are also the part and parcel of this process. Proper record for the goods received are essential. A liasion has to be maintained with other departments for proper disposal of the goods purchased. Without the assistance of office, the Purchase Department may not be able to function properly.

Offices and Sale Department

Selling the goods or services is an important aspect of business and the most ticklish job involving a lot of publicity compaign, skil of salesmanship, information, tact and efficiency. A good saleman can create a market for the worst type of goods whereas an inefficient person may not be able to sell the best of goods or services. In the Sales Department, much depends upon the uptodate information about market trends, tastes and liking of consumers and their capacity to pay for the goods. Latest sophisticated and the most modern modia for publicity are required to be utilised but the cost of sales has to be kept at the minimum. The Cash and Accounts Departments have to be quick in receiving payments for sales and apprising the customers' accounts position within no time, A co-ordination with the Production or Purchase Department has to be closely maintained for finding out the availability of stocks for sale. The Correspondence Department should be ready all the time for giving reminders, price-quotations, acknowledging orders etc. Thus, the functioning of Sales Department largely depends upon the efficient working of office. In turn, the office has to perform a lot of work for the Sales Department. Hence, a close liasion with the office is essential.

Office and Accounts Department

In smaller Organisations, the Accounts Section may form a part of the office but, in bigger Organisation, the Accounts Department has a separate entity and independent set-up. Since 'Accounting' involves keeping a systematic record of financial transactions of business and also analysing and interpreting them, the functions of an Accounts Department as a separate entity may be in preparing the books of accounts, balance sheets, financial statements, reconciliation of bank accounts, cost accounting, financial accounting, management accounting etc. All these functions are related with the office because the office collects or receives data or details for accounts, keeps a proper record of purchase/sales invoice copies, supplies vouchers or documents useful for the Accounts Department. The necessary works of typing, duplicating, mailing, filing and indexing etc. are done at the office. The correspondence in connection with opening bank accounts, applying for credit facilities, furnishing information to the Bank etc. may be efficiently done with the assistance of office only.

Office and Personnel Department

The Personnel Department is one which handles the matters pertaining to persons working in the Organisation. The recruitment promotions, transfers, termination, dismissal, taking disciplinary action against them or maintaining the records of leave, salary etc., all these functions are performed by the Personnel Department. Although Personnel Department is a part of office, yet, in many bigger Organisations, this Department functions as a separate entity other than the General Office. Under such circumstances, the Personnel Department has to depend upon heavily on the office in matters of receiving or collecting information, recording information and communication of information. The Office arranges to release advertisement for vacant posts in the daily newspapers ; purchases, stores and issues stationery items and other supplies used in the Personnel Department and works as a communication channel. Thus, the two are inter-linked with each other.

QUESTIONS

1. State the duties of Office Manager in relation to (i) Top management and (ii) Sub-ordinates. (*B. Com. Pass, Delhi, 1983*)
2. (a) Explain the importance of office to an organisation. State the challenges that the office faces in the near future in our country,

   (b) State the need for training office managers. Also describe briefly the methods of training office managers. (*B. Com. Pass, Delhi, 1982*)
3. What do you understand by office management ? Discuss the functions of an Office Manager. (*B. Com. Pass, Delhi, 1980-1987*)
4. What do you mean by Organisation ? Discuss the main principles of Organisation.
5. Bring out the qualities of an efficient manager. (*B. Com. Pass, Delhi, 1987*)

3

OFFICE LOCATION AND ACCOMMODATION

If someone is entrusted with the task of setting up of a new office, he or she may have to come across with the following problems :-

(i) Where or in which locality the office may be set up ;
(ii) What type of accommodation or premises be procured or acquired for the office ?
(iii) How the arrangement for seating of personnel and/or placing the office machines and equipments be made ?
(v) Why and how best the physical conditions of work be created so that there is maximum efficiency ?

Out of the above, the first two aspects have been discussed by us in the present chapter and the latters are given in the following chapters.

Location of office

For an office, any building or part thereof is required. The situation or location of the office building is an important consideration for the office management because the personnel working in office have to come there and work, the visitors have to visit the office, the postal and other communication services may have to be availed of and so on. It will mean that the office should be ideally situated at a place where there is no hindrance to the office working and, at the same, the operating expenses of office are the minimum. Though there is no hard and fast rule as to where the office building is to be located, yet all the practical aspects of working shall have to be pondered over for the purpose.

Factors for Location of office

The following points should be considered in connection with the location of office :-

(i) **Convenient approach** : It should be borne in mind that the persons working in the office as well as the outsiders may easily and conveniently reach the office. The office should be situated at such a place where all sorts of vehicles may easily be taken. There should be the proper facility of parking of vehicles also. The narrow streets, no direct thoroughfare, far off places inconvenient to persons etc., would create problems in the office working. As such, the place must be selected after taking into consideration the accessibility.

(ii) **Transport facilities :** Transportation is the means which makes the movement possible, both for persons as well as the goods. The transport facilities like the city buses, trucks and other vehicles should be available near the office. If adequate transport facilities are available, even a little distance from the main city will not become a hindrance.

(iii) **Service facilities** : An office itself is service and to render efficient service by the office, it is necessary that the facilities of post office, bank, insurance company etc., should be readily available near by. Every time, the mail is to be received and despatched or dealings with the bank are to be made. If these facilities are available at a distance, it will be inconvenient, risky and uneconomical.

(iv) **Peaceful neighbourhood** : Since office work is directly related to the application of brain and the same requires attention and concentration, it is necessary to ensure that the sorrounding area of office is not noisy and there is not too much of disturbance otherwise it will entail too many clerical errors, Though the outside noise can be prevented through artificial measures like sound-absorbent partitions or making the building air-conditioned yet too much noise in the surrounding area cannot be prevented. Therefore, the necessity of peaceful surrounding area.

(v) **Close to other units** : If there are other units or branches of the same organisation and the office has to perform centralised work for all of them, it is necessary that the general office should, as far as possible, be situated near to other units so that effective control may be exercised and the efficient service is rendered to all.

(vi) **Nearness to related trades** : From business point of view, it is also necessary that the office should be located near to other related trades so that uptodate information about the market trends etc,, is readily available.

(vii) **Basic Amenities** : Before finalising the site for the office, it should be ensured that water, power, electricity, natural light, air and other infrastructural facilities are available. Without these, the office working will not be possible.

OFFICE ACCOMMODATION

After deciding the location of office, the next problem before the office manager is that of building of premises in which the office is laid out. The building may be *owncd* or *rented.* In case the building is purchased or constructcd on a plot of land owned by the management, it is convenient to get the desired hall or rooms. At the same time, additions and alterations to the building are easy. But, in case of the rented building, the permission of the landlord has to be souhgt for and the terms mentioned in the rent or lease deed have to be followed. The office should preferably be set on the ground floor of the building because that is convenient from all angles. If it is on the first floor, second-floor or above, there should be proper arrangement for the stairs or lifts. Though there is less noise and minimum disturbance on the upper floors, yet it is inconvenient for the movement of staff and machines etc., and much expenditure has to be incurred on taking and bringing the material. Particularly, in big cities or towns, there is a paucity of space and various problems connected with the aecommodation have to be faced.

Factors for accommodation

The following are the various factors determining the suitability of the office building :

(i) **Office Lay-out** : The office building should be such that it fits well into the lay-out plan of the office. If open lay-out is preferred, the building should have a big hall and a few separate rooms. If closed lay-out is desired, then the building should have many small rooms. Overall, the building should be such that the seating arrangement of persons and that of placing the machines/ equipments may be convenient so that there is smooth flow of work and the efficiency is attained to the maximum.

(ii) **Facility for renovation** : Even if the building is not exactly similar to the lay out, the purpose may be served if the facility of renovating or restrueturing the building is available in the sense there are not many restrictions from the side of the municipality or other Government bodies. The wooden partitions may also serve the purpose.

(iii) **Working environment** : Physical facilities like the light, ventilation, safety, cleanliness, provision for toilets, colouring of walls etc., constitute the environment for office working. The building should be such that all these facilities could be easily provided. Though there are artificial means for providing light, air and ventilation, yet the natural sources are of greater importance.

(iv) **Facility in expansion** : Once the building is fixed up, it is not easy to shift again and again to other places. That is why, the building should be such as to provide additional space, if needed, at any time in furture. The additional space may be created by constructing additional floors, mazannine floors etc.

(v) **Cost** : The cost of office building is an important consideration. If the accommodation is available at a very high cost which cannot be afforded, it is no use. If it is cheaper, larger area may be occupied but the same should not be far off from the main centre of business activities. Hence, the building should be acquired at the reasonable average cost.

(vi) **Safety and Security** : The building should be safe and secured from the point of view of theft, burglary, dacoity etc. Normally the buildings which are situated at lonely places far away from the madding crowd are unsafe.

(vii) **Storage facilities** : In the office building, there should the facility of creating a store or records room for keeping the records of paper and documents. The filing cabinets, racks or almirahs full of papers or records may be easily kept, Records are an important assets of office. Hence, the facility for their storage is required. For this purpose, the construction of building should be solid and sound.

QUESTIONS

1. Discuss the factors to be considered in the selection of an office accommodation ?
2. What points would you keep while selecting the location office ?
3. 'Office location is a key factor for the success of modern office', comment.

4

OFFICE LAY-OUT AND WORKING ENVIRONMENT

OFFICE LAY-OUT

When the accommodation or space for an office—whether rented or owned—is acquired or fixed up, the next problem comes as how to make the seating arrangement for all persons and how to set up the various equipments or machines in the office so that the work of office can be carried out smoothly and efficiently. This is the subject of office-layout.

Office lay-out may be defined as "the arrangement of men and equipment within the available floor-space."

Office lay-out refers to the arrangement and placing of men, materials, machines, furniture and equipment within each section or department of the office in such a way that the best possible utilisation of available space is achieved."

From the above definitions, we come to know that office lay-out is concerned with the arrangement of the men and equipment in an office within the available floor space in such a manner that the office work may be done easily and without inconvenience to anyone.

Special Features

The office—lay out involves mainly the following :-

1. The determination of correct space for each person and the machines and equipment and also the furniture used by them.

2. The arrangement of furniture, equipment and machines in such a way that those could be utilised in a better way.

3. The provision of the best working conditions or physical conditions like light, air, ventilation etc.

Objectives of Office Lay-Out or Advantages of a Better Office Lay-Out :

In case sufficient space is allotted to each one and the right arrangement of machinery, furniture equipment is done, the following advantages are derived :-

1. **Efficiency or Effective Work Flow** : Which means that the work would pass through the various desks effectively and there would be better efficiency if the office lay out is scientific and better.

2. **Economy** : There will be no wastage of time and energies and a lot of money can be saved.

3. **Comfort** : In a better lay-out everyone feels more comfortable and the work can be performed without any difficulty.

4. **Balance** : A proper balance may be maintained between the various desks by equally dividing the work amongst various persons.

5. **Easy Supervision and Control** : When the correct arrangement for sitting and placing of machines and equipment is done, it becomes easy to control and supervise the entire work of an office.

6. **Flexibility** : In case there is little increase in work or even a little decreaes in work, the same may be easily performed with the same men and machines and without effecting any material change in the set-up.

7. **Securacy and Security** : The entire things in an office can be kept secret and safe if there is a proper lay-out of an office because these are kept in view while laying down an office.

8. **Minimum Interference** : There is very less disturbance in work if the lay-out of an office is proper because each section of department is set-up in such a way that there is no hindrance to others. The inter-connected departments are kept together.

Principles of Office Lay-Out

The arrangement of men, machinery, furniture and equipment is always made by following certain set rules or principles, which are :

1. **Inter Departmental Relationship** : It is always kept in view that the works which are inter-connected or dependent upon each other, the same are kept side by side. For example, cash and accounts. The cash section cannot work without accounts and vice-versa.

2. **Btter Flow of Work** : All the sections of an office are set up in such a way that the entire series of steps to complete a work may be easily carried on without much wastage of time and energies. By 'Flow of work' we always mean the speed with which the work passes from one hand desk to another.

3. **Office Systems and Routine** : There are certain set procedures or systems for performing the office work. While making the office lay-out it is kept in view that those systems and procedures may be followed easily.

4. **Requirements of Space for Staff and Equipment** : While making an office lay-out, it should be kept in view that adequate space is provided for seating and movement of staff and also the machines or equipment so that those could be conveniently operated upon or used.

5. **Flexibility and Expansion** : The future requirements about the space should also be kept in mind because the organisation may expand sufficiently after sometime and it is not possible for us every time to change the office premises. As such sufficient space should be provided in each section so that any expansion in the near might be easily absorbed without any material change.

6. **Service Facilities or Amenities** : Human beings are always subject to certain requirements like water, air, food etc. For that purpose, complete provision be made in the office about the light, air, ventilation, canteen, drinking water, toilets etc.

However, for a proper lay-out of an office, the above rules or principles should be kept in view so that there is no problem and the office work may be performed easily and efficiently.

Types of Office Lay Out : Open Office and private office :

Thre are two types of Office-layout :—(i) Open offices and (ii) Private or closed offices. Any one of them may be adopted in an office or both may be used in one office, depending upon the availability of floor-space and the requirement of work.

Open Office

An "Open office means a large room where the staff and equipment of all departments or sections are accommodated without partitions".

It may be called a Japanese system of office lay-out also. Under this system, the tables and chairs of all persons working in the office are arranged in a big hall in such a way that there is no partition/s between any section or department. A lot of space may be saved and all persons get the maximum of natural light and air.

There are certain advantages and disadvantages of 'Open office'—

Advantages of Open Office

1. It results in better utilisation on office space.
2. There are economies in office cost and the office space.
3. There is free flow of natural light and air.
4. The communication becomes easier and economical.
5. There is greater flexibility. A little increase or decrease in office work may be adopted within the same means.

Disadvantages of Open Office

1. No secrecy may be maintained in the open office lay-out.
2. The attention and concentration to the work cannot be done.
3. It has un-business like appearance.
4. It creates impersonal atmosphere.
5. There is an adverse effect of accumulated noise on the efficiency of workers.
6. There is minimum movement of staff.

Private or Closed Office

'A Private or Closed Office means small rooms or cabins which are separated from similar other rooms by full or half partitions'.

Under this type of office-lay out, separate closed rooms are provided to each section of an office and the work is carried on separately by each section of an office and the work is Carried on separately by each Section or department within the four walls of the room.

Advantages or Uses of Private Office

1. Prestige in the eyes of empioyees and visitors.
2. The work of confidential nature may be easily performed.
3. The work requiring attention and concentration of mind may be easily performed in private offices.

Disadvantages of Private Office

1. There is much wastage of space on partitions and corridors.
2. Supervision becomes difficult and costly.
3. It prevents free flow of natural light and air.
4. Supervision and control of work becomes difficult and costly.
5. There are problems of communication of information.
6. There is lesser flexibility as compared to open offices.
7. There is increased movement of staff and personnel.

Sketch of a Better Office Lay-out

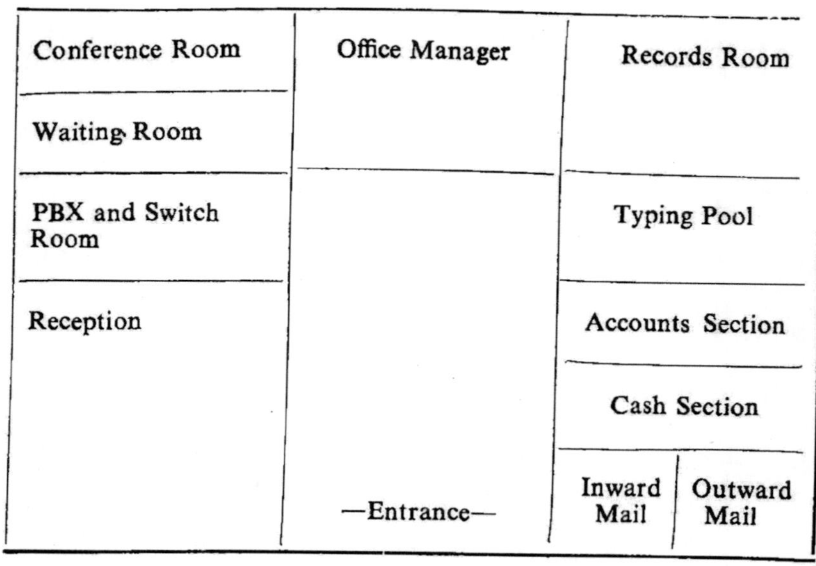

WORKING ENVIRONMENT OR WORKING CONDITIONS

Meaning

By working environment of office, we mean the physical conditions of working i.e. providing such an atmosphere that the office work may be easily performed.

For good working in an office, certain physical conditions are to be provided like good lighting, proper ventilation, decoration etc. All these things have a great impact on the working of an office.

Importance

Providing physical facilities in the office is very important because of the following points :-

1. It gives lesser fatigue to workers.
2. It results in fewer errors in work.
3. The efficiency of office workers is increased.
4. The absenteeism of workers is reduced, because everyone likes to work in a good atmosphere.
5. The morale of workers is boosted upon.
6. There is good image of the organisation in the eyes of workers as well as outsiders.

Factors or Elements of Working Envirnoments

There are many factors which affect the working environment in an office, as under :-

(i) **Interior Decoration** : There should be proper decoration inside the office. The interior decoration includes the following :

(*a*) Colouring of walls ; (*b*) Furnishings ; and
(*c*) Floor coverings.

The place or room where office workers are sitting for hours, should having a good combination of colours on the side walls, ceiling and flooring. Where one has to stare long, the colour should be light green. The ceiling should be white so that it supports light. Like this, light and sober colours should be used in painting of walls, roof etc. The scheme of colour combinanion has assumed such an importance that it has become a separate subject of Science known as *Psychromatics*.

The 'Furnishing' include providing curtains, posters, pictures, rare paintings etc. including the false ceiling, wooden coverings etc. The floor coverings include providing matting, carpets or other such type of coverings on the floor so that when people in an office walk over, it does not create noise and disturb the other workers and at the same time the outside dirt and filth does not come in.

Objectives of Interior Decoration

The 'Interior Decoration' in the office is done with the following objectives in mind :

1. Prestige in the eyes of outsiders and staff.
2. Health of workers.
3. Boosting up of morale of workers.
4. Increased Efficiency.

2. **Office Lighiting** : Proper lighting should be provided in the office. The lighting may be of two types :—

(*a*) Natural Lighting—through sunrays; and (*b*) Artificial Lighting, which may be provided through bulbs (or incandescent) and flourescent tubes.

The *Artificial Lighting* may be of the following types :

(*a*) Direct Lighting—When the bulb or tube is provided with a thick cover and the entire light is cast upon the table where work is performed.

(*b*) Semi—direct Lighting—When the bulb or tubelight is provided with a transparent cover and the major portion of light comes directly and some light is cast upon through the ceiling or side walls.

(*c*) Indirect Lighting—When the reflection of light is not directly cast upon but the entire light comes through the side walls or ceiling. The bulb or tubelight is fitted behind some object and the light comes indirectly.

(*d*) Semi-indirect—Where the reflection of light does not come directly but through the side walls or ceiling and some light comes through the transparent cover.

(*e*) Global Lighting—It is a round light i.e. with a round transparent cover fitted to the bulb or tubelight and, thus, the light comes on all directions.

However, for a *good lighting system*, the following *characteristics* should be there :

1. There should be sufficient quantity of light.
2. The proper density or intensity of lighting should be there.
3. There should not be any glaring or dazzling, otherwise it adversely effects the eyes of workers.
4. There should be no contrasts i.e. no light at one place and more light at other places. The light should be evenly spread over.

Advantages/or Importance of good lighting

1. It results in lesser fatigue to workers.
2. It results in fewer errors or mistakes.
3. It helps in increasing the efficiency of workers.
4. Good Lighting always creates good image of the Organisation.

3. **Sanitation and Cleanliness** : There should be proper arrangements of cleanliness, sanitation and sweeping in the office. For this purpose; besides sufficient number of scavangers or sweepers, there should be a provision of spitoons, drinking water, canteen, toilets, clock and rest-room for the staff.

4. **Ventilation** : Ventilation helps in sucking of bad air from the room or place of working and bringing in fresh air for breathing. When many persons are working at one place, there is suffocation. The fresh air should always be allowed to come in. For this purpose ventilation is provided by two means-by keeping necessary windows and doors ; and by use of exhaust fans.

5. **Office Furniture** : For the purpose of sitting well and working a provision should be there for good type of furniture. The office furniture may be divided into three categories—(*i*) Executive Furniture ; (*ii*) Clerical Furniture ; and (*iii*) Special Furniture.

However, for selecting office furniture the following *factors* should be taken into consideration :

1. It should be attractive and modern.
2. It must have the facility of work performance.
3. The furniture should be adaptable to multi-purpose uses.
4. The cost of furniture should be reasonable.

5. It should be safe and durable.
6. There should be sufficient quantity of furniture in the office.

6. **Reduction of Noise :** Since the office work is paper or clerical work it requires attention and concentration of mind, without any disturbance. The noise may be created from two sources :

(*a*) *Internal*, like clicking of tapewriters, telephone bells, rustling of papers etc. and (*b*) *External*, like street sound, moving vehicles etc. In order to avoid noise in an office, sufficient provision be made of the door-closers, sound-proof walls or partitions, floor coverings, use of buzzers instead of call bells etc.

7. **Safety and Security :** For the purpose, there should be a provision of Fire Extinguishers, First-aid boxes, Security Guards and also the Fidelity Guarantee Insurance Policy for employees working in the office.

QUESTIONS

1. Explain the importance of good working environment for the staff. (*B. Com. Pass, Delhi, 1981*)
2. (a) "Layout is very important for office operations." Explain.
   (b) Discuss the advantages and disadvantages of an open office. (*B. Com, Pass, Delhi, 1981*)
3. (a) What are the principles of office lay out ?
   (b) Discuss the provision of adequate lighting and ventilation in relation to lay-out plan for office. (*B. Com. Pass, Delhi, 1980*)
4. (a) State the importance of proper Layout in planning an office.
   (b) Why is proper office environment considered essential for promoting efficiency of office operations ? (*B. Com. Pass, 1987*)

5

HANDLING THE MAIL

Meaning

The word 'Mail' or 'Dak' is used to denote the bulk of letters which are received in an organisation and the letters which are sent out. The handling of mail implies as to how these letters are properly dealt with or disposed of and despatched. The 'Mail' or 'Dak' may be broadly classified under *two catagories* :--

(*a*) Inward Mail—which represents the letters received.
(*b*) Outward Mail or Dak Despatched—which represents the letters outgoing

A private Secretary should know the efficient handling of both types of Mail—the Inward Mail and the Outward Mail,

Inward Mail

The day, in an office, starts with the letters received from various sources—the customers, suppliers, debtors, creditors, other sections of our own organisation or other outside agencies. For efficient handling of inward mail or dak, there is a certain set procedures in every organisation which, in general, must be known to a private secretary. The following *steps* are generally taken in an office for handling inward mail :

Acknowledging the receipt of letters : The letters may be received through post—ordinary, registered, registered A.D., post bag, post box etc. or those may be received by 'hand delivery' through some messenger. Whatever may be the source, the letters are daily received. For many letters, you have to sign a separate receipt or sign in the hand dak delivery book but, for the letters received by ordinary mail, there may not be any necessity of giving signatures. Where the receipt is required, the same should be given by affixing the rubber stamp of the office (which contains the name of organisation, its postal address, date and time of receipt of letter). Usually, the private secretary has to make his/her own signatures for the letters adressed in the name of boss or the office. Before making signatures, the private secretary should verify that the letter is actually addressed to his/her own office or in the name of boss. Even, for personal letters of boss, the private secretary may receive them and give the acknowledgment.

Opening Envelopes The next step is the opening of letters received. For this purpose, there may be the availability of letter opening machine, otherwise the ordinary office-knife may be used. For opening envelopes, care should be taken that all the contents of envelope are taken to one side and the envelope is teared/broken from one side corner and then the contents are taken out. It should be ensured that all the papers, documents etc. are properly taken out of the envelope. After this, the envelope may be put into the dustbin or, in some cases, the envelopes are also retained and pinned together with the contents for the purpose of verifying the post office marks about the date of posting and the date of delivery etc. Confidential and personal letters are generally not opened by the private secretary unless authorised to do so.

Sorting The entire letters are properly sorted out into ordinary, registered, urgent, confidential etc. Those may also be arranged department-wise or subject-wise.

Affixing Dak Receipt Stamp Every business organisation has its own dak received rubber stamp on which the name of the oganisation, date, serial number, signatures etc. are inscribed. The date in this rubber stamp may be changed every day. The specimen of this rubber stamp is given below :

A.B.C. COMPANY
New Delhi.

DAK RECEIVED
28 FEB. 1987

No.——————————

Sig.——————————

The 'Dak Received' Stamp should invariably be affixed on each and every letter received. It should be put on all letters in such a way that the contents of letter are not distorted or obliterated. It should preferably be affixed towards the left-hand upper corner of a letter or in between the date and body of letter towards the right-hand side or at any other blank space available in the letter. Care should also be taken that this rubber stamp is not affixed on any cheque, draft or any other legal document, otherwise the same might become invalid.

Recording : Generally, all letters received in an organisation are recorded in a particular register called 'Inward Mail Register' or 'Dak Received Register'. In many Organisations, it is the practice that only letters received through registered post may be recorded in the register. As a matter of rule, all letters whether received by ordinary mail or otherwise, should be recorded in the above register. In general, the Dak Received Register has the following columns :

INWARD MAIL REGISTER

Date	*S. No.*	*From whom Received*	*Subject*	*Initials*

How disposed of	*Initials*	*Remarks*

The date of receipt of letter is recorded in the abovc register. The serial numbers generally commence from 1 to any number in a progressive manner. Every year usually this serial number may start from 1. The particulars are noted down in the relevant columns of register and the receiving clerk/official makes his/her initals in token of having received the letter. The same serial number, on which a particular letter has been entered in the above register, is put on the letter received at the space available in the rubber stamp already affixed. The column of 'Disposal' is left blank for the time being but at the later stage we have to make notations as to whether letter filed. replied or any action taken on it and the concerning official has to put his/her initials with remarks in token of having disposed of the letter.

Disposal : After all the letters are recorded in the inward mail register, a private secretary should secrutinize the contents by reading and/or underlining the important details. Necessary remarks ar notations may also be made by the private secretary in the left-hand margin.

All the letters must be kept inside a separate file cover or folder inscribing on it 'DAK RECEIVED'. These should not be taken loose to the boss without the folder. Amongs the letter received, there may be some routine letters/dak which the private secretary may prepare and type out a reply of and the same should also be enclosed with the original letter. The personal or confidential letters may by sent separately to the boss.

Whatever action is taken on the letters received in the office, the necessary remarks should be written against each letter in the inward mail register e.g. seen and filed, replied, sent to such and such person etc. The disposal column of the inward mail register should not remain blank, otherwise any important letter might remain to be replied and the same may remain pending unnecessarily for longer periods.

Outward Mail or Despatch

'Outward Mail' consists of all such letters which are going out of your Organisation. These letters may either be replied to the letters received by you or the letters originating from your office.

There are *two aspects* of outgoing mail—

(*i*) Preparing letters or making the letters ready after drafting, typing and signatures of the Boss.
(*ii*) Despatching letters.

Preparing Letters : The outgoing letters are first of all drafted, then typed and got signed from the Boss. The letters may be prepared through *two sources* :

(*i*) Letters dicated by your Boss ; and
(*ii*) Letters drafted and typed by yourself as a private secretary. It may be noted here that only those letters are usually dictated by a boss which require a special skill of drafting or wherein special care is required or those are important letters requiring some crucial decision or policy matter. However, the routine business letters may be drafted by the parivate secretary himself hereself. Routine letters may include making enquiries, calling quotations, placing an order, acknowledgments etc. Such letters are almost stereo-type and may be easily drafted by private secretary directly on a typewriter.

Boss's Signature : After the day's letters are duly typed it is necessary to take the signatures of your boss on such letters which are ready for despatch. Please note that no letter should go out unsigned otherwise it is not authentic and also that the recipient of letter gets a bad image of inefficiency of your Organisation.

For taking the signatures of Boss on letters which are ready, the following procedure may be followed :

1. Prepare a separate folder or file cover marked as 'FOR SIGNATURES'.

2. Keep all ready letters properly inside the folder. The office copy of each letter should also accompany the original letter. The boss should make his full signatures on the original letter and put initials or short signatures on the office copy.

3. Ensure that all the enclosures are kept duly pinned

with the original letter and the necessary notation about the enclosures is made on the original letter e.g. Cheque No. 002341 Rs. 200/- etc.

4. Take the folder by hand yourself to the boss's desk for getting his signatures on letters meant for despatch. If you are busy in work, you may send the folder through a messenger. Preferably you should take boss's signatures in your presence because if he wants any clarification, you can at least give the same instantaneously and he would face no problem in making his signatures on all letters.

5. When the folder containing letters duly signed by the boss is received back by you you, should ensure that all letters are duly signed by boss and also initials are available on office copies.

6. Take out the original letters, duly signed by boss, by separating from the office copies. You may make notation on respective office copy about the file number etc. so that the office copy may be filed properly and in the correct folder.

7. If any correction, like additions/deletions etc. have been made by boss at the time of signing the letter, the private secretary should ensure that those corrections are also carried out in the respective office copy of letter.

Addressing Envelopes (Writing address on Envelopes)

As soon as the letter is ready, it is checked and signed by the authorised signatory. Then envelopes are prepared for posting them. The envelopes used for this purpose are generally of *two* types :—

(*a*) Window Covers
(*b*) Plain envelopes

Both the above types of envelopes are available in different sizes—smaller or bigger—depending upon the requirements of the Business Organisation.

The 'WINDOW COVERS' have some space for display of address through a transparent thin paper. The letter is folded and put into the envelope in such a way that the Inside Address inscribed on the letter, comes exactly in the window and is visible. There is no necessity of writing address separately on the envelope.

However, it is necessary to write or type out separately the address including the full name and complete postal address on the PLAIN ENVELOPES. While doing so, it is necessary :

(*i*) That the name and address on the envelope should be written or typed *legibly* so that it could be read by all.

(*ii*) That the address on envelope should be *complete and correct* so that there is no delay in delivery of letter to the addressee.

(*iii*) That the display and spacing while writing address on the envelope should be prominent and *attractive*.

In order to achieve the above objectives, the following *Rules* should be observed while addressing the envelopes :

1. Sufficient blank space should be left at the upper half portion of the envelope so that the postal stamps could be affixed easily.

2. The name and address of the Addressee should be correctly spelt out and at the same time it should be complete in all respects like number of building, name of road/street. Town or City together with the correct princode number etc. The name of City or Town should preferably be written typed in bold capital letters and/or underlined. The name of State or Country should also be written writhin brackets.

3. As far as possible, the name and other particulars of address should not be abbreviated to avoid confusion. For example, for New Delhi, we should not write NDLI or so.

4. The mailing notations or directions and other notations like 'Regd. A.D.' 'Express', 'Personal', 'Confidential' etc. should preferably be written/typed at the top towards left-margin of the envelope.

5. For good display and attractive appearance, the style of writing an address on envelope may be fully-blocked or indented. It should be written in single line spacing or double-line spacing depending upon the matter of address. (The styles have been explained in separate chapter).

6. Sender's name and address is usually printed on the envelope towards the left-hand bottom corner or on the back/reverse ef envelope usually with the words 'From' or 'If undelivered, please return to'.

In case the sender's same and address is not printed on the envelope, we should invariably write or type the same in the manner explained above.

An example of addressing the envelope is given below :

REGISTERED A.D.
CONFIDENTIAL

M/s Verma & Company (P) Ltd.,
B-I,[Connaught Place,
New Delhi-110001.

From :
M/s Singh & Sons
Mall Road,
Delhi

(Addressing envelope in Block form)

REGISTERED A.D.
CONFIDENTIAL
To

Messrs. New Delhi Traders,
B-I, Connaught Place,
New Delhi-110001.

From :
M/s Prashant & Co.
City Market,
Bangalore.

(Addressing envelope in Indented form)

Entry in Despatch Register and Numbering—All the outgoing letters are recorded in a register called the 'Outward Mail Register' or 'Despatch Register. This register has generally the following columns :...

S. No.	*Date*	*Name and Address*	*Contents*	*Postage used. Rs. P.*	*Balance*	*Remarks*

It is used for letters sent through the post.

The serial numbers in the above register start from 1 and written progressively for every letter despatched. Every year the serial number re-starts from S. No. 1. All the particulars of an outgoing letter are filled in by the despatcher. The serial number on which a particular letter has been entered, the same serial number is also written on the letter—the original and the office copy.

It should be noted that before recording letters in the above register, the outgoing letters are sorted out in the categories of ordinary mail, registered etc. and then the entry is made in the register.

For the letters to be sent through messenger service, there is a separate 'Local Dak Delivery Book' or 'Hand Delivery Book' or also called as 'Peon Book'. In this book, the following are the various columns—

Date	*S. No.*	*Name and Address*	*Contents*	*Signatures.*

(Specimen of Local Dak Delivery Book)

All the letters to be sent by hand delivery through a messenger are recorded in the above register separately. The peon or messenger delivers the respective letter after obtaining the signatures of recipient on this book.

Affixing Postage Stamps—The postal stamps of the requisite denomination, as per the rates prevailing, are affixed on all envelopes in which the outgoing letters are placed inside.

The postage stamps may be affixed manually by getting the postal tickets from the post office and pasting them on the concerned envelope or by using the FRANKING MACHINE. In the modern organisations we find mostly the postal stamps affixed through the Franking Machine, because the first process is cumbersome, dirty and the chance of manipulation of funds are also there. With the help of a Franking Machine, the postage stamps are printgd in red-colour on the envelopes.

The exact amount of postage incurred is always recorded in the Outward Mail Register, explained above. The total amount of postage used is written every day in the register and the balance amount, in the form of cash or postage stamps, is also recorded. While using the Franking Machine, the opening balance/number is recorded in the register as well as the closing reading of the meter of franking machine. The balance is tallied with postage incurred during the day.

In respect of the letters sent through registered post, the number of receipt issued by post office is also inscribed against the individual letter recorded in the outward mail register. A separate file may be maintained for preserving all the post office receipts of registered letters.

While pasting or imprinting the postal stamps on the respective envelope, care should be taken that those are affixed in such a way that no matter of the envelope is disfigured or obliterated. We must affix the postal stamps towards the right-hand upper corner of the envelope on the front side where address is written.

The Letter Box—At the end, all the envelopes are carefully pasted and put into the letter-box. Only the ordinary letters may be put into the letter box available nearby your office. The registered letters are always sent to the post office and they accept all such letters. There are separate letter·boxes for Q.M.S. (Quick Mail service), under which all letters carrying the pincode numbers of addressee are put, and for packets/parcels or other letters.

Machines and Equipments used for Despatch of Letters

In the outward mail section of the modern business organisation, the following equipments/machines may be used :

1. Postal Franking Machine	—for affixing postal stamps
2. Weighing Scale	—for ascertaining postage amount
3. Addressing Machine	—For writing addresses
4. Pigeon-hole or Docketing	—for sorting of letters
5. Post Office Guides	—for ascertaining postal information about the post offices in India, the services rendered
6. Letter folding machine	—by post offices and the current postal rates etc.

We shall discuss the above, briefly, in the following paragraphs.

1. Postal Franking Machine—This Machine is used for affixing, rather imprinting the postal stamps on envelopes containing outgoing letters. It may be purchased from an authorised manufacturer or may be hired from the post office. It is directly licensed and controlled by the respective post office in India. The machine has to be taken to the post office and the initial amount, for which postage is to be incurred, is deposited in lump sum into the post office, The postal authorities, on receipt of amount, fix up the meter of the machine upto that exent and seal it. For using this machine in an office, first of all, the denomination of postage stamp to be used, is fixed with the help of knobs fitted in it. Then the concerned envelope or letter on which postage stamp is to be affixed is put below a box in the machine and then a handle is rotated once. And the postal stamp of the denomination, already fixed by you, will be printed on the envelope/letter. This machine may be manual i.e. operated by rotating the handle or electric i.e. operated with the help of electricity/power, There is a dial in the machine which shows the accumulated total of postage incurred uptodate. This machine is very useful in offices as the printing of stamps is quick, easy and attractive. It also protects from any sort of manipulation or fraud etc because no cash is handled by the despatcher while using it. But it is costlier,

2. **Weighing Scale or Machine** : It may be used for weighing the envelope containing outgoing letter, paper or documents, for the purpose of ascertaining as to how much for postage may be used. The machine may be small, medium or bigger. Since the postage in India is charged according to the weight of the envelope, this machine is useful in ascertaining the correct amount of postage to be incurred. This machine has a small tray to keep the envelope and the meter indicates the exact weight of the envelope for calculating the postage amount. For weighing parcels, we may use the bigger weighing scale/ machine.

3. **Addressing Machine** : Available in various models and sizes, this machine may be used for addressing the envelopes containing outgoing letters. It may be manually operated or through power. For using this machine, we have to get metal plates or rubber sheets inscribing the correct name and complete address of the addressee. All these master plates rest on a stand fitted to the machine. There is a ribbon which runs through in between the master plate and the envelope. Simply put the envelope at the appropriate place and press the plate over it and the address may be printed. It works much faster and many addreses may be inscribed in much less time. But, this machine is useful only where the addresses are of regular customers, suppliers, shareholders, policy-holders etc. because to such persons regular communications are made and the same master plate may be used again and again. This machine has no use where there are frequent changes in the addresses, because every time the new master plate may be required which would be costlier and not workable. However, the addressing of envelopes with the help of this machine is accurate, legible and attractive.

4. **Pigeon-hole or Docketing** : Generally, for sorting letters in big organisations, it is one of the old methods of filing also. Under it, there is a wooden box in which there are many cages or compartments, like the one used in post office or fitted in R.M.S. railway compartment. Each cage of wooden almirah may be allotted to a particular alphabet and the letters pertaining to a particular alphabet may be put inside the cage. This way, all the letters may be sorted out quickly and conveniently. In bigger organisations, where hundreds of letters are despatched daily, this equipment may be very useful. Otherwise also, it is not costly and easy to use.

Post Office Guides : These are printed books published by the postal authorities in India, containing all details about the post offices – day and night services, the various facilities available to public and also the current rates of postage (inland and foreign). These may be readily available from any main post office on payment of certain amount. These may be used to get any information about the post office services in India and abroad. Every office should obtain and keep the copy of post office guides for use in the Despatch Department.

The post office guides are information booklets which contain the various rules and regulations relating to the inland and foreign post. Starting in 1960, the post office guide is now printed in three volumes, instead of a combined guide before then. The names and periodicity of the *three* parts of post office guides are given below :

(*i*) **Part one**—Containing the rules and regulations relating to the inland post, it is published every five years.

(*ii*) **Part two**—Containing the rules and regulations relating to foreign post and prohibitions etc., it is printed every five years.

(*iii*) **Part three**—Containing the list of post offices, it is published in two volumes *annually*.

All the above volumes/parts of post office guide contain the rules and conditions which have been notified in the Indian post office rules framed by the Government of India.

The contents of the post office guide include the types of poor offices, including night and mobile post office, the business hours of post offices and the various rules regarding payment of postage ; posting of letters ; addressing methods, delivery of letters, recall of articles, enquiries and complaints etc. The various notes for public information are also given in the post office guide. Now-a-days, these post offiee guides are printed in bi-lingual i.e. first Hindi and then English. These are very useful to the public for their general information about the post and telegraph services rendered by post offices in India, as well as foreign countries.

Post Office Services

The letters may be despatched in two ways : (*i*) By hand delivery through a message, and (*ii*) By, Post i.e. through the Post Office. In India, the postal authorities offer various facilities for letters, parcels etc. as well as other communication services like Telegram, Telephone, Telex etc. besides the remittance of funds from one place to another through money orders, telegraphic money orders, postal orders etc. We are giving below some of the important services offered by post offices in India in respect of the outward mail :-

Ordinery Post : The post cards, inland letters and envelopes are included under this heading. If the message is ordinary and very less, the same may be written. typed or printed on a postcard available from the post office at a nominal cost of 15 paise. In case the matter is little more, an inland letter costing 35 paise may be sent. An inland letter may take more message as compared to a post card and the information may also be kept confidential because the inland letter is like a closed cover. Besides the above two, the matter written on a separate paper may be sent under a closed cover called the envelope available from the post office presently at a cost of 65 paise. If a private envelope is used, the postage of only 60 paise may be affixed on it.

Under a Postal Certificate (U.P.C.)

Where the sender of an ordinary mail requires a documentary evidence in token of having posted the letter, this facility may be availed of. Under it three letters (post-card, inland letter or envelope) at one time may be sent to different addresses with an additional postage of 25 paise. What you have to do is that the ordinary letters with requisite postage stamps are taken to the post office. The names and addresses of the receivers are written on a separate piece of paper and a postage stamp of 25 paise is affixed on it. The Post Office takes those letters and affixes its stamp with date in token of having received those letters for posting. The receipt issued by post office may be kept as a documentary evidence. Earlier such a certificate was recognised by Courts of Law in India but now it is not recognised.

Registered Post with/without A.D. (Acknowledgement Due)

Under this facility, the postal authorities assume responsibility of sure delivery of letter/parcel to its receiver. The postage is many times more than the ordinary post. Presently, the minimum charges are Rs. 2.70 and may vary depending upon the weight. The letter has to be taken personally to the post office where they receive it and issue a receipt separately printed out for the purpose. If the sender wants to have the signatures of the addressee, an acknowledgment (which is a printed form available from the post office) is attached to the registered letter. At the time of delivering the letter to addressee, his signatures are obtained by the postman on the acknowledgment and that is a sent back to the sender. The charges for A.D. are extra.

Quick Mail Service (Q.M.S.)

Under this special service, the ordinary letters may be delivered quickly at the place of destination. For this purpose, the sender has to write down the postal pincode number and the letter reaches earlier. Though no extra postage is to be incurred for this purpose, yet presently this facility is limited to big towns only.

Postal Insurance

Under this facility, the registered letter/article may be insured on payment of prescribed insurance premium in addition to the registration charges of the post office. If any envelope contains any costly document or item, this facility may be availed of. If the insured article is lost in transit, the post office would pay the full amount for which the article was insured. The insured articles may be properly packed and sealed before delivering to the post office. The sender has to indicate the amount, on tbe evelope, for which the article has been insured against.

Value Payable Parcel/Letter (V.P.P./V.P.L.)

If the sender wishes to recover the amount before delivering the letter or parcel to its receiver, it can be done through this facility. The letter or parcel is properly packed and sealed. The amount, which may be recovered form the receiver, is also indicated on the envelope. The sender has to fill up the prescribed form available from the post office for the purpose and deliver it alongwith the article/parced/letter. The postal charges for V.P.P./V.P.L. are extra because these include the cost of money order also through which the money may be remitted to the sender.

Post Parcels

Persons sending goods through the post office may avail of this facility. There is a certain limit of bulk weight and upto which post office may accept parcels for delivering it to the addressee. The charges are recovered according to the weight and bulk. A parcel may be sent as an ordinary one or may be resistered. The charges are different in both the cases. Usually, goods having lesser weight and bulk are sent under this facility.

Book Post

For sending the printed material, samples and patterns etc., the facility of book-post may be availed of under which the charges are very less. The envelopes or packets containing the printed matter, books, newspapers, etc., are not closed but properly packed and delivered to the post office with indications—'Book-post'. The size and weight of envelopes/packets are alsy prescribed.

AIR-MAIL SERVICE

This facility is available from the post offices in India. Under this service, a person can send the letters or parcel from India to other countries of the world. For letters, the AEROGRAM is also available, which presently costs Rs. 3.75 only. The Aerogram is just like an Inland letter, which may be sent to any other country of the world. Under the Aerogram, no paper is put, only the written matter may be communicated to any one sitting in any part of the world.

For envelopes, to be sent to other countries by Air-mail Service, the postage rates are different for different countries. For example, for U.K. the minimum charges ase Rs. 4/25 for envelope weighing 10 gms and Rs. 4/90 above that. Similarly, for U.S.A., the minimum postage is Rs. 4/50 and above 10 gms the charges are Rs. 5/40.

The parcels or packets may also be sent to countries outside India through Air-mail. The parcels should be properly attached and packed or duly sealed. Alongwith the Air Parcel, one DECLARATION FORM which is printed and available from the post office, is also filed in and signed by the sender in *quadruplicate* i.e. four copies. This Declaration Form is No. EP-19 and is meant for Customs Declaration. This Form has the columns for Name and Address of Sender, Sender's Referencel, his Name and Address of Sender, Sender's Referencel, his Name and Address including the country of destination, country of origin, number of items, detailed description of contents, weight, value etc. of the parcel.

However, in case the value of goods contained in the air parcel is more than Rs. 50/-, then the permission from Reserve Bank of India is also obtained and a copy of such permission is given to the post office alongwith the parcel. For obtaining, Reserve Bank permission, there is a prescribed form which is filled in and signed in a set of *three*.

The main *advantages* of Air-mail service are : (i) the letters or parcels reach to the destination quickly : and (ii) it is convenient to send and message or goods below the value of Rs. 50/- without completing much of the formalities.

However, the *disadvantages* of Air-mil service are that itis costly and, at the same time, for sending articles valuing over Rs. 50/ many formalities are to be completed.

RAIL PARCEL SERVICE

It is the service performed by railways, under which there is facility of sending goods through railways from one place to another. The goods or articles, to be forwarded, are properly packed and sealed in a packet or bundle and delivered to the parcel office at the railways station. Besides proper packing, it is also necessary that correct address of the sender and receiver of parcel should be inscribed on the packet or parcel. At the railway station, a printed form which is called 'FORWARDING NOTE FOR GENERAL MERCHANDISE' available free of cost from the parcel office of the Railway station, is duly filled in and signed by the sender of parcel and alongwith it the parcel is delivered at the railway station for booking. The Forwarding Note for merchandise contains the columns of name and address of consigner, consignee Station to and from, number of articles and description/marking of goods etc. The *maximum weight permissible* is 1½ Quintals. The size of packet or parcel should also not be more than the following dimensions -

1½ Mt. × 2 Mt. × 1¼ Mt.

i.e the maximum length of parcel is 2 Mt. and the maximum height and width is 1½ Mt. and 1¼ Mt. respectively. The railway authorities generally do not accept any parcel beyond the above dimensions, because of the capacity of parcel van in the train.

The charges for sending parcels through railways are of two types—Superfast trains and Ordinary trains. The charges for superfast are little more than the other trains. Usually from New Delhi and any other big station, the parcels are sent through superfast trains. The charges are also made according to *mileage*/kilometer basis and per quintal, depending upon the weight of the parcel to be sent. The minimum charges are Rs. 8/- for ordinary and Rs. 10/ for the superfast.

The *advantages* of rail parcel service are :

(*i*) It is easy and convenient to send goods through railways because not much formalities are completed :

(*ii*) It is cheaper means to forward goods to any station throughout the country and at any time ;

(*iii*) For bulky and heavy goods having lesser value, rail parcel service is the only means for sending packets or parcels of merchandise.

However, the *disadvantages* are that it takes comparatively more time for the goods to reach to the beneficiary and (ii) also that mishandling of parcels by railway staff results in damages or breakage of goods besides pilferage and theft.

However, on delivering the parcel or packet at the sending railway station, the railway authorities issue a Railway Receipt which is an acknowledgement of goods for transmission. The goods or parecls may be taken delivery of at the destination. On production of the railway receipt.

Post Box

The Post Office Authrities allow the bigger Organisations to take on rent a post box having a distinctive number for a full year or part of the year on payment of requisite charges, An application on the printed prescribed form obtained from the post office may be submitted to the main post office of the area together with the necessary fees. A delivery ticket and a key to the box is allotted to the holder. The duplicate key is retained at the post office. All letters bearing the post box number allotted to a person, are put into the concerned box and locked. The owner of the box may collect such incoming letters from the post box during the working hours of the post office. A representative of the post box owner may also visit the post office for clearance of the incoming mail. The Post Box facility ensures quick delivery of letters and to the right person. It is also not costly as the charges are nominal.

Post Bag

Under the post box facility, there is one disadvantage and, that is, the letters may be dropped on the way while collecting from the post office and taking to your place. To avoid this, the post office may allot a bag in which all the incoming letters may be preserved and the bag, containing incoming letters, may be taken to your place. This bag may be locked. One key remains with the hirer and the other with the post office. The post bags are also allotted distinctive numbers like the post boxes. The Post Box and the Bag may also be taken together on payment of the requisite charges to the post office. The post bag may also be used for sending dak to the post office. The facility of Post Bag carries many advantages:

(*i*) There is safety and security of letters in transit from the post office to the place of hirer of the post bag ;

(*ii*) The delivery of incoming letters is comparatively quik and sure ;

(*iii*) There is the facility of sending outward mail to the post office. However, the disadvantage is that in case the messenger or representative of hirer of post bag does not reach in time to the post office, the delivery of *dak* may be delayed. Moreover, an additional expenditure on payment of rent to the post office is incurred.

Still, both the above facilities are of greater importance to traders and businessmen under the present-day conditions.

Poste Restante.

Whenver there is no fixed address on which a letter may be delivered through the post just as in case of travelling sales representatives, the letters may be sent marked care of Post Master concerned. The Post Master keeps all such letters with him. The addressee of such a letter may contact the Post Master and take the delivery of letter. This facility is available to public free of cost but the identification has to be made before taking delivery of letter, When the Post Master is stisfied that the addressee of a letter is the same person, he may deliver the letter. But such letters may not be kept for over 3 months with the Post Office. Thereafter these are returned to the senders respectively.

QUESTIONS

1. Outline the procedure for handling 'including' and 'Outgoing' mails in an Office. Do you think centralisation of mailing department will improve the efficiency in handling mails ?
   (B. Com. Pass, Delhi, 1986)
2. Give an outline of the routine that should be followed in bussiness office for opening, distributing and recording of inward mail. *(B.T.E., Delhi, Ist Yr. 1987)*
3. Write short notes on :
   (a) Peon Book
   (b) Rail Parcel Service
   (c) Airmail Service *(B.T.E., Delhi, SP, Ist Yr. 1987)*
4. Compared to Rail Parcel Service, what are the advantages of Air Mail Service Give a brief account of the Air Mail Service operating in India. *(B.T.E., Delhi, SP-I, 1984)*
5. Describe the procedure of work in the Mailing Department of a modern business office. Do you think centralisation of the Mailing Department will improve the efficiency in handling mail ? *(B.T.E., Delhi, SP-I. 1981*

6

EFFICIENT COMMUNICATION

Meaning

The word 'Communication' has been derived from the Latin word COMMUNIS which means common. Anything which is common may be called commnuication. The most common thing in every walk of life is giving and taking information to which we may call as communication. In the day-to-day ordinarily speaking lanaguge, the communication implies 'passing on of information from one person to another.' In other words, "It is an exchange of facts, ideas, opinions or emotions by two or more persons." (Newman and Summer) The term 'Communication' has also been defined as under :

"It is the process of conveying information from one person to another through post, by telephone, by messenger service or by any other means."

According to Oxford English Dictionary, 'communication' means "imparting, conveying or exchange of ideas. knowledge etc. whether by speech, writing or signs."

According to the American Management Association, communication' means "Any behaviour that results in exchange of meaning."

A more detailed definition may be given as under :

"Communication, simply stated, means the process of passing information from one person to another. It is the process of imparting ideas and making oneself understood by others. Thus communication is the conveying of information from one person to another."

From the various definitions, given above, we may come to know that 'communication' is the process of passing on of information from one person to another in such a way that the other person, who receives the information, should understand it in the same sense in which the communicator wants it. However, the communication has no value if the information is not correctly interpreted by the recipient of information. It is a wide term and includes even gestures or symbols signifying something.

Salient Features

From the above definitions of 'communication', we may derive the following special features of 'communication' :—

1. It is the *process* of exchange of information between two or more persons.
2. It is the *means* to convey information from one person to another.
3. It involves both the information and the understanding.
4. It is the major function of office.

Qualities of a good communication system or Factors for selection of communication system :—

The information may be exchanged by any of the means—telephone, verbal discussions, writing letters or by any other means but, for a good system of communication, certain qualities must exist :—

Speed	Accuracy	Secrecy	Safety
Distance	Records	Cost	Impression
Expansion			

The above points may be explained in brief here. The communication of information should be fast, correct and it should not be leaked out in the process. It should be safe and must reach to any distant place. There should be a facility to keep a record of it. It shonld not be very costly. Ii must leave a good impression over the recipient. It must be flexible in order to adopt the increasing requirements of future.

Communication Process-Steps

As we have already discussed, 'communication' is a process,

As such, a series of steps are taken to complete it. The various *steps* taken to complete the process of communication are as under :—

1. **Perception** : The first step is that the ideas or thoughts come to the mind of a certain person, called the 'Communicator'. The ideas are conceived or perceived.

2. **Encoding** : The ideas or thoughts are put into some symbols or channels so that those could be conveyed to the receiver.

3. **Transmission** : Then the communication symbols are conveyed to the receiver through some mechanical or manual devices.

4. **Receiving and Decoding** : The information is received by the receiver and that is translated into the day-to-day ordinary language for interpretation and action.

5. **Responding** : Finally, the action is taken by the receiver of the message. He acts upon it.

When all the above steps are taken the process of communication is complete and the message or information is said to be communicated.

Objectives

The communication is done for the following purposes :—

1. **Information** : i.e. the receiver is to be given some information or taken some information from him. An information may be anything which is usefull for any purpose any time.

2. **Advice or Counselling** : When someone is to be advised, we make the communication.

3. **Order-operation** : When any direction is to be issued and, to ensure its compliance, the communication may be made.

4. **Suggestion** : When something is to be suggested, the communication may be made.

5. **Persuasion** : When someone is pursuaded or motivated to do something, the communication may be done.

6. **Education** : It implies general awareness in the various fields of knowledge, for which communication may take place.

7. **Warning** : Communication may also be done in order to give a caution or signal against any risk of danger, e.g. displaying on a board 'Danger 440 volts' etc.

8. **Raising morale** : For the purpose of boosting up the morale of workers in an organisation, the up-to-date information may be furnished or communicated to them.

Types of Communication ;

COMMUNICATION

- Internal
  - Oral
    - Face to-face
  - Written
    - Messenger Service
    - Centralised Mail
  - Mechanical
    - Pneumatic Tubes
    - Conveyor Belts
    - Intercom
    - Speaking tubes
    - Dictaphone
  - Staff Location System
    - Bells and Buzzers
    - Lighted Signals
    - Public addressing
    - Wireless
    - Signs and Posters
    - Television
    - Teleprinter
    - Telex and Telephone
- External
  - Oral
    - Personal visit
  - Written
    - Messenger service
    - Post Office Services
    - Telegrams
  - Mechanical
    - Telex
    - Telephone

(N.B. The mechanical communication may be both-oral as well as written).

INTERNAL COMMUNICATION

It consists of passing on information or message inside or within an organisation. The internal communication may be within one department or section, between the employees of the one department, or it may be from one department to another department within the same organisation. It may be upward, i.e. from the lower level staff to the upper hierarchy management or down-ward, from the top management to the lower level staff, or vice versa. Whatever may be the direction of communication, the internal communication may be oral/verbal, written, mechanical or staff location systems.

In the *Oral or Verbal* Communication within an Organisation, the face to face communication is the best. Under this, the communicator may call or visit the receiver of message and convey or discuss the matter fully well. The communication, under it, is very easy, convenient, economical, efficient and effective but the only disadvantage of 'face to face communication' may be that it is not suitable where the information, rather the same information, is to be conveyed to various parts or persons and, also, that much time may be wasted under this types of communication.

Written Communication may take the form of writing letters, memorandum, reports etc. In Internal communication, the written communication offers various advantages like accuracy, exactness, details, records and reference, widest coverage and avoiding the personal visits. But, the written internal communication suffers from many disadvantages, like disputes, red tapism and depriving the recipient of the opportunity to explain. Still, most of the internal communication takes place in writing in offices and, for that, *messenger services* may be utilised, in which the peon or messenger takes the letters to the recipient. However, in bigger organisation, there may be a centralised section where the entire letters are received and then distributed to all concerned.

Amongst the *Mechanical devices* for internal communication, *Pneumatic Tubes* may be used. A cylindrical pipe connects the various offices or departments of an organisation by means of which cylinders, containing papers or documents etc., are conveyed by section from one department to another or wherever required. This system is useful where the services of peons or other such staff may be avioded to carry the written letters, documents etc. However, Pneumatic tubes are not much in vogue in our country.

Conveyor Belts are also one of the types of mechanical device for internal communication. These are wider belts fitted to a motor and through which the dak or documents may be carried from one department to another. It is the same type of system as we may see at the airports for carrying luggage of passengers. However, this system may be used where the destination is fixed and extra space is available in the office.

Teleprinter and Telex are the machines which work on the electromagnetic system. Written messages may be passed on through these machines very quickly. There is the combination of typewriter and the telephone. When the line is connected by means of dialing, message may be typed fast and, at the same time, the same message is automatically typed at the other end. However, in Teleprinter, the message can only be given one-way, whereas, on telex, the massages may go both ways. Even the reply may be obtained instantaneously. However, written may be given quickly on both the machines. These machines may be purchased or hired from the Post Office. These are easy to instal and operate upon. Any typist may operate upon both the machines conveniently and without much of skill or training.

Telex—It is the mechanical device through which written messages may be communicated from one place to another within the country or even outside the country. It has a key-board like that of a typewriter and a telephone like dial. The number of the other subscriber is dialled like a telephone and when it is connected, the machine starts working. The message may be typed and the same text is automaticaly typed at the other end in bold capital letters. The telex machine may either be hired from the post office or it may be owned by a subscriber. It is very commonly used machine in the modern offices.

There are various *advantages* of a Telex. The message is passed on in writing and, as such, the documentary evidence of message may be kept. Besides it, there is the facility of getting instant reply also. The receiver of message may type out the reply and the same would be received at the sender's telex machine. The only *disadvantage* of Telex is that it is a costly machine and expensive also. Hence smaller organisations cannot afford to use it.

Any ordinary typist can operate upon the Telex machine with a little knowledge about the various keys used for changing the line, spacing and calling back the receiver. No special training is required. The messages are typed on a continuous paper-roll fitted to the machine.

Intercom—It is a private Inter-Communication system which may be used as a mechanical device for oral communication within an organisation. This system may be operated by electric power or a battery. Under it, the various extension lines are provided and the telephone like instrument is provided for each extension. A separate number is allotted to each extension and the communicator has simply to push the button of the concerned extension number. The other person picks up the receiver like telephone and may talk with the communicator. The various manufactures have designed intercom systems differently and the size of system depends upon the requirements of the organisation. There may be 10, 20 or more extensions. However, this system can be installed only where a number of separate rooms are provided to different sections within an organisation. It is simple, easy to instal and inexpensive but the initial cost of installation of this system is high.

Staff Location Systems—Under the Internal Communication, it is a device through which the required persons are located or found out or called, Usually. the messengers, clerks or assistants are located by the officers in the office through the various systems outlined below : –

1. **Bells or Buzzers** : These are installed outside the cabins or rooms of the officers, who just push the button and the bell or buzzer makes sound to call a particular person. These are mostly used in every office.

2. **Lighted Signals** : Under this system, there is the sound like ringing of buzzer and at the same time the lighted signal also comes in.

3. **Public Addressing system** : Under it, the messages are conveyed with the help of mike or loudspeaker.

4. **Wireless** : It is used to flash the messages quickly from one place to another. It works on the same lines as transistors or radios.

EXTERNAL COMMUNICATION

It involves sending information outside the organisation—to customers, suppliers, creditors or other outside persons. Such communication is not confined to a particular organisation but to anyone outside the organisation.

Messenger Service is one of the means of communication under which the letters written and addressed to outsiders are sent through the peons or messengers. The letters duly written and signed are put into the covers or envelopes and address is also written. Then these are recorded in a 'Hand Delivery Book' or 'Peon Book'. The messenger takes all such letters and takes the signature of the recipient in token of having delivered the letter. This system ensures quick and definite delivery of written message but where the addressees are sporadic and many, then this system cannot be adopted and becomes useless.

Post Office Services also play an important role in the external communication. In India, the post offices provide various services for sending and receiving written messages. These have been discussed elsewhere.

Telegrams are also used for sending written messages quickly from one place to another. These may be ordinary or express and both of them may be reply-paid also. Written messages are immediately conveyed over the machines with the Telegraph Department.

Telephone

Telephone is the means of oral/verbal communication. It may be used both for internal as well as external communication. The facility of telephone is provided by the Telephone Department to a subscriber who can either own a telephone under the OYT (Own Your Telephone) Scheme by depositing a sum of money with the concerned department or obtain the same on rental basis in India. The details about the various types of telephones, telephone calls and handling the same are given in the chapter 'HANDLING TELEPHONE' which may be perused by the reader.

Barriers to Communication

It is necessary that the communication should be smooth and perfect so that the message communicated by the communicator reaches well to the receiver and he understands it fully and acts accordingly in the right sense. But, in practical life, it seldom happens that the message is correctly received and rightly interpreted because of the following reasons which we may call as *barriers or bottlenecks to communication* :—

1. **Bad Expression** : If the communicator is not able to express himself properly, the message cannot be passed on to the other end and the result is that there is miscommunication or communication gap.
2. **Inaccurate Translation** : In case the message is wrongly translated by the receiver, then also there are chances of mis-communication.
3. **Poor Retention or Loss in Transmission** : If the persons or channels through which the message passes on, is/are not able to keep up the full text of the message, then also there is mis-communication or communication gap.
4. **Inattention** : If the persons through whom the message is passed on, are not attentive, the messages not properly passed on to the other end.
5. **Vague or Unclarified Assumptions** : If people take vague assumption prior to the receipt of actual message, then also there are chances of miscommunication.

6. **Inadequate Period of Adjustment** : In case reasonable time is not allowed to the communicatee for making adjustment to the changed conditions, it is not possible to respond to the message rightly.
7. **Distrust** : When the persons through whom the message is routed, do not keep trust or full faith in each other, there is every chance that the interpretation of message is not correctly read.
8. **Fear** : When fear prevails between the persons—the communicator and the communicatee—then also the full and complete/correct details are not reaching and the result is that there is always a communication gap.
9. **Failure to Communicate** : Many times, the message is not sent from the communicator's side at all, the result is that there is no communication.
10. **Language Barriers** : Many a time, the problem of different languages in between the process of communication also arises due to which the communication is not proper and incomplete.
11. **Mechanical Barrier** : When mechanical devices like telephone, telex etc. are used for communication of messages and those machines suffer from distortions, filterings and overloading etc., then also the communication is not smooth and it results in miscommunication of information.

MEASURES TO OVERCOME BARRIERS

However, the following measures may be taken to overcome the various barriers to communication outlined earlier :—

1. **Shortening the Line of Communication** : So far as possible, we should reduce the number of hands through which the message is passed on. It may overcome the various barriers like retention, inattention, distrust etc. The communication should, therefore, be direct and not many intermediaries be involved in it.
2. **Use of Simple and Meaningful Language** : So that everyone may easily understand the message and respond to it.
3. **Developing Patience** : One should have the for bearance and power to listen and understand others in the right

earnest. It would improve the quality of communication. There should not be any haste, rather reasonable time be devoted for receiving and responding the information.

4. **Developing Mutual Trust** : It is also necessary that we should not be unnecessarily suspicious about everyone unless and otherwise there are valid and solid reasons therefor. It would result in smooth sailing.

Many times, the informal communication also plays an important role in the organisation, which we may call as GRAPEVINE. It consists of gossiping and informal discussion between the employees during off hours of office.

QUESTIONS

1. Distinguish between the following :
   (a) Internal Communication and External Communication.
   (*B. Com. Pass, Delhi, 1985*)
2. What are the different systems of mechanical communication available in a modern office ? Describe the advantages and limitations of telex-communication.
   (*B.T.E. Delhi, SP-II, 1987*)
3. What do you mean by communication ? What media would you suggest for a modern large-sized organisation for oral communication ? (*B.T.E. Delhi, SP-II, 1987*)
4. Write short notes on :
   (i) Telephone Directories (ii) Encyclopaedias
   (iii) Railway Time Table (iv) Year Books
   (v) Forms & Stationery (*B.T.E. Delhi, SP-II, 1984*)
5. Outline the different methods used for communication in an office. (*B. Com. Pass, Delhi, 1987*)

7

FORMS AND STATIONERY

Meaning

Since office work is primarily the paper or clerical work, it involves the use of a lot of papers, envelopes, printed letter-heads, printed forms, and a number of other small articles. These may be used in the office for completing the work and may be called as 'Office Stationery'. In the mordern office, there is a variety of stationery items used, depending upon the requirements and styles of working. The term 'stationery' may be defined as:—

"Those small articles/items which are used regularly in an office".

In other words, "stationery" denotes papers, printed forms accessories used in an office as a device to complete the office work.

From this definition, we can come to know that stationery refers to many items like printed letter-heads, plain papers, carbons, pencils, eraser, sharpner, stencil papers, correcting fluid and typing ribbons etc. All these items are useful in the day to day working of an office because most of the clerical work is performed with the help of the above items.

A modern Private Secretary has to take care of all the stationery items provided in the office because a major portion of the office cost, say, about 40% of the total office cost, excluding the expenses on salary, comes on stationery items. As such, a greater control has to be exercised in respect of the office stationery.

Advantages

The main advantages of using office stationery are as under :

(i) A lot of time and labour may be saved if proper stationery is available in adequate quantity.

(ii) It brings an efficiency in office operations.

(iii) It facilitates speedy use of various office machines.

(iv) By use of stationery, it is possible to apply the office procedures into practice on account of proper designing of office forms etc.

(v) It helps in bringing uniformity and standardisation of work.

Types of Stationery

Briefly, the following are the various items included in office stationery:

1. **Printed Forms**—These are printed papers or cards which provide space for entering the details of information or instructions in the columns or cages according to the laid down plan. In the printed forms, the necessary information is printed and for obtaining other details, the blank space is left which may be completed by hand or on a typwriter. The printed forms make it easy to give detailed and correct information without much problem. They are almost standardised and the requisite information is planned in advance and printed therein. Now-a-days, there is an increasing use of printed forms in the offices, because these forms facilitate giving or taking the information accuratcly and much quicker.

For designing and printing the forms, a number of *principles* are followed, which may be explained as under:—

(i) The forms should be simple and facilitate easy use. These should be so designed that the users do not feel difficulty in giving information. At the same time, the sorting etc. should also become easy. The display and spacing arrangement in each form should be such that all information or instructions are clearly visible.

(ii) The forms should be in different colours for different purposes so that the identification becomes easy.

(iii) The forms should be designed and printed in such a way that there is a proper facility of punching or perforating them, when required.

(iv) Every form should be given a name and the number so that it becomes easy to remember them.

(v) The form should not be larger than necessary to accommodate the required matter. For determining the size of forms we should take into consideration the length and breadth of column for writing digits or description and also to make the required entries.

(vi) The paper used for the forms should be selected after giving consideration to the frequency with which the forms may be used and the period for which those are to be preserved as well as the cost of paper and printing.

(vii) The forms should be divided into various parts, depending upon the requirements.

2. **Continuous Stationery** : It may be defined as a device whereby office forms are produced in continuous strips and where separate forms are divided by perforation or in the form of *rolls* like the paper rolls used on a cash register or adding and listing machines on which the information may be continuously printed with the help of machine. The other type of continuous stationery may be called *interfold*, where a complete sheet of paper is folded or separated in between. Both these portions might be used as the original and the office copy. The third type of continuous stationery may be *fanfold*, in which a single sheet may be divided into various parts and all the parts may be used for various purposes.

3. **Other Supplies** : The stationery may include other small articles like pins, pens, pencils, carbons, typing ribbon, eraser, papers, envelopes. etc. Since it is not possible here to explain, in detail, each and every items, we are giving below the summary of important items of stationery:—

(1) Papers : The paper used in an office may be typing papers, duplicating papers, etc. These are available in various sizes and makes. The common sizes of paper used in an office are given below :—

(1) Foolscap—8″ × 13″ approximately
(2) Quarto —8″ × 10″ approximately
(3) Octavo —5″ × 8″ approximately

Besides the above, there are even much bigger or smaller sizes of papers which may be obtained from the market depending upon the requirements of office ? The typing and duplicating papers are available in the market in reams, one ream containing 480 to 500 sheets.

(2) Printed Letter-Heads : Every modern business organsisation has got the printed letter-heads, which contain the name of the firm, nature of business, address, telephone number, telex number, telegraphic code address etc. The printed letter-heads are attractively set out and nicely printed. These are used for writ ing or typing thc letters emanating from the office. The sizes of the letter-heads are also like that of papers given earlier.

(3) **Envelopes** :—The various types and sizes of envelopes may be used in an office. These are made of ordinary paper and may be either 'window' covers or 'plain' envelopes. The window covers are such envelopes in which a certain portion is cut and wrapped with transparent thin paper. There is no necessity of writing address separately on the envelope but the letter is folded and put inside the envelope in such a way that the address is visible through the window. The most commonly used sizes of envelopes, used in India, are as under :—

$6 \times 3\frac{1}{2}$" approximately

$8\frac{9}{10} \times 3\frac{8}{10}$,, ,,

$9\frac{9}{10} \times 4\frac{4}{10}$,, ,,

$10\frac{8}{10} \times 4\frac{8}{10}$,, ,,

Priniciples of Stationery Control

As the major portion of office cost is involved in stationery, it is necessary that a proper control should be exercised on all the stationery items which may be purchased, stored, or consumed in the office. For this purpose, the following principles may be followed :—

1. **Purchase of Stationery** :—Usually, the starionery is purchased at one place for the entire organisation because it saves a lot of office cost if it is purchased in wholesale. For the purpose of purchasing, we should remember the following points :

(i) What type of stationery should be bought?
(ii) How much stationery should be bought?
(iii) How it should be bought?

The answers to the above three questions are given hereunder :—

Only the right type of stationery should be purchased for the offices. Only those items be purchased which are actually used for the day-to-day office working. Irrelevant purchases should be avoided otherwise it will entail dead investment of money. We should purchase only that much quantity of stationery which may be consumed during a short period. For the right quantity of stationery, we should take into consideration the actual consumption of stationery, the time taken for procuring it, availability of storing space, the availablility of finance and the risk of stationery items becoming obsolete or out of date. If we keep these factors into consideration, we can certainly buy the right quantity of stationery for our office.

For purchasing the stationery for the organisation as a whole, we should always make centralised purchase by calling the tenders. or price quotations from various dealers or manufacturers. Which ever quotation or tender is found lowest or most competitive, we may place the order for supply of stationery.

2. **Upkeeping and Storage** : There should be adequate space available, in the office for storage of stationery purchased. For this purpose, the slotted angle-racks are generally used on which the different types of stationery items are arranged properly and stored. However, the important items of stationery may be keept in a cupboard or almirah under the safe custody of an authorised official. Care should be taken that stationery could be saved from dampening or insects and, at the same time, it should not be exposed to dust and sunrays.

3. **Issuing Stationery** : From the centralised stationery department, proper arrangement should be made to issue stationery to various departments or sections. For this purpose, the requisition slips, lists, or indents may be called for. An indent is the technical name given to the list of stationery and which may contain the quantity issued, consumed, balance, and the fresh requirements of stationery. A proper control should always be exercised while issuing the stationery. Otherwise it will result into wastage of stationery.

4. **Controlling Consumption** : The last principle is how to control of stationery in the office. There should always be a check by surprise visit of senior officers or authorities in order to ensure that there is no unnecessary wastage through misuse or by carrying away the stationery items by the workers to their homes.

QUESTIONS

1. Enumerate the benefits which are derived by the management from forms control. *(B. Com. Delhi, 1986)*
2. How can control over office stationery be exercised ? *(B. Com., Delhi, Paper VI, 1986)*
3. What are the essential elements of a sound system of stationery control ? *(B. Com. Pass, Delhi, 1985)*
4. (a) Write a note on standardisation of office stationery.
   (b) Write short note on designing office forms. *(B. Com. Pass, Delhi, 1983)*
5. Write short note on objects and steps in forms control. *(B. Com. Pass, Delhi, 1982)*
6. Discuss the significance of forms : What are the principles of form designing ? *(B.T.E., Delhi, SP-II, 1987)*
7. Why is it necessary to have a proper control over stationery in a big business organisation ? Suggest a system of sound control over issue and storage of stationery. *(B.T.E., Delhi, SP-II, 1987)*
8. State the advantages of using continuous stationery in a modern office. *(B. Com. Pass, Delhi, 1987)*

8

DUPLICATING AND PHOTOCOPYING

In an office, there may be the necessity of reproducing many copies of a single document or paper. The system of typing the same matter again and again has become outmoded. Hence, a number of methods are now used for reproducing multiple copies.

DUPLICATING

It is the process of reproducing many or multiple copies of a letter or document, where all the copies are alike and as good as the original, The word 'Duplicating' should not be confused with copying because in copying the first copy is the original and the other one is an extract of the original. Actually, in the duplicating process, a master copy is first prepared and then the multiple copies are reproduced from that.

Methods—

There are various *methods* of duplicating. The commonly used methods in offices have been discussed in the following paragraphs.

(i) **Hectorgraphy or Spirit duplicating** : Under the process, a master copy is prepared with the help of a special carbon known as 'Hectograph'. When the paper is written or typed, a reverse impression is obtained on the back of the master copy. Coloured carbons may also be used for preparing the matter yielding a coloured reproduction. After preparing the matter, it is clipped at one end to the machine called the duplicator. The copy paper is now fed through the machine which is damped and after a contact with the master copy may be obtained. This process is generally used for taking copies of documents or lay-out maps of building etc.

(ii) **Offset Lithography** : Under it, a master copy is prepared on a slab of stone or on metal sheets and rotary type of duplicator is used to take out copies. The machine works on the offset lithography principle which is antipathy of grease or oil and water. Firstly, the damped rollers and then inked rollers are applied to take the impression from the master. Though it is simple and cheap form of duplicating, yet it is treated as the cumbersome and obsolete method of duplicating in the modern days.

(iii) **Carbon Copying** : Under this process, the copies are taken by putting carbon papers Separate carbon papers are available for typing and for writing by hand. With the help of a ballpen or hard pencil, the matter may be written by hand or many copies may be taken on a typewriter. The First copy is called the original and the others are carbon copies. Though it is very simple and cheap process, yet many copies cannot be taken out by this process. If it is an electric typewriter, we may take upto a maximum of 15 copies otherwise 3-4 copies can only be taken with this process.

(iv) **Stencil Duplicating** : It is the most commonly used process of taking out multiple copies in the offices. According to this process, first of all, the stencil paper is cut either writing by hand or on a typewriter. A stencil paper is a wax paper over which the matter may be written with a hard nib pen called 'stylus'. For typing on stencil paper, care is taken that the ribbon of type-writer is not working or not used while typing. For corrections of mistakes or errors, a special type of fluid called the 'correcting fiuid' is used, which is applied on the wrong matter and correct matter may be written or typed. However, the stencil paper should be properly cut so that the perforation is good.

After cutting the stencil paper the same is pinned to a machine called 'Stencil Duplicator' or 'Cyclostyling Machine'. In this machine, there are two trays, In one tray the blank papers are kept and the machine is rotated manually or electrically. One by one the blank paper goes inside the machine and after getting a contact with the stencil paper, the printed copy comes out on the other tray of the machine.

There are many *advantages* of this process—(i) It is the simplest process, (ii) it is economical, (iii) many copies may easily be taken out (iv) the copies are legible and attractive ; (v) the stencil paper may also be retained and re-used after some time.

However, the *disadvantages* are : (i) It is uneconomical if the copies are beyoned one or two thousand ; (ii) the exact impression of emblem or the Photograph cannot be taken ; and (iii) the equipment & papers are also not easily available.

Overall, it is the most practical and useful method of duplicating in the modern offices.

Now-a-days, there is an electronic process of cutting the stencils which is a very quick process but little costlier.

PHOTOCOPYING

It is the process of taking out the photographic impression of a document on a separate plain paper. It comes exactly the same as the original. Even the emblem, signature or any other sign or symbol on the original document comes as it is. The machines used for photocopying have been explained separately under the chapter on 'Office Machines and Equipments'.

The following are the main *advantages* of photocopying :—

1. There is no necessity of preparing separately the master with which the copies may be reproduced but only the photo impression of the original document is taken. Hence, it saves a lot of money and time. Within minutes, the copies are ready and at a very less cost.

2. Photocopying avoids human errors. There is no need of checking the original, because exact photocopy of the document is taken.

3. It saves a lot of labour, rather the machines themselves reprodce the copies, It is difficult to take out a copy of the original document other than photocopying.

4. With the help of photocopying, it is possible to take out the copies of sketchs, diagrams, signs etc. which may not otherwise be possible by any other means.

There are certain *drawbacks* of photocopying. Only a limited number of copies may be taken with the photocopying process. If a large number of copies are to be photocopied, it becomes expensive. Moreover, the life of the photocopied matter is short and it fades away after sometime because the chemicals are used for photocopying and with the lapse of time, the impression becomes weak.

Photocopying Methods

The following are the various methods of photocopying :—

(i) **Diffusion Transfer** : Under this method the first exposure is taken on a negative and then it is processed in the machine to get a readable copy immediately. Actually, under this process, a positive and the negative are fed together into the machine with the original document. The original is taken out after exposure and the positive and negative both are used to take out a copy immediately. This process gives one copy in a minute and is comparatively a slow process. It may be used for preparing charts, sketches and maps, etc.

(ii) **Reflex** : Under the method a-negative copy is prepared. and after processing, the positive copies are taken out by further exposure, developing and drying them. It is comparatively a better process than the earlier one.

(iii) **Blue printing or Dye-line** : Under this method, the original is transferred to a transluent sheet and then it is placed in contact with a special dye-line paper and subjected to a sharp and brighter light. The positive copy is developed by soaking it in three or four solutions and then dried up. It is a simple process and not very costly. However, it can produce only a limited number of copies.

(iv) **Electrostat** : It is a dry process under which the impression of the original document is translated on a plain paper with the help of electrical rays. The original document is projected on a coated plate fitted into the machine. The plate is charged through electricity. The plain sheet of paper is placed on it and the image comes exactly on it. This proces is instant and direct.

(v) **Microfilming** : The most modern method of photocopying is preparing a negative film with the help of a camera which is fitted into the machine called the Microfilmator. The photographs of the documents are taken with the help of a camera and then the film is developed in order to retain it as a part of records. There is a projector fitted into the machine over which the film may be played and one can read the contents of the photocopied document. This method is used for keeping the records of a Business Organisation. The original papers or documents are not preserved but the film is prepared and kept on record. With this method, the space problem is solved. The roll of film may be stored by preparing suitable index of all the film rolls.

Difference between Duplicating and Photocopying

If one thinks minutely, the duplicating is different than photocopying though both the methods may be used to reproduce multiple copies. The points of differences are :

1. In duplicating, basically one master copy is prepared and from that the multiple copies are reproduced and all the copies are similar. In the photocopying, no master is prpared rather the exact impression of the original document is taken again and again.

2. In duplicating, it is possible, to imprint a large number of copies, say 500, 1000 or more but in photocopying it is not possible. Generally, a limited number of copies are taken with the help of photostat or electrostat machines.

However, both the processes are very useful for modern offices and these save a lot of time, energy and money.

QUESTIONS

1. What is 'Duplicating'? Explain the various methods of duplicating used in a modern office. (*B. Com. Pass Delhi, 1987*)
2. What is the difference between Photocopying and duplicating ? List the different methods of duplicating and explain the working of any one of them. (*B.T.E., Delhi, SP-II, 1987*)
3. Name the various methods of duplicating and photocopying Explain briefiy the working of any three duplicating machines used in an office. (*B.T.E., Delhi, SP-II, 1986*)
4. Write a deiailed note on Photocopying methods followed in a good office.

9

FILING AND INDEXING

Meaning

In all the offices, we have papers and documents like original letters received, copies of letters sent out, debit and credit vouchers, agreements and other papers which are useful for business either for reference at some future date or for taking some action. We call them 'Records'. Strictly speaking, '*Records refer to the vast bulk of letters received and copies of letters sent out and other papers or documents.*

Filing is a system of keeping the records. It means that according to any system when we keep up the letters, papers or documents etc., we call it filing. The following are the definitions of filing :—

1. "Filing is the system of record-keeping".

2. "Filing is the process of arranging and storing records so that they can be easily available when required."

3. "Filing is the placing of papers in acceptable containers according to some pre.determined arrangement so that any paper can be located quickly and conveniently, when required."

—George Terry

From the above definitions, we can come to know that filing is the process with which we can place the paper in some containers and we can easily locate any paper whenever required for use at some future date. All the papers or documents are properly arranged in some order and then placed inside some cabinets etc. in such a way that we should be in a position to find out any paper, out of the bulk, at time in future.

Salient features

From the above definition, we come to know that filing has the following salient features :—

1. It is the process of placing the papers.
2. There should be some container in which the papers are placed and those containers should be acceptable to our requirements.
3. There should be some pre-determined arrangement of placing the papers.
4. The papers should be located, i.e. traced out quickly and conveniently. Not much time be wasted in locating the papers.

Objects or Purposes

Why we use filing? There is some purpose behind it. The following are the various objects or purposes of filing :—

1. Systematic arrangement of records.
2. Proper safety and security of records.
3. Easy availability of records at the point of need.
4. Economy of space and the cost.

Functions

The filing performs a number of functions as under :—

1. **Library Function**—Just as we get books in a Library for reference purposes, the same way, in office, we have files for reference purposes. All records are well-arranged and we may refer to any paper without much trouble.
2. **Historical Function**—History is a subject of study of the past events. Similarly, filing performs this function of giving us awareness of the past events. Files contain records of the past events.
3. **Administration Functian** —Administration is concerned with the execution of policies framed by Management. Filing helps in performing day-to-day Administrative functions. Correspondence and communication become easier.

4. **Information Function**—An office is the information centre and the entire information is kept by way of files in the office. If there is proper filing, we can get all information conveniently.

Importance or Advantages of Filing

Filing is of greater importance in every office because of the following facts :

1. **Efficient Correspondence**—It becomes easier and efficient to make correspondence if the filing is there, otherwise locating the papers takes longer time and the efficency cannot be maintained.
2. **Documentary Evidence**—With the filing, it is possible to keep written records of transaction and such written records be produced anywhere as proof or evidence.
3. **Ready Reference**—A reference to any paper or document becomes easy and quick if proper files are maintained.
4. **Safety of Records**—The papers or documents may be kept safe from fire and theft because the modren filing equipments are having the locking device and are fire-proof.
5. **Prompt Decision Making**—The decisions may be taken quickly if proper files are maintained because the information necessary for the purpose is readily available.
6. **Follow-Up Action**—The matters may be easily pursued if the files are maintained in an office because the records are properly arranged and with the help of reminder-diary we can take out the relevant file and issue reminder etc.

Essentials or Characteristics of good filing system

Whatever may be the system of keeping records, the same should have the following qualities : (All the points may be easily remembered by the word—SAFESCIP)

1. **Simplicity**—It should be simple and easily understandable.
2. **Accessibility**—The filing system should be such that

it is easily approachable to all members of the office. If the files are kept aloof at a distant place, it would be inconvenient.

3. **Flexibility**—If there is any increase or decrease in records, the same may be accommodated within the same filing equipments.
4. **Economy**—The filing system should not be costly. Also it should not unnecessarily engage more space.
5. **Safety**—The records should be kept safe from fire or dust or insects, etc.
6. **Cross-Reference**—A good filing system should have the facility of referring to a paper pertaining to two or more departments.
7. **Indexing**—There should be the facility of maintaining a list of all files so that the location of papers becomes easy.
8. **Proper Classification**—Before keeping papers inside the folders it is necessary that those should be classified or arranged on some common basis, say, alphabetically or subjectwise or chronologically, etc.

Classification and Arrangement of Files

Before we keep the office records into folders, cabinets or containers, it is necessary that we must classify all the papers on some common basis, which we call as classification of files.

"*Grouping of papers, doouments or records on some common basis is called the classification and arrangement of files.*"

The following are the various systems of classification :—

(1) **Alphabetical order** : Under this, we have to keep all the files on the basis of alphabets like A, B, C, D, etc. Each file is allotted an alphabet. We may keep one file for a name or subject commencing from a particular alphabet. In case there are many files under one alphabet, we may sub-divide them according to the vowels, e.g. a, e, i, o, u, etc. followed by the concerned alphabet. The Alphabetical order may be of two types :—

(a) **By Name**—The personal files pertaining to all office-workers may be kept by name. Just as the names are arranged in a telephone directory, the same way we may keep the files by names starting from the concerned Sirname. Where two synonymous names are there, we may take into account the name of father or Sir-name, etc.

(b) **By Subject.** The files may also be classified according to the subject like sales file, purchases file, payments file. The starting alphabet of the subject is taken into consideration for arranging the files.

Following are the *advantages* of alphabetical order :—

1. It is the most natural and simple classification and may be understood easily.
2. It is flexible, as new names/subjects may be easily added or deleted.
3. It is self-indexing. There is no need of preparing a separate index where the files are classified according to alphabets.

However, the *disadvantages* of alphabetical order are :

1. There are difficulties when the names are mis-spelt.
2. The difficulty arises where two common names are there.
3. It is not useful where large number of files are prepared.

(II) **Numerical Order** : Under this system, the files are arranged by giving serial numbers, e.g. 1, 2, 3, 4, 5, etc. This type of classification may be sub-divided into the following :—

(a) **Consecutive Numbers**—Like 1, 2, 3, 4. and so on serially.

(b) **Terminal Digits**—i.e. the digits are terminated at particular point, e.g. : 01, 001, 0001 and so on. It is useful where the number of files is large.

(c) **Dewy-decimal Points**—There is one main number and it is followed by the decimal point, e.g. 1.1, 1.2, 1.3, 1.4, 2.1, 2.2, 2.3, 2.4 and so on. Just as the pages are numbered in a book in modern days, similarly the system is used for filing. It is useful where there are innumerable files or sub-files.

The numerical classification is used by transport authorities in respect of registration numbers allotted to vehicles and for giving numbers to invoices by the accounts department of any business organisation.

Following are the advantages of numerical classification

(i) It is simple and easy to understand ; (ii) the location of files becomes easy ; and (iii) there can be unlimited expansion of files.

The *disadvantages are* : (i) Separate index has to be prepared ; (ii) it may be used as a part of reference number of file ; and (iii) it is costly as a separate index has to be maintained while using this classification.

(III) **Alpha-Numerical Order**—According to this system of classification of files, the arrangement is done according to the alphabets and then each alphabet is allotted a number, e.g. B1, B2, B3, B4, etc. Generally one subject is allotted to one alphabet and then the same alphabet is sub-divided into many numericals. It is the most flexible system of classification and a combination of both —the alphabetical and numerical. Hence, this system has got the advantages of both the systems. It is used by bigger and expanding organisations like banks etc.

(IV) **Geographical Location**—This system is adopted where the records are required to be kept areawise. All records of one particular area, division or region are kept in one folder like Northern Region, Southern Region etc. or it may be kept according to the States or Countries etc.

Though this system is easy and simple to use, yet there are difficulties in using this system because the clerks handling this system must be fully trained in knowing the location of different places.

(V) **Chronological Order** : Under it, the papers are put in a folder as soon as these are received—datewise. This can be done in two ways. Firstly, by putting the latest paper at the top of all papers and, of the oldest date at the end or vice-versa, i.e. keeping the oldest letter at the top and the latest at the bottom.

Though this system is very simple to use, yet it is useful for all smaller organisations only where the number of papers to be filed is very less.

Factors for selecting a particular system :

Out of the various systems of classification and arrangement of files, which one would be select for our organisation ? This would depend upon various factors given below :—

1. **Volume of Records**—If records are bulky, we may use numerical, alpha-numerical or any other system, otherwise subject-wise or neme-wise.

2. **Simple in Use.** Any system which is simple to use and easy to understand may be selected.
3. **Convenient**—Whichever is convenient to use in the organisation, we may select that system.
4. **Speed of Reference**—i.e. the speed with which we are required to refer to the papers. If more speed is required, we may avoid that system which requires an additional reference to index etc.
5. **Accuracy**—i.e. the correctness and exactness in using the files.
6. **Expansion**—We should keep in mind as to how much the work is to be increased in the near future—and which system is more flexible.

Filing Methods and Equipments

Now we shall discuss about the various methods or equipments for filing the papers. We may conveniently divide them into the following broad heads :—

(a) Old Methods—*i.e.* those used for past times or from ages.

(b) Modern Methods—*i.e.* those used in the modern days.

OLD METHODS

Amongst the old methods of filing, the following are the various types of files and equipments :—

(*i*) **Spike, Wire or Post-to-pillar Files** : It contains a simple piece of wire made of steel which has a knot at the bottom and the upper portion of wire is moulded a little to facilitate the same to be hanged on a peg. The papers, to be filed, are punched with the help of the paper portion of the wire. The papers rest one over the other in horizontal position. The wire may be hanged on a peg or it may be kept inside an Almirah or at any place convenient. It is called 'post to pillar' or 'pillar to post' file because in between the two ends of the wire, the papers are filed. It is the most simple method of filing used from the olden times. Still in offices, this method may be used to preserve the papers. It is very cheap as the cost of wire is nominal. However, the drawbacks of this type of filing are that the papers are exposed to dust and sunrays and there is possibility of papers being lost since those remain loose and anyone may take out any paper easily.

(ii) **Clip or Metal Holders** : These are metallic clips or holders to hold the papers together. The letters or papers are put together and the clip is pressed from the rear and its mouth is opened for keeping the papers inside. Though it is very simple, cheap and convenient method of filing, yet it cannot be treated as a regular method, because it may be used for temporarily holding the papers. As there is no tagging system in it, there are chances of misplacing the papers. Very less papers may be filed under this method. Still, clips or metal holders are used in all offices to hold the bunch of papers.

(iii) **Box file** : Under this method, card-board boxes 8 to 10 cms deep and of the foolscap size are used to keep the papers. These boxes may or may not have the cover. In order to press the papers kept inside the box, there may be a provision of the spring which keeps all papers pressed. It is cheap and simple method of filing but not many papers can be filed and at the same time the papers are likely to be misplaced as there is no tagging system. However, these types of files are used to serve as in-tray and out-tray at the officer's desk.

(iv) **Pigeon-hole or Docketing** : It involves a box or cupboard made of wood and having many cages or holes. These cages are deep and have sufficient space in order to keep the papers inside. All cages are allotted different alphabets, etc. and the papers are kept inside the respective cage. Though it is an old system of filing, yet the post offices are using it for sorting letters. In bigger Organisations, pigeon-hole filing is used in dak despatch section for sorting out the letters before despatch. This method is cheap, simple, convenient but there are chances of loss of papers because those are kept loose inside the holes. Also, many letters/papers cannot be stored. Rather, it is not a permanent method of filing, but useful for sorting out records.

(v) **Press-copy book** : This system is used to serve as the evidence of the letters sent out by an organisation. Under this, all letters to be sent out are copied in a book by putting the carbon paper for making office copies and those remain in the book in chronological order.

(vi) **Bound book** : Under this system, all papers etc. are pasted in the bound book in chronological order to avoid the possibility of loss or misplacement. Since not many papers can be accommodated, this system is not of much utility now-a-days.

MODERN METHODS & EQUIPMENTS

With the advancement of science and technology, some new methods have been invented in order to cope with the increase in work and records. These are :

Horizontal Filing

Under this method, the papers are inserted into a folder made of thick paper or plastic and these folders are kept inside the almirahs or cupboards one over the other in a horizontal or flat position after arranging the papers in chronological order. The important files used in horizontal method are as follows :

(a) **Flat Files** : These are ordinary folders or covers made of thick paper, cardboard or plastic sheets with metal hinges for fastening the papers or with one hole at the left hand upper corner. A thread tag and a punching machine may be used to make holes and to fasten the papers. We may use a punching machine to make two holes in paper towards the left-hand margin. All the papers related to a particular folder are arranged chronologically and fastened. These folders/files are placed in drawers or cup boards horizontally. These fiat files are mostly used in offices in India.

(b) **Lever or Arch or Era-File** : These are thicker folders made of cardboard and operated by a lever with a double spring arch. When any paper is to be inserted, the same is punched and lever is moved upward so that the mouth of arches is opened and the paper can be placed in the arches. This file is like a big binder and can accommodate quite a large number of papers. Because of lever arch system, such files eliminate the need to take out papers while referring but we can see the papers in the file itself.

Advantages of Horizontal Filing : The following are the merits of the horizontal filing :

1. It is a very simple method of filing, because the papers are punched and placed inside the folders and those folders may be placed in cupboards etc. one over the other.
2. It is economical so far as cost is concerned because there is no costly equipment required for it.
3. There is safety of records as the papers are not kept loose but inside the folders.
4. It has got easy accessibility as any one can easily approach to the records.

Limitations

The following are the drawbacks of horizontal filing :

1. There is inconvenience in filing the papers and taking out the folders as these lie one over the other and much trouble is taken in taking out any particular folder out of the bulk.
2. It is more time consuming because of the position of files.
3. There is lesser flexibility under this method.

Vertical Filing

It denots the position of files or folders which are kept upright down and side by side. Under this method, the papers are first arranged in some order and placed in folders. Afterwards these folders are placed inside a steel filing cabinet which has deep drawers.

Three things are required for vertical filing :—

1. **Cabinet.** It is the steel filing cabinet with two, three or four deep drawers and automatic locking device.. The drawers are deep and spacious to accommodate the folders in upright position.

2. **Folders.** These are ordinary file covers made of thick paper or plastic sheet for placing the papers inside.

3. **Guide Cards.** These are made of thick paper and in various colours. These are placed with the folders in order to select a particular folder inside the cabinet.

It is one of the modern methods of filing in which quite a large bulk of papers may be easily accommodated and retrieved much quicker. The steel filing cabinets are fire-proof and safe. If the space is less, the filing cabinets may be placed one over the other in two-tier or three-tier system.

Advantages

1. The files are readily available for reference purposes because not much time is wasted in filing or retrieving the papers.
2. There is economy in space as the cabinets may be placed one over the other as a two-tier or three-tier system.
3. There is more flexibility under this system as any number of folders may be added or taken out easily.
4. It has got maximum safety of records from fire and theft.
5. This method has got adaptability, as the filing cabinets

may also be used for keeping other things like cash, books etc.

Limitations

Vertical filing has got only two drawbacks as under :—

1. The equipment used in it is costlier.

2. There is fear of movement or misplacement of folders as these are kept loose inside the filing cabinet.

Horizontal Vs. Vertical Filing

The above two types of files are different from each other on the following points :

1. **Placement of folders** : In Horizontal filing, the folders are placed one over the other but in vertical filing, the folders are placed side by side or in upright down position.

2. **Location of files** : It is much quicker in vertical filing to locate the popers as compared to the horizontal filing because in vertical every thing is systematically arranged whereas in horizontal the files are arranged one over the other.

3. **The space requirement** : It is less in case of vertical filing and it is more in case of horizontal filing because of the position of files.

4. **Grouping & regrouping of papers** : It is easy to group or regroup the papers in caso of vertical but not in case of horizontal filing.

Suspended Filing

It is an improved method of vertical filing. Under it, the papers are placed inside the folders and the folders are placed in upright down position or side by side inside the deep drawers of the steel filing cabinet but these foldes are suspended from one another by means of metal strips which are fitted inside the drawer on two metal bars fitted on both sides of the drawer. On metal strips, the particulars of folders may also be inscribed.

This methed has got all the advantages of vertical filing plus the advantage that the folders are not misplaced as these are suspended with the help of metal strips fitted inside the drawers of the cabinet. Rather, this method obviates all the disadvantages of vertical filing.

Lateral Filing

It is another kind of vertical filing, as the folders are placed vertically inside the shelves of a cupboard. The papers are placed inside the folders and the folders are hanged in hooks in the shelves of a steelcupboard having three or four drawers like that in an Almirah. The folders are hanged in hooks just like hanging clothes in a wardrob. The tops of foders are fitted with title indicators. This type of filing is less expensive as it engages much lesser space and the removal and replacement of folders is also swift and quick. No space is required for opening the drawers.

Open-Shelf Filing

It is a commonly used method in libraries. Just as books are placed in the open shelves, similarly the folders may be placed in the open shelves separately. The files are kept vertically in the open shelves. This method offers almost all the advantages as those of lateral filing but the open shelves are more economical and cheep and open shelves accommodate more files as compared to lateral filing. The limitation of this type of filing is that it requires dust-free-area in order to protect the records from dust and sunrays.

Microfilming

Under this method, we do not preserve the original records but we take photo of the records and keep the negatives like a film roll. The rolls are properly & carefully indexed and whenever any paper is to be referred, the same is placed on a machine and the enlarged form in readable position comes on the screen and the purpose may be served. At the same time a lot of space may be saved as the folders etc. are not there as a means of retaining information by using any method of filing. It is simple and most modern. It saves a lot of space.

Factors for Selection of a Filing Method or Equipment

Out of the various filing methods or equipments discussed earlier in this chapter, which one would we select for our Organisation, it would depend upon the following factors which may be considered before selecting any one particular method :

1. The **nature and type** of records being stored. If maps or sketches or bigger size of papers are to be stored, we may select horizontal filing otherwise vertical or suspended, etc.

2. Frequency with which the records are retrieved, *i.e.* kept back. If frequency is more, we may select vertical filing otherwise horizontal filing may be used.

3. Duration for which the records remain active *i.e.* in use at the office.

4. Location of filing equipment—centralised. For centralised filing, we may use any of the modern methods of filing.

5. Space available for storage of records. If more space is available for keeping records, we may use horizontal filing otherwise vertical.

6. Lay-out of office—open office or closed type office : In open office, we may use any of the modern methods like vertical or horizontal but in closed offices only lateral or microfilming may be used.

7. The importance of *protecting* the records—Vertical filing is the best because it has got locking device and the cabinets are fire proof also.

CENTRALISED VERSUS DECENTRALISED FILING

In an Organisation, we may keep the entire files pertaining to different sections at one place called the filing section or we may allow the respective departments to maintain their own files themselves. The former is called 'Centralised' filing system whereas the latter is called 'Decentralised' filing.

Centralised Filing

"It implies location of filing equipment and personnel in a single section or area of office which is easily accessible to other departments."

Advantages of Centralised Filing—(i) Uniformity of methods and equipments of filing may be adopted ; (ii) Supervision and control becomes easy ; (iii) Economy in cost and space may be effected and (iv) Efficiency in operation may be achieved.

Disadvantages : (i) There is delay in keeping and locating the files ; (ii) It is the most inconvenient system for the management ; and (iii) There is no use of centralised filing where the records are frequently required for reference purpose.

Decentralised Filing

"Decentralised Filing implies the location of filing equipment and staff within each department or section."

Advantages of Decentralised Filing : (i) There is no delay in location of files ; (ii) It is more convenient system for the management ; and (iii) It is useful where the files are frequently required.

Disadvantages of Decentralised Filing : (i) There are chances of duplication of equipment ; (ii) There is little scope for specialisation ; and (iii) There is difficulty in filing papers pertaining to more than one department.

However, for selecting any one of the centralised or decentralised system of filing, we should know that for a smaller organisation, there is no question of decentralised or centraliied filing because the number of files is small. For a bigger Organisation, we have to compare the relative advantages and disadvantages and then select any one of them. However, both the systems may also be used in one Organisation—frequently required files may be decentralised and the rest may be centralised.

FILING AIDS

Whatever may be the system of filing or whatever may be the filing equipments used in office, the private secretary may handle it efficiently only when proper tools etc. are available. These filing aids may include the following :—

1. Punching machines
2. Folders
3. Paper Containers like filing cabinets, racks etc.
4. Stapling machines
5. Proper index of files.

In the modern days, mostly the folders are such that in between the two plastic or metal hinges/strips each paper is tagged after making two holes on the left-hand margin of paper. The two holes may be made with the help of punching machine. The paper is put into the machine from the centre of left-hand margin and by pressing the lever of machine, the two holes may be easily made after which the paper is placed into the folder. Whenever two or more papers pre kept together in a file like the original letter and its reply-copy, thc stapler may be used so that the two papers are not separated. The punching machine and the stapler, both of them, are available in various sizes and makes. Whatever may be, such punching machines are also available which can make only one hole in a paper. The folders are the covers made of thick paper or plastic sheet in which the papers are kept inside duly tagged so that the papers are not misplaced. It is also necessary to have an up-to-date list of all the files, called an Index. The index helps in tracing out or locating a particular folder easily and quickly.

All the above filing aids tools should be always kept ready and in proper working condition so that the private secretary can handle filing efficiently and without wasting time unnecessarily. Though the aids mainly depend upon the filing equipments used in an office yet the above said aids are required in general for any system of filing.

INDEXING

Meaning

Indexing may be anything which indicates or points out. In other words, "Indexing is the process of determining the name, subject or other caption under which the documents are filed."

In simple words, indexing is the process through which we may find out the subject, name or other details of files. In an office, there may be hundreds of files and thousands of papers lying in various files. It is difficult to find out a paper out of the bulk. To facilitate this, an index is prepared which may indicate at a glance that a particular paper or document is available in a particular file. Such type of index is always prepared everywhere particularly at places or occasions where we have to locate something. For example, if we have to find out in a book whether a particular topic is included and, if so, on which page, we may refer to the index of the book and easily locate it. Similarly, in offices, where there are innumerable files or folders, we might not know by word of mouth as to which file contains what ? The Index of files would tell us at a glance that a particular file number contains a particular topic and, if so, on which page. We may refer to the index of the book and easily locate it. Similarly, in offices where there are innumerable files or folders, we might not know by word of mouth as to which file contains what? Index of files would tell us at a glance that a particular file number contains a particular subject or matter. Hence, we may say—

"Indexing is an aid to filing"

An index is the list of the contents and it assists the reader to locate 'what is where'. A Telephone Directory is an example of index which contains the telephone numbers of different persons arranged in alphabetical order and at a glance one can find out a particular telephone number of a particular person. Similarly, we may have an index on ledgers, the diaries etc.

Objectives or Purposes

An Index may be used for the following purposes :

1. To facilitate easy location of the required paper or document or file.
2. To present an orderly list of papers and documents.
3. To store the key information in a condensed form.

From the above points, we may say that the primary purpose of indexing is the easy location of a paper out of the bulk at a glance and the other purposes are to arrange and store the information. As a matter of fact, indexing is very much used in offices where there are many files on different subjects and files are frequently required and retrieved.

Cases where Indexing may not be required

Though Indexing is required in every office, yet it is not necessary that in all cases we should prepare an index. We may not require an index in the following cases :

1. Where the files are kept alphabetically—*i.e.* either subjectwise or namewise. In such cases, the files may be located without the help of an index because files are arranged according to the subject or by name.
2. Where the files are arranged according to the Geographical classification—*i.e.* according to area, state region etc. In such a case also, the index is not necessary because there are few files arranged as per the geographical location. Hence, index might not be required.

Characteristics of a good Indexing system

In whatever way we prepare the index for our Organisation, a good indexing system should have the following characteristics :

1. **Simplicity** : The indexing system should be quite simple so that everyone could easily understand. There should not be any complication or roundaboutness in the system of indexing.

2. **Accessibility** : The indexing system should be well within the reach of everyone so that it may be used conveniently at the point of need. If the index is kept within some lock or at a separate place where no one can easily approach, the index system might not be used at the point of need.

3. **Flexibility** : It is also necessary that the indexing system

should be flexible so that any new name may be added or deleted whenever required, without having any material change.

4. ECONOMY : The indexing system should be economical so far as cost or the space is concerned. If more money is spent on preparing the index system for the organisation, it would not be feasible.

5. SAFETY : The indexing system should be safe from theft and should not be exposed to any risk. As the system has to be preserved for longer periods, it is necessary that it should be safe.

TYPES OF INDEX

Bound Book Index : Under this system, the names of persons, documents or files etc. are first arranged alphabetically and written on different pages. These pages are bound in the form of a book or register. Different pages are allotted to different alphabets. When the names are more under one alphabet, we may allot more than one page. While making such an index, the prefix like Mr., Miss., Dr. or Prof. are not considered and surnames may be taken into consideration while deciding a particular alphabet. If two similar names are there, father's name or surname may be used for writing them on priority. This type of index is also known as alphabetical index. Special type of registers are also available in the market on which the index may be prepared. From right hand certain portoin of the page is cut in such a way that different alphabets are visible at a glance.

Advantages

The bound book index has the following advantages :—

1. It is the most simple system of indexing.
2. It is economical as the registers etc. are not costly.
3. It is compact and handy as the index book/register can be easily moved from one place to another.
4. It is safe and there is no danger of pages being lost or misplaced.

Disadvantages

1. The system is not flexible. If page of a particular alphabet is exhausted, it is not possible to add more pages to it.
2. A lot of time is wasted in locating a particular name if the names are more on a particular page.

However, the bound book system is most useful for smaller organisations as the names, etc. are comparatively fewer with them. The telephone directory is a good example of bound book index.

Vowel Index : In book index, explained earlier, it is the disadvantage that when there are so many names under one alphabet, it becomes difficult rather more time-consuming to locate any particular name. To overcome it, the vowel index may be prepared Under it, first of all the names are divided according to alphabets and then under each alphabet, there is classification according to the vowels, *e.g.* Be, Bi, Bu, etc. The vowel next to the alphabet is considered for classification purpose. The name **Bano** will be written on the page allotted to **Ba** ; and **Benazir** would be written on the page allotted to **Be**. Hence, this index facilitates easy location of any name in the alphabetical classification. It has got all the advantages and disadvantages of Book Index plus the additional advantage of easy location of name.

Fixed Index : Instead of making a separate register or bound book, as explained earlier, when a few pages are separately allotted and attached to the book or ledger and on those pages the index is written, we call it the fixed index. It is a part of the book or ledger and not a separate index. Such an index appears either a the beginning or at the end of ledger or book. The fixed index may have two forms :

(*a*) **Self-index** : Where the leaves of the book are cut in such a way so as to show each alphabet at a glance.

(*b*) **Extended Index** : Where it is bound in the form of a book and so arranged in a way as to open outside the area of a book or the register concerned.

Loose-leaf Index : Under this type of index, separate loose leaves or paper-sheets are fitted into metal hinges or screwed in a binder. Index is prepared alphabetically on loose sheets. Any number of loose sheets may be inserted or taken out and the index may be kept always alive. This type of index has got all the advantages of bound book index plus the additional advantage that any number of new sheets may be inserted or taken out so as to keep the index always alive. Also that the loose sheets may be locked properly so that the index remains safe. However, the limitation of this index is that only limited names etc. may be accommodated in it.

Card Index : It is one of the modern methods of indexing. Under this system, separate paper cards, available in different sizes, are allotted to each piece of information, *e.g.* customers, account-holders, documents etc. All cards are of uniform size. The important information may be written by hand or typed and then the cards are serially arranged—numerically or alphabetically—and kept in a drawer or cardex cabinet etc. The card index has many *uses* :

(*i*) It may be used as a catalogue of books in a library.
(*ii*) It may be used to contain the specimen signatures of account holders in a bank.
(*iii*) It may be used to contain the addresses and other particulars about the customers in a business organisation.
(*iv*) It may be used to keep a record of bio-data or particulars of employees working in an organisation.
(*v*) It may be used to maintain a record of store items, documents or investments, and accounts of customers.

Advantages

The card index has the following advantages :

1. It is most flexible as any number of cards may be inserted or removed without disturbing the sequence.
2. It is easy and convenient to handle.
3. The cards contain all important information in a condensed form at one place and at a glance.
4. The cards may be grouped or regrouped in any manner or order.
5. It is always alive because unused cards may be taken out and fresh cards may be added.
6. The operating cost of the card indx is lower.
7. It is adaptable to multi-purpose uses.

Disadvantages

1. There is a danger of cards being lost or misplaced, because the cards are kept loose.
2. There is a chance of fraudulent substitution of cards.
3. The equipment used in it is costly, *e.g.* the steel cardex cabinets etc.

Visible Card Index : Under this, the cards are kept in pockets and laid flat in a metal tray overlapping each other in such a manner that the important information of the card like account number, name etc. is visible through the pocket. There is a plastic strip in each pocket through which the important information is visible. The pockets have cages to insert the card and the pockets are attached to the metal tray in such a way that these cannot be taken out. There are many flat drawers in the card index cabinets and in one drawer 150 to 200 pockets are there. It is the most modern method of indexing and has multi-purpose uses. In Banks, it may be used to keep the account opening forms and specimen signatures of savings bank account-holders.

Advantages

1. The visible card index is compact and takes small space.
2. It has got all the advantages of card index like efficiency, multi-purpose uses etc.
3. The cards lie safe inside the pockets and there are no chances of loss or misplacement of cards.
4. It is easy to handle and the metal trays/drawers may be taken out easily and then re-inserted. It has got locking device also.

Strip Index : In this type of index, the important particulars are written on a paper strip and these strips may be arranged and pasted on a card board. The information may be typed or written by hand and separate strips may be pasted in proper order at a prominent place so that the index is easily accessible and visible at a glance. Such type of index may be found at the important Bus Stands or Railway Stations. The advantages of Strip Index are—(*i*) It is not costly but cheap; (*ii*) It may be prepared and displayed easily ; and (*iii*) The entire information is available at a glance. However, the disadvantage is that it can accommodate only the limited information.

Wheel Index : Under it, special paper cards are kept inside the transparent folders or envelopes and these are fitted on a rotating wheel. The wheel may be rotated by hand or mechanically also. Whenever any particular information is required to be referred to, we may rotate the wheel and refer to the information. This type of index may be having a wheel to move horizontally or vertically. This index is used at such places where the space is very less and much-more information is required to be indexed.

However, out of the various types of indices, discussed above, we may select any one for a particular organisation, depending upon the nature of work, volume, cost, convenience, safety, flexibility, etc. Overall, the card index and the visible card index systems are most modern and useful, as these have the multi-purpose utility and convenience also.

QUESTIONS

1. Explain the importance of filing in a modern business office. (*B. Com. Pass, Delhi, 1986*)
2. Distinguish between classification and indexing. (*B. Com. Pass, Delhi, 1985*)
3. Write explanatory note on vertical filing. (*B. Com. Pass, Delhi, 1985*)
4. What is Indexing? What are its objects? State briefly the advantages of a good system of Indexing. (*B. Com. Pass, Delhi, 1984*)
5. Write a note on decentralised filing. (*B. Com. Pass, Delhi, 1983*)
6. What is Classification? State the factors which affect the choice of the methods of classification. (*B. Com. Pass, Delhi, 1982*)
7. State the various methods of classifying files and discuss in brief their advantages and disadvantages. (*B.T.E. Delhi, SP-II, 1987*)
8. What do you understand by a good Filing System? Briefly discuss the modern methods of Filing. (*B.T.E. Delhi, SP-I, 1985*)
9. Explain briefly the Card-indexing system and give its relative advantages and disadvantages. What are the other uses of the Card-indexing? (*B.T.E. Delhi, SP-I, 1984*)
10. Distinguish between Horizontal and Vertical methods of filing. What are the main advantages of vertical method of filing? (*B.T.E. Delhi, SP-I, 1983*)

10

OFFICE MACHINES AND EQUIPMENTS

Mechanisation of Office Work

We know it very well that the office work is the paper or clerical work. When the same is performed with the help of machines, we call it "Mechnisation of office work". For example, writing of letters may be done by hand and the same might be done on a typewriter. To the first, we call manual and the latter we call as mechanical. Like other things being done with the help of machines as using a Grinder and Mixer in a kitchen, the work of office may also be performed with the help of various machines. Taking totals of amounts in a cash book with the help of an Adding Machine, preparing cash memo or bill with the help of a Cash Register machine ; typing letters with the help of typewriter or taking multiple copies with the help of a duplicating machine—all these are the examples of mechanisation of office work.

'Necessity is the mother of invention' is the saying which holds true in office work also. The more we advanced towards the scientific age, the necessity of performing office work at a speed was felt and now is the time when most of the office work is performed with the help of machines. Even the sophisticated machines like computers etc. are being used in office. But one thing is certain that, all the works of office cannot be performed with the help of machines because of their nature and variety. Only those types of office works can be performed with the help of machines which are routine, repetitive or stereotype of works like taking totals, opening the envelopes, reproducing written matter etc. Other work like planning or management cannot be performed with the help of machines because these require the application of brain and are done differently under different situations.

Objectives/Purposes

Still most of the office works are performed now-a-days with the help of machines and the manual operations are being replaced with mechanical operations, because of the following objectives in mind :

1. **To save labour** : Labour involves strain on nerves and physical fatigue, which may be avoided by using the machines. It is torturous to put manual labour and cumbersome also. When machines are used, we may save that labour.

2. **To save time** : Time is the factor to be taken into consideration while doing office work. Time runs very fast and to cope with its speed. we have to use the machines so that more work may be performed within less time.

3. **To increase efficiency** : Efficiency denotes the ability to work with quantity and quality. Both of these can be very well achieved while we use machines for doing the office work.

4. **To promote accuracy** : The office machines are used to bring in correctness or accuracy in work, because the machines are very honest. Whatever information is fed in to a machine, it gives the result accordingly. During the manual operations, no one may commit more mistakes but the machines help in eliminating the mistakes.

5. **To minimise the chances of frauds etc** : Frauds involve wilful misrepresentation of facts with a view to deceive others. Machines are provided to check over the manual operations and not to leave any margin for playing frauds in the organisation. For example. a Cash Register is used to keep a control over the cash receipts. A cheque-writer is used to check alteration on the amounts of cheques or drafts.

6. **To have good impression or look** : The machines are also used with a view to leave a lasting impression over others. This improves the moral of employees and at the same time leaves a good impression over others. For example, a typed letter is more effective and impressive as compared to a letter hand-written.

Advantages

While we use office machimes, the following advantages are derived :—

1. Office machines are labour-saving devices and overcome the drudgery or dullness of manual working and, at the same time lead to saving of wages or salaries paid to employees.
2. The machines increase the speed of work and increase the efficiency of office operations.
3. Machines help in bringing out standardisation and uniformity in work.
4. Machines ensure accuracy of work and eliminate chances of mistakes.
5. Machines also relieve the employees from the monotony of work.
6. The use of machines minimises the chances of frauds being played in an organisation.
7. Machines bring in economy of total office costs because the more work may be performed within the less time.
8. Machines help in giving good display and appearance of work and help in bringing the effectiveness of work.

Disadvantages/Limitations

There are certain disadvantages of office machines as under :—

1. Machines are *costly* and the smaller organisations cannot afford to purchase them. Even a typewriter may cost around four to five thousand rupees.
2. The machines *require* special *skill* for operation. Non-skilled persons cannot operate upon the machines.
3. Machines create unemployment and there is resistance from the workers.
4. The machines are wasteful and uneconomical if these are not used upto their optimum capacity.
5. Machines are exposed to the risk of obsolescence whenever there is change in methods and styles.
6. There are other risks and problems like noise and space also.

Factors for selection of office machines

Whenever any machine is to be purchased or selected for use in an office, a number of factors are to be considered. These may be defined as under :

1. Nature of work : First of all, we have to consider as to which type of work is going to be performed with the machine.

Suppose we are to purchase a typewriter, we should think whether we have to type out letters only or reports and statements also. If only letters are to be typed, we shall select the typewriter with a smaller roller. In case the bigger reports and/or statements are to be typed, we shall purchase a typewriter with a bigger roller.

2. **Volume of work** : How much work is to be performed with the help of machines. If the work is less, we shall purchase the manually operated machines. In case the work is more, we shall purchase the machines which are electrically operated and could cope with the larger volume of work.

3. **Operating cost** : Before we select a particular machine, we have to take into consideration the costs of its operation. The operating cost comprises of the money to be spent for working of the machine, e.g. the cost of electricity consumed, salary payable to the operator and/or other things which are to be required for operating the machine in an office. We should think whether our office may afford to bear all such costs. Many a time, the printed stationery is also required for using the machine. Whether we can afford to spend on it also.

4. **Durability** : It consists of the period for which the machine can remain in the working position with the organisation. Generally the durability is always taken into consideration before the machine is purchased.

5. **Adaptability** : Whether a particular machine may be used for other purposes also ? As we have already discussed, for example, a typewriter—whether it may be used for letter-writing and also for statistical work of balance sheet etc. If the machine is confined to a particular purpose and cannot be used for other works, generally we do not purchase such a machine. It is necesary to consider that the machine may also be utilised for other similar works.

6. **Flexibility & Expansion** : The organisation is always subject to expansion and the work continuously increases. Before we select a particular machine, we should keep in view whether the same machine may cope with the increased work in future.

7. **Service Facilities** : Every machine-requirs a regular servicing, oiling, overhauling etc, Whether sufficient arrangements for its repairs and maintenance are at your door-step. If the service facilities are not there and there is a problem in working of the machine, the entire work is held up and there is no use of the machine.

8. **Style** : Style is the dress of thoughts. Every Organisation

has its own style of working. Before we purchase a particular machine, we have to ensure whether the machine conforms to the style adopted by us. Suppose we use italics type words on a typewriter. When we purchase a typewriter, we have to ensure whether the typewriter is of the same style or not.

9. **Cost** : The initial cost of machine is usually heavy. Before we purchase a particular machine, we have to ensure whether we can afford to purchase it.

After taking into consideration all the above factors, we may select a particular machine for use in our office.

TYPES OF OFFICE MACHINES

The various types of machines used in an office are listed below :

1. Typewriter
2. Dictaphone or Dictating Machine
3. Computing, Accounting & Tabulaxing machines:—
   (*i*) Adding & Listing Machines (*ii*) Calculators
   (*iii*) Cash Register (*iv*) Coin-handling machines
4. Duplicating machines
5. Mailing Machines :—
   (*i*) Postal Franking Machine (*ii*) Addressing Machine
6. Misc./other machines :
   (*i*) Time-recording machine
   (*ii*) Numbering Machine
   (*iii*) Cheque-writer or Protectograph
   (*iv*) Photostat & Electrostat machines

There are other machines also which are used in offices for performing the work in an office like Billing Machines, Accounting machines or even computers, but we shall concentrate our discussion to the commonly used machines.

Typewriter

It is the most common machine used in offices to reproduce the written matter in a legible and attractive manner. The first practical typewriter is said to have been manufactured somewhere in the year 1873 but originally it was a blind typewriter, i.e. the matter typed could not be seen by the typist while typing. Later on the improvements took place and now-a-days we have many sophisticated typewriters. The following types are common:—

(*i*) Standard Typewriters—of the full size and operated manually or by electricity or even electronic.

(*ii*) Portable Typewriter—which is small in size and may be easily carried from one place to another.

(*iii*) Noiseless Typewriter—which does not create noise while typing.

(*iv*) Electric Typewriter—which may be operated with the help of an electric motor fitted in it. It runs very fast and the typist also feels very less fatigue.

However, the *advantages* of a Typewriter are :—(i) The written matter may be reproduced legibly and attractively ; (ii) The matter may be reproduced at a fast speed ; (iii) There is very less fatigue to the writer; (iv) Many copies of a single letter of document can also be obtained by using carbons. On an electric typewriter even upto a maximum of 15 copies may be obtained at one time. The *disadvantages* are :—(i) It is a costly machine and very small organisations cannot afford to purchase it ; (ii) The skilled typist has to be appointed whose salary is to be paid ; and (iii) There is a problem of noise and space for it.

Overall, the typewriter is a popular machine and is very commonly used in every office.

Dictaphone or Dictating Machine

This machine is used for giving dictation to a steno-typist in an office. Many times, it happens that either the boss is busy or the steno-typist is not available. In that case it is difficult to give dictation. To avoid this problem. Dictaphone is used. Whenever the Boss or Executive finds time, he gives dictation to machine and later on the steno-typist can take the matter for typing. This machine may also be used to pass on messages to the others in the office. The information is first recorded like on a tape-recorder and then the same may be played by using the speed control device also. In India, this machine is not very commonly used but in western countries, is it much in vogue. The metallic cassettes or plastic discs are used. The earlier dictation may also be get omitted if desired and the fresh information may be recorded. The speed may also be controlled.

There are many *advantages* of Dictating Machine : (i) We may save the running cost because in some cases the steno-typist may be dispensed with ; (ii) Lengthy debates or meetings' proceedings thereof, may easily be recorded; (iii) It may also be used for recording telephonic conversations; (iv) It is much convenient for the boss as well as for the steno-typist.

The *disadvantages* are : (i) The addition or alteration in messages becomes very difficult and cumbersome; (ii) There is a lack of personal touch when the machine is used; and (iii) It requires skill and training of both the boss and the typist before the machine may be properly utilised.

DUPLICATING MACHINES

The 'duplicating process' has been discussed in detail in the chapter entitled as 'Duplicating and Photocopying'. The different types of machines are used for various duplicating processes and are available in the market.

For 'Stencil Duplicating', the following are the important machines :

Mimeo Stencil Duplicator—Actually the term 'Mimeo' is used to denote the common office system with which the stencils are cut by typing directly. After the stencil is cut over a typewriter, the duplicator is used to reproduce as many copies as required in the office. In this machine, there is a drum/cylinder over which there is a place to fasten the stencil paper. This drum or cylinder rotates with the handle fitted to the machine. The duplicating ink, which is like the printing ink and available in the form of a paste, is applied on the upper side of the cylinder and with its rotation the ink is spread over and comes through the perforated portions of the stencil paper. There are two trays fitted to the machinc on both the sides. 'On one tray' the blank or plain sheets of paper are placed. When the machine is rotated, one by one paper goes inside the machine and with the contact of stencil paper, the printed sheets of paper come out on the other side tray. This machine may be operated manually by using the handle and also with the help of an electric motor fitted into the machine. There is a meter also which can be fixed to take out the requisite number of copies. The machine automatically stops when the required number of copies are taken out. This machine is handy and used in every big office for reproducing multiple copies. The famous manufacturers of stencil duplicator, in India, are 'Gestetner', 'Shourie', 'Roneo' and 'Kilburn'. Though this machine is little costly, yet the process of taking out multiple copies is comparatively very simple and cheap.

Typeset Duplicators—With this machine, the matter to be printed, is set out on a drum by letter press which may be operated like a typewriter. Once the matter has been set up, a high quality printing work is possible on a long-run. But, the process of type-setting is slow and requires special skill. However, the machine is costly but it may be efficiently used for printing purposes.

Electronic Stencil Duplicator

An electronic stencil duplicator is an improvement over the ordinary stencil duplicator and it is the most modern machine used for duplicating. The photographic copies of any document or matter may be obtained with an electronically produced stencil. It takes very little time in producing a stencil through the electronic process. With the help of stencil, which is affixed on a cylinder in the machine, thousands of copies may be easily reproduced on this type of duplicator. The electronic duplicator has additional advantages over the ordinary one as it can produce copies more fast and accurately. Moreover, the photographs or sketches etc. may also be reproduced with the help of this machine.

Spirit Duplicator

It may also be called a Gelatine duplicator. It is used to take out multiple copies from the master prepared with the help of a hectographic carbon. The process has been explained elsewhere in this book. This machine is used where it is desired to reproduce the graphs, sketches, lay-out maps etc. The master is fastened to the machine at one end on a drum. The copy paper is fed into the machine which is damped and moistened in the process and after coming in contact with the master copy, the printed copies come out immediately.

This machine is very useful as the papers and carbons used for it are not very costly. The master copy may be prpared easily. The duplicated copy may be taken out in many colours simultaneously However, there are certain drawbacks also like the one that many. copies cannot be taken out with good impression as further copies are fade and not so clear. This machine cannot be successfully used for the written running matter. If the mistakes are there in the master, it is difficult to rectify them.

PHOTOCOPYING MACHINES

The process of photocopying has been discussed separately in the chapter entitled as 'Duplicating and Photocopying'. However, two types of photocopying machines are generally used in our country. These are :

Zerox or Xerographic Photostat Machine : With this machine the exact photo of a letter or document may be taken out by using a camera and the chemicals. First of all, a photo of the document is taken by focus of light on a metal plate on which the chemiclas are applied. Afterwards, the metal plate, containing the impression, is dried by keeping it inside the machine. Then a plain paper is kept over the plate and the exact impression comes out on the plain paper. Though it is very easy to operate this type of photostat machine ; yet the process is cumbersome as the operator has to set and take out the plate again and again. Moreover, only two copies can be easily taken from one photo impression. After that, again the photo of the document is required to take more copies. Though this machine is mostly used every-where to take copies, yet it has become outmoded. Many companies are manufacturing and marketing this machine in our country.

Electrostat Machine : This machine is the modern invention in the line of photocopying and an improvement over the earlier photostat machine. This machine is available in various sizes and models, depending upon the requirement of the user. There are two tray fitted to this machine. One contains the plain sheets of paper and the other may be used to keep ready copies. The document, of which the photocopying is to be done, is kept on a glass frame and covered. The machine is switched on and through the automatic electrical rays, the impression comes on the plain paper. It is rather an instant process. One by one the plain paper goes inside the machine and comes out at the same time duly carrying the impression of the document. Now-a-days, every big organisation is having this machine. Its operation is easy and automatic. This machine has got all the advantages of the photostat machine plus others like speed, accuracy etc. However, it is a costly machine.

Adding and Listing Machines

These machines are used to prepare a list of figures of amounts and taking totals of the same. Used for accounting work, these machines may be manunal, electric or electronic and of the various sizes including pocket model or table model. There is a key board like a typewriter giving the digits from 1 to 0. The other keys are for addition of figures and substraction. There is a provision for cancelling the wrong figures. Whatever number or figure is desired, the relevant keys are pressed and then the handle is rotated manually or electrically and the result is printed on a paper patti slip fitted on the roller of machine. The correct totals are taken with a speed. These machines may be used for listing of invoices, cheques, preparation of trial balances, totalling receipts or payments, and checking of balances etc.

The *advantages* of these machines are—(i) Correct totals may be taken (ii) It may give totals with speed and may increase the efficiency of work in an office ; and (ii) It has multi-purpose use as given above.

However, the adding and listing machine is costly and in those organisations where there is lesser volume of work and they cannot afford the cost, these might not be used. Otherwise, these are most commonly used machines in banks and accounts departments of business organisations.

Calculating Machines or Calculators

These are used when the calculation, division, squares etc. have to be made on a large scale. In adding machines, only the totals or substractions may be done but with a calculator, the engineering calculations upto a number of decimal points may be done accuratety and with a speed. These Machines contribute greatly to business efficiency by eliminating routine and tiring mental work, and by eliminating errors etc. They also bring in economy and generally increase clerical efficiency. The calculators are also manual, electrical or electronic and available in various sizes right from the pocket model to table model. Many standard machines are non-listing and have a full key—board and show the answers on a dial. The main *advantages* of these machines are—(i) There is simplicity in operation of these machines ; (ii) These may be easily ported from one place to another as these are handy ; (iii) These are economical as the consumption of power, battery etc. is very less ; and (iv) These are dependable as the answers are given correctly and with a speed.

Cash Register

This machine is used for taking the correct total of cash received during the day. It is a form of listing and adding machine. Whenever any cash is received, the total is taken and the machine accumulates the total of entire cash received during the day. At the end of the day, whatever total is shown by the machine, the cash received is tallied. In this machine, there is a key board like an adding machine and the operator presses the relevant keys and takes the totals. This machine is mostly found at the Telegraph office for taking stock of the money received on account of telegrams. At railway platforms, this machine is used for issuing the platform tickets and tallying the total cash received at the end of the day. This machine is also used at Super Bazars or at bigger co-operative stores where the receipt of cash is frequent. This machine helps in keeping a control over the cash receipts and reducing the chances of frauds etc.

Coin Handling Machine

This machine is used for handling the small coins of 10 paise, 5 paise ; 25 paise or 50 paise. The mixed change is poured into the machine and that is also sorted out denominationwise automatically. Whenever the balance amount is to be returned to a customer in terms of small coins, the relevant keys are pressed and the coins come out in a disc fitted at the bottom of machine. These machines are mostly used at retail stores where there are frequent transactions in terms of small coins.

The *advantages* of this machine are:—(i) Greater speed in handling small coins ; (ii) Relief from the monotony of the job of separating and counting coins ; (iii) Accuracy in calculation and balancing the change etc.

Addressing Machine

These machines are used for writing addresses on the envelopes or postcards meant for despatch. The metal plates or rubber sheets are used on which the correct and complete name and address of the addressee is inscribed with the help of a special machine and these plates are put in a stand fitted in to the machine. One by one the addressed plate is pressed with the help of a handle and the address is printed on the envelope. It may be manually operated as well as electrically operated. It is estimated that this machine can print around 1000 addresses during a period of one day whereas it takes a lot of time of the typist or writer if the addresses are written by hand or typed. The Addressing Machines are available in various models—the small and big. These are used by Insurance Companies, Electric Supply Undertakings, Water Departments or Limited Companies where frequent communications are addressed to regular consumers.

The *advantages* of addressing machines are :—(i) There is a lot of saving of time as the addresses are printed with a speed ; (ii) It eliminates the necessity of checking as the mistakes are rare and a through checking is done at the time of preparing plates ; and (iii) It is very easy and simple to operate this machine.

However, the *disadvantage*s are : (i)The cost of installation is high and (ii) It is difficult to change the address frequently because it i s expensive to prepare a fresh address-plate.

Franking Machines

These are postal franking machines used for imprinting postal stamps on envelopes or postcards. Instead of getting the postage stamps from the post office and pasting the same individually on envelopes, this machine can imprint the postage stamps. It is controlled and licensed by the post office. At periodical intervals, the machine is taken to the post office where, on deposit of lump sum money, the meter is adjusted by the postal authorities. The machine automatically stops when the postage stamps of the full value are consumed. The postage stamps are not pasted with the help of this machine but these are printed on the envelopes or postcards. It may be manual or electrically operated. The letter or envelope to be stamped is inserted into the machine and the handle is rotated. The machine marks the letter with the required denomination of postage stamp. There is a provision for printing the insigma or emblem or any slogan along side the postage stamp.

The advantages of a postal franking machine are :—(i) It is simple to operate ; (ii) The accounting of postage is simplified because there is no necessity of keeping a separate record for the stamps ; (iii) It saves a lot of time in affixing the postal stamps; (iv) It eliminates the errors in stamping ; and (v) The chances of frauds etc. are reduced to the minimum because there is no handling of cash when this machine is used.

However, the machine is costly and of no use where the letters for despatch are few.

Time Recording Machine

This machine is used for recording the time of arrival and departure from office or factory of an employee. In this machine, there is a wall-clock and the cards are used. The concerned worker or employee takes out his/her card and puts into the machine and pulls the lever. Whatever time is shown by the clock, the same is printed on the card. When the employee leaves the office, he again puts the card into the machine and pulls the lever, the time is printed on the card in another column of the same card. As such, the machine is used for keeping a control over the timings of workers and facilitates the calculation of their wages or overtime on hourly basis. Mostly this machine is used in factories where the workers are paid hourly wages.

Cheque-Writing Machine or Protectograph

This machine is used for writing amounts on cheques or drafts. It is a very small machine and hand operated. When the cheque or draft is prepared, the amount is inscribed on it with the help of this machine. It imprints, rather perforates the amount in red ink. As such, the chances of altering or changing the amounts on cheques etc. are reduced. This machine is mostly used in banks for inscribing the amount on bank drafts and in other organisations for writing the amounts on cheques.

Numbering Machine

It is a small machine used for writing serial numbers on pages of accounts books or on papers in files. It is hand operated and numbers can be set to print each number once, twice or thrice repeatedly. The machines are fitted with a self inking device and change the number automatically after it is pressed against a paper. Book-binders also use this machine for printing numbers.

Secretary Using the Word-Processor

In an office, most of the typing work contains typing of letters, memorandum, reports etc. which are almost of the same nature. Many times, the same type of letters are sent to different persons and the poor typist has to put more labour in taking out the same typ of matter again and again. Though cyclostyling may be used for taking many copies of the same letter, yet the cyclostyled copies are not so impressive and effective. To overcome the above problem and for taking out many letters with speed, accuracy and attactiveness, the word-processor machines are used by the private secretary, with the help of which many copies may be taken out either with the same contents or with the same contents and different addresses.

The word-processor has got two aspects—the first is the computer on which the matter is composed by feeding the necessary information or data, or then the second thing is a printer which prints at a fast speed the matter composed on the computer. This process is very fast and accurate.

The word-processor system consists of :—

(1) The central processing unit (CPU)
(2) The memory
(3) The peripherals

The simple and most common peripherals in a computer system are the keyboards, the display unit and the printer. The key board is similar to the key board of a typewriter. It is just like ear when you use the key-board, you communicate with the CPU. If you want to instruct the computer to do something, you will have to type your message on the key-board. This message will also appear on the Display Unit (the Television Screen).

Display Unit is basically a TV screen. A television at home may also be used as a display unit. Monitors are, however, normally supplied by the manufacturers. Just as a message appears on the screen after it is typed on the key-board, it can be passed on to the printer with certain commands which are made known to the operator at the time of training.

Printer—What appears from the display unit, can be instantly printed out on the printer which is connected to the CPU. There are many types of printers. Their sizes, speeds and kinds of mechanism are diverse. For example, printer speed ranges from 10 letters or characters per second to 1000 letters per second.

A few weeks' training to a private secretary can equip him/her with complete knowledge of operation of the word-processor unit and turn out comparatively cleaner and accurate letters and other typed matter. The present cost of the entire system, including the printer, is approximately Rs. 20,000 or so in India. Almost all the modern business organisations have started using the word-processor for the secretarial work as it can cope with the increased work of typing and reprography and at the same time the cost of printing matter is also ultimately reduced to the minimum.

However, the word-processing unit is the most modern development for successfully performing the secretarial and other works in an office and every private secretary must have the knowledge and training of operating this system.

Punched Card Machines

These machines are used for processing the data. The basic information is recorded on the cards by punching holes on them over the machine. The cards are specially designed for facilitating punching over the machine.

Punched Cards Machines are multi-purpose as those may be used to perform any of the following functions :—

(i) Keeping accounts of receivables or creditors
(ii) Preparing wage-sheets or stock-reports
(iii) Classification, tabulation and analysis of statistical data
(iv) Invoicing the goods sold or purchased.

The *advantages* of these machines are that these are simple to use, multi-purpose and the facility of grouping and re-grouping of information is available. However, the operation requires technical handling and special type of stationery like the cards of uniform size with cages.

E.D.P. (Electronic Data Processing)

The Electronic Data Processing is a device in which the electronic rays are used mechanically for finding out the results. In other words, the processing of data is done through electronic computers. The basic information is fed into the computer in coded form and the results are obtained after automatic arithmetical calculations inside. The results are achieved in the form of reports or documents in code language. The record of details may be retained in file or memory. Separate cassette discs may also be used for filing or repeating information for a long time. The entire processing work is performed at a very high speed and with accuracy. Now-a-days, various models of computers are available in the market with different number of terminals. Any one of them may be selected as per the requirements of the Business Organisation.

The E.D.P. carries the following *advantages* :—

(i) The processing of data or calculations may be done at a very high speed as compared to manual or any other system.

(ii) It brings an utmost accuracy in results provided the basic information is fed accurately.

(iii) The facility of storing the data for repetitive use is available.

(iv) Larger volumes of transactions may be classified in batches and the results may be achieved in a single run.

(v) The operations are automatic. Only the basic details are required to be fed carefully.

However, the *disadvantages* are :

(i) Electronic Equipments are costly and heavy initial investment is required.

(ii) The maintenance costs are also comparatively high as sophisticated spares and specialised servicing is required which involves a higher operating cost.

(iii) Care and caution is required to be exercised while feeding the information to the equipment used for processing.

Still, we find that most of the modern offices are using E.D.P. as a tool for efficient working. It sounds the management information and a lot of time may be saved by using this process.

QUESTIONS

1. Write explanatory notes on any two of the following :—
   (a) Is office work Unproductive ?
   (b) Objects of introducting machines in an office.
   (*B. Com. Pass, Delhi, 1986*)
2. Write explanatory note on the uses of office machines.
   (*B. Com. Pass, Delhi, 1985*)
3. What are the objects of mechanisation in the office ? How would you determine whether a particular machine is needed in the office ? (*B. Com. Pass, Delhi, 1984*)
4. Write short note on Addressing Machines.
   (*B. Com. Pass, Delhi, 1983*)
5. Write short notes on—
   (i) Postal Franking Machine
   (ii) Dictaphone
   (iii) Electronic Stencil Duplicator
   (iv) Cash Register
   (v) Time Recording Machine.

11

OFFICE SYSTEMS, PROCEDURES AND METHODS

The three terms viz. Systems, Procedures and Methods are frequently used in the office management and there is a greater importance of these also because of their close connection with the performance of work. An Office Manager should always bear in mind that the clerical staff is not exactly similar to factory workers because the clerical or paper work pertains to the application of brain and it is not homogeneous in nature.

OFFICE SYSTEMS

A system may be defined as a *broad guide to action.* In other words, a system gives us a broad and vague idea as to how the things are done. For example, if some one asks you what is the system of recruitment in your organisation, you give him an idea that the vacancies are published in the newspapers, applications are invited, written test is held, ineterview is taken and thereafter the final selection is made. Thus, the system refers to the various operations or procedures conducted to do a particular work. In other words, we may say that the various procedures or operations are collectively known as systems. While giving the definition of office systems, *J.C. Denyer* has stated as under :—

"The term 'Office Procedures' is used to describe office systems and such 'procedures' are said to be made up of 'Operations', an operation being the smallest step in a procedure, although the amount of work involved in an operation will depend on circumstances."

From the above, it is clear that 'system' is comprised of the various procedures and the procedures are made up of 'operations' which represent each of the steps taken to complete the job.

As such, office system is a broader concept which draws a complete picture of personnel, records, machines and equipments involved in completing the major aspects of office work. Actually speaking, office system is a planned approach to complete the office activities.

Importance or Advantages of office systems

Why are office systems necessary or why systems be applied while taking up office activities ? The answer to this question lies in the following points :—

(i) Office systems help in avoiding delays and fruitless efforts on the part of office staff. These also help in speedy disposal of office work.

(ii) It becomes easy to understand the work if the same is systematically outlined.

(iii) It becomes easy to mechanise and standardise the work. That is, mechanisation and standardisation of office activities is made possible if the same is systematic.

(iv) The supervision and control becomes easy and effective, because the work performance can easily be measured with the standards fixed under the systems.

(v) The co-ordination between the different persons or sections becomes possible because each one of them follows the rules or guidelines laid down under the systems.

(vi) Good systems avoid the chances of clerical errors and may protect the organisation from fraud etc.

(vii) Office systems reduce the office costs to the minimum or assist in curtailing extra expenditure.

(viii) Training to staff becomes easy.

Characteristics of a good office system

The following features must exist in a good office system :—

(i) It should be simple and easy to understand for all concerned. A complicated system is difficult to apply.

(ii) It should have accuracy, i.e. the chances of errors

should be reduced to the minimum and it should give exact results.

(iii) It should be result oriented, i.e. it must serve the purpose for which it is meant.

(iv) A good office system has the maximum practical utility, i.e. it may be applied into practical use without any problem.

(v) It should be economical. It's no use in incurring heavy cost for making the office systems.

(vi) The office systems should be flexible in the sense that the same may be capable of applying for future expansion of the organisation.

(vii) Good office systems should be clear-cut and well-defined.

(vii) With the good systems, it is possible to train the office staff in work and fix up their responsibility.

Principles of Office Systems

There are certain general rules or principles which should be followed while making the systems for an office and these may be as under :—

(i) **Good flow of work**—By flow of work, we mean the speed with which the work passes on from one desk to another desk. That flow of work should be constant and quick. This fact should always be kept in mind while designing the systems for the office.

Minimum movement of staff—(ii) It should be kept in mind that the movement of staff from one place to another within office premises or even outside is the minimum, otherwise they will unnecessarily waste time and may not give the desired output.

(iii) **Minimun paper work**—Unnecessary paper work may be avoided so that most of the office services mighi be rendered efficiently. Rather, exact procedures should be adapted.

(iv) **No duplication of work**—It should also be kept in mind that there is no need of unnecessarily doing the same work again and again. In other words, repetition of work may be avoided while designing the systems for an office.

(v) **Encouragement to use machines**—Office mechanisation results in many advantages like saving labour, time, speed, accuracy and protection from frauds etc. Hence, the office systems should involve mechanisation of work to the maximum possible extent.

(vi) **Work Simplification**—The systems should be laid out in such a way that they make the work more simple to perform.

(vii) **Efficient service**—The systems should be geared up in such a way that they bring in prompt and efficient working in office.

(viii) **Specialisation and Standardisation**—The systems must be based on the principles of specialisation and standardisation of work and machines.

(ix) **Avoiding unnecessary checking**—The systems should be based on definite internal checks so that further futile checking may be avoided.

Designing Office Systems

For efficient working in an office, it is necessary that suitable Systems be outlined before-hand and revised from time to time keeping in view the latest developments and the scientific principles of office management. The work of planning, preparing and designing the office systems should either be entrusted to a competent management consultant engaged for the purpose or by forming a special committee of the internal management or by appointing a special O & M officer. The system, as a whole, should be bifurcated into different procedures and norms be laid down keeping the policy framework of the top management in mind.

However, the following steps are generally taken for planning the office systems in an organisation :—

(i) A study of the various printed forms, used in the organisation should be made on the basis of overall survey of working.

(ii) Installation of new machines, equipments and controlling devices be made on the basis of study of forms.

(iii) The flow of work may be checked on the basis of lay-out plan of office.

(iv) Appropriate methods of work based on the systems analysed should be planned.

(v) A Procedure Manual be prepared and the systems decided upon may be suitably outlined in seriatim.

OFFICE PROCEDURES OR ROUTINE

'Routine' is something which is repeatedly done in the same

way like the daily routine. Similarly, the office routine signifies a sequence of operations made in the office almost in the same way every day. The office routine is called the office procedure because the procedure refers to the planned sequence of operations of the various office activities like mail-handling, typing, filing, indexing etc. As we have discussed earlier, the 'procedure' involves a number of operations or steps. When the steps are taken in a process. it completes the procedure. Actually the office procedures are made to complete and control the clerical operations in an office.

Difference between Office Systems and Procedures or Routine

The two terms, viz. system and procedure may be distinguished on the following lines :—

(i) The system is used in a broader sense to signify the broad guide to action, whereas the routine or procedure is used in a narrow sense to complete a particular work only.

(ii) A system is a plan of work comprised of procedures or routines whereas the procedure is comprised of various clerical steps or operations.

Advantages of office procedures

By formulating the office procedures, the following advantages are derived :-

(i) It brings in uniformity and standardisation in office work and machines or equipments.

(ii) It works as a source of information and guidance for efficiently performing the routine works of office.

(iii) It helps in training the clerical staff.

(iv) It brings in economy for the Organisation by avoiding wastage, delay and duplication of work.

(v) It brings in efficiency in clerical operations.

OFFICE METHODS

Generally speaking, a method is the manner in which the work is performed. To be more specific, a 'method' is the manual or mechanical means by which clerical operations are performed. For example, the work of writing a business letter may be performed by writing a letter by hand or over a typewriter. Office methods also represent the means through which office routine is completed.

Office Methods are altogether different from the systems or procedures because the former is a means to achieve the latter ends.

Areas where methods may be applied

The following are the different important areas of office routine where the methods may be applied :—

(i) Correspondence and other records including forms
(ii) Filing and Indexing
(iii) Office machines and equipments
(iv) Commuication and office reports
(v) Office procedures
(vi) Office Personnel

However, the use of office methods largely depends upon the nature and volume of business handled by the organisation for whom the office work may be performed.

QUESTIONS

1. Write explanatory note on the importance of office systems and routines. (*B. Com. Pass, Delhi, 1986*)
2. Distinguish between office systems and office routines. (*B. Com. Pass, Delhi, 1985*)
3. What do you understand by Office Systems ? Explain. (*B. Com. Pass, Delhi, 1983*)
4. (a) State the importance of the institution of office systems. Outline the steps needed to plan office systems.
   (b) You are the O & M Officer of a large office. What principles would you take into consideration for the O & M Work ? (*B. Com. Pass, Delhi, 1982*)

12

WORK SIMPLIFICATION, MEASUREMENT AND CONTROL

In office mangement, the important aspects are making the office work simpler and measuring the work-performance through a number of control devices. All this has to be done by an efficient office manager who does not only look after the daily routine but also takes effective measure, in improving the office working.

In the present-day world of science and technology, the principles of scientific management are followed for the mangement of office. Based on the phenomenon that there is always a possibility in improvement in working, methods, machines and equipment, the concept of work simplification or work improvement has been developed.

By work simplification or work improvement, we mean finding out the ways and means through which unnecessary parts of work are eliminated and necessary aspects are combined in such a way that there is good flow of work and maximum efficiency is attained. In other words. work simplification is the process through which better and easier methods of working are applied in carrying out the various office operations.

In big modern offices, it is the pratice that the time and motion studies are conducted on regular basis either by a special department called the Organisation and Methods Department (O & M Deptt.) or through a management consultant engaged for the purpose. On the basis (of survey and study, new or cut-short methods are suggested to the top management or administration and then applied in practice. All this is aimed in improving the efficiency of office operations.

Objectives and Importance

Work simplification is carried out with some objectives in view or there is the importance of work simplification in office management on account of the following :—

(i) **Elimination of wastes**—The parts of work which are wasteful or futile, are eliminated from the procedures through the process of work simplification.

(ii) **Avoiding Duplication**—Wherever it is felt that there is double performance of the same work, such areas are taken out and not allowed to be repeated.

(iii) **Improvement of Methods**—By studying the present methods of work, the new methods are invented which are certainly better and more efficient than the present ones. As we know, methods are the manual or mechanical means of carrying out the actual office operations. Through work simplification, the old or stale methods are discarded or cut short and modern methods are applied for day-to-day office routine.

(iv) **Printing in speed and accuracy** — Working is simplified with a view to bring in speed in work because time is the more valuable factor in the modern days. At the same time, the aim is that the errors may be reduced to the minimum.

(v) **Reducing fatigue of workers**—The work is simplified because the workers may not feel too much of fatigue and the output may be increased without effecting material changes.

(vi) **Reducing Costs**—The process of work simplification is adopted because the office costs on labour, stationery, machines and equipments etc., are reduced to the minimum. More work may be performed within the least possible time.

(vii) **Improvement in communication**—When office forms, equipments and procedures are simplified, it is possible to effect efficient communication at all the levels and the management information system is developed well.

(viii) **Increased efficiency** — The performance of office operations becomes good in terms of quantity and quality. It becomes easy for the workers to understand the procedures and implement them practically without much of the problem.

(ix) **Easy supervision and control**—When the work is simplified there is no problem to the supervisor in fixing up the norms or standards and then measure the actual work with the standards already fixed up.

Thus, the importance of work simplification or improvement is increasing day by day, particularly in the field of office management. The modern office manager is expected to know thoroughly well the various devices through which the work may be made very easy and convenient for all those concerned.

Procedure for Work Simplification

For the purpose of simplifying the office operation, a namber of *steps* may be taken which are enumerated as under :—

(i) Studying and identifying the areas of office operations which involve higher costs or where the interruptions are too many. This can be done by closely watching the office routine works.

(ii) Collecting statistical data or detailed information by further studying the various office records or documents on the basis of which the areas have been identified for work simplification.

(iii) Critically analysing the data through discussions with staff and experts or through independent sources.

(iv) Devising simpler and economical new methods of working on the basis of study and critical analysis made earlier. If necessary, the new methods may be well tested before putting them into practical use.

(v) Implementing the methods developed through study analysis and tests, etc.

WORK MEASUREMENT AND CONTROL

One of the important functions of an Office Manager is to control the office operations and that involves fixing up the norms or standards of performance, comparing them with the actual work performed and taking the corrective measures in order to avoid any deviation from the standards in future. This process may be applied for each and every operation carried out in the office.

Work Measurement is a part of the controlling of an office manager. It involves determining the time required to complete a particular job. In other words, it is the technique designed to establish the ideal time rate required to perform a particular office operation. We may call it a time study also. The work measurement helps in deciding the optimum workload for the workers in general,

Objectives or Importance

The work measurement or control is dene with a number of objectives in view or the same is important for a number of reasons enumerated hereunder :

(i) **Deciding optimum workload for each worker**—How much volume of work may be allotted to a worker under the norml conditions so that the worker may easily complete the work, this can be decided on the basis of work measurement only. On this basis of trial or time study, the manager comes to know the time factor of an average worker and accordingly he may allot the optimum work to the worker.

(ii) **Manpower Planning**—On the basis of time study, it is possible to plan out the requirements of men in an office. The recruitment and placement of personnel may be done on the basis to work measurement. By divding the total work with the time factor, the exact number of persons required may be ascertained.

(iii) **Assessment of Efficiency**—The efficiency in office work or of the organisation as a whole may be adjudged through the work measurement techniques. As efficiency involves quantity of quality-work, both these things may be measured through time study.

(iv) **Basis for office systems and procedures**—It is the basis on which the systems and procedures may be adopted in the day-to-day working because the practical utility of systems or procedures may be adjudged through work measurement.

(v) **Basis for incentives**—The work measurement is important because the incentives to workers may be granted on the basis of their work performance which is measured through time study. Incentives may include appreciation, cash rewards, promotion or higher assignments for the good work performance. For this work measurement is the only deciding factor.

Techniques or Methods of Work Measurement

There are a number of methods or techniques adopted for measuring the work performance in an office. The important amongst them are as under :—

(i) **Rule of Thumb or Subjective Method**—Under this method, the individual guess or judgment is taken up as a standard of performance and the actual work is measured in relation to that. Though it is a simple methods, yet cannot be scientific because it is not based on any study or research but simply an estimated one. As such, it may not be practical also.

(ii) **Past Performance Method** : Under it, the past performance of the average worker is taken as a standard for measuring the actual work done in the present. If the output is found to be the same, it is considered to be efficient otherwise not. Though this method is based on the traditional values and is very simple, yet it does not take into account the time and motion study of work and, as such, it may not be fool-proof.

(iii) **Time and Motion Study Method** : This method is based on the principles of scientific management enunciated by Taylor and Fayol. According to this method, a study is conducted of the various operations or aspects separately and the ideal time taken for each operation is decided upon. Thereafter the actual performance is measured, The time study is conducted after the motion study and the rates or scales of pay or wages are determined. It is comparatively a better method and promotes inducement amongst workers. It is more accurate but much time and money is wasted in conducting the studies.

(iv) **Random Sampling Method** : Under this method, a direct personal observation is made of the activity or group of activities and the sample is taken out on random basis. The sample taken on the basis of direct personal observation is fixed as a standard for work performance and the actual work is measured in relation to the standard determined on the basis of random sampling. This method is simple, easy, economical and more popular in the modern days but it is lesser accurate than the time and motion study method.

ORGANTSATION & METHODS (O & M)

For the puspose of bringing in the top level of efficiency and saving time, labour and energies in office operations, a new concept has emerged in the modern office management and that is known as O & M. In bigger Organisations, we find a separate full-fledged department known as O & M Department which makes study from time to time of the various forms, machines, equipments, organisation of office, procedures and methods used to perform the so-called office operations and suggests simplification and improvements in the present working.

In view of the above, Organisation and Methods may be defined as an activity of work simplification with an objective to eliminate waste of time, energy and space, etc. and bringing in maximum efficiency at the minimum costs. In other words, it is an organised activity undertaken to find easier and better ways of working in an office. Generally, it is concerned with the organisation and administration of office operations. It forms part of the continuous working of an Organisation. Abbreviately it is known as O & M.

Objectives or Importance

The O & M has the following objectives or its importance can be adjudged from the following points :—

(i) **Elimination of Wastes** : Whatever superfluous or unnecessar parts of work, forms, space, equipments etc. are found, the same are omitted or cut short so that all sorts of economies are effected. The overall working is made smooth and without any hurdle.

(ii) **Maximum Work Output** : The O & M takes care to ensure that the work output of office is the maximum, so to say, optimum as a result of better utilisation of men, material, machines, methods and money.

(iii) **Constant Improvements** : The very purpose of O & M is to be on the job of making improvements in the office working on regular basis. Hence, its importance.

(iv) **Prompt and efficient service** : Since the office work is a service, it is the object of O & M that the office services may be rendered promptly and efficiently. That is why, form designing, data-processing, mechanisation of office work is done at the instance of O & M.

(v) **Helping Mechanisation of office work** : The latest and most machines are introduced for performing office routine operations of the repetitive nature for quicker results. O & M helps in it, because the primary objective of this is maximum efficiency with least cost.

Limitations or Drawbacks

However, O & M suffers from the following disadvantages ;—

(i) It is a costly affair because additional expenditure has to be incurred on staff, survey, studies etc.

(ii) The workers or employees are upset because O & M always finds fault in their working and forces them to adapt to new methods and procedures time and again.

O & M Department

As we have said earlier, larger Organisations create a seperate section or department called the Systems Department or Organisation & Methods Department. This department functions as a corollary to office and looks after the office organisation, lay-out, administration, working procedures, methods, equipments and machines etc. This department is headed by an expert or specialist in office organisation and planning techniques. He or she is assisted by a number of assistants or other staff. This Department is treated as an important one in the whole of the Organisation. Its functions are carried on simultaneously with the working of the organisation as a continuous and regular process. Its functions are almost the same as the procedure of work simplification.

Its Functions

The important functions performed by the O & M Department may be outlined as under :—

(i) Determining the objectives or areas for which the department will have to work. Generally, the areas which involve higher costs or where interruptions or overlappings are discerning, the same are chosen by it for study or survey and making suggestions for improvement.

(ii) Planning the assignment i.e. deciding the course of action well in advance for the purpose of simplifying the work and procedures.

(iii) Collecting statistical data or detailed information from the office records or documents for the purpose of studying and analysing the facts.

(iv) Analysing or processing the data collected from different sources and arrive at the concrete conclusions.

(v) Devising the new methods/procedures inculcating the improvement over the existing methods or procedures.

(vi) Suggesting the improvements to the top-level management or administration by submitting proposals, in writing, giving facts, figures and basis on which improvements have been suggested.

(vii) Looking after the implementation of improved methods or procedures and analysing the progress achieved in the field.

The above points may also be narrated while the steps involved in Organisation & Methods are asked for. Actually, these are the various elements involved in the process of organisation and methods. The same are the functions performed by the O & M Department.

QUESTIONS

1. Write explanatory note on the importance of work measurement. (*B. Com. Pass, Delhi, 1986*)
2. Explain the importance of work measurement as a tool of management. (*B. Com. Pass, Delhi, 1987*)

13

OFFICE PERSONNEL RELATIONS

Dale Carnegie in his book 'How to win friends and influence people' has rightly stated:—

"When dealing with people, let us remember, we are not dealing with creatures of logic but the creatures of emotion bristling with prejudices and motivated by pride and vanity."

The above lines should be remembered by the office manager when he has to deal with personnel working in office After all, office manager cannot alone do the entire office work. He has to take work from people and get the things done through them. They are not to be treated like machines but they are governed by their whims and desires. It is the duty of the office manager to ensure that good inter-personal relations are maintained throughout so that they co-operate and strive for achieving the organisational goals. If the relations are not harmonious, they may not co-operate and the result will be that they may not give the desired output of work, rather create problems for the management.

An important aspect of handling office personnel is understanding the human behaviour at work, i.e. to understand how people behave and why they behave in a particular manner at a particular time. This, in turn, calls for understanding the important principles of 'Human Relations' which involve humanizing the incentives, i.e. the rules for allowing incentives to human beings at work, without that it may not be possible to take work from them.

These incentives may include—delegation of authority, discipline, impartiality. counselling, boosting morale etc.

MORALE

The literal meaning of the term 'morale' is increasing or boosting the moral of workers. Moral has no definite meaning but it may be defined as the state of mind or attitude of a person towards the work so as to show his willingness to co-operate in achieving the organisational goals. A person having a good moral extends his co-operation of his own whereas the others have to be motivated for getting their co-operation.

It is the duty of office manager to keep up or boost up the morale of office personnel and the same may be done by providing security of job, recognition, giving them the feeling of being important, welcoming their suggestions and so on. By giving such incentives, the morale of employees remains at the high level otherwise the low level of morale results in low rate of productivity, high rate of absenteeism, higher labour turnover, too many complaints, labour unrest, too much resistance, frictions and grievances etc. On the other hand, a high morale may bring more productivity, lesser labour turnover, discipline and good working atmosphere etc.

Morale and Productivity

It is generally said that morale and productivity go together and these are co-related with each other—'*High morale, high productivity and low morale, low productivity*'. Productivity is the power, ability or capacity to produce work by the employees and the morale has a direct connection with the mental ability of workers to co-operate in achieving targets of work for the Organisation. Therefore, when the morale of workers is high, their capacity to produce will increase as they will work happily towards that end. On the other hand, if the morale is low, the production level will also be low. But, it is not true always. There may be cases where low morale may fetch high productivity because of strict supervision and control, punishments for erring personnel and other factors, but such a situation does not go a long way because strictness cannot bring good results in the long-run though it may do in the short-run similarly, under the conditions of high morale, the personnel may feel happy and satisfied but they may be lacking interest towards the work or they might become careless. That is why, even with the high morale of workers, the management should exercise proper supervision, control, frame proper rules for working and impose penalties for blunders. Then only the high morale may bring higher productivity

Measures to boost up Morale :

It is said, "morale requires regular attention, diagnosis and treatment just as health does". This has a meaning that just as health is to be maintained by regular exercise, check-up and treatment etc., in the same way the morale of workers in the office has to be paid attention, diagnosed and treated regularly by the management. That means, regular measures deserve to be taken for keeping up the morale. Some of the important measures are as under :—

(i) **Effective and flawless communication** : Communication involves the process of exchanging information between the management, employees, outsiders and all concerned. In a good office, communication channels are so adopted that there is no mis-communication or that there is no communication gap and the things are understood in the same sense in which the communicator wants them. Thus, effective communication brings in all-round efficiency in working. When there are barriers to communication, the expected results may not be achieved because the employees might not be mentally prepared to take up the work.

(ii) **Staff Meetings** : One way to keep the morale of workers is arranging meetings or get-together of all the staff members and discussing the progress achieved and or discussing their problems or complaints about the work and assuring them of the best co-operation from management's side. Generally, once a month such a meeting should invariably be called and informal discussions may also be held with staff. This fosters a general feeling amongst personnel that they are participating in management of affairs of the company.

(iii) **Personal discussions** : It is also necessary that the office manager may call, in turn, each person and ask his or her problems or difficulties which he or she might be facing while working. Many people are not able to speak during meetings or conferences and when they meet personally, they are able to express themselves well. This keeps up the morale of office personnel at the highest level.

(iv) **Regular follow-up** : The office manager should continuously pursue the progress achieved by each of the member of staff. This keeps up the tempo of work amongst workers and, at the same time, they have a feeling that if they do not work, it may be checked and any problem might arise for them. If there is no regular follow-up, the employees might not be mentally prepared to accomplish the work. The follow-up may be done through work-sheets or work diaries maintained for the works completed. The office manager may call the diary or sheet and check the same with the actual work performed.

(v) **Encouraging group activities** : It is also necessary that group activities like picnic. sports, informal get-together etc., of the employees may be arranged from time to time so that all of them have a feeling of the team spirit. They maintain the pace of progress and help achieving the goals.

(vi) **Regular incentive schemes** : In order to prepare the employees mentally for the high morale and productivity, it will also be beneficial that the special schemes of cash rewards or other benefits, be chalked out and circulated amongst the members. It will make their moral of the higher level and they may strive to get the incentives.

(vii) **Welfare Activities** : These comprise of the various fringe benefits extended to the employees on account of the fact that they are working in the Organisation like pension, medical aid hospitalisation, tiffin, free education to employees children and so on with these facilities the employees always keep their morale high because they know that they would be entitled to such benefits if they work well and achieve promotions. The detailed description of the staff welfare activities is given in the following paragraphs.

STAFF WELFARE ACTIVITIES

Those benefits, facilities or services which are extended by an employer to its employees with social objectives in view and which do not have a direct connection with the productivity or work output but have a mental bearing on the employees, may be called the staff welfare activities. These may include leave travel concession, medical aid, educational facilities to employees' children, contribution to provident fund, family pension. recreation facilities, subsidised food arrangements etc. Some of them may be of the economic nature while the others may be recreational, facilitative or fringe benefits. These are different in different Organisations, their nature and quantum depending upon the profitability of the Organisation concerned and/or the policies of the management.

Classification

Depending upon the nature of staff welfare activities, these may be broadly classified under *three* heads :—

(i) Economic benefits : (ii) Recreational Facilities and (iii) Physical comforts.

(i) **Economic Benefits** : In addition to wages, salaries or overtime, whatever other benefits are granted to employees in terms of monetary benefits. These may include—

Credit facilities : In most of the Organisations, loans are granted for the purchase of consumer items like TV, furniture, refrigerator, almirahs etc. at concessional rate of interest. Advance against salary is granted. Housing loans are granted at lower rates of interest for purchase of plot of land or built up house etc. Such loans are granted on easy terms and repayable in monthly instalments by deducting a fixed sum from the salary every month. On the eve of big occasions like Diwali, Christmas or Holi, the festival advances are also granted to employees in order to meet their extra expenditure on the festivals. These are mostly given free of interest.

Credit and Thrift Co-operative Societies : Many organisations allow their employees to form such societies who enrol their members out of the employees by offering them the shares. The co-operative stores are opened for selling the consumer items at no-profit-no-loss basis. Loans are also granted to the members from time to time by these societies. These societies also inculcate the habit of thrift or saving amongst the employees.

Group Insurance : Many employers arrange to take life insurance policy for the employees as a group and pay insurance premium from their side. This gives a feeling of security to employees and keeps up their morale. If any employee meets with an accident or dies, the compensation may be made available by the insurance company.

Under the group insurance scheme, many times, a blanket fidelity guarantee policy may also be obtained which covers the entire risks of employees while at work.

Hence, group insurance has many *advantages* like covering the risks of individual employees at work, availability of timely compensation, increasing efficiency and morale of employees, no burden on individual employes for payment of premium amount, no burden on employer for payment of compensation in case of mis-happening etc. However, the *disadvantage* is that the employer has alone to bear the loan of premium, the difficulty arises in ascertaining or sharing the amount received from the insurance company on completion of period of insurance. The employees may also take undue advantage of the facility.

Retirement Benefits : While an employee leaves the service after completion of a certain period of service, he or she may be entitriled to benefits like *contributory provident fund*, under which a fixed sum is deducted every month from the salary while the employee is working and the same amount is paid by the employer, the amount with interest is payable on retirement and even the loans may be granted there against. *Gratuity* may also be paid on retirement, which represents the amount equivalent to average salary last drawn. The lump-sum amount is paid in cash to the employee on retirement.

Pension is the amount of allowance paid to an employee every month after his retirement from service. Particularly, in government service, there is a provision for pension and *family pension* under which a fixed sum is paid every month to the employee on his retirement and even after the death of the employee to his family members. This type of scheme is much beneficial as it enables the employee even after his retirement to pull on the day-to-day expenditure. However, it may be a permanent burden on the employer for an indefinite period.

(ii) **Recreational Facilities** : Many Organisations promote the services pertaining to the recreation, entertainment or enjoyment of their employees so that they are keeping a good health. Under this head, the facility of providing *indoor games* like carom, table tannis, chess etc. as well as *outdoor games* like cricket, football, volley ball, hockey etc. is provided. The games material is purchased by the Organisation at their own cost and provided to the employees. The bigger Organisations also make a provision of the play-ground under or adjacent to the working compound. Tournaments may also be arranged and prizes distributed to the best players.

Outdoor picnics may also be arranged from time to time when the family members of employees get-together and arrange for group recreation at the cost of the organisation.

Leave, Travel Concession is the facility extended by most of the employers, under which the employee is allowed to take reimbursement of actual travel expenses for visiting the place of domicile or to any place in India once in two years or once in four years for the purpose of taking rest and recuperation. The leave is also allowed vis-a-vis L.T.C. and leave encashment facility is also extended.

This way, the employees get an opportunity to remain away from work for certain period and take mental rest alongwith their family-members. After that, when they come for work, they are refreshed and work with more efficiency.

(iii) **Physical Comforts and other Facilities** : Under this group of welfare, many facilities like providing free furnished or unfurnished housing accommodation, reimbursement of medical expenses or hospitalisation expenses, provision for canteen, water coolers, toilets etc., may be included. Besides these, the facility of appointment of sons or daughters in the organisation or educational facilities to employees children are also included. The facility of *tiffin* or payment of income-tax on behalf of employees by the employer may also be included.

In a nutshell, the above said benefits or facilities are provided by the employers in addition to the regular-salary, overtime or bonus etc. All these are mainly aimed at providing incentives for better working conditions, comforts and ultimate better productivity with efficient working.

Staff-Welfare and Productivity

Though staff welfare and productivity are not directly related as there is no such thing that the worker will produce this much and will be allowed that much of welfare, and it should not be treated as charity from the employer's side or a matter of right from employee's side, yet the welfare has a psychological effect on the employee. Many Organisations attract workers due to the fringe benefits. Normally, the labour turnover is less in such Organisations where welfare activities are sufficiently extended. The absenteeism is also comparatively less. The workers feel happy and satisfied and their efficiency increases to a greater extent. Where the facilities for housing accommodation etc., are available, the workers have not to worry much about their familities and they do not resort to malpractices and work with devotion and integrity, One more thing is that the workers become more loyal to an Organisation where fringe benefits are available to them for bettering their living standards. With the retirement benefits, the future of workers is secured and they work with devotion throughout the service period. Overall, the staff welfare activities on the part of employer have certainly a good impact over the productivity although the same might not be realised in direct terms. These activities certainly help the employee to settle their family problems and, thus, keep them mentally saturated so that they strive to achieve the organisational goals.

HANDLING THE GRIEVANCES OR COMPLAINTS

'Grievances' refer to that state of mind of employees when they feel discontented or dissatisfied over certain matters and consequently they resort to complaints or resentment. They have a feeling that they are not treated fairly and some injustice is done to them. It is all *relative* because any particular matter may be a benefit to someone whereas a grievance to some other person. The grievance may be on account of anything while working in the Organisation. It may be on account of poor working conditions, promotions, transfers, fresh-recruitment, disciplinary action and so on.

Whenever there is some grievance with any employee or a group of employees, they either resort to or form a destructive attitude towards work or adopt work to rule. Consequently, the productivity or output starts declining. Many times, the work is totally held up due to which the management has to suffer a lot. In order to avoid any conflict or untoward incident, it is the duty of the management to deal with the redressal of grievances without any further loss of time.

The aggrieved employee or group of employees, generally, adopt any of the two ways to represent or express the grievances—(i) They make a representation to the Competent Authority through proper channel, i.e. through their immediate boss and have a dialogue with the management, or (ii) They may approach the Union of Workers and the leaders of workers hold discussions/meetings with the top executives. If the things are unsettled through dialogue, they may take the shelter of Court of Law for the redressal of grievances, which is, of course, the last resort when nothing else works.

Generally, the management prefers making a dialogue with the concerned employee or the representatives of their Union and tries to settle the disputes arising out of the grievances. None of the management can afford to wait for long and create disturbances in the working. The ultimate result is the loss of production or work. A 'Grievances Committee' may also be formed for the purpose.

STAFF UNIONS

A Staff Union is the organised body or association of workers formed for the purpose of collective bargaining with the management and thereby protecting the interests of the member-workers. These may be termed as *Trade Unions*-also. Actually, the workers elect their representatives who form the governing body of the Union. The membership of the Union is obtained by paying a fees by each of the employee. Whenever there is any grievance, the representatives arrange to hold dialogues with the management and settle the issues. In case the disputes are not settled with simple dialogue, a call for the strike or work-to-rule may be given by the Union and all the workers follow the instructions given to them of their leaders.

In bigger Business Organisations usually the employees form various Unions under separate banners and those may be recognised by the management. The registered Unions are generally recognised by the management.

Advantages

There may be many advantages of the Staff Unions like:—

(i) Most of the disputes are settled with amicable dialogue with the management and the individual employee has not to suffer much. The Union Leaders are competent to satisfy the management easily as compared to an individual employee.

(ii) The bargaining power of employees increases because the unions are supported by a large team of workers. Hence, the management generally agrees for reasonable things without much of the problem.

(iii) It is through the Unions that the management may get better or improved productivity of workers. The trivial grievances do not come to the higher management because the union leaders get them settled on the spot. The Union can compel the workers to work for better prospects.

(iv) It encourages participation of workers in the management of an Organisation because the interests of workers are linked with management policies or vice versa.

In most of the government bodies, there is a representative of workers in the Board of Directors.

Defects

There may be various disadvantages of the Staff Unions e.g.—

(i) With the existence, generally, a hostile attitude is adopted by the workers whenever there is some change in the management policies or set-up. That disturbs the management in introducing new systems, techniques etc.

(ii) Most of the workers who become leaders in workers' Unions, do not work well because they have to spend much time in the union activities.

(iii) The chances of strikes and other slow tactics are enhanced where the staff unions are formed and the management cannot work with freedom.

Overall, the staff Unions take an active part in handling the grievances of employees and also help in developing better working relationship between the management and the workers. The role of the Unions has been widely recognised in the business circle.

OFFICE COMMITTEES

An Office Committee may be defined as a group of persons, representing the management or workers, who discuss the various office matters and may take certain decisions for the common interests. The Office Committee may be any *Ad Hoc Committee*, constituted for a specific purpose or a *Standing Committee*, having permanent members. There may be *Joint Consultative Committees* also which are formed by the representatives of a management as well as the workers for resolving various office matters like providing better working conditions or improvement in productivity or office routine problems etc. Whatever it may be, the committee is formed for the specific purpose and the members have to tape up the task, study it, collect details and, finally, submit the report to the appropriate Management Authority.

The main aim of forming Office Committees is joint consultation with the persons representing diverse interests and achieve maximum efficiency in working or in management of office affairs. These help in removing prejudices or vested interests in taking decisions because they work independently in resolving specific issues only.

Advantages

The following are the various advantages of Office Committees :—

(i) The concentration of power is removed because the working of office committees is based on democratic principles involving opinion of diverse people.

(ii) It leads to pooling of ideas and the balanced judgment on office matters.

(iii) The office committees safeguard the interests of both the management as well as employees because they work independently.

(iv) These help in developing mutual understanding as the opportunity is given to all for discussions and representing their respective interests.

(v) It helps in maintaining harmonious inter-personal relations in office because the office workers feel that the committee would give decision after taking into account all the aspects.

However, the office committees may suffer from the following defects or *disadvantages* :—

(i) The committees members may waste a lot of time and energies in prolonged discussions and consultations, putting a burden on the exchequer of the concerned Organisation.

(ii) Since the members of the committee may go on stressing their own vested interests, the decisions may be wrong many times.

SUGGESTION SYSTEM

In many bigger Organisations, there is a system of installing 'Suggestion Box' or 'Complaints Box' and through them the management invites suggestions from workers and others. When letters are received to this effect, the same are handed over to the special Cell created for the purpose of studying and finding out whether the suggestion may be implemented in actual practical routine. Many times, the information is circulated throughout the workers and their consents are sought.

This may help the management in bringing about the improvement in working of office. Many useful schemes or tips may be obtained without incurring any cost for the same. But, most of them are a simply waste and spoils the time of officers. Still, the management is obliged to invite suggestions independently with an open heart so as to give opportunity to everyone in the Organisation for active participation in management.

QUESTIONS

1. What are 'Office Committees' ? Explain the functions of such committees. (*B. Com. Pass, Delhi, 1986*)
2. Write explanatory note on Employee Morale and Productivity. (*B. Com. Pass, Delhi, 1986*)
3. Write explanatory note on the Advantages of Employees Group Insurance. (*B. Com. Pass, Delhi, 1985*)

4. Write short note on the Credit Societies in the office.
(*B. Com. Pass, Delhi, 1984*)
5. What is Group Insurance? Explain its advantages to the employees and the management.
(*B. Cam. Pass, Delhi, 1981-1987*)
6. Describe briefly the various staff welfare measures which are generally extended by the employers.
(*B. Com. Delhi-II, NS, 1986*)
7. Discaurs the following :
Causes of employce-grievances. (*B. Com. II, Delhi, 1987*)
8. Write explanatory notes on—
   (a) Meaning and purposes of work measurement.
   (b) Emyloyees Co-opertaive credit societies.
(*B. Com. II, Delhi, 1987*)

14

CORRESPONDENCE AND OFFICE REPORTS

We know it very well that no business worth the name can run without proper means of communication. The 'communication' refers to the process of exchange of information, ideas opinions and thoughts etc. between two or more persons. This communication of information may be done in many ways like face to face conversation, by telephone, telex etc. or even by writing letters. Thus, letter writing, in business, is one of the means of written communication and it is preferred most out of the various means of communication because letter-writing is the cheapest, most convenient, facilitates keeping record for reference any time in future, helps in maintaining goodwill and reputation and is also having a wider approach. Due to the above reasons, writing letters in business has become very important and the need of the hour in modern days. It is, therefore, essential for a private secretary to know and learn the art of writing letters, in business, official, social and personal life. Many important letters are dictated by his/her Boss whereas the other routine letters, a private secretary should be able to draft and type independently because the boss is mostly is very busy in his official assignments and he does not have so much time that he could dictate even the day-to-day ordinary routine letters. As such a successful private secretary is supposed to know and be able to draft independently all such routine letters. The routine letters of business may include acknowledging a letter, making an enquiry, calling a quotation, sending quotation, placing an order etc.

However, for the purpose of drafting routine correspondence a private secretary must know the various principles of good letter-writing, the lay-out of the letter and also the various styles of letter-writing (i.e. the rules for display and spacing in a letter) besides knowing the opening and closing sentences for different types of routine letters. All these things would help him/her in drafting a good business letter.

Types of Letters

Broadly speaking, the following are the various types of letters :—

1. **Personal Letters**—These letters are written by individuals in connection with the family, friendship or other social matters. These are purely personal and are written differently by individuals without being formal. The examples of such letters are—letters between two friends, son writing to father, or a nephew writing to uncle. Such letters are very much informal in nature and could be written in any way.

2. **Business Letters**—These letters are formal in nature and are written between firms, associations or bodies of persons, concerning the matters of trade or other business activities. In such type of letters, we have to complete certain formalities, conform to the formal lay-out and follow the conventional discipline or decorum required in business.

3. **Official Letters**—These are written in Government, Semi-Government or other offices on subjects concerning the administrative and/or policy matters. Such letters have a different tone and style of writing, depending upon the position/designation of the official or person writing the letter.

4. **Miscellaneous or Other Letters**—These letters comprise of the letters written on miscellaneous matters. These are written differently than personal, business or official letters. Such letters include circular letters, sales letters and application for the jobs etc.

Business Letters

Business letters can be broadly classified into two main groups:

(a) **Routine Letters**—Which are written in day-to-day business life almost in the same fashion all the time, concerning the ordinary matters like making business enquiries, calling for quotations, sending quotations, placing an order for goods or other items, acknowledgments etc. Such letters must be known to the clerical or other secretarial staff in business organizations.

(b) **Letters requiring special care or attention**—These are usually drafted by the person having special skill or responsibility, because such type of letters involve important business decisions or policy making or crucial events. These types of business letters require logical presentation of facts and are usually dictated by Executives or Managers or Bosses to a steno-typist and involve careful drafting.

Kinds of Routine Business Letters

The following are the various kinds of business letters :—

1. Enquiries
2. Status-enquiries
3. Quotations
4. Order for goods
5. Complaints or claims
6. Adjustments
7. Settlement of Accounts
8. Collection of Bills
9. Sales Letters
10. Circular letters
11. Letters of Introduction
12. Banking letters etc.

BUSINESS CORRESPONDENCE

Essentials or Qualities of a Good Letter :

In order to serve the purpose for which a letter has been written, it is necessary that a letter should be correct, complete, concise, courteous etc. There are certain essentials of a good letter which may be discussed in the following paragraphs :—

ABC of a Good Letter

For a layman, there are three essentials of a good letter. We may call them as ABC. where :—

A stands for Accuracy,
B stands for Brevity, and
C stands for Courtesy.

Seven Cs

There are seven essentials or qualities in a good business letter, which may be explained as under :—

1. **Correctness** : The letter should be correct in all respects like the spellings of words, construction of sentences, grammar etc. The name, address, number and other facts and figures should also be correctly reproduced in the letter. Any mistake in it would adversely reflect the efficiency of the whole Organisation.

2. **Courtesy** : A business letter has to be polite and courteous. There is no place for coarseness in a business letter, because the businessman can never afford to have enemity with any one. The courtesy does not only consist of respectful titles or use of words like 'please', 'Thanks' etc. but also showing promptness in attending to any matter.

3. **Conciseness** : So far as possible, the letter should be short and brief. A letter is different than a story or an essay. Hence, all the facts should be given in short and summarised form but at the cost of brevity, the letter should not become ambiguous.

4. **Completeness** : All the facts should be included in a letter. Nothing should remain unwritten. If complete information is not given in a letter, it would involve unnecessary queries from the receiver of your letter.

5. **Commercialese** : The use of commercial words, phrases or terminology should be avoided in a business letter. The language of a letter should be that of day-to-day ordinary use and not commercial one. In the good old days, there used to be letters containing commercial terminology like 'I beg to submit for your kind consideration' or 'I beg to enclose herewith' etc. In modern days, there is no place for such a commercial language.

6. **Clarity** : There should not be any round-aboutness or ambiguity in the language of a letter so that a single word or sentence may have many meanings. It should be crystally clear, otherwise many times the results of ambiguous language are horrible. For bringing clarity, we must use proper punctuation marks, etc. This point has been discussed in detail in the following paragraphs.

7. **Continuity** : In order to avoid any monotony in a letter, the matter should be represented as a link-chain, giving the most important fact first followed by other relevant facts in continuation. The entire letter may be divided into various paragraphs and one paragraph must contain only one type of information. All the paragraphs should have close link with one another.

GENERAL RULES/PRINCIPLES OF GOOD WRITING

While drafting a business letter, certain rules or principle may be followed in order to make a letter more attractive and impressive. These may be defined as under :—

1. **Writing Naturally**—A business letter is a piece of conversation by post. Hence, it should be written in such a way as if two persons are sitting together and discussing. It would bring in the naturalness in writing. No artificiality should be depicted. For example, if two persons are talking to each other and one asks the other, "When are you sending my goods." The other person would reply, "You will get them during the next week." The reply would never be, the "The goods would bc received at your place during the next week." See the difference. Similarly, the business letter should be written in a natural tone, using the day-to-day ordinary speaking languages used in conversation.

2. **Writing Clearly**—The ideas presented in the form of a letter should be crystally clear and there should not be any ground for taking out many meanings of the same word or sentence. There is a famous saying about the clarity. One judge gave a judgement and at last hc wrote, "LEAVE HIM NOT HANG HIM". The judge wanted to say that the accused is innocent and he should be left free but he forgot to put fullstop after the first, him, and the next-day morning the typist inadvertently put the fullstop after the word NOT. The result was that the poor person, who was to be freed, was hanged. Like this, there may be many instances where, the clarity is very important. On a road, there was a sign-board telling—GO SLOW WORK IN PROGRESS. The hyphen was wrongly put after the word Go instead of SLOW and the result was that many accidents took place at that site. As such, the letter should necessarily be quite clear for which care must be taken to ensure proper punctuation in the letter and the ambiguity may be avoided.

3. **Writing Completely**—All the facts should be included in your letter. In case incomplete information is given, there may be unnecessary queries from the correspondent which would waste the time of both—the writer and the receiver of letter. As an example we may quote one instance where an order was placed with a book seller, stating—'Please send me four books on Business Correspondence and Private Secretary'. Here, the reader could not make out whether the orderer wants two books each or any other number. Also the name of author was not given. As such, the order could not be complied with. In order to avoid any disappointment or inconvenience, it is necessary that your letter should contain compelete details so that there is no unnecessary shunting of letters.

4. **Courtesy**—As explained earlier, courtesy implies using the polite language and respectful titles in a letter and also showing promptness in writing or replying to any letter. Courtesy has got a vital role to play in the business-life as no business may run without it. One cannot afford to use rough or coarse language in a business letter. Wherever possible, the use of words like 'Please', 'Thanks', 'Sorry' etc. be made in a letter. Moreover, the reply to the letters be sent immediately so that the correspondent is not kept in abeyance. He should be satisfied that you are seized of the matter.

5. **Avoiding Jargon of Words**—A business letter is not like an essay or an article from literary point of view. Hence, it is essential that the language of a business letter should be simple with short sentences and easy words of every-day vocabulary as no business man has time to consult dictionary for translating difficult words. Hence, using the extempore or difficult words must be avoided altogether. We should avoid bookish and verbose style of writing in a letter. For example, instead of writing 'Apropos to your letter', we should write 'Refer to your letter'.

6. **Avoiding Use of Commercial Words**—While writing a letter, it is also essential that so far as possible, we should avoid using commercial terms or phrases like 'Your letter of 5th ultimo' or "I beg to acknowledge receipt of your letter' or C.O.D. (i.e. cash on demand), C.I.F. (Cost insurance and freight) etc. These types of terms or phrases have become obsolete and out of date. Though some commercial terms are so important and such that there is no substitute for them, still efforts should be made to avoid using commercialese.

7. **Avoiding Monotony**—A business letter is said to be effective when it is easily understood by the reader and the contents fully followed. For this purpose, it is necessary that our letter should be precise, relevant, concrete and consistent. All facts, to be conveyed in a letter, should be arranged in such a way that one fact which is most important, is written first and followed by other fact in continuation so that the entire letter becomes a link-chain. For this purpose, we can divide the letter into different small paragraphs and each paragraph should contain one type of information only. However, the letter should not be so short also, that it might loose sense. Rather, we should have a mediocre approach of combining brevity with completeness of information. We should write whatever needs to be written and then stop. This way, we can avoid

monotony or dullness in a business letter.

8. **Planning the Letter**—Planning, in business correspondence, means 'thinking before writing'. By doing so, we can ensure that all the facts are included in the letter and that they are so arranged that the business letter become useful and result-oriented. For planning a letter, we have to take the following step :—

(*a*) **Collecting Facts/Information**—which means making available all the relevant information or facts to be included in a letter. These are jotted down on a piece of paper before-hand.

(*b*) **Selecting the Right Approach**—which implies the way of starting the letter. However, a letter could begin with any of the three approaches or styles—direct, indirect or persuasive. In the direct approach, we bounce upon the main topic at the beginning, without preface or ground or without introduction. The routine business letters, like those of inquiries, quotations, orders etc. are always written with a direct style. Under direct style or approach the letters are started with a direct question or a point. Indirect approach involves first making ground for the main information be given thereafter, like the one used for writing collection letters, for realising payments, in which we first narrate the necessity for payment and then request for our dues. A persuasive approach is one where the reader is motivated by attracting attention, arousing interest, creating desire and stimulating action. This type of approach is usually used for writing sales letters and in such type of letters we have to behave like a good salesmen for persuading the customer. Whatever may be the approach of writing a business letter, we can use any one of the above approaches depending upon the situation in which we are writing letter.

(*c*) **Arranging Facts**—In planning, it is also important that the collected facts should be arranged properly in such a way that the entire letter becomes a link-chain and the letter ends with satisfaction.

9. **Checking the Letter**—Lastly, we should thoroughly check the business letter before signatures and despatch. For this purpose, we should check spellings, punctuation, completeness of information, tone, way of approach etc. so as to assure accuracy, clarity, impressiveness and effectiveness of a business letter.

LAYOUT/STRUCTURE/FORMAT OF A BUSINESS LETTER

Layout of a letter refers to "the logical arrangement of information in a business letter".

While we look at the business letter, we find that it has many parts like the sender's name and address, reference number, the name and address of Adressee, subject-heading, various paragraphs etc. The lay-out involves arrangement of different parts of a letter in a logical manner. It becomes an ideal form of a business letter. The lay-out may also be called as 'Format of a business letter'.

Parts of a Business Letter

A business letter can be divided into various parts and the logical arrangement of these parts of a letter is the subject-matter of layout.

Before we discuss the details of each part of a letter, the first thing is the selection of right size of note, paper or printed letter-head on which the letter is typed or written. It depends upon the quantum of information included in a letter. We may use any size of sheet for typing or writing a business letter, depending upon the size of information. It is always better to select the right size of paper or sheet based on the quantum of information, otherwise the appearance of letter is not attractive. Suppose we have to type out only 3-4 lines in a letter, we should select the smallest size of paper or printed letter-head. If we type or write 3-4 lines on a foolscap paper, then the letter would look very odd. However, in case the information or matter is lengthy, we may use 'continuation-sheets.

Letter-Heading (or Sender's name and Address)

Usually, the first and most important part of a business letter is the *heading,* which contains the name and address of the sender firm. The name is usually printed in bold Capital letters. The nature of business and complete address of sender is written, giving the correct number of building, name of road/street and place or town accompanied with the correct pincode number. The telephone number, telex number and telegraphic code address, if any, may also be given. All these details form part of the letter-heading. There is no specific style of writing the letter-heading and the Business Concerns get the latter-heads printed in any way they like, depending upon the convenience. Some letter-heads contain address on the upper right-hand side whereas, in others, it is written in the centre and a few concerns get the address printed at the bottom.

Sender's Reference Number

Next to letter-heading, we usually write the reference number of the sender, which represents the number of file, where the office copy of letter sent out, would have been kept on record.

The above reference number of the sender firm is written for easy location of paper out of the bulk of records. The usual way of making a reference number, in, Business Firms is, first, they take the initials of firm's name, then name of department, year and serial number of despatch register. All these details are necessary to make a complete reference number, like—

AVON ENTERPRISES

Ref. No. AE/Sales/85/4903

The above reference number is always quoted by the person replying the letter.

Date

It represents the date when the letter is writen/sent by the sender. The date may be written on the right-hand upper corner of paper, of below reference number, depending upon the style followed for letter-writing.

The date may be written in any way like—12/4/1987 or April 12, 1987 or 12th April, 1987. In some countries, the first digit is always treated as a month and not the day. Hence, it becomes confusing if the date is written in figures. The best way of writing the date on a business letter is 15th April, 1987 or April 12, 1987.

Inside Address

The name and address of the person, whom the letter is addressed to, may be written after the reference number and the date. It contains the correct name of the person or firm, number of building, name of street/road and the town or city together with the pincode number. So far as possible, there should be no abbreviation for the name and other particulars. Where the letter is addressed in the name of a firm, we should prefix the words 'Messrs or M/s' with the name of the company or firm.

The inside address is written on the left-hand margin. Sufficient space should also be left above and below the inside address because of convenience. However, the inside address should be written completely, legibly and attractively.

Salutation

The salutation is a token of respect shown in business letters. The usual form of writing a salutation in 'Dear Sirs' when we address to a firm/company, 'Dear Sir' when we address a letter in personal name or by designation, 'Madam' when the letter is addressed to a lady, and 'Mesdame' when the letter is addressed to a group of ladies. The salutation is written on the left-hand margin below the inside address after leaving two-lines space from inside address. We should avoid writing 'Gentlmen' or any other word for salutation as those have become obsolete.

Subject-heading

Like giving a topic for an essay or precis, we may write the subject heading in a business-letter, giving the short title to the subject matter of the letter. Suppose we are writing about the order for goods, we may write subject as 'Supply of Goods' or 'Placing an Order'.

The subject-heading is written after salutation in a business-letter. However, in official letters, we may write subject before salutation. The subject should preferably be written in bold capital letters and/or underlined so that it is prominently displayed in a letter. It should be either written in the middle or towards the left-hand margin.

The words like 'Sub', 'Reg' or 'Re' may also be prefixed to the subject-heading. In the most modern letters, people avoid using these prefixes. The examples are given below :—

Dear Sirs,

SUB : QUOTATION

Or,

Dear Sirs,

PAYMENT OF BILL

Body of Letter

The body of a letter denotes the various ines or paragraphs of information included in a letter. The body of letter consists of opening sentences, paragraphs and closing sentences.

The opening sentence consists of a few words in the beginning of a letter. These are different for different kinds of letters, depending upon the approach to the main subject-matter.

After writing the opening sentence, the rest of the information is divided into suitable convenient paragraphs. Each paragraph should cantain one type of information only. The paragraphs should have a sequence. The paragraphs should be short and few in number. However, the letter is closed with a suitable closing sentence, which may contain a closing suggestion from sender's side about the future course of action. The closing sentence should also be impressive so that it leaves the lasting impression on the reader and he should be tempted to take an early action on our letter.

Subscription or Complimentary Close

It is necessary that a business letter should be closed with a suitable complimentry words, like 'Yours faithfully', 'Yours truly' or 'Yours sincerely' etc. However, in a business letter, we should write 'Yours faithfully' as complimentary close. The others like 'truely' or 'affectionately' are used in personal letters and 'sincerely' is generally used for demi-official letters. The subscription in a business letter is written at the end, either on the right-hand bottom margin or on left, depending upon the style of writing a business-letter. It is also accompanied with the name of the company or firm.

Signature

It should also be remembered that the business letter be signed by the authorised signatory of the firm. An unsigned letter is not authentic and leaves a bad impression on the recipient firm.

Other Miscellaneous Matters

There are certain other matters also which form part of lay-out of a business letter. These are :—

Enclosures

If any paper or document is attached to the letter, it is called an enclosure. For this, we should clearly indicate in the letter as to how many papers/documents etc. have been enclosed with the letter. The usual way of writing it is as under :

Enc : Four.
Enc : AS ABOVE.

Mailing Directions

Any specific direction or instruction for posting a letter like

'Registered', 'Registered A.D.', 'Express and 'Confidential' etc., may be marked at some prominent place at the top (near the letter-heading) or in between the date and body of letter towards the right side. These mailing directions may be written/typed preferably with red ink and/or underlined.

Where the sender wishes to draw the attention of a particular person, the same may be done by putting the remarks 'For Personal Attention of Mr......'. The same may be written or typed preferably in the blank space available on the right side in between the date and body of the letter.

Carbon Copy Notations

Whenever the copy of a letter is to be addressed to others also, a number of extra copies of that letter may be taken out by inserting carbon papers. It is necessary that the requisite notations may be made on the letter itself, preferably at the end, by writing in the following manner :—

Copy to :	C.C. to :
(*i*) M/s X.	(*i*) M/s X.
(*ii*) M/s Z.	(*ii*) M/s Z.

In official language, we call the above as 'Endorsement'.

P.S. (Post-Script)

If any information or facts remain to be included in the letter or some matter is to be incorporated without re-typing the letter, the same may be done by writing the words 'P.S.' (which means the matter written afterwards) at the end of your letter. Please ensure that such a matter, which is written afterwards, is invariably signed by the original signatory of your letter. Though it is not a good practice, yet the purpose may be served if the necessity arises.

A private secretary should always remember that while drafting or typing a business letter, he/she should conform to the lay-out and follow the various principles of lay-out of a letter. The different parts of a business letter may be arranged and re-arranged in accordance with the style followed for letter-writing. The specimen lay-out of a business letter is given on the next page for the guidance of the reader.

LAY-OUT OF A BUSINESS LETTER

Gram : ABCOL | Tel : 565554
Tlx : 021-2156

Letter-Heading

YOUNG ENTERPRISES
(Cloth Merchants)
10/10 W.E.A. Karol Bagh,
New Delhi-110005.

Reference No. & Date

Ref. No. X/S/87/9114 25th April, 1987.

Inside Address

Messrs. Beauty Corner
Chawranghee,
Calcutta.

REGISTERED A.D.
URGENT/CONFIDENTIAL
FOR PERSONAL ATTENTION
OF MR...............

Salutation

Dear Sirs,

Subject-Heading QUOTATION

(Opening Sentence)...
....

Body of Letter

(Second paragraph)..
....
(Closing sentence)..
....

Subscription or Complimentary Close

Yours faithfully,
For Young Enterprises

ENC : AS ABOVE.

Sd/-
Partner/Proprietor

P.S.
....
....

Sd/-
(Signatures)

Carbon Copy Notation

C.C. to—

(*i*) M/s Verma Bros.....................
(*ii*) M/s Sharma & Co..................
for information & necessary action.

DISPLAY AND SPACING

(*Styles of Letter-writing*)

It is necessary that the letter should have a good appearance or look. For this puryose, we use various styles in writing letters and these styles conform to the rules of spacing and margin etc. A STYLE is the dress of thoughts in a letter. Just as a well dressed man appears to a great advantage, similarly a well-dressed letter is also very useful. The manner of dressing our thoughts in a business letter is called the 'Style' of letter-writing. We may also call it as the FORM OF LAY-OUT.

The styles, used for writing business letters, may be broadly classified into the following :—

Indented :

It is the traditional style of letter-writing. Under this style, the lines are indented 5 to 10 spaces inside the left-hand margin. The date and subscription are written on the right-hand side towards the middle of paper. Reference Number is written on left-hand side. Inside Address is also indented and the subject heading is written towards the middle. With all this setting or matter, the letter becomes well-balanced. Much care is taken of the full-stops, commas and the other punctuation marks.

The salient features of *Indented Style* are as under :—

1. A margin of about 1½" is adopted on both sides of paper.

2. Inside address and paragraphs (in body of letter) are indented 5 to 10 spaces inside. The first line is started after 5 to 7 spaces inside from the left-hand margin and rest of the other lines are not to be indented.

3. Date and Subscription are written on right-hand side of paper.

4. All paragraphs in the letter are separated by double-line spacing.

It is the most traditional style of letter-writing.

Tel : 732743

S. KUMAR SALES CORPORATION

18-V. Old Gupta Colony, New Delhi

18th March, 1987.

Ref. No. SSC./Sales/87/1029.
Messrs, Sunita Brothers,
76, Green Park Extension,
New Delhi.

Dear Sirs,

SUB : YOUR COMPLAINT

We thank you for your letter No. SB/Pur/87/876, dated 8th march, 1987.

We are surprised to know that the contents of our books, supplied to you, are not clear and not lagible at some pages. It is difficult to understand why the books, sold to your customers have given trouble. Normally we dispatch the books after thorough inspection at our end.

We understand your problem but regret that we cannot accept your suggestion to take back all unsold stocks from you, since it is unlikely that the number of faulty books can be very large. We would, of course, replace any book found quite unsatisfactory.

However, we are prepared to allow you a special discount of 9% on this consignment, particularly to compensate your trouble.

We trust that you would accept this as being a fair and reasonable solution of the matter.

Yours faithfully,

For S. KUMAR SALES CORPORATION
(PARTNER)

Modified Indented : In this form of lay-out, all things are like fully-indented, as explained above, except that the inside address is written as fully-blocked and there is no indentation in the inside Address. All other things remain the same.

SUPERT INDUSTRIES
Bapu Road
BANGALORE

Grams : 'SUPERB' Tel. 242613
Ref. No : RI/Gen/87/109 20th January, 1987

M/S International Crockeries,

D.N. Road,

BOMBAY.

Dear Sirs,

QUOTATION FOR THE CROCKERY.

Will you please send us your lowest quotation for the following ?

1. 12 Doz. Cups & Plates (China make)
2. 12 Doz. Cups & Saucers (Roshni make)
3. 30 Doz. Full Plates (Roshni make)
4. 30 Doz. Quarter Plates ('Bela' make)

If your prices and other terms compare favourably with others, we may send you an order for supply of above items.

Yours faithfully,
for SUPER INDUSTRIES
(Managing Partner)

Fully Blocked :—It is the most modern style. We start every line from the left hand margin. Right from the sender's reference number to the date inside, address, every line of the body of letter as well as the complimentary close—all are commencing from the left-hand margin. There is no indentation or inside spacing for the lines of paragraphs. Besides, the open pattern of punctuation is followed (which means that the use of full-stops and commas is very much restricted) while writing a letter under the fully-blocked form of lay-out of a letter.

The salient features of this style are :—

1. All parts of a letter are written/typed towards the left-hand margin of paper.

2. Open pattern of punctuation is followed i.e. the use of full-stops and commas is very limited. These are placed only where it is absolutely necessary.

3. The date and subscription are written towards the left-hand margin.

GRAM : ASHOK Telex : 02-021
Tel : 313921

ASHOK KUMAR & SONS

1, ASHOKA ROAD, NEW DELHI-110001

Ref. No. AKS/P/87/1102
4th December 1987,

M/s. Bhagat Ram & Sons
6, Mall Road, Simla,
(HIMACHAL PRADESH.)

Dear Sirs,

As desired vide your letter No. BRS/Misc/87/1238, dated 1st December, 1987 we are giving the names and addresses of the trade references with whom we have dealings since long along with the names of our bankers :

1. M/s Rajan Babu & Sons
   F-4, Connought Place, New Delhi.

2. M/s Joginder & Sons
   24, Chandani Cowk, Delhi.

Our banker are : United Bank of India,
Parliament Street, New Delhi-110001.

If you require any other information, we shall be glad to supply you the same.

Yours faithfully,

For ASHOK KUMAR & SONS

PROPRIETOR.

Semi-Blocked : While using this style of letter-writing there is neither too many indentation nor is the matter entirely blocked towards the left-hand margin. Some matter is blocked and the other parts, like date and subscription, are written towards the right-hand side. Hence, it is called half blocked and half unblocked i.e. semi-blocked. The letter is neither one-sided heavy nor fully indented.

The salient features of Semi-Blocked Styles are :—

1. The reference number, inside address, salutation, subject-heading and all paragraphs of the body of letter commence from the

left-hand margin like that in fully-blocked form. The Subject, however, may also be typed in the middle.

2. The date and subscription or complimentary close are written/typed towards the right side.

3. Open pattern of punctution, like that in fully-blocked, may be used.

Tel : 368292

LECTROMEDIK PRIVATE LIMITED
35/59, Industrial Suburb, Yeswantpur
BANGALORE-560022.

Ref. No. LPL/GEN/87/1206 18th March, 1987

Messrs. Bullworker Private Ltd.
5, Mathew Road,
Bombay-400004.

Dear Sirs,

SUPPLY OF BULLWORKER ON 'APPROVAL OR RETURN' BASIS.

Several of our customers have expressed interest in the new bullworker manufactured by you, and they are enquiring about its durability and price etc.

We shall feel obliged, if you please let us know, whether you can supply us 100 Bullworkers—full size, on sale or return basis. If the quality and prices are found to be satisfactory, we expect to purchase 100 bullworkers from you on regular basis. But, before we place our regular order for the above, we would like you to send us 5 Bullworkers on approval or return basis. We hope there will be good sale of the item. However, any of the same remaining unsold within a period of 2 months, from receipt of the goods, would be returned to you at our expense.

We hope to hear from you very soon.

Your faithfully,
For Lectromedik Pvt. Ltd.
DIRECTOR

Hanging Paragraph

The Hanging Paragraph Style is said to be the reversal of Indented Style of letter-writing, because in Hanging Paragraph, the first line is blocked and rest of the other lines are indented 5 to 7 spaces inside whereas in indented the first line is indented and the remaining lines are blocked.

The salient features of Hanging Paragraph Letter-Style are :

1. Reference number is written/typed as usual on the left-hand upper corner and the date is typed towards the right middle side of paper. The inside address may be written as either fully-blocked or the first line is blocked and the rest of the other lines are indented inside.

2. First few words of each paragraph are typed from the left-hand margin like that in fully-blocked and the remaining lines are typed 5 to 7 spaces inside the left-hand margin.

3. The subscription is in the normal position towards the right middle and/or may be written in a hanging way.

Though the Hanging Paragraph Style of letter-writing is very seldomly used, yet for letters containing many topics or paragraphs this style is useful. The disadvantage of this style is that it takes much more time of the Typist due to many indentations. At the same time, the paragraphs of the letter also do not look attractive.

Ref. No. EP/Pur/87/950 6th April, 1987
M/s. Sikri & Company,
Asaf Ali Road,
New Delhi-110002.

Dear Sirs,

Please let us know whether you can supply us six numbers of 'Smart' Celling Fans 48. If so, please quote your current prices and other terms and conditions.

We shall feel obliged if you please let us know whether your fans carry a Guarantee for 5 years against any manufacturing defect.

Please also inform us whether you can arrange for a free-demonstration of the same before we place our large regular order with you for the same.

Please note that we have a regular demand of celling fans for our various offices in Delhi. In case we find your prices and other terms competitive, we may divert all or future orders to you.

Yours faithfully,

For Smart Manufacturing,
Mg. Partner.

Memorandum :—Also called the most blunt and simplified style of letter-writing, it is mostly used for inter-office correspondence. Under this style, there is no salutation and no complimentary close. The matter is written directly in a simplified manner. However, for typing the body of letter fully-blocked style may be used.

The salient features of this style are :—

1. The formal salutation like 'Dear Sir/s' etc. and also the subscription like 'Yours faithfully' etc. are not used.
2. The subject-heading is generally typed in blod capital letters and or underlined.
3. The body of letter is generally typed in fully-blocked form by staring every line from the left-hand margin and the usual double-line spacing is given between the paragraphs.
4. Sender's name and designation are typed towards the right-hand side after leaving 3-4 lines from the last line, in bold capital letters. The Typists' initials and/or initials of officer writing the letter are typed in abbreviation towards the left-hand bottom corner.

No. AEL/Admn/87/265 7th April, 1987
The Branch Manager
Naraina, New Delhi.

Supply of Ceiling Fans to your branch.

This is to inform you that we have made enquiries from M/s Bajaj Electricals Ltd. in respect of ceiling fans and we are placing an order with them.

As soon as we receive the same, we shall be sending you the required quantity immediately.

DIRECTOR.

Out of the various style of letter-writing explained hereinabove we may use any one of the style. Mostly the fully and semi-blocked styles are used now-a-days. People are still going far away from the conventional or traditional styies of letter-writing and adopting other modern ways of writing for good display and saving in time.

Rules for drafting routine business letters

As we have already discussed, a private secretary may himself herself draft the routine letters directly without taking dictation from the boss. For this purpose, the private secretary should remember the *following points* ;—

1. Try to immitate the bose's style or way of writing the letters. It can be done by keeping carbon copies of such type of earlier dictated by the boss. These may become 'Form Letters' which the private secretary may store in a separate file cover kept in his/her desk under the personal custody.

2. When the letter is already drafted and typed and before you pass it on for the signatures of boss, ensure that the letter is clearly, neatly and impresively typed out.

3. Check spellings construction of sentences, style, etc. and ensure that it contains all the details required to be included.

4. Prepare the envelope by writing addressee's name and complete address or mailing or other notations. The addressing of envelope should be accurate, legible and impressive. Keep the envelop duly prepared by you alongwith the letter.

5. Always make the required number of copies of the letter drafted and typed by you, depending upon the practice followed in your office and the requirements, by inserting requiste carbon papers. It is necessary always to keep a carbon copy/office copy of each and every letter. Nobody would tell you but you have to do it yourself.

CIRCULAR LETTERS

A 'Circular Letter' is a form of business correspondence which carries a message for so many persons at one time. In other words, it is a letter which circulates or goes to a large number of persons carrying the same message at one time. It is usually cyclostyled or printed in order to make out many copies.

The main objectives of writing a Circular Letter may be to give publicity/advertisement or gaining popularity of any goods, products or services amongst a large number of people. The other objectives may be to inform different classes of people simultaneously about some event or cause for which all the readers may be made interested and impressed.

Generally, a Circulur Letter may be written on many occasions like opening a new business/branch, change of place of business, change in the constitution of firms, granting or withdrawing of 'per pro' authority of a person and obtaining announcing an agency/dealership/distributorship of some thing etc. For these occasions, the circular letter may contain the different types of information but the basic rules/essentials of drafting a circular letter remain the same.

The essentials for drafting a circular letter are as under :—

1. A Cirular Letter should be written in a general form because the same contents are read over by different classes of persons at one time.

2. The information should be brief and compact so that the reader may get full information without being bored.

3. It should attract the attention of the reader so that he is tempted to read the contents of a circular letter.

4. All the necessary details be included in a circular letter so that the reader should not feel the necessity of making further queries.

5. The co-operation and patronage of the reader may be sought at the end.

Lay-out or Structure

Usually the lay-out of a 'Circular Letter' is similar to a business-letter except that the inside address is either not written at all or 2-3 lines are drawn for writing inside address separately on individual copies and the saluttaion is in general form e.g. 'Dear Customer/ Patron' or 'Dear Sir Madam'. Rest of the parts are arranged similar to those of a business-letter. However, we give blow the specimen lay-out of a 'Circular Letter' :—

Lay-out of a Circulat Letter

Ph. 323130

FRIENDS INTERNATIONAL
F-1,/Connaught Place, New Delhi-110001

Ref. No Dated......

...

...

Dear Customer/Patron,

...

...

...

....

Yours faithfully,
For Friends International,
Managing Partner.

Enc. as above.

'FORM' LETTERS

A 'Form Letter' is a standard printed or cyclostyled letter containing a particular type of information with a few blank columns to be filled in by hand or otherwise to make it a complete letter to serve the purpose.

In business routine, many letters are written every time contain ing almost the same type of matter. In order to save time and energies, such stereotype letters are got cyclostyled or printed. Only a few blank columns are left so that the relevant details may be filled in and then it becomes a comylete letter to serve the same purpose as if a fresh letter is made out. Such a 'From Letter' may be used for acknowledging letter/document, remittances, reminders, confirmations, quotations, collection of dues, calling a person to an office and for other matters of similar nature.

A Private Secretary may also have to use a 'Form Letter' in the day-to-day business/official life. If these are available, in office, one may use them at the point of need, otherwise the same may be prepared and kept on record. The process is very simple. Whatever letters are written almost in the same fashion again and again in your office, take out a proforma and get it cyclostyled or printed but ensure that a few blank columns are created in such a way that the same form letter may be used for addressing it to different types of persons serving the same purpose. There is no use of preparing a form letter for such communication which may be used very limited.

There are many advantages of preparing a 'Form Letter'. It saves labour, time and energies because the full letter need not be prepared again and again the same way. It brings in speed in correspondence. It is economical because the printing or cyclostyling of so many copies of a letter is cheaper than making a fresh letter everytime. It brings in accuracy also because at the time of printing or cyclostyling, the entire matter is thoroughly checked once and thereafter the chances of mistakes are not there.

However, there are certain disadvantages also. A 'Form' Letter is not so impressive upon the reader because he feels that it is a routine thing to send him a printed/cyclostyled matter. It lacks the personal touch. Moreover, a 'Form Letter' has got the limited use, because it may be used only for matters which are repetitive. Lastly, the initial cost of printing or cyclostyling is heavy because these have to be printed/cyclostyled in bulk.

Lay-out of A 'Form Letters'

A.B.C. ENTERPRISES
D-1, Connaught Place, New Delhi.

Dated.........

No.........

Dear Sir,

We acknowledge with thanks your letter No date together with...enclosuies/without enclosures. The same is receiving our best attention.

Yours faithfully,

TELEGRAMS AND CONFIRMATION LETTERS

A 'Telegram' is one of the means of written communication through which the messages are passed on from one place to another much quickly. A printed form is obtained from the Telegraph Office free of cost and all details are filled there in. The telegram form, duly filled in and signed by the sender is passed on to the Telegraph Office, who in turn, pass on the message over the machines to the place of destination. Then the message is immediately delivered to the receiver at the place of destination.

The telegram is of two types-(i) Ordinary and (ii) Express. The charges of the ordinary telegram are less as compared to the express one in which the charges are just double than the ordinary telegram. However, the express telegram is given priority in respect of passing on of messages.

The charges for a telegram are made per word. As such, efforts should be made to draft the message/text of telegram in as few words as possible. The commonly used abbreviations may be written but the figures are always written in words and the care is taken that the message is quite clear.

The details of addressee and the text of message should preferably be typed on the telegram form, using the capitals and a carbon copy of the same may be retained for office records. Immediately after giving the telegram, we must ourselves prepare a 'Telegram Confirmation Letter', the details of which have been discussed in the following paragraphs.

The language of a telegram may be either (i) Enclair or (ii) Cypher or Code. The Enclair telegrams contain the language which is very clear and of day-to-day ordinarily speaking way, which everyone can read and make out the sense. The Cypher or Coded Telegram is one which has the private language comprised of some code words which are known only to the sender and the receiver of a telegram and to no one else. The Coded telegram is cheaper, secret and safer, particularly for the matters involving finance the messages are passed on through the Coded Telegrams.

Drafting a Telegraphic Message

The following points should be remembered while drafting a message to be conveyed by telegrams—

1. The matter should be as brief as possible because every word/letter is charged.
2. The message should be clear. Strict punctuation be followed. There should not be any ambiguity in understanding the sense.
3. The figures should always be written in words in the message in order to avoid any misinterpretation.
4. For addressing telegrams, if gram or telegraphic code address is available, the same should be used for lesser cost of telegram and sure delivery of message at the correct address.
5. The words 'Ordinary' or 'Express' be written on the printed form at the space availadle therein.
6. The message conveyed through a telegram/telephone/telex should always be confirmed immediately by writing a separate letter in this behalf.

A *Telegram Confirmation Letter* is written *mainly* for three reasons :—

1. The telegram might not be or not at all received in time This usually happens in practice ;
2. The message might not have been clearly conveyed ; and
3. In order to keep authoritative evidence of the telegraphic message.

We give below the SPECIMEN of Telegraphic Message and a Confirmation Letter :—

TELEGRAM—

To

Class	JABINCO
ORDY.	FORT, BOMBAY

REF OUR ORDER DT 8TH.
DESPATCH GOODS IMDTLY. EVERGREEN CO.

Sender' Name and Address (Not to be telegraphed) Ph. 272728

EVERGREEN CO.

34, CHANDNI CHOWK, DELHI.

CONFIRMATION LETTER FOR THE ABOVE MESSAGE

EVERGREEN COMPANY

Ref. No. FAC/Mise/87/1267
Messrs. Jaya Bharat Company,
Fort, Bombay.

34, Chandni Chowk,
DELHI 110006.
Date.........

Dear Sirs,

We confirm our Telegram/Telex/Telephonic Message of date...... reading as under :-

"REF OUR ORDER DT 8th. DESPATCH GOODS IMMDTLY"

Yours faithfully,
For EVERGREEN COMPANY,
Partner.

OFFICIAL CORRESPONDENCE

It is necessary for a private secretary to know the drafting and writing of letters in office. The Official Correspondence broadly refers to the letters written between one office or department to another office or department of Government, Semi-Government of Public Sector Undertakings. It may also consist of letters written within one section or department of the same Organisation.

Forms of Official Correspondence

The Official Correspondence may be made in any of the following forms-

1. Official Letter
2. Demi-Official Letter (or D.O. Letter)
3. Office Memorandum (or inter-departmental memo)
4. Office Order
5. Endorsement
6. Circular

7. Notice or Notification
8. Resolution
9. Press Release or Press Communique

In this small book, it is not possible to discuss at length each and every form of Official Correspondence. Still, efforts would be made to impart complete idea and knowledge of the routine official correspondence.

Before we discuss the above forms of Official Correspondcne, it is necessary to know the difference between the Official and Business Correspondence. The main points of difference between both the types of correspondence are as under:—

1. The language in Official correspondence is almost authoritarian and is based on the official position of the writer, whereas the language of a business letter is always very courteous, friendly and business-like.

2. The business letters are mostly written or typed on attractively set-out printed letter-heads of business firms, whereas most of the official letters are written/typed on plain paper.

3. The lay-out or structure of official letters is very much different from that of a business letter in the sense that the various parts of a letter are arranged differently in both types of letters separately as is evident from the lay-out of an official letter given separately in this chapter.

4. There is an absence of sales-punch (i.e. canvassing and convincing) in an official letter, whereas the same exists definitely in a business letter.

Official Letter

An Official Letter is one which may be written by one Government to another or one office to another on administrative or routine matters. Such a letter serves the purpose of external communication in writing in the offices.

Lay-out of an Official Letter

SENDER'S OFFICE ADDRESS—	Government of India Ministry of Works and Housing Nirman Bhavan, New Delhi.

REFERENCE NO. AND DATE.
Ref. No. AXI./F. 32(523/LAND/DO/84-85.
New Delhi, the 10th March, 1987.

NAME & OFFICIAL DESIGNATION OF SENDER— From : XYZ Land and Development Officer.

To :

INSIDE ADDRESS—.........
BY NAME AND...........
OFFICIAL DESIGNATION—......
SUBJECT-HEADING— **Sub : Sale Permission**
SALUTATION—
OPENING SENTENCE—

Sir,

I am directed to acknowledge the receipt of your letter No......dated...........and inform you that......

2. ......

PARAGRAPHS NUMBERED-

BODY OF LETTER.

....

3. ....

....

Yours faithfully.

SUBSCRIPTION or COMPLIMENTARY CLOSE-

(XYZ)
Land and Development Officer.

From the above specimen lay-out of an Official Letter, the students will notice the following special features which go to make an official letter written differently than a business :-

1. The name and address of Sender and the Addressee are respectively written with the prefix of words 'From' and 'To' and also that the personal name and official designation are used.

2. The reference number is little complicated and lenghthy as compared to that of a business-letter. The date is always

written following the name of place. e.g., New Delhi, the 10th March, 1985.

3. The usual way of salutation in an official letter is 'Sir' and that the same is written after the subject heading, whereas in a business letter, we may use 'Dear Sir/s' for salutation and the subject heading may be written after salution.

4. The body of an official letter is divided into various paragraphs and mostly each paragraph is serially numbered consecutively.

5. The usual way of subscription or complimentary close is 'Yours faithfully'. After this, a blank space is left for signatures and below that we have to write the name of official within brackets followed by his official designation.

Demi-Official (D.O.) Letter

A Demi-Official letter is one which is written by a person in his personal-cum-official capacity and is also addressed to another person by name and his official designation. Since such a letter is partly official and partly personal, we call it 'Demi-Official'. In an office, a private secretary may be required to draft and/or type such letters frequently. Hence, a complete knowledgen of the same is essential.

Lay-out of a D.O. Letter :

A Demi-Official Letter may be written/typed on a printed personal letter-head or on a plain paper in the following format :—

Personnel Manager

S. BHASKAR A.B.C. COMPANY LTD.,

B.Sc.,LL.B. 5, Parliment Street,

No...... New Delhi-11001.

Dear Mr. Singh,

Dated.........

......
......
......

Yours Sincerely,
(S. BHASKAR)

Shri B.K. Singh
7A/12, W.E.A.
Karolbagh, New Delhi.

From the above specimen lay-out of a Demi-Official Letter, the student would find the following special features :—

1. Sender's personal name, designation and address etc. are written at the top on both sides of paper.

2. The D.O. letter commences with the salutation to be written 'Dear Mr......' or 'Dear Shri......'.

3. The body of a D.C. letter is written using the first-person i.e. using 'I' instead of 'we' because it is a letter in the personal capacity.

4. The usual way of subscription or complimentary close is 'Yours sincerely' or 'Sincerely yours' and the sender has to sign the letter below it.

5. The name and address of the receiver are usually written as towards the left-hand bottom corner.

Uses of a D.O. letter

A.D.O. letter is comparatively more useful as it involves the personal attention of the sender and the receiver, resulting into getting the information much quickly. Secondly, it helps in keeping the information quite safe, secret and confidential because no person other than the sender and receiver may read its contents. The persons concerned may utilise their official designation/position for getting the work done at personal-leve.

Office Memorandum or Inter-office Memo

It is a form of Official Correspondence which may be used for internal use in an office on matters like appointment, confirmation leave and salary adjustments etc. It is written differently than a letter. While writing a memo, we do not generally use the traditional salutation and complimentary close as in a letter. However, the name and/or official designation of the sender and addressee have to be written.

Lay-out of Form of a Memo

A.B.C. COMPANY LTD.,
MEMORANDUM

No.........	Dated...
From	To
....	...
...	

It has been decided to transfer Shri Ashwani Kumar, presently working as an Officer at our Connaught Place, New Delhi Branch to Chandni Chowk, Delhi branch with immediate effect.

Body of Memo

· He should, therefore, be relieved immediately, with instructions to report for further duty at Chandni Chowk, Delhi branch. His salary, leave and other personal records may be sent to the same branch.

PERSONNEL MANAGER.

(ii) To
From
Sub...

From the above specimen lay-out of Office Memorandum, it may be observed that—

1. The name, designation, address of sender and receiver are written with the prefix of words 'From' and 'To'.
2. There is no salutation and the usual complimentary close.
3. The language of a memo is also in third-person and indirect.
4. Typist's initials may be written on/towards the left-hand bottom corner.

Office Order

An Office Order is a form of written communication in an office which may be used to convey decisions or instructions of higher authorities to all concerned for the purpose of complying with them. The non-compliance of an office order may result in the disciplinary action against the concerned persons. However, the office order may be written or typed directly without any salutation or complimentary close, as per specimen given below. It should invariably be signed by the issuing authority and routed by the persons who are to comply with the office order.

Lay-out of An Office Order

Dated.........

No. OFFICE ORDER

It has been decided to conduct the final examinations w.e.f. 1st April, 1925. The concerned Lecturers are, therefore, advised to prepare question papers in their subjects of study and submit to the under-signed on or before 15th of March, 1985.

1. Mr. X
2. Mr. Y

PRINCIPAL.

Endorsement

It is the form of official communication through which the earbon copy of any original letter may be sent to the other person/s simultaneously with the original addressee. While making endorsement on any letter emanating from the office, it is the practice to give a reference number and the date also. The endorsement is usually made at the end of official coummunication, as per the example given below :—

Ref. No. AX50/P/F. 54 (901)/85. New Delhi. 11th of March, 1985.

Copy forwarded for information and necessary action :—

(*i*) The personnel Manager, H.O. New Delhi.

(*ii*) The Manager, Inspection Department, H.O. New Delhi.

Sd/-
SECRETARY.

The endorsement on a letter should necessarily be signed by the person signing the original letter, otherwise it is not authentic.

Circular

It is another form of official communication which may be used to carry the same message to a large number of persons, including the members, units, sections or departments or branches of the same Organisation, at one time. Mostly Circulars are written for internal use within the same Organisation and are cyclostyled or printed so that the required number of copies may be taken out and circulated amongst all those who are concerned with it.

A 'Circular' is different from a 'Circular Letter'. The main aspects of different between the two types of communication are as under :—

1. A circular may be used for internal use of an Organisation, whereas a circular letter may be sent to persons outside the Organisation.

2. A Circular is usually used in offices whereas the circular letter may be used by Business Organisations for the information of outsiders.

3. The language of a Circular is authoritarian and official, whereas the language of a circular letter is business—like!

4. The inside address on a circular may be in the form of—, 'To ALL BRANCHES/DEPARTMENTS' whereas we may write inside address on individual copy.

Lay-out of a Circular

A.B.C. CORPORATION OF INDIA
H.O. 1, Connaught Place, New Delhi.

No, AX1/P/86—87 15 the March, 1987

TO ALL BRANCHES/DEPARTMENTS

Sub :

It has been brought to our notice that most the members of clerical staff are not attending the office on time, despite the clear-cut instructions to this effect.

All the members of staff are hereby informed that they should attend the respective offices on time, failing which necessary disciplinary action may be taken against them.

This may be brought to the notice of each and every staff member in your office for strict compliance.

STAFF MANAGER.

Notification

It is the formal announcement in order to inform the general public. In Government Office, the notifications are usually published in the Gazette of India and in order offices, it may be published or displayed as a notice on the Notice Board. The notification may be written/typed on a plain paper, giving the necessary reference number, date and official designation of the authority issuing it. The matter should be brief and to the point. There is no salutation or complimentary close but it is signed by the issuing authority.

Resolution

It is a from of official communication whereby the decision/s of the Government are conveyed to the public for general information, It may also be published in the Government Gazette.

Press Release/Communique

It is rather a form of informal communication through which the important annoucements/decisions of the government are handed over to the Press Reporters for publication in the daily newspapers for the purpose of general information to the public. The nature and contents of a Press Release are almost the same as those of a notification but the former is meant for passing on to the press reporter for publication in daily newspapers whereas the latter is meant for publication in the Government Gazette. There are various advantages of a Press Release, e.g. the information reaches to the public much earlier and also that the coverage or circulatio of a Press Release is many times more than a Gazette.

However, this form of communication may be frequently us in Government Offices.

SOCIAL AND PERSONAL CORRESPONDENCE

Besides the letters written in day-to-day business and official life, there may be other letters also which may have to be drafted by a private secretary for his/her Boss. These may include inviting a person to attend some function or occasion, accepting invitation given by others, expressing inability in attending to any function, writing to a firiend on any matter, sending personal greetings for Christmas, Digali or New Year and/or reciprocating others' greetings and so on and so forth. All these may be included under the social and personal correspondence.

It may be noted here th t the social or personal letters are very much informal in nature and these may be drafted in any way depending upon the social or traditional customs or practices prevailing at the time of writing such letters. However, the basic theme of such letters is the same and the idea behind drafting such letters is that the purpose of conveying any information may be served. Hence, such letters should necessarily be correct, clear, complete, courteous and meaningful. These may be written in any form and the way of addressing, salutation or complimentary close may be different in different types of letters. For example, the Boss may address a person as 'Kanwar ji' or to the other person as 'Shri Kanwar Lal'. The entire thing depends upon the degree of affection, affinity, or personal relations with the concerned reader of the letter. Still, the private secretary should know, in general, as to how these letters are drafted and made more meaningful and attractive.

In this chapter, we shall discuss, in general, the drafting and writing of different types of social or personal letters for and on behalf of the boss in order to shaw as to how a successful private secretary may handle such correspondence independently.

Lay-out or Structure

A social or personal letter is quite different than a business letter so far as its format, lay-out or structure is concerned. We do not write or type out such a letter on an attractively set out printed letter-head of the business firm or enterprise but either on plain paper or on a personal letter-nead of the Boss/Executive on which the presonal name, qualifications address and designation etc. may be printed. Mostly such letters are written as Demi-Official (D.O.) letters, written in the personal-cum-official capacity of the Boss/Executive.

Lay-out of a Personal/Social Letter

SENDER'S NAME AND ADDRESS B. SINGH Chartered Accountant. 7A/12, W.E.A Karol Bagh, NEW DELHI-11005.

DATE— Dated...

SALUTATION— Dear Shri Verma,

...

...

...

BODY OF LETTER— ...

...

DOMPLIMENTARY DLOSE OR SUBSCRIPTION— Yours Sincerely,

(Signatures)

INSIDE ADDRESS—Shri B.R. Verma
M-65, Kirti Nagar,
New Delhi.

From the above lay-out of a social or personal letter, it may be noted that the sender's name and address is written differently than in a business letter, the inside address i.e. the name and address of the receiver is written to wards the left-hand bottom corner at the end of letter, and the usual way of subscription or complementary close may be 'Your Sincerely' or 'Yours truly' or 'Cordially yours' etc. The salutation in such a letter may also be different in different types of letters, as we have already expained that the salutation depends upon the closeness, affnity, afiection and relationship of the boss with receiver of the letter. Usually, no subject-heading is written. If needed, a short subject-heading may also be written. Since these are purely personal letters, no formality is completed while writing such letters but we have given the specimen lay-out, in general, taking the same from the practical life.

Display and Spacing (style of writing) :

The different styles of business letter—writing have already been discussed by us in the earlier chapter. Out of the various styles of letter-writing, we may suggest that the MODIFIED INDENTED, SEMI-BLOCKED or FULLY BLOCKED styles of letter-writing are mostly preferred while writing or typing social or personal letters.

However, we are giving below a few examples of social or personal letters derived from the practical life in India and these would give a clear idea of drafting such letters to a private secretary under similar situations. Tee essentials for drafting have also been given separately under each sub-heading.

Letters of Appreciation or Congratulations

There are various occassions for congratulating persons in business and social life like marriage of any staff member or friend, birthday, success in examination, promotion or any special achievement etc. On such occasions, there lies an opportunity to wish with warmth and naturalness. Similarly, if someone has done any good work for the organisation, there is an opportunity to appreciate the work. For this purpose, the letters may be written by a Boss in his personal and/or official capacity. We may call such letters as 'Letters of Appreciation or Congratulations'. There are many advantages of writing such letters, such as, motivating the concerned person to work still better, showing a personal touch and helping to maintain good inter-personal relations.

While drafting such letters, a private secretary scould remember the following points :—

1. Expess pleasure for the occasion which deserves congratulations or appreciation.
2. Be like a sincere friend and do not show any envy.
3. Do not write any thing detracting from the occasion.
4. The letter should be short and to the point.

Congratulations for success in an Examination

Dear Shri Singh,

I note with pleasure that you have come out successfully at the M. Com. Examination conducted by the University of Meerut. I congratulate you upon your success.

May you as well as the Institution you serve be benefited by added qualifications.

Yours sincerely,

Appreciation for Personal Achievement

Dear Shri Singh,

I am in receipt of your letter dated 1st March, 1915 and have noted the contents.

I quite appreciate the labour that you have put in towards the development of your branch and also your work as the first Branch Manager. I have absolutely no doubt that you would continue to devote yourself whole-heartedly in furthering the development of the Branch you are working for and the Institution as a whole.

Yours sincerely,

Letter of Congratnlations on a Marriage

Dear Mr. Ashok,

Please accept my heartiest congratulations on the auspicious occasion of your marriage to take place on the 10th of March, 1985. I wish you a long happy married life.

With best wishes,

Yours sincerely,

On a Birth-day

Dear Mr. Shekhar,

Please accept my sincere congratulations on the eve of your birthday which falls on the 20th of this month. May I wish you a very happy long life.

Yours sincerely,

On a Promotion

Dear Mr. Singh,

I am happy to note that you have been promoted as Director in your Organisation. Please accept my heartiest congratulations on this occasion.

May I pary the Almighty to give you a very happy and prosperous long life full of achivements all the time.

Yours sincerely,

One a new job

Dear Mr. Friend,

I am delighted to note from your letter that you have secured the new job as a Lecturer in the University. I am sure that you would continue to show your experienced capabilities in the field of education. Lots of success and happiness in the new job.

Yours truly,

On a Personal Achievement

Dear Mr. Ramesh,

I am happy to know that you have achieved the target of business fixed for your Branch for the ensuring quarter, much before the stipulated period. Please accept my heartiest congratulations for this big achievement. May the Institution be benefitted under your able stewardship.

I look forward for ever grater accomplishments in the years ahead.

With regards,

Yours sincerely,

Greetings and Good Will

A letter expressing good wishes may be called the 'Greetings'. Similarly, a letter containing the atitude or kindness towards a person may be called a letter of 'Good will'. Such letters are mostly written for establishing, maintaining and fostering good public relations.

While drafting such letters, a private secretary should keep in mind the following points :—

1. Express pleasure for the occasion or accomplishment.
2. Extend heartiest felicitations or greetings from the core of your heart.
3. Wish for continuing good relationship between the writer and the reader of your letter.

4. Offer assistance without hope of any immediate return.

Greetings for New year

Dear Shri Mada,

I wish you a very happy and prosperous NEW YEAR. May the New Year bring you new hopes and lots of achievements.

Yours sincerely,

N,B.—The above Greentings may be written differently as per specimen given below and in it there is no necessity of signatures of the Boss. The private secretary may send it himself/her-self.

Mr. C.S. Verma wishes you a happy and prosperous NEW YEAR and extends his heartiest congratulations for the same.

Greetings for Diwali or Christmas

Mr. A.K. KALRA wishes you a happy DIWALI/CHRISTMAS and extends his heartiest felicitations for the same.

Reciprocating a Greeting

Whenever a letter of card containing greeting for the new year, Diwali or Christmas, it is a social custom or practice to acknowledge and reciprocate the same by writing the following letter.

Dear Shri Gulati,

I acknowledge with thanks your greetings for the NEW YEAR DIWALI/CHRISTMAS and heartily reciprocate the same.

Sincerely yours,

Welcoming a New Employee

Dear Mr. Saarma,

I am pleased to learn that you are joining my Organisation as a Development Officer. You will be working with many of the nice people. I know them for the last about five years. I am confident that you will find them all intelligent and able workers.

After you set in your office, let us try to get together for a lunch any time during the next week. Meantime, please let us know if I can be helpful in any way.

Sincerely yours,

Pesonal Greeting

Dear Mr. Singh,

It gives me a great pleasure in sending you my warm personal greetings on the occasion of opening of the new Branch of our Organisation at Connaught Place, New Delhi of which you have been designated as the first Branch Manager.

You have been working with us since 1975 and since then held the positions as Officer, Accountant and Branch Manager of various branches. Thus, you have acquired sufficient experience of the routine work as well as developmental activities at the branch level. With this, it will not be difficult for you to estabilish a firm foot-hold in the area of operation of this centre. The expert advice of your Executives is always available to you.

I once again wish you all successes in your new assignment.

Yours sincerely,

Invitations

The people may be invited for a tea party, lunch, dinner or to attend a marriage or a social get-together. For this purpose, the letter may be written. While drafting the letters of invitation, the private secretary should remember the following points :-

1. Express pleasure for the occasion.
2. Write the exact day, date and time fixed for lunch/party etc.
3. Request that his/her presence is solicited.

SPECIMEN

Shri and Smt. Harbans Lal Kharbanda requests the pleasure of your company at LUNCH on Monday, the 11th March, 1985 at 1.30 P.M. at R-2, New Rajinder Nagar, New Delhi-110060.

Invitation to speek/attend a Seminar

Dear Mr. Singh,

The Association of Rajinder Nagar Residents is organising a two-days seminar on the 'policy of charging house-tax by the Municipal Corporation of Delhi' on Sunday and Monday, the 10th and 11th March, 1985. The emphasis will be on helping the landlords of the area in getting the correct assessment of the house-tax on residential property. As an educated young man, you must have the knowledge and experience which will benefit the participants and stimulate new thinking on the subject.

I am, therefore, writing to you to enquire whether it would be convenient for to be one of the speakers at the seminar.

I shall feel grateful if you kindly convey your acceptance, in writing, at the earliest so that I may issue the necessary circular.

With kind regards,

Yours sincerely,

Accepting an Invitation

Smt. and Shri Prem Kumar Chopra,
accept with pleasure your invitation to
LUNCH on 11th March, 1985.

Refusing or expressing regret to the invitation

Dear Smt. and Shri Kharbanda,

I acknowledge with thanks your kind invitation to lunch on 11th March, 1985 but regret that owing to prior engagement, I am unable to accept the same.

Yours sincerely,
(Prem Kumar Chopra)

Smt. and Shri Harbanslal Chopra
C-40, Lajpat Nagar III,
New Delhi.

Accepting invitation (in another Form)

Dear Shri Singh,

I thank you very much for your invitation to lunch on Monday, the 11th March, 1985.

I am looking forward to meet you on the appointed day, date and time

Sincerely yours,

Hotel Reservation

Whenever any room or accommodation in a Hotel is to be booked, a letter may be addressed to the Reservations Manager of the concerned Hotel making a request for the purpose. Such a letter should be brief and to the point, but it must contain all the necessary details like the date/s, the name and address of the person staying in and mode of payment of hotel charges etc.

The specimen letter is below :-

Dear Sir/Madam,

I shall be grateful if you kindly book one single-room with at—tached bath from 11th March to 15th March, 1985 (total five days), A cheque for Rs. 1,000/- is enclosed. The bill may be made out in the Company's name and sent to my office.

Please confirm the booking by return of post.

Yours sincerely,

Enc: Cheque No. 00420
for Rs. 1,000/-

In Another Form (Specimen)

Dear Shri Sharma.

Please book one double,bed air-conditioned suite for Mrs. and Mr. P.K. Chopra, the Chief Executive Officer of our Company, from 11th to 12th March, 1985 (two days). The bill will be paid by Mr. Chopra himself.

I shall be grateful if you please confirm the booking by return of post.

Yours sincerely,

Shri A.K. Sharma,
Manager,
Hotel Siddhartha,
Pusa Road, New Dilhi.

Reservation for Air-travel

Dear Sir,

This has a referenc to my telephonic conversation with you this morning.

Please reserve for me one seat by Air-bus flight No. 1A-303 leaving Delhi at 603 hours for Bombay, on 15th March, 1985. A crossed cheque for Rs. 910/- is enclosed.

I shall be grateful if you kindly confirm the ticket and arrange to send the same to my office.

Thanking you,

Yours faithfully,

Enc : As above.

Reservation for Travel by Train

Dear Sir,

I shall thank you to please book one berth for me in A.C. Ist class of 2 Dn. Rajdhani Mail leaving New Delhi for Bombay Central at 1600 Hrs on 25th March, 1985. I am sending the required reservation form duly filled in and signed by me alongwith the money for the tieket per bearer.

Yours faithfully,

Letters of Sympathy and Condolence

On the sad occasions like prolonged sickness, injury, accident, death or something like that, it becomes a matter of courtesy or sympathy to write a letter in order to gain goodwill and gratitude for you and to share the sorrow of others. Such letters should be extremely brief and be able to convey your sincere and heart-felt expressions.

While drafting such letters, the following points should always be remembered :

1. Express your sorrow on whatever has happened in as few words as posible.
2. Show your sympathetic attitude in a realistic manner but do not become too much sentimental or emotional.
3. Officer your assistance only where it is realistic.
4. Address the letter to the next with and kin of the deceased (applicable in case of condolence on death).

Condolence on a Death

Dear Mr. (Mrs...

I am really shocked to hear the untimely sad demise of Mr. . . who was closely associated with me for the last about five years. I express my heart-felt condolences and pray the Almighty to bestow patience and courage to all other family members to bear this irreparable loss.

Yours sincerely.

Another Letter of Condolence

DearMrs, Ketker,

I am really shocked to learn that your husband expired on Sunday, the 10th of March, 1985.

I know that he was sick for past some time but had no idea that we would loss him suddenly.

My heart-felt feelings are shared by my colleagues and all those who know him. They have joined me in conveying to you our sympathy. We all pray to God to let the soul rest in peace and give you strength to bear the loss.

If there is anything, we can do to lighten your burden, please do let me know.

With kind regards,

Yours sincerely.

On an Accident or Injury

Dear Mr. Suresh,

I was shocked to learn of your accident on when you were coming to office on your two-wheeler scooter, but I am relieved to learn that through your injuries are painful, yet they are not dangerous and you are recovering speedily.

Please let me know if there is anything I can do to help you or your family during your convalescene.

Yours sincerely,

On serious illness

Dear Mr. Joan,

I am sorry to learn that you are suffering from (illness) which your Doctor has reported to be serious. Please get it checked up from a specialist Doctor and take his treatment in the right earnest. I hope you would be all-right very soon.

Please let me know if I can help you or your family in any matter.

Yours sincerely.

Seeking or Giving an Appointment

Whenever your boss wishes to call on someone in connection with any matter, he may tell you to take a prior appointment for him by writing a letter. Similarly, the other persons may also call on your boss by fixing a prior appointment through a letter. In both the cases, the private secretary should draft a letter as per the specimen given below.

While drafting such letters the following points may be kept in view :—

1. Make a polite request for appointment.
2. State the probable time or exact date of appointment.
3. Mention the nature of business for which the appointment is sought or given.
4. Send a thanks-giving letter after getting an appointment.

Seeking an Appointment

Dear Sir

The undersigned wishes to call on the Chairman and Managing, Director in connection with the development of business, on any day during the next week. Please arrange to fix up an appointment with him at your earliest convenience under intimation to me.

Yours faithfully,

Giving an Appointment

Dear Sir,

This has a reference to your letter number——————— dated———requesting an appointment with our Chairman and Managing Director. He is pleased to give you an appointment on 31st March 1985 at 3.00 p.m. Please make it convenient to call on him as per schedule.

Yours faithfully,

Thanks-Giving

Dear Sir,

I thank you for giving me an appointment for 31st March 1985 at 300 p.m. when I shall be calling on you for discussing about the development of business.

Thanking you,

Yours faithfully,

OFFICE REPORTS

A private secretary should be able to report any matter to his/her superior. He/she should also be in a position to assist his/her superior in perparation of draft form of Reports, Agenda and

Minutes of a meeting etc. The skill that a private secretary can show in this regard will be a great plus point in his/her ability.

Reporting

'Reporting' may be defined os the process of describing, narrating or writing an account of whatever has been observed through enquiry, investigaiion or probe in one's own language. Actually speaking 'Reporting' is a very wide term and it includes in itself not only passing on of a telephonic message or telling a gist of telephonic conversation, but also conveying a summary of talks held with outsiders, a gist of discussicns a private secretary had with the officers etc.

Reporting a Telephonic Message

Sir. Dated

Mr. G.S. Srivastava, Managing Director, Textiles Corporation, Bombay rang up at 12.30 P.M. He would be calling on the 25th March, 1985 forenoon to discuss the set-up of a chemical plant. He has asked me to confirm the appointment by telephone.

Sd/-
Private Secretary.

Printed Message Slip

In some Organisations, the printed message-slips are available which may be filled in and passed on to the Boss Executive. A specimen is given below :—

MESSAGE

For
From
of
Telephone No

TELEPHONE	PLEASE RING
CALLED TO SEE YOU	WILL CALL AGAIN
WANTS TO SEE YOU	URGENT
MESSAGE	

—

Date Time

While reporting, care should be taken that all the relevant details are furnished so that the information is complete and may be clearly understood. Whenever the message is lengthy, it should be made short by using your-skill of drafting. The day date, time and the nature of business may be clearly stated together with full details of the caller.

Reports

A 'Report' is an account or statement containing the results of enquiry, observation, discussion, speech, meeting etc.

A private secretary should be in a position to prepare the draft form of a 'Report' and assist his/her superior in this regard. In practical life, the report-writing is the job of an executive but a private secretary has to help him in making it out. The rough draft may be prepared by a private secretary and the same should be got approved from the executive. Even an executive may furnish the necessary details and ask the private secretary to prepare the draft of report on certain lines. Many times. the reports may be strictly confidential and the private secretary may be entrusted with the work. The reports may also be dictated and the private secretary may be asked to type them. In all cases, it is necessary that a private secretary should possess a thorough knowledge of Lay-out, structure and styles of reports.

However, for preparing a good report, a number of steps are taken, e.g. collecting necessary details/data, analysing the data, arranging them in a proper order/sequence and then finally preparing the draft of a report. An efficient private secretary must know all the details and procedures and be able to type the report. Generally, a report may be typed on plain papers of foolscap size and the entire matter is reproduced in an attractive and systematic manner so that the important details are visible at a glance. The display and spacing are also important while typing a report.

The report may be *verbal/oral,* when told anything by word of mouth. It may be *written,* when the matter is reproduced in black and white on a piece of paper. It may be *individual or personal,* when addressed to a person in his individual capacity by name. It may be *official*, when addressed to an official by designation or to an organisation. It may be *formal.* when a formality is observed while writing a report. It may be *informal,* when no formality is observed while writing. It may be a *routine* report when written at periodical intervals in the same fashion every time or *special* report, when it is about a specific matter or for the specific purpose.

The routine reports are mainly prepared on the printed proforma and the report-writer has not to write it separately but put a tick-mark against the items which are relevant in the printed form. The examples of such reports are : Inspection Report. Confidential Report (C.R) on an employee, Progress Reports, Laboratory Reports, and Inventory Reports etc. However, the formal or special reports are drafted and typed out separately following certain *basic rules* which are given as under :—

1. The report should bear on top a clear title relvant to the subject-matter.

2. It should bear the name and/or official designation and address of the receiver.

3. It should bear the name and address of a person submitting the report as an individual. official or committee.

4. The terms of reference should be clarified, as to who asked for a report, on what matter and under what authority.

5. The matter, in a report, must be discussed in continuity as a link-chain.

6. It may bear at the end definite recommendations and suggestions, if necessary.

7. The report should invariably be signed by the person authorised to submit the same and dated.

Lay-out of a small Formal Report

Place
The Chairman, Dated

—

—

Sir,

Sub :

We, the undersigned, were appointed, vide office order No
dated , to report on
In this connection, we have to report as under :

Paragraph

—

Conciusion

Recommendations

Yours faithfully
Sd/-

Lay-out of a Large Report

Report Number————

A.B.C. COMPANY LIMITED
(H.O. : Parliament Street, New Delhi)
A
REPORT ON
REDUCTION OF NOISE IN THE OFFICE
Prepared
for the Chairman and Mg. Director
By
A.B. SINGH
Office Manager.
Dated————————

CONTENTS :

MAIN REPORT

Introduction——————————————————
——————————————————————————

Pragraphs————
——————
——————
————

Conclustions——
Recommendations———

Sd/—
(A.B. SINGH)
Office Manager.

The specimen lay-out of reports, given in the preceding paragraphs, would certainly give an idea to the reader as to how the reports are drafted and prepared so that, whenever there is an occasion, a private secretary may successfully handle this work.

QUESTIONS

1. Explain the importance of business correspondence to a modern business organisation.
2. Write explanatory note on Purposes of Office Reports.
   (B. Com. Pass, Delhi, 1985)
3. Discuss the qualities of a good Report.
4. Distinguish between business and official correspondence. What are the various forms of official correspondence ?
5. What is the importance of social correspondence for a private secretary ?

1

THE SECRETARY—MEANING AND TYPES

MEANING OF A 'SECRETARY'

In the ordinary language, 'Secretary' is a person who performs the works of secret (or confidential) nature. However, the dictionary meaning of the word 'Secretary' is as under :

"Person employed to send letters, keep papers and records, etc., for another or for an Organization."

Actually, the word 'Secretary' has been derived from the Latin word *Secretarius* which means a 'Confidential Officer'.

From the above definition, we can say that 'Secretary' may be any person who does the works of confidential nature for and on behalf of another person or an organisatiou. Thus, we come to know about the *three* special features of a 'Secretary' :

1. The Secretary is a person (male or female).
2. He/she should be able to perform the works of confidential nature.
3. He/she works for another person or an organisation.

The use of 'Secretary' has been made from the olden times when the kings, rulers or dignitaries used to appoint the persons of confidence do to the work on their behalf. The kings never used to do the work themselves, rather get the work done through their trusted persons. Since then, the use of 'Secretary' came into being. Like the kings, now-a-days, the business executives, political persons, e.g. Members of Parliament or ministers and other authorities are keeping their secretaries and getting the asisstance in their works. Now, in every field of activity whether business, social, political or others, we find that almost every V.I.P. is keeping the 'Secretary' for sharing the workload. The Minister has his own secretary, the chairman or executive has his own secretary, the company has a secretary and so on. The basie idea behind keeping a 'Secretary' is that there should be a person who can assist these authorities in carrying out the details of their works so that all matters could be handled in confidence and with utmost efficiency.

By and by, the dependence on secretaries has been increasing and, in modern times, the role of a 'Secretary' has tremendously changed and become so vast that he/she no longer handles only the confidential correspondence or other routine matters but does much more, including the public relations, administration, conducting meetings and drafting of reports and speeches etc. Hence, the secretary occupies an important and pivotal position in the modern business. The secretary has become indispensable in every field of activity. More so, the Secretarial Practice has become a specialised subject of study. Particularly, in business, the role of a secretary has become so Important that not a wheel turns without the consent of a secreatry in the business office.

TYPES OF SECRETARIES

The following are the various categories of Secretaries :

Secretariat of Government of India

Under the administrative set-up of machinery of the Government of India, there are different grades of secretaries like the Secretary, Additional Secretary, Special Secretary, Joint Secretary, Deputy Secretary, Under Secretary, Private Secretary, etc. The chart on page 217 shows the administrative set-up of machinery of the Government and the position of various types of secretaries in the Government Secertariat.

The category of Government Secretaries enjoys certain delegation of powers by the Government to act for and on behalf of the President of India. The Secretaries are the chief executives and the authorities in the Government. They work under the Cabinet Ministers. The Cabinet Ministers give instructions to the Secretaries as to the policy to be followed and the Secretaries examine the policies and execute them. The Minister is an elected representative and the member of the Cabinet, whereas a Secretary is an Executive. He has the powers delegated to him by the Minister. He is the representative of the President of India. In brief, therefore, the Minister has got no executive powers while a Secretary of Gevernment has.

Secretary
|
Additional Secretary/Special Secretary
Joint Secretary
|
Director/Deputy Secretary
|
Under Secretary
|
Section Officer
|
Assistant/Private Secretary/Personal Assistant/Stenographer
Upper Division Clerk
|
Lower Division Clerk

Thus, the Secretaries in the Government have various grades of working at the different levels—the Chief Secretary. Joint Secretary, Deputy Secretary and so on. The delegation of powers to these various grades, under the Secretary, are the powers delegated to them by the Secretary.

In India, the senior civil servants are generally attached to the different Ministers of the Government and they act as the administrative head of the concerned Government Department, e.g. Finance Secretary. Home Secretary, Foreign Secretary, etc. Below the rank of Secretary comes the Joint Secretary, Deputy Secretary and the Under Secretary, etc.

Company Secretary

Every joint stock company, particularly a public company, has to appoint a secretary as per the provisions laid down under the Indian Companies Act, 1956. He must be a qualified person. Thus, a company secretary is an individual possessing the prescribed qualifications like G.D.S. (Government Diploma in Secretaryship) etc. and he is required to perform all works as required under the Act, called statutory duties, for observing all legal formalities in formation and day-to-day working of a public company and also maintaining the proper books and registers of the company.

Every company, having a paid up capital of Rs. 25 lakhs and

over, is required to appoint a qualified company secretary who should have the membership of the Institute of Company Secretaries of India or the membership of the Institute of Chartered Secretaries and Administrators, London. In case of any other company, the person to be appointed as a secretary should be possessing the degree in Law, or membership in of the Institute of Chartered Accountants of India or Indian Cost and Works Accountants, a post-graduate degree or diploma in management or company secretaryship or diploma in company law.

Duties and Functions of a Company Secretary

The duties and functions of a Company Secretary, in brief, are as under :

1. **To carry out Statutory Duties** : The include observing the all legal formalities as a principal officer of the company in order to ensure that the various provisions of the Indian Companies Act 1956 are observed by the Company for propers maintenance of books of accounts and registers of the company, preparation and authentication of resolutions, preparing and filing the returns and documents with the Registrar of Companies ; supervision of issue, allotment, transfer and forfeiture of shares and debentures and safe custody of common seal of the company.

2. To carry out the instructions of board of directors and exercising the powers delegated to him by the board of directors of the Company.

3. To protect and serve the best interests of the share-holders and debenture-holders of the company.

4. To act as Liaison Officcr between the board of directors, staff and others.

5. To organise, supervise and co-ordinate the works of office of the company, and handling the routine matters of accounts, filing records, etc.

However. a company secretary enjoys, various positions such as administrator, executive and principal officer of the Company.

Secretary of a Voluntary Organisation, Society, Club or Association etc.

There are voluntary Organisations or Associations of persons like the Co-operative Society, Club, Traders Associations, etc. Such organisations, associations undertake the works for and on behalf of their members and for the mutual benefit of all. These institutions have a secretary, either elected representative of members or an employee. The main functions of such a Secretary include managing, directing and controlling the entire affairs of the concerned organisation and also to ensure that the interests of members are watched and protected. He does the entire correspondence with the Government and other outside agencies and administers the routine matters.

Private Secretary

Private secretary, is a *secretary to an individual official*, administrator or chief executive of a business firm etc. and he/she works as his confident. The duties of a private secretary, therefore cannot be *succinctly* defined as he/she has to assist his/her superior in whatever way his her assistance is required. To be an efficient Private Secretary, therefore, the requirements will be a thorough knowledge of the English Language besides other languages, a sense of understanding the rules and regulations governing his office, a capacity to draft ordinary letters, a good general knowledge, a good personality and more than that the pleasant manners to keep up the standard of high public relation.

Hence a Private Secretary is the person who assists a boss, superior or executive in carrying out the details of his work. A private secretary performs all the works for and on behalf of a particular person, called the superior, boss or executive. The private secretary's position is like an independent loyal right-hand of the boss. Though he/she may be treated like a personal assistant to the boss, which is not necessarily correct all the time because the senior private secretaries work like an independent office executive, yet is sure that he/she is the loyal right-hand of the boss or superior because for all routine works of office and other things, the boss has to depend upon his private secretary. Rather the main objective in appointing a private secretary is that he she should make the boss free from all sorts of monotonous routine jobs like handling mail. making correspondence, typing, filing etc. Not only this, a private secretary has to render all sorts of assistance so that the works of the boss could be effectively and efficiently be carried out. Many senior secretaries are delegated with certain authority to carry out a few works as an independent incharge. Overall, the position of a private secretary is very important and is closely linked with the boss. His her job is mainly to assist a boss, executive or superior in the day-to-day business rountine. Thus a private secretary is the person who assists and works for a superior, called the boss or executive, and no one else.

The term 'Private Secretary' should not be confused with a Company Secretary' because the company secretary is the principal officer of a company, supervising and controling the legal aspects about the formation and day-to-day working of a company, whereas a 'private secrety' is attached to an officer and undertakes all sorts of works required to be performed in the official discharge of his duties. The private secretary is simply to assist his her superior in carrying out the details of his work. A person performing the duties as private secretary needs to understand the office procedures and methods besides the techniques of handling people. The term 'Secretarial Practice' is used to denote the procedures and methods of work adopted by a private secretary. In the present-day world, we find that bebind the success of every Executive/Boss/Manager, there is an efficient private secretary who acts as the "Loyal right-hand" to him. Usually, the executive or boss is a male and the private secretary a female. There may be female top executives also and the male as her private secretary. As such, there is no such criteria that an executive boss may be a male and the private secretary a female or vice versa.

The modern private secretary, also known as 'executive secretary' or 'office secretary', has to play a vital and pivotal role in the business life of an executive/boss/superior by making him !ree from the monotony of routine office works like typing, filing, handling mail etc., attending the telephone calls and handling visitors without disturbing him. Not only this, the private secretary has to make travel arrangements, hotel reservation, drafting speeches, notes and reports for the boss besides a lot of other works required to be performed in order to make the boss's works simpler, easier, correct and complete. As such, the scope of work of a private secretary is not only confined to the routine office work but also in doing many more works for and on behalf of the Boss.

A private secretary is *not mcrely a steno-typist* but more than that. Rather, we may say that the persoas having attained sufficient experience as a steno-typist and office assistant, may aspire to become a perfect private secretary. Beside being a fast and accurate steno-typist, he/sne must have the capacity to handle the visitors, telephone calls and keep the matters secret in addition to handling the routine office matter officiently. He/she must be able to work without interruptions and without prodding or supervision. He/she has to take initiative for any sorts of office works. He/she must be able to cope with the rush of work without worrying. Many of such qualities, required in a private secretary, have been discussed in the succeeding is chapter.

DUTIES AND FUNCTIONS OF A PRIVATE SECRETARY

Usually, a private secretary is employed to perform all the works of office for and on behalf of his/her boss, which may include handling mail, making correspondence, filing, handling telephone, telex etc. and also other works in the personal-cum-official capacity of the boss. However, there cannot be any rigid or watertight compartment in which we may define the works of a private secretary, because his/her duties or functions may depend upon the nature of work ond the responsibilities shouldered by the boss who apyoints the private secretary. Any way, we many classify the duties or functions of a private secretary into the *following groups* :

(*i*) **Routine office duties** :—These may include all sueh works which may be performed in an office as a matter of routine, e.g. handling mail, drafting routine letters, taking dictation in shorthand and typing, keeping proper records, filing, indexing and handlıng the various office machines or equipments etc.

(*ii*) **Receptionist's duties** : These include all such works as receiving telephone calls, making outgoing telephone calls, welcoming and screening the visitors or in-person callers, taking appointments, engagements, etc. for and on behalf of the boss.

(*iii*) **Literary duties** :—Under this head, we may include the works requiring special skills of drafting the reports, speeches, briefs, notes, agenda and minutes of meetings, etc.

(*iv*) **Financial duties** :—These comprise the handling of cash and bank transactions by a privare secretary, i.e. depositing cash and cheques into the bank, withdrawing amounts from the bank, receiving or paying cash and also recording and reconciling the transactions for and on behalf of the boss or his office.

(*v*) **Private duties** :—Such duties consist of the works in the personal-cum-official capacity of the boss, e.g. handling personal bank accounts of boss, arranging payments of water, electricity or telephone bills of the residential accommodation of boss, handling his personal tax matters, arranging tours and travels, making hotel reservations, arranging parties, meetings, conferences, etc. Though all these works are purely personal of the boss, yet the private secretary has to perform these as private duties in order to help the boss in his official and business life.

(*vi*) **Miscellaneous** :—Besides the duties enumerated in the earlier paragraphs, a private secretary has to perform all other works for and on behalf of the boss, depending upon the exigencies and the requirements of boss's business. These may include taking the family members of the boss for a sight-seeing visiting tours, others as a representative of the boss, etc.

The following Chart shows the details of private secretarial duties.

Secretarial Duties

Routine Office Duties	Noting and Drafting	Receptionist's Duties	Financial and Accounting Duties	Other Duties
Handling Mail.	General Drafting of Reports	Handling Telephone, Telex etc.	Petty Cash	Travel Arrangements
Correspondence.	Notice	Handling Visitors.	Banking Transactions.	Hotel-reservations, etc.
Typing, Dictation and Transcribing. cribing.	Agenda and Minutes	Appointments and Engagements.		
Duplicating and Photocopying				
Handling. Office Machines and Equipments.				
Filing and Indexing.				
Handling Communication Systems.				
Handling Office Stationery and other supplies.				
Organising Office and the work.				

However, the following *list* shows the *detailed duties* of a private secretary, which the reader may take as a guide to understand the entire duties of a private secretary :—

1. Taking dictation in shorthand and transcribing it in the best possible manner.
2. Maintaining, in good order, the papers required by the officer to be retained in his room.
3. Screening telephone calls received.
4. Fixing up appointments, and where necessary cancelling those already fixed.
5. Keeping an accurate list of engagements and meetings etc. and reminding the officer *in good time* for keeping them.
6. Visitors : Both official and non-official—screening them in a tactful manner.
7. Keeping track of papers and progress of action taken by the subordinates on important matters as required by the officer.
8. Processing of cases of confidential and secret nature which the offieer does not wish to be sent to the office.
9. Thoroughly familiarising oneself with the procedure and practice followed in Government Offices specially with regard to tours of officers.
10. Have a good knowledge of noting and drafting and preparation of agenda, briefs and minutes or reports connected with the meetings or the various conferences.
11. See to the interests of the officer first, then the public or his clients. It is the officer who pays you, not the public.
12. Always do a little extra than what is required from you. Supply other information connccted with the business in hand, provided it is relevant.
13. Don't pass mistakes made by others uncorrcted. The responsibility is yours, otherwise don't accept a file if there is a mistake in it.
14. Little points like numbering of pages, putting the file in a neat and tidy appearance.
15. Maintaining a Diary of the officer's engagements.
16. Always connect up notes etc. with the previous ones, filling in references, if necessary, with flags sticking out to make the relevant pages prominent and easily traceable.
17. Engagements/invitations—certainly refuse on them on behelf of the officer politely in his absence when you know that he will not be in station, that date. No use

absolutely for his to deal with on him arrival back from the tours.

18. Remind the officer *in time* about the renewal of motor car driving licence, insurance premia, cooking gas payment, etc.
19. Get to know the files in the officer's room, and make out a summary or precis of some files, when time permits. The main thing is to be ready *before* he makes a request for it. This goes a *longway*.
20. Anticipate what the officer wants and, if necessary, when you know he is going wrong, correct him politely.
21. Whenever in doubt, don't let the thing pass, but *check up* from all available sources the correctness of the information you have, e.g. addresses of persons. Don't just copy what is given to you.
22. You must use your discretion and sense of judgement and not just follow the practice.
23. In deciding what to do in certain cases, don't just go by **precedent.** Have some originality.
24. A private secretary is a trusted individual on whom the officer relies, but there are certain things he may wish to keep secret from his private secretary. Don't try to find out those secrets from his papers. Keep your eye and ears open, but don't be inquisitive into his private affairs.
25. Never tell his wife or his family of the officer's visitors and engagements, lunch etc. You can easily teil them that he has gone out for a meeting or something of that kind.
26. Before meetings, inform the officer in time and get all the files and papers, etc. ready and mark the files like this : "Rcquired for the Annual General Meeting on such and such date at such time.
27. **Telephone**—Make a list of telephone numbers and names of the officers and sections the officer usually phone to, and place a copy af this list on his table and you keep a copy for your reference. Include in it some other important numbers like Taxi Stand, Railway enquiries, Club, Hotels, Home, Friends, Police, Fire Brigade, Grocer, Office T'ffin Room, Aerodrome, Air Booking Office, Post Office, Bank, Hospitals, etc.
28. P.B.X.—Get acquainted with the working of the different line etc.

28. Phonograms (Telegrams to the telegraph office over the phone). Make use of it in urgent cases.
30. Direct connections (S.T.D.s.) Make a list of such places where trunk-calls can be replaced by Ensure direct dialing to give time.
31. Payment of Telephone bills in time or telephone will be disconnected. No notice will be sent for payment of telephone bills. If not received by a certain date, ask for the bill or duplicate copy.
32. Secret or other files maintained by the officer—Make a list of files.
33. Officer's bank accounts : (*a*) Overdrafts (*b*) Periodical payments for donations etc. } Bank to be informed.
34. Keep upto date list of postal rates (Inland and foreign). Postage, Money orders, Parcels, Registrations, By air and By rail etc.
35. **Complaints :** Remember and also note down in your desk index the phone numbers for complaints about—Telephone, Electric lights, Water, Municipal Corporation's office.

An all-rounder

Looking at the multifarious functions of a private secretary, as explained above, we may duly say that a modern private secretary is expected to be an all-rounder i.e. jack of all trades. He/she has to perform all sorts of works which facilitate the boss or executive in carrying out the details of his work. The private secretary is like an independent loyal right-hand of the boss. His/her activities may include right from typing and taking dictation to drafting routine official or business correspondenee, reports, Agenda and Minutes of Meetings, etc. He/she may have to receive, sort out and record the incoming mail and then putting the same for the information and action to be taken. It is also his/her duty to attend the incoming telephone calls and receive the visitors, to fix appointments on behalf of the boss in consultation with him, dialing the telephone number for the boss and to put necessary communication between the boss and the outsiders. He/she is supposed to remind the boss to keep up the appointments or meetings/conferences. He/she has to supervise the work of the office where other staff members are also working. He/she has to ensure that all the records are maintained properly and to look after the stationery and other supplies of offlce. He/she has also to attend the work connected with meetings/conferences and to fix up so many details about the programmes, including the tour/visit of the boss to any place within the country or outside the country. Not only this, when the boss is away from office, he/she has to keep the office running smoothly. In addition to the above, he/she has to handle many other works depending upon the exigeneies. The objective is that he/she should make the boss free from all worrics of routine works. Hence, he/she has to be an all-rounder, i.e. competent to perform any work by maintaining the confidence of the boss. The task is really challenging but dignified and paying.

QUESTIONS

1. Who is a Secretary ? Discuss the various types of Secretaries.
2. What is the meaning of a Private Secretary ? How a private secretary may be distinguished wiih other Secretaries ?
3. What are the secretarial functions ? Discuss them. *(Board of Technical Education, Delhi, 1987)*
4. Discuss the nature and scope of secretarial duties in brief. *(B.T.E, Delhi, 1986)*
5. What are the main types of secretaries found in a modern Organisation ? Briefly discuss the functions of a Private Secretary. *(B.T.E. Delei, 1985)*
6. Mention some of the principal types of secretaries. Discuss the main functions of a private secretary. *(B.T.E. Delhi, 1984)*
7. What do you mean by Private Secretary ? Discuss the main functions of a Private Secretary. *(B.T.E. Delhi, 1983)*

2

THE COMPANY SECRETARY

In the previous chapter, we have discussed about the meaning of a 'Company Secretary' and his functions or duties. Thus, we know that a company secretary is an important person in the eyes of law. Section 2 (45) of the Indian Companies Act, 1956 (as amended upto date) has defined the company secretary as an individual who possesses the prescribed qualifications appointed to perform the duties which may be performed by a secretary under the Act and any other ministerial or administrative duties. It is further stated that the company secretary must possess the qualifications as prescribed by the Central Government from time to time. However, based on the various rules, the company secretary must generally possess the following qualifications :—

(i) The membership of the Institute of Company Secretaries of India or the membership of Institute of Chartered Secretaries and Administrators, London. (It is compulsory in case of a company having a paid-up capital of Rs. 25 lakhs or over).

(ii) Degree in law from any recognised University.

(iii) Post-graduate degree in commerce from any recognised University.

(iv) Diploma in Company Law from the Indian Law Institute.

(v) Post-graduate degree or diploma in management from

any Indian University or Indian Institute of Management, Ahmedabad or Calcutta.

(vi) Post-graduate diploma in company secretaryship from the Institute of Commercial Practice, Kashmeregate, Delhi.

It may be pointed out here that for a company having a paid-up capital below Rs. 25 lakhs may appoint a person as a company secretary possessing one or more of the qualifications given above from (ii) to (vi). However, in case of a company having paid-up capital of Rs. 25 lakhs and over, it is a must that the person concerned must be the member and a qualified secretary from the Indian Institute of Company Secretaries or an Associate of Institute of Chartered Secretaries and Administrators, London.

Besides the above prescribed qualifications, the nature of company secretarial duties require the following general qualifications :—

Knowledge of Company Law Matters : Primarily, the company secretary is supposed to know the matters relating to company law and practice because he has to ensure completion of the various formalities in connection with formation and day-to-day working of the company. Up-to-date amendments or changes must also be known to him.

Knowledge of Office Administration : The company secretary has to supervise and control the office activities and put into practice the polices of management. For this purpose, knowledge of organisation, administration and management of office is essential. He has to be competent to deal with the practical problems arising out of working of office and guide the subordinates appropriately.

Knowledge of Office Procedures and Methods : These are the tools for an executive. Without the knowledge of basic procedures and methods, it may not be possible for the Company Secretary to have a smooth working of his office.

Knowledge of Accounts and Finance : It is under the supervision of a Company Secretary that the books of account of the company are well maintained. At the same time, he may have to deal with the financial aspects of his office. Hence, the knowledge of both these aspects is essential.

Knowledge of Correspondence and Report-writing : Making corresondence with various offices of Company Administration Management and others is a routine matter which has to be dealt with by the company secretary. At the same time, he may have to prepare the various types or Reports etc. For this purpose it is necessary that he should have the complete knowledge of the same.

General Knowledge : It consists of a general awareness of what is happening in and around the country. That will be helpful in chalking out the various improvements or effecting changes in the state of affairs of the company. That is why an up-to-date knowledge in general matters is essential.

Command over language/s : To deal with effectively with people of all sorts, it is essential that the company secretary must know the national language, must have fluency in speaking 'English' as one of the most popular language of the international level and proficiency in one or two at least regional/foreign languages.

Personality Tra its or Qualities

It makes one's own personality if certain good personal qualities are possessed by him/her. Particularly, the personification of image in the eyes of staff and others can be reflected if the Company Secretary has a good common sense, tact, sense of humour, honesty, discipline, devotion, hard-working punctuality, regularity, good manners and habits etc. These are invaluable things of great importance in practical working because these things impress others and make the subordinates to follow suit. These are helpful in dealing with others effectively and getting the work done through others.

IMPORTANCE AND STATUS OF A COMPANY SECRETARY

Looking at the various functions and duties which a company secretary is required to perform under the law as well as general administration of a limited company, we may say that the Company Secretary is not a mere servant or an employee of the company working under the instructions of the Board of Directors (through he has to abide by them) but an independent administrative officer or executive dealing with company matters and ensuring that the company functions strictly in accordance with provisions laid down under the Companies Act, 1956. At the same time, he has to keep his office well, up-to-date and working efficiently for achieving the goals. Within his own area of operation, he has the powers to take independent decisions and/or delegate authority to other persons working under him and fixing up their responsibility. In the eyes of law, the company secretary has to meet all the legal obligations thwarted upon him, otherwise he may be held personally liable and penalty may also be imposed upon him.

Hence, the work and status of a company is of vital importance for (i) the Board of Directors of a Company, (ii) Company Law Administrators, (iii) Staff working in the Company, and (iv) Outsiders interested in the company. With the efficient working of the Company, the shareholders may get a higher rate of dividend and the creditors may safely lend money to the company. With the sound general administration, the company can be saved from any sort of fraud, pilferage of mal-practice. The profitability of the company may be ultimately increased and the revenues of the Government from taxes on profits may be enhanced. Staff may get higher emoluments and perks. Thus, the importance of a company secretary may be adjudged from all these angles.

The role of a Company Secretary has also been recognised as a principal authority for Tax administrative requirements under the Income-tax, Sales Tax, Stamp Duty Act, Factories Act, Shops and Establishment Act vis-a-vis the Companies Act, because the Law Authorities look at the Company Secretary as an Executor, ensuring fulfilment of obligations required under the various provisions laid down under different Acts. The Monopolies and Restrictive Trade Practices Act recognises the Company Secretary as the 'Principal Officer' in relation to the body corporate owned by a group of persons. The Company Secretary's authentication made on statutory declarations, company documents, statements, lists, Balance Sheet & Profit and Loss Account etc., are recognised by Law.

Hence, we may say that the company secretary, as an important official of the company, assumes a tremendous importance in the eyes of law as well as in the general administration of a Joint Stock Company.

APPOINTMENT AND DISMISSAL

Under the provisions laid down under Companies Act, 1956 every company having a paid-up capital of Rs. 25 lakhs and over has to appoint a whole-time Company Secretary and that no person can hold the post of a Secretary in more than one Company. His name may be included in the Articles of Association of the company concerned.

However, in case of a newly promoted company, any person out of the promoters may be appointed as the first secretary of the Company, also known as pro tem secretary (secretary for the time being).

The authority for appointing a regular full-time Secretary vests with the Board of Directors of the Company and they may appoint a person fulfilling the norms and qualifications prescribed by the Government from time to time and possessing the requisite general qualifications etc. by exercising the powers in a Board Meeting through passing a Resolution unanimously or by a vote of majority. The two major formalities to be completed in connection with the appointment of a qualified company secretary are :

(i) Passing a Resolution in the Board Meeting : The matter for appointing any particular person as the Secretary of the Company, is placed before the Directors in the Board meeting through the formal Agenda, discussion or voting. The Resolution in the following manner is passed :—

"Resolved that Shri X be and hereby appointed as the Secretary of the Company with immediate effect, at a monthly salary of Rs. 2000/- puls the usual allowances and perquisites admissibles under the Company Rules in force from time to time, subject to the usual terms and conditions of appointment."

"Further resolved that the nccessary appointment letter be and hereby issued and communicated to Mr. X and that the formalities of executing service Agrement etc., be completed."

On the basis of the above Resolution, the Company Secretary may be appointed and asked to join duties on fulfiling the requisite formalities. The Authority to sign the appointment letter may lie with any of the Directors or the Chairman and Managing Director. Before joining duties, the person concerned may be required to sign and execut the Service Agreement which may contain the duties, conduct and service regulations of the Company.

(ii) Filing with the Registrar of Companies : On appointment of a Secretary, it is obligatory under the company Act, to fill in the particulars on Form Not 32, in duplicate, and file the same with the Registrar of Companies within a period of 30 days from the date of appointment.

Afterwards, an entry is also required to be made in the Register regarding particulars of drectors, managers and secretary.

From administration point of view, the company secretary may be treated as an officer employee of the company and will be subject to conduct and disciplinery Rules in force from time to time.

In case of breach of any of the service regulations, the services of a company secretary may be dismissed with or without notice by the Board of Directors or any other competent Authority as mentioned under the Articles of Association of the Company. As per the recent amendments, no prior notice is required for dismissal of services.

RIGHTS, POWERS AND LIABILITIES

By virtue of his official designation and position as an officer employee of the Company, the Company Secretary may exercise generally the following rights and powers :—

(i) To supervise and control the office activities including the office personnel, records, equipments etc.
(ii) To sign letters, papers or documents for and on behalf of the company and those requiring authentication,
(iii) To do any one or all acts by exercising authority in respect of the general administration of the company.
(iv) To claim his salary as a preferential creditor in case of winding up of a company.

However, there are some restrictions in exercising Secretary's powers and rights, which may include—

(i) No right to make allotment or transfer of shares to any person without being specifically authorised to do so by the Director/s of the Company ;
(ii) No right to make any representation on behalf of Company or to make contracts without express authority of the directors.
(iii) No right to borrow amounts in the name of the Company.

If the Company Secretary does any work for which he is not empowered or authorised by the directors, he may be held personally liable for any loss to the company on his account.

The *Liabilities* of a Company Secretary may briefly be stated as under :—

(i) Under the Companies Act, 1956, a company secretary is liable personally for any default, omission or commission in respect of not complying with the provisions applicable to companies concerned, in respect of—

—failure to submit timely returns, statements or documents to the Registrar of Companies ;

—failure to submit copies of the annual Balance Sheet, Profit & Loss Account ;

—failure to maintain the proper books of account of the company ;

—default in holding the statutory meetings and failure to circulate the Statutory Report ;

—Default in holding the Annual General Meeting, giving due and proper notice for the same and circulating annual report ;

—failure to give due and proper notice for the Board Meetings ;

—failure to maintain proper minutes book and circulating the copies of minutes amongst the members ;

—default in getting certain Resolutions and Agreements registered, required to be made under the law ;

—default in getting ready the share certificates or debentures within a period of three months from allotment and/or transfer them within a period of two months from the date of application for transfer ;

—failure to maintain proper registers of members and/or debentureholders as required under the Act ;

—failure to maintain the register of directors, managers etc., as required under the Act ;

—default in submitting the details of charge created over the assets of the company in favour of banks/creditors ;

—any other default or failure in complying with the provisions laid down under the Companies Act, 1956.

(ii) Under the Income-tax regulations, the Company Secretary is liable to deduct income-tax at source and its payment to the Government Authorities in respect of the payments made by the company on account of dividends to shareholders, salaries to staff and corporate tax as per latest rates in force.

(iii) Under the Indian Stamp Act, the Company Secretary is liable for payment of actual stamp duty to the Government on the documents or deeds executed by the company.

(iv) Under the Monopolies & Restrictive Trade Practices Act, the Company Secretary is liable to verify the statements made under various forms of the Company and also for giving due notice for various matters.

(v) The Company Secretary is liable to complete necessary formalities or submit papers under the Sales Tax Act, Factory Act,

Above all, a Company Secretary is liable to maintain utmost secrecy of company matters, obeying the orders of the board of Directors and discharge his duties with reasonable care and skill as a prudent person. If he does anything contrary, he is liable to compensate the damages to the company occured on account of his negligence. He is also personally liable to pay penalties or face punishments.

QUESTIONS

1. Who is a Company Secretary ? Explain briefiy the duties of a company secretary.
2. Give the functions of a Company Secretary ?
   (*B. Com. Pass, Delhi, 1986*)
3. (a) How is a Company Secretary appointed ?
   (b) "A company Secretary is an Advisor, an executive and a liaison officer." Discuss. (*B. Com. Pass, Delhi, 1985-1987*)
4. Who can be appointed a Company Secretary ? Discuss his liabilities. (*B. Com. Pass, Delhi, 1984*)
5. State the liabilities of the company secretary. Can he be dismissed ? (*B. Com. Pass. Delhi, 1983-1987*)
6. State the liabilities of the company secretary. Also state the rules regarding his remuneration. (*B. Com. Pass, Delhi, 1982*)
7. (a) How is Company Secretary appointed ?
   (b) How is the appointment of a company secretary recorded ?
   (c) How can a Company Secretary be dismissed ?
   (*B. Com. Pass, Delhi, 1981*)
8. Discuss the liabilities of Companv Secretary.
   (*B. Com. Pass, Delhi, 1987*)
9. State the parocedure for the appointment of a Company Secretary.

3

JOINT STOCK COMPANIES

Introduction

For carrying on a business at the large-scale, much capital is needed. It is not possible for any one individual or a few persons to arrange for capital at a large-scale. Therefore, some such form of business organisations is needed which can amess or collect huge sums of money for doing business. Leaving aside the case of the Government which can arrange huge funds easily for any purpose, the private form of business organisation can collect huge sums of money only when the members of the public co-operate and majority of them become ready for giving money for business. With this idea in mind, the 'Joint Stock Companies' were formed as an organised sector during the nineteenth century in India. The name itself signifies that the capital for doing business is divided into various units and each of such unit may be called 'stock'. All the units combined together in collective form used to be called 'joint stock'. That is how the joint stock companies came into existence. With the passage of time, this form of business organisation became more and more popular because through this form it became possible to collect large sums of money for doing business and the liability of the joint stock owners was kept limited to the amount of 'stock' contributed by each individual.

The Joint Stock Companies became an organised sector in India during late 1800s and, for the first time, an Act was promulgated for directing and controlling the activities of these companies in the year 1850. Later on, the Indian Companies Act, 1956 was passed, which till date governs the formation, working and winding up the company form of business organisation. The amendments are made in the Act from time to time in accordance with the needs of country and corporate sector. Presently, all the Joint Stock Companies are formed and set up as per the provisions laid down under the Act and the Government administers and controls the affairs of business of companies through this Act.

Meaning

A Joint Stock Company may be defined as *an association or incorporate body which is an artificial person created by law, having a common seal and perpetual succession.* It has a meaning that the Company is a different type of association of persons which is the creation of law and that the same cannot be seen or touched but it can be sensed with the 'Common seal' (a stamp containing the name and registered office address of the company). Such a form of organisation is incorporated under the law i.e. Companies Act, and it never dies i.e. its existence is continuous and permanent.

The abovesaid definition gives us an idea that some persons get-together and approach the Government authorities under the Companies Act, 1956 to incorporate a separate body known as a 'Company'. Thereafter, the capital may be collected from the public or other persons in the form of 'share capital' i.e. the capital divided and distributed into many units of fixed amount, called the 'shares'. The business is carried on in the name of the company after completion of certain formalities as required under the law. The affairs of business are controlled by the representatives or persons holding the shares but the management is done at the hands of persons separately employed by the company, other than those who own 'shares' of the company. Whatever profits are earned by doing business in the form of the company, those are distributed in the form of 'dividend' on shares to the holders of those shares.

Thus, we find that the company form of business organisation is literally separate and different than the sole proprietorship or partnership, because the company organisation is the creation of law, though manual efforts are put in to create it, and it may be called an 'artifical person' different than the actual person or persons in the other forms of business organisation.

However, *Section 566* of the Companies Act, 1956 defines a Joint Stock Company as under :—

"*A Company having a permanent paid-up or nominal share*

capital of fixed amount divided into shares also of fixed amount or held partly in the other, and formed on the principle of having for its members, the holders of *those shares or that stock and no other person.*"

According to the above statutory definition of a company, the words 'company' and joint stock company' are used similarly in a a sense that it has a permanent share-capital base which is contributed the members or shareholders. The shares are of the fixed ε̲no-unt and those persons who purchase or own those stocks or shares are called the members or shareholders of the company.

The law takes a view that the company may be formed by registration under the Act. It takes a broader view of the fact that company may have permanent paid-up share capital (i.e. the company limited by shares) or may have a nominal share-capital (i.e. the company not having share-capital but may be limited by guarantee etc.). Thus, the companies registered under the Companies Act may be (i) companies limited by shares and (ii) companies limited by guarantee.

However, both the definitions given initially and the one that is given under the Act enunciate the point that a 'company' or a 'joint stock company' is the creation of law and it can be formed by registration under the law. Both the definitions confirm the fact that the capital of the company is divided and distributed into 'stocks' or 'shares' of the fixed amount and the owners or holders of shares are called the members or shareholders of the company. They may be treated like owners who have a separate entity than the managers of the company.

Special Features or Characteristics

From the definition of a joint stock company we derive at the following main characteristics :—

(i) **Creation of Law or an Incorporated Association**—A company can be cneated only after completing certain formalities as provided under the Companies Act, 1956. Actually, the person or persons who wish to form a company, have to approach the company law authorities, prepare certain papers or doccnments and file them with the appropriate Authority for getting the name of the Company registered or incorporated. The Company can do business only after it is incorporated or registered under the Act. That is why, a company may be called a legal person.

(ii) **An Artificial Person**—Anything which cannot be physically seen or touched, may be called an artificial person. Like it, the

Company is also an artificial person because its existence can be felt only by its name and registered oce, otherwise it is invisible.

(iii) **A 'Common Seal'**—To know a company is through its common seal which is a rubber or brass stamp containing the name and registered office of the company. When the common seal is affixed on papers or documents together with the signatures of its officials, then only it is recognised. Hence, a company is known by its common seal.

(iv) **Perpetual or Continuous Succession**—It has a meaning that a Company never dies. It remains for ever like a continuous link in the chain. If any person dies, the other takes over. When the second dies, the third takes over. Like that the shares of the company are freely transferable from one person to another but the share amount is never refunded throughout the life-time of the company.

(v) **Separation of ownership than management**—The set-up of a company is such that the ownership and management lie in different hands. Generally, the members or shareholders are treated like owners because they own the share-capital of the company and they are concerned about their money and dividend thereupon. They are least concerned as to how the company is managed and by whom. Generally, the managers of the company are its paid employees and they have no direct link or connection with the shareholders or members. Hence, the two are separate entities.

(vi) **Limited Liability of Members**—The members or shareholders are liable only upto the amount of shares owned by them. In case the company goes into liquidation or is wound up, each of the shareholder shall have to forgoe the amount paid by him for purchase of company's shares. There is no other liability other than that even if the company incurs huge losses any time. In proprietorship or partnership, the liability is unlimited because the proprietor or each of partners shall have to pay entire amount of loss, if any, even by selling the household utensils. That is not the case with the shareholders of the company.

Difference between Partnership and Joint Stock Companies

The two forms of business may by distinguished on the following points :—

Partnership	*Joint Stock Companies*
1. A minimum of two persons	1. A minimum of two in case

and maximum 20 (10 in case of banking business) may form a partnership.	of a private company and 7 in case of a public company form a company. However, the maximum number is 50 and no limit in case of private and public companies respectively.
2. Registration is not necessary for a partnership firm	2. Registration under the Act is compulsory.
3. A partnership does not have a separate entity other than the partners.	3. A company has a separate legal entity.
4. The partnership is based on the partnership deed or Agreement made verbally or in writing.	4. The company is based on the Memorandum and Articles of Association. In the absence of Articles, the company may adopt Table 'A' as given in the Act.
5. The liability of partners in a firm is unlimited.	5. The liability of members is limited upto the amount of shares owned by each member.
6. The ownership and management are one as any number or all of the partners may manage the business of partnership.	6. The ownership is separate from the management in case of the company.
7. The partnership comes to an end at will or when a partner retires, becomes insolvent or dies.	7. The company has a perpetual succession and it is more stable in nature.
8. No partner can transfer his share or interest in the firm.	8. The shareholder may freely transfer shares to others in case of public limited company.
9. The partnership works independently watching the interests of partners as well as the firm.	9. The company works within the scope of its Memorandum of Association.
10. The audit and publication of accounts is not required.	10. The audit of accounts and publication by the public company is compulsory.
11. No formal or legal meetings are required to be held.	11. Formal meetings are held for taking decisions on policy matters.

Kinds of Companies

Generally, the Companies are of the following types—

(i) **Chartered Companies** : Those companies which are formed or incorporated under a special royal charter of the King or State, may be called 'Chartered Companies'. The examples are Bank of England or the East India Company formed during the British regime in our country.

(ii) **Statutory Companies** : The companies which are formed by passing a special Act in Parliament or under a legislation promulgated in the public interest, are known as 'Statutory Companies'. Their examples are—Reserve Bank of India (formed under R.B.I. Act, 1934) or State Bank of India (formed under S.B.I. Act, 1955) etc. Such companies may or may not use the word 'limited' against their names.

(iii) **Registered or Incorporated Companies** : Such companies are incorporated or registered under the Indian Companies Act, 1956. The Promoters of such companies have to complete certain formalities as per the provisions laid down under the Act and then only those are incorporated. These types of companies may be sub-divided under the following heads :—

(*a*) Companies limited by shares, i.e. the members having limited liability upto the amount of shares.

(*b*) Companies limited by Guarantee, i.e. carrying the guarantee of the member with or without nominal share-capital.

(*c*) Unlimited Companies, i.e. the companies in which the liability of its members is not limited upto the amount of shares purchased by them.

The *Companies limited by Guarantee* are generally formed for setting up the non-trading concerns like Schools. Hospitals, Clubs etc. Under these companies, the liability of each of the member is limited upto the amount the member has guaranteed to contribute in case of winding up of the company. The amount of guarantee is fixed at the time of incorporation but no payment has to be made until the winding up of the company. This type of Company may or may not have share-capital or even the nominal share-capital may serve the purpose. However, it is necessary for such a company to use the words 'Limited' or 'Pvt. Ltd.' as the last word of its name. The Central Government may grant a licence to such a company and exempt it for using the words 'Ltd.' or 'P. Ltd.

Government Companies

Section 617 of the Companies Act, 1956 defines a Government Company as a "company in which not less than 51% of the paid-up share-capital is held by the Central Government or by any State Government or Governments, or partly by the Central Government and partly by one or more State Governments and includes a Company which is a subsidiary of a Government Company as thus defined." The functioning of such companies is governed by the various rules and regulations provided under the Companies Act or the Central Government may enact any of the provisions by notification in the Government gazette. However the major control rests with the Comptroller and Auditor General of India who conducts the audit of these companies. Indian Telephone Industries Ltd., Bharat Heavy Electricals Ltd. Hindustan Steel Ltd., N.C.D.C. Ltd., are some of the examples of Government Companies.

However, certain provisions of Companies Act, 1956 do not apply or apply with exceptions to the Government Companies. The exemptions to Government Companies have been granted in the following matters :—

(i) Appointment of Managing Director, whole-time Directors and their remuneration. (Sections 198, 259, 268, 269, 310 and 311)

(ii) Appointment and Retirement of Directors. (Sections 255 to 257)

(iii) Previous approval of the Central Government for entering into contracts by it with any other Govt. Company. (Sec. 297)

(iv) Transfer of unpaid dividend to a special account (Section 205-A)

(v) Disclosure of beneficial interest in shares of a company. (Section 187-C)

(vi) Reduction of Capital by a Company. (Section 100 to 102 applicable with modification)

(vii) Amalgamation of Companies. (Sections 391, 392 and 394 applicable with modification as the Central Government may deem fit).

In case of *Foreign Companies*, which have been incorporated outside India but have a place of business in India, it is necessary that they should inform to the Registrar of Companies, within 30 days of their setting up in India, the details of their registered office, a copy of charter, memorandum and articles of association, person/s authorised to act on behalf of the Company in India etc. No provision of Companies Act shall apply to them, except for controlling purposes.

Difference between Government Company and Non-Government Companies

As we know, a Government Company is one in which not less than 51% share capital is owned by the Central Government or any of the State Governments or both combined. When the company is a private organisation, it may be called a non-Government Company. The Non-Government Company may be both—a public company or private company.

However, the two forms may be distinguished on the following points :—

Government Companies	*Non-Government Companies*
1. Not less than 51% of the share capital is owned by the Government.	1. The share capital is owned by private persons, in toto.
2. The Audit of accounts of a government company is done by the Comptroller and Auditor General of India.	2. The audit of accounts may be done by a private practising auditor at the discretion of the Board of Directors.
3. Certain provisions of Companies Act, 1956, are not applicable like those of appointment of Mg. Director/whole-time Directors, their age, remuneration may be applicable with modification by the Central Govt.	3. There is no such exemption to the non-government companies.
4. The annual reports of Government Companies are submitted to the Parliament or to the special committee formed for the purpose.	4. The annual reports are not required to be submitted to the Parliament.
5. Permission of the Central Government may be required for entering into contract with any other government company.	5. No permission of the Central Government is required for entering into a contract with any government company.

The Companies limited by shares may be broadly sub-classified into two :—

(i) **Public Companies** : A Public Company or Public Limited

Company is that form of Business Organisation, the membership of which is open to all members of general public. It can invite the general public to subscribe to its share capital. The minimum number of persons to commence business as a public company is seven but there is no limit to the maximum number of persons who can become members of the public company. Its shares are freely transferable from one person to another. But, there are certain restrictions imposed by the Government on the Directors 'remuneration, age and the number' of companies to which a person can become the director. Otherwise, the Public Companies can be incorporated under the Companies Act, 1956 on completion of necessary formalities required under the Act. Such companies may commence business after obtaining the certificate of commencement of business and not earlier than that. The public companies have to adhere strictly to the rules or provisions laid down under the Act in respect of their formation, functioning, conducting meetings, winding up etc.

(ii) **Private Companies** : According to Section 3(i) (iii) of the Companies Act, 1956, a private company means a company, which by its Articles—

(a) restricts the rights to transfer the shares to any member of the public ;

(b) limits the number of its members to 50 (not including the persons who are in the employment of the company) ; persons who having been formerly in the employment of the company were the members of the company while in that employment and have continued to be members after the employment ceased ;

(c) cannot invite the general public to subscribe to its share capital or debentures.

Such a company can be started with minimum two persons as its members and the maximum limit of members is 50. It cannot make public invitation for its shares and the shares are also not freely transferable. However, the private companies are exempted from the restrictions to commence business or the directors' age, remuneration etc. but the liability of its members is limited.

Privileges enjoyed or Exemptions granted to Private Companies :

(i) The private companies may be incorporated or registered with two members only, the maximum being 50 only.

(ii) It needs not issue a Prospectus or Statement in lieu of

Prospectus or file it with the Registrar of Companies for the purpose of allotment of shares.

(iii) It is not necessary for the private company to obtain a certificate of commencement of business rather it may start business as soon as it is incorporated.

(iv) There are no restrictions in respect of allotment of shares of minimum subscriptions.

(v) It is not necessary for a private company to hold the statutory meeting (as in case of a public Co.) or file the statutory report with the registrar of companies.

(vi) Restrictions regarding further issue of capital do not apply to them.

(vii) There is no restriction as to the written consent of Directors to act as such or to pay for the qualification shares before appointment.

(viii) It is not required to maintain a separate index of members because the number of members is restricted to 50 only.

(ix) The minimum number of members for deciding the quorum in a company meeting is only two.

(x) It may issue any class of shares and need not restrict itself to the issue of only a particular class of shares.

(xi) The provisions of Sections 171 to 186 in respect of holding general meetings of the company are not applicable to private companies. They may hold the meeting independently as per provisions in their respective articles of association.

(xii) Since the shares of private companies are not freely transferable, it is not necessary to register transfer or transmission of shares.

With all the above privileges, the private companies can function more freely and independently than the public companies, but the only disadvantage is that such companies cannot collect more funds by way of selling their shares to the general public.

Distinction between Public and Private Company

Public Companies	*Private Companies*
1. Minimum seven persons can form a public company.	1. Minimum two persons or members may form a private Co.
2. There is no limit to the maximum number of members.	2. The maximum limit is 50 members.

3. It can commence business only after obtaining a certificate of commencement of business.	3. It can commence business as soon as it is incorporated or registered.
4. It is required to issue a Prospectus or statement in lieu of prospectus and publish the same in daily newspapers.	4. It needs not issue the Prospectus or statement as it cannot invite the general public to subscribe to its share-capital.
5. It is necessary to hold the Statutory General Meeting within the stipulated period.	5. It needs not hold the statutory meeting.
6. At the time of Annual General Meeting, it must send all the members a printed copy of Annual Balance Sheet/Profit & Loss A/c and other reports.	6. It needs not send a copy of Balance Sheet or other financial statements to the members.
7. Minimum five persons are needed to complete the quorum in a company meeting.	7. Only two persons can complete the quorum for the meeting.
8. There should be at least three directors in a public company.	8. It may have two directors.
9. There are restrictions about the age-limit of Directors, number of companies to which one person can act as director holding the qualification shares and consent of the Central Government in appointing the Mg. Director, remuneration and loans to directors etc.	9. It is free from all these restrictions.

Conversion of a Private Company into a Public Company :

The facility of converting a private company into a public company or vice versa is provided under the Companies Act, 1956. The Act also provides for automatic conversion of a private company into a public company through the process of law under certain special circumstances.

So far as conversion of private company into a public company is concerned, it can be done if the company alters its Article of Association in such a monner that it no ionger works as a private company, changes the name, capital and objects clause in the Memorandum, files a Prospectus or Statement in lieu of Prospectus within 30 days of such a conversion, passes a special resolution in the extra-ordinary general meeting of shareholders and the decision to this effect is taken at the board meeting. The restriction on transfer of shares, limitation on maximum membership and the prohibition to invite the public to subscribe to shares has also to be removed from the articles of association. The decision to this effect has first to be cleared through the special resolution passed in the meeting of Board of directors and then the matter is to be placed before the shareholders in the extra-ordinary general meeting of the company. Thereafter all the documents duly altered or prepared together with the special resolution have to be filed with the Registrar of Companies.

The Registrar, if satisfied with the statements or documents submitted to him for the purpose, may accord necessary permission.

The Act also provides that if a default in filing the Prospectus or a Statement in lieu thereof within the stipulated period as stated herein above, or if the particulars given in the Prospectus or in any of the documents filed with the Registrar are found untrue, the company and every officer of the company in default shall be punishable with a fine upto Rs. 500 for every day of continuous default and the person authorised for filing the Prospectus or Statement shall be punishable with imprisonment upto two years or a fine upto Rs. 5,000 or both if the particulars filed with the Registrar are found to be untrue.

Secretarial Participation :

That is why, the Company Secretary must take utmost care and caution in dealing with the conversion of the company. He must perform the following duties :—

(i) In consultation with the directors of the Company, he must arrange to convene a Board Meeting immediately by preparing the agenda by fixing up the day, date, time and place therefor.

(ii) He must convene an extra-ordinary general meeting of the shareholders in which the special resolution to alter the Articles of Association and Memorandum of Association etc. is to be passed.

(iii) He must arrange to file with the Registrar within 30 days the copies of the altered Articles of Association etc. and the Prospectus together with the copy of the special resolution passed in the extra-ordinary general meeting of the shareholders.

(iv) He must also file with the Registrar an application requesting him to issue a fresh certificate of incorporation with the altered name etc.

Special Circumstances for Conversion :

The following are the special circumstances under which a private company automatically gets converted into a public company :—

(i) Where not less than 25 per cent of the paid up capital of the private company is held by one or more corporate bodies ;

(ii) Where the average annual turnover of the private company is not less than Rs. one crore.

(iii) Where a private company holds not less than 25 per cent of the paid up share capital of a public company.

However, in computing the above percentage, the shares held by a banking company shall not be included or if the shares are held by it as a Trustee, Executor or Administrator.

The provisions laid down under section 43-A of the Companies Act, 1956 are applicable for such an automatic conversion. However the Act provides that the information to the above effect shall have to be furnished to the Registrar within a period of three months.

For conversion of a public company into a private company, the procedure remains the same as outlined above except that the approval of the Central Government is required for the purpose.

FORMATION OF A JOINT STOCK COMPANY

A Joint Stock Campany is said to have been formed when it has been incorporated or registered under the Indian Companies Act, 1956, after completion of the formalities as required under the Act. Actually, a lot of preliminary work or works are to be performed before the Company is brought into existence and before it commences doing business for which it is formed. For convenience, we may divide the entire work into the *four stages* : (i) Promotion Stage. (ii) Incorporation Stage, (iii) Issue of Share

Capital and (iv) Commencement of business. We shall discuss them in the following paragraphs in detail.

(i) Promotion of a Company :

First of all, a company has to be promoted. 'Promotion' is a technical term used in respect of the joint stock companies and it denotes *a number of business operations through which a company is brought into existence.* In other words, it may be defined as *a process by which a specific business enterprise is created with the new and untried ideas.*

Actually speaking, a few persons get-together initially with an idea to do business at a large-scale for which huge capital is required. They try the idea with market survey and a detailed study or investigation and prepare the necessary infra-structure inclning the documents required to form a joint stock company under the provisions of law. All these works are included in the promotion stage of the company. The following steps are usually taken in promoting a Company :—

(i) Conceiving the new and untried ideas for business and deciding the nature and volume of business to be carried on as a company form of business organisation.
(ii) Making the detailed investigation through market survey and other independent sources.
(iii) Assembling the required data, information or papers for the proposed project of business.
(iv) Making arrangement for initial financing of the proposition through their own sources.
(v) Preparing the necessary documents in consultation with the solicitors for filing them with the Registrar of Companies for the purpose of formation of the company.

The persons who take up the work of promotion of a company may be called the 'Promoters' of the company. They are the pioneers in the line and, through their efforts, make it sure that the company is brought into existence. The various *functions* performed by the promoters may be summarised as under :—

(i) Planning or deciding the nature, volume, scope or extent of business proposed to be undertaken in the company form of business organisation.
(ii) Arranging for initial funds or capital required for promotion of a company.

(iii) Instructing the Solicitors or Legal Advisor or Chartered Accountant to prepare the necessary documents, viz. the Memorandum and Articles of Association etc., for filing them with the Registrar of Companies for incorporating a company.

(iv) Selecting the persons who can become the directors of the company.

(v) Any other work which may be required to be done for promoting a company.

(vi) Signing the preliminary contracts for taking over the existing business in the company organisation.

Thus, the Company Promoters play a vital role not only in bringing a company into existence but also in developing business for the country as a whole. If the promoters are not there, the company cannot be set-up and the proposition may not be materialised. It is through their efforts only that the preliminary legal formalities are completed and finance is arranged for promotion purposes. Not only this, they form the new ideas for the business and take pains in investigating the viability or profitability of the proposition.

(2) Incorporation of a Company :

A Joint Stock Company is said to be incorporated when it gets a certificate of incorporation from the Registrar of Companies. In other words, incorporation is the process through which the company is got registered or incorporated with the Government authorities administering the Companies Act, 1956, called the Registrar of Companies.

For this purpose, it is necessary to file the following documents with the Registrar of Companies tegether with payment of necessary fee :—

(i) Memorandum of Association of the proposed company.

(ii) Articles of Association.

(iii) List of persons who have consented to become the directors of the company.

(iv) The written consent or undertaking of the directors who have agreed to act as such.

(v) Any other information which the Registrar may require for the purpose of incorporation of the company.

On filing the above documents or papers, the Registrar may scrutinize them and on finding them satisfactory, may issue a certificate called the "certificate of incorporation."

Memorandum of Association

It is an important document of the Company in the form of a printed booklet required for the purpose of incorporation or registration under the Companies Act, 1956. It sets out the charter or constitution of the company and lays out the structure of the Company. On reading it, any person can know as to what the company is and what is the scope for its working. That is why, it is said that the Memorandum of Association lays the foundation stone of the company on which its structure is based, because the basic information of the company, viz. name, address, capital, objects etc.

Section 15 of the Companies Act, 1956 provides that the Memorandum of Association must be printed and the contents be divided into paragraphs and each of such paragraph should be consecutively numbered and that it must be signed by each subscriber and witnessed by at least one person, both of them would add the name and complete address under the signatures.

The *main contents or clauses* in the Memorandum of Association are as under :—

(*i*) **Name Clause** : The Memorandum of Association, firstly, contains the full name of the company with the word 'Limited' and Private Limited' respectively for public and private companies adjoined at the end, viz. Kitco (India) Private Limited.

The name for the company can be selected by the promoters and the same is informed to the Registrar of Companies, who has to verify that the proposed name is not synonymous or exactly the same as kept by any other company incorporated earlier. A fee of Rs. 10 is deposited with such an application. The Registrar may suggest any alteration, if any, in the name before it is found acceptable to them. *Section 147* of the Companies Act, 1956 lays down that the name of the company must be painted on the signboards and displayed on every office of the company. It must be engraved clearly on the common seal of the company and printed on the letter-heads, bill books, invoices, registers etc.

(*ii*) **Situation Clause** : The Memorandum must contain the complete postal address of the registered office of the company by giving the details of building number, road, street or city preferably with the pincode number. It indicates the place of domicile, nationality and the jurisdiction of the Court. Hence, the importance of 'situation clause'. This clause may be worded as under :—

"The Registered Office of the Company will be situated in the Union Territory of Delhi."

However, *Section 146* of the Act lays down that it is not necessary to give the address at the time of filing the Memorandum with the Registrar of Companies but it has to be communicated within 30 days of registration of the company.

(*iii*) **Object Clause** : The main objects for which the company is established are given in the Memorandum of Association. Besides the main objects, the objects ancilliary to the main objects and other objects are also contained. This clause must also specify the State or States to which the objects will extend. It must also not include any object/s which are illegal or against the public interest. Thus, the objects clause states the ambit of powers which are given to the company by law.

(*iv*) **Liability Clause** : This clause in the Memorandum of Association contains a clear statement that the liability of members, in a limited company, is limited upto the amount or face value of shares owned by each of the shareholders. Section 45 of the Act provides that at any stage the number of members should not fall below the minimum prescribed (viz. two for a private company and seven for a public company). If the company carries on the business with less than the minimum limit of members for more than six months, the liability of such members may be several for payment of debts of the company incurred during this period.

(*v*) **Capital Clause** : The law states that Memorandum of Association of a Company must contain the amount of share capital and division thereof in shares of fixed amount. Each type of share, i.e. reference or equity should be specifically mentioned.

(*vi*) **Association or Subscription Clause** : The Memorandum must also contain a statement of agreements entered into by the company with others and the purpose thereof. The number of shares in the share capital of the company taken by each of the associate or subscriber must also be shown in the memorandum of Association.

Alteration in the Memorandum of Association :

Since the Memorandum of Association is the document of

utmost importance for the company, any alteration in it is not possible in the ordinary course of business and much easily. However, in exceptional cases where specific provision is made in the Act, alterations are possible, e.g. alteration in the name clause, situation clause or the capital clause can be made but by following a certain set procedure which has been outlined in the following paragraphs.

ALTERATION IN NAME CLAUSE

As per the provisions laid down under *section 21* of the Companies Act, 1956, a oompany may alter its name by passing a special resolution and with the approval of the Central Government. If the Central Government directs any company to change the name as suggested by it, then it can do so by passing an ordinary resolution within a period of 3 months of such a direction., and any default made in the direction shall make the defaulting officer of the company liable for punishment of upto Rs. 100 per day of such period of default.

Briefly, the *procedure* for alteration in the name is that the Company Secretary should—

(*i*) Make an application to the Registrar asking him whether change in the name is desirable or possible. The necessary fees should also be deposited along with such an application.

(*ii*) Forward an application to the Central Government for its approval.

(*iii*) Convene the Board meeting to recommend the changed name to the members. In turn, the Board of Directors may call an extra-ordinary general meeting of the shareholders and shall pass a special resolution therein.

(*iv*) Take out the copies of the special resolution and forward the same to the Registrar of Companies, maximum within a period of 30 days from the date of resolution.

(*v*) Incorporate the change in the Memorandum, articles of Association etc., and send a copy of the altered ones to the Registrar within a period of three months.

(vi) Incorporate the change in name in the books or registers of the company.

(vii) Get the new common seal of the company with the

changed name and get it approved from the Board of Directors.

(viii) Notify the alteration to all the concerned parties of the company.

ALTERATION IN SITUATION CLAUSE

If a company wishes to change the place of its registered office for attainment of its main objectives or for increasing business or for abandoning any objective or for amalgamation with some other company, it may do so by following the procedure laid down under the Companies Act which may be summarised as under :—

(i) Where the change in location of the registered office is proposed within the same city from one locality to another locality, the resolution to this effect may be passed at the Board Meeting and filed with the Registrar for necessary approval, within 30 days of the date of passing such a resolution. And a public notice may be released for the information of shareholder and the general public.

(ii) Where the shifting is proposed from one place to another (two different cities) but within the same state, a special Resolution may be passed at the extra-ordinary general meeting and the copy of such a resolution must be filed with the Registrar within 15 days. The notice to this effect may also be released and a copy of notice must also be filed with the Registrar within 30 days of the date of notice.

(iii) Where the change in location is desired from one State to another State, a special resolution has to be passed in the extra-ordinary general meeting. The permission of the Company Law Board has to be obtained necessarily before giving notice to the concerned parties and the geueral public. The copies of the altered memorandum of association should be forwarded to the Registrars of Companies of the respective States together with the certified copy of the Company Law Board Order allowing the alteration or shifting.

The Company Secretary must take all the necessary steps as per the procedure defined herein above, viz. convening the meetings' passing special resolutions, taking necessary permission from the Authorities, filing the copies to the Registrar giving public notice and furnishing the copy of notice to the Registrar of Companies and other works connected with it.

ALTERATION IN OBJECTS CLAUSE

The alteration in the 'Objects Clause' of the Memorandum of Association can be possibly made for the purpose of enabling the company to increase the efficiency of business, to carry out its operations more economically, to attain the main objectives by new or improved means, to abandon or restrict any of its objects, enlarge the area of operations, amalgamate with any other company and/or sell wholly or partly the undertaking of the company. For altering the objects clause, the following procedure must be adopted :—

(i) Filing a petition with the Company Law Board informing the alteration proposed and satisfying them that the alteration is desired in the best interests of the company and each and every party of the company will be duly informed about the change.
(ii) Passing a special resolution in the Board as well as extra-ordinary general meeting of the company.
(iii) Filing with the Registrar a copy of the order passed by the Company Law Board and that of the special resolution together with the altered copy of the memorandum, A certificate to alteration has also to be obtained necessarily from the Registrar.
(iv) Giving notice to shareholders, creditors and other concerned parties of the company.

In case of default in complying with any of the provisions of law, the defaulting company officers shall be liable to penalty.

ALTERATION IN SHARE CAPITAL

There are various types of alterations which may be made in the shares capital of the company, viz.—

(a) Reduction in the amount of share capital,
(b) Increase in the amount of share capital,

(c) Changing the denominations of shares into lower or higher ones.
(d) Conversion of shares into stock or their re-conversion.
(e) Cancelling the unused share capital.
(f) Any other alteration for better availability of funds for company's business.

For any of the above types of alteration in the share capital, the company shall have to follow the procedure as laid down in its Articles of Association. If any alteration is sought for which there is no provision in the Articles of Association, the Company may first alter the Articles of Association and then effect the alteration in the share capital. As such, it is necessary that proper provisions are made in the Articles of Association of the Company, without which it might not be possible.

As per the provisions provided in the Articles of Association, the Company Secretary should follow the same procedure in altering the share-capital of the company. An ordinary or special resolution may be passed in the General Meeting of the Company by convening the same. A copy of the Resolution together with the explanatory statement of the alteration, must be filed with the Registrar of Companies with a period of 30 days from the date of passing the resolution. Necessary changes may by made in the Memorandum & Articles of Association and other records of the Company. A notice to the creditors and other parties may be given by the company. However, in case of reduction in capital, the company may file an application with the Court and the copy of order of the court must also be given to the Registrar, Necessary steps should also be taken to settle the claims or objection of the creditors, if any.

ARTICLES OF ASSOCIATION

It is an important document, in printed form, containing the internal rules, regulations or bye-laws of the Company. Like Memorandum, of Association, this document is also of great importance and it is required compulsorily for incorporation purposes. It is useful for internal management of the company.

Section 26 of the Companies Act, 1956 lays down that a Public Company, limited by shares, may or may not have its own Articles of Association. Instead, it may adopt Schedule I, Table 'A' as given in the Act. But, a private company must have Articles of Association of its own.

The Act also provides that the Articles of a company shall state the number of members with which a company is registered and in case of a company not limited by shares the Articles must be in any one of the forms given in Tables C,D and E of Schedule I or near to it.

Contents :

The Articles of Association of the Company generally contains the following important matters relating to—

(i) The share capital of the company and its division into various classes of shares;
(ii) Calls, transfer, transmission, forfeiture and surrender etc. of shares ;
(iii) Alteration (increase or reduction) in capital;
(iv) Appointment, dismissal, remuneration, duties, powers etc. of the Directors of Company ;
(v) Appointment of Managers or Secretary;
(vi) Borrowing powers of the company;
(vii) Declaration of dividend ;
(viii) Procedure for conducting company meetings ;
(ix) Maintenance of books of accounts and registers of the company ;
(x) Audit of Accounts ;
(xi) Common Seal of the Company ;
(xii) Share Certificates, Share Warrants and/or Debentures;
(xiii) Procedure for winding up, amalgamation of the company ;
(xiv) Rules regarding Notice, Capitalisation of profits and Distribution of property etc.

However, the Articles of Association should not include any point which is contrary to the provisions of Companies Act and the Memorandum of Association.

The use of Articles of Association lies in the fact that it governs the internal management and administration of the affairs of a company.

Preparing the Articles of Association

Section 20 of the Companies Act, 1956 lays down that the Articles of Association must be printed and the information must be divided into paragraphs and consecutively numbered. The members who have signed the Memorandum must also sign the Articles of Association together with name, address and occupation in the presence of witness and that it must be stamped as per the provisions of the Indian Stamp Act. While preparing the Articles of Association, it must also be ensured that none of the information is written contrary to the provisions of the Memorandum and Table A of Schedule I of the Companies Act. Each information should be specific and clear so that there is no ambiguity in it. At the end it must be filed alongwith the Memorandum of Association with the local Registrar of Companies for registration.

Alteration in Articles of Association

Any alteration in the Articles of Association can be made by following the procedure laid down for the purpose. But the alteration is permissible, if the alteration is not contradictory to the Memorandum of Association or it does not increase the liability of any member without written consent from the member or it is not contrary to the provisions of the Companies Act, 1956 or it has the effect of converting any public company into a private company without the approval of the the Central Government or it does not commit a breach of contract with any outsider or it does not keep up the interests of the Company as a whole.

Keeping in view the foregoing facts, for altering the Articles of Association, the following procedure should generally be adopted :—

(i) For altering any provision of the Articles of Association, a Board Meeting must be held to decide and recommend the Articles of Association.

(ii) The Extra-ordinary general meeting of the shareholder's should be convened for passing a special resolution about the alterations.

(iii) The copy of the altered Articles must be filed with the Registrar of Companies within a period of 30 days from the date of passing the resolution in the extra-ordinary general meeting of the company.

(iv) If the Articles have been substantially or completely altered, a new printed copy of Aritcles of Association must be filed wlth the Registrar of Companies.

(v) The consent of all the directors, who have signed the Articles of Association, must be obtained for the alterations made.

The Company Secretary should take all the abovesaid steps and/or do any other act in that connection as may be deemed necessary for effecting the alteration/s.

Difference between Memorandum and Articles of Association

The two documents of the Company may be distinguished on the following lines :—

Memorandum of Association	*Articles of Association*
1. The *contents* of a Memorandum are : Name, Address, Objects, Capital, Liability etc.	1. The contents of the Articles of Association are : internal rules and bye-laws.
2. It is *useful for* the outsiders.	2. It is useful for the internal management of the company.
3. It must be registered by *filing* the same with the Regsitrar of Companies.	3. The Company may adopt Table 'A' of Schedule I of Companies Act, 1956.
4. For alteration of any of the clauses in it, a direct resolution may be passed.	4. For altering any of the provisions of Articles, the clauses of memorandum have to be kept in mind.

(iii) Raising Share Capital

The third stage in formation of a Company is the stage in which a public company collects its share capital from the public for carrying on business.

As we have earlier discussed, a private company may commence business as soon as it is incorporated or registered under the Act. However, a public company cannot do so unless it obtains a certificate of commencement of business from the Registrar of Companies and that can be obtained when all the formalities of issue of share capital by the public company are completed.

As a matter of practice, generally, the promoters of a company call a meeting of the Directors immediately after the incorporation. In that meeting, they decide to appoint the Bankers, Share-brokers, Underwriters, Auditors, Solicitors and Secretary of the Company. If any Company Secretary has already been appointed in the promotion stage, the new Board of Directors of the Company may confirm the appointment by fixing up the terms and conditions of service for the Secretary. If the bankers or solicitors have also been appointed earlier in the promotion stage, a confirmation to that is also obtained from the directors in their first meeting and those may be continued as a fresh appointment.

Opening a Bank Account

Whenever it is contemplated to open a new current account of the Company in a Bank (for a public company, it is necessary that it should be a scheduled commercial bank in India), certain formalities are required to be completed for the purpose. Those *formalities* are—

(i) Obtaining a prescribed printed account Opening Form from the concerned Bank. Generally, all banks have their different printed forms for opening current accounts by joint stock companies. The Companies are not permitted to open savings bank account for their day-to-day business operations because the number of withdrawals or deposits are much more in number.

(ii) The details in the form are filled in and completed. These may include the name of the company, its registered, office, particulars of Directors, Branches or other offices of the Company and names of persons authorised to operate upon the Bank Account. The Common Seal of the Company is also affixed on the Account Opening Form and the Authorised Signatories have to put their signatures at the place meant for the purpose.

(iii) The Account has to be got introduced from any other person or business firm known to the Bank or having any account with that Bank.

(iv) A printed copy of the Memorandum of Association and Articles of Association should be enclosed with the Account Opening Form.

(v) A copy of Resolution passed in the meeting of the Board of Directors for opening the current account with the concerned Bank has to be enclosed with the Account Opening Form of the Bank. Given below is the *specimen Resolution* to be passed at the meeting for opening a bank account :—

"Resolved that a Current Account in the name of the Company be and hereby opened with State Bank of India,...... Branch to be operated by the Chairman, viz. Mr.........and the Secretary, viz, Mr.........under their *joint* signatures, and that the Bank be and hereby empowered to honour cheques, drafts, bills etc., drawn by the aforesaid persons under their joint signatures.

Further Resolved that the Secretary be and hereby authorised to complete all the formalities for opening the bank account."

(vi) A copy of the certificate of incorporation should also be enclosed with the Account Opening Form and submitted to the Bank.

The Company Secretary has to ensure that all the above formalities are completed and the account with the Bank is opened. On Opening the Account, the Bank may issue a Cheque Book in the account which should be obtained by signing a separate application/requisition slip for cheque book and kept under lock and key by the Secretary.

PROSPECTUS

For subscription of share capital, a public company has to prepare a printed document called the Prospectus. It is in the form of a notice, circular, advertisement or often as a printed document inviting the public to subscribe to its share capital. Section 2(36) of the Companies Act, 1956 defines a Prospectus as 'any document described or issued as a prospectus including any notice, circular, advertisement or the document inviting deposits from the public or inviting offers from the public for the subscription or purchase of any shares in or debentures of a body corporate.'

The above definition gives us the idea that the Prospectus is a company's printed document and issued for the purposes of inviting deposits from the public, issue of Shares and Debentures by the Company. It is published in the daily newspapers and a printed form for application of shares or debentures is also annexed with it, in order to facilitate the general public to apply for shares or debentures immediately as soon as they are satisfied about the company's position on reading from the Prospectus.

In order of the fact that the Prospectus serves the purpose of invitation to the public for deposits, shares or debentures, the *contents* of the Prospectus should be clear, complete and self-explanatory. It must include the following :—

(i) *Details of Capital Structure* of the Company, giving the nature, number and particulars of shares or debentures for which the company is authorised to issue and the proposed issue of shares of debentures.

(ii) *Terms of Payment* including the amount to be paid on application, allotment and any further call and the procedure to be followed for default.

(iii) *Particulars of Board of Directors*, giving the name, ddress, occupation and directorship of other companies, in respect of each of the Directors of the Company.

(iv) *Particulars of Bankers to the Issue*, including the name, Head Office and addresses of branches of Banks authorised to collect the amount.

(v) Name/s and Address/es of Share Brokers and Underwriters.

(vi) Particulars of Legal Advisors, Auditors and Managers to the Issue.

(vii) Brief History and Developmental Plans of the Company.

(viii) Nature and Scope of Company's Activities.

(ix) Management of Staff of the Company.

(x) Working Capital Arrangements made by the Company.

(xi) Financial highlights, i.e. prospects, profitability and dividends proposed by the Company.

(xii) Particulars of Assets of the Company, including the fi ed and current assets and other properties.

(xiii) *Other Statutory and General Information*, inculding the main objects of the 'Company and Directors' Interest and Qualification shares owned by them, Powers of Directors, particulars of the Managing Director, Discount or Premium on Shares etc.

However, the Companies Act requires that the 'Reports' as mentioned in Part II of the Second Schedule, must also be contained in the Prospectus. These Reports include—A Report from the Auditors giving the position of profits & losses, assets and liabilities of the Company for the last five years preceeding the issue or a Report of the Accountants giving the particulars of proceeds applied for purchase of any business by the Company during a period of five years proceeding to the issue.

After preparing the Prospectus on the lines mentioned above, the same should be got printed and then it must be got registered with the Registrar of Companies.

Legal Provisions regarding Registration of Prospectus as mentioned in *Sections 55 to* 58 and 60 of the Companies Act, 1956 are as under :—

(i) Unless a copy of the Prospectus is delivered to the Registrar of rregistration purposes, it cannot be issued to the public. Rather, it can be issued within a period of 90 days from the date of delivery to the Registrar.

(ii) It must be signed and dated by all the directors or their agents whose names are given in the Prospectus.

(iii) Any statement made or consent given in the Prospectus must be obtained in writing.

If any reports are made by Auditors or Accountants, that must also be obtained in writing and their signatures should be obtained;

(iv) The reports and written consents of persons must be filed with the Registrar along with a copy of the Prospectus to the Registrar of Companies.

In case the Prospectus is not registered or any of the provisions of Companies Act, 1956 are not complied with or the Prospectus is issued later than 90 days of the date of delivery to the Registrar, then every officer responsible for it may be punished with a fine upto Rs. 5,000. However, a director, promoter or any other person will not be held liable if it is proved that he had withdrawn his consent to become a director of the company, the prospectus was issued without his knowledge or he became aware of any untrue statement in the Prospectus and withdrew his consent or any untrue statement was purported to be a true statment or any other circumstance which made to believe that he is not a defaulter.

A STATEMENT IN LIEU OF PROSPECTUS

In the absence of any Prospectus, any statement filed with the Registrar giving the same information as a Prospectus, may be termed as a 'Statement in Lieu of Propectus'. Whenever the promoters or directors of a company feel that they might collect the necessary share capital of the company from their friends and relatives or the underwriters, they may not need the public to subscribe to the Company's Share Capital, in that case the Company is required to file for registration with the Registrar of Companies, a statment similar to the Prospectus but not actually the Prospectus. Such a statement must be filed at least three days earlier to the particulars as set out in Schedule III of the Companies Act which are virtually the same as in Prospectus. It must also be signed and dated by the directors whose names are given in the statement and the other persons whose consent is reproduced, the same consent must be obtained in writing from them. Only a public company can file the statement in lieu of prospectus and it is not allowed to allot any of the shares or debentures unless the statement is filed with the Registrar of Companies. It may be published in daily newspapers with clear wording that it should not be treated as a prospectus.

Listing of Shares

Whenever a new Company is floated and it issues the shares in the public, the Company gets its name registered with the Stock Exchange for the purpose of buying and selling of its shares, such a process is called 'Listing of Shares'. In other words, it is the process through which a new company gets the name of its shares on the list of Stock Exchange so that the shares may be easily bought or sold in the open market of securities freely.

There are many advantages of 'Listing of Shares' viz. (i) The shares may be easily bought and sold in the securities market ; (ii) It creates market for the shares : (iii) It brings instability to the prices of shares ; (iv) The investors get a confidence of investing their funds in those states ; (v) The demand for shares may be created through speculative activities on the stock exchange. However the *drawbacks* of 'Listing of Shares' that a lot for getting them enlisted at the Stock Exchange. The procedure is also cumbersome and costly.

Generally speaking, the following procedure is to be followed in respect of listing of shares :—

(i) An application has to be made, requesting the Stock Exchange Authorities to enlist their shares ;
(ii) Copies of the Memorandum of Association, articles of Association, Prospectus and the Agreement with Underwriters have to be filed with the Stock Exchange Authorities along with the application.
(iii) Specimen copy of share certificate, allotment letter, transfer deed etc., have to be submitted.
(iv) Particulars of the Capital Structure of the Company are furnished.

(v) Particulars of shares, which are to be listed, shall have to be furnished.

(vi) The necessary security, as required under stock exchange rules, has to be deposited for the purpose of listing of shares.

But, for listing of shares purposes, the *following preconditions* must be fulfilled by the Company :—

(i) The Company must have offered at least 49% of its shares to the public for subscription.

(ii) The Company should have a broad-based capital structure with a fair size of its working.

(iii) The Articles of Association of the Company must not allow any lien on the fully paid up shares.

(iv) No dividend rights shall be accorded to advance payments.

(v) The transfer of shares is not registered by the company except with a proper instrument of transfer as required under Companies Act, 1956.

After listing of shares by the Company, a mention to this effect be made in the Prospectus, giving the names of Stock Exchanges where the shares may be dealt with.

The Company Secretary should perform his duties in such a way so as to ensure proper formalities for listing of shares. The provisions of Companies Act, 1956 must also be complied with.

Underwriting of Shares

Underwriting is the process through which a Company makes it sure that whatever shares are issued to the public the same would be subscribed by the public or by the person, firm or Institution underwriting the capital issue. It is an agreement entered into by the Company wishing to issue shares and the financier (a person, firm or a Financial Institution) called the Underwriter in which the latter party gives an assurance for a sum of money paid by the former, called the under-writing commission, to the former that if the Share offered for subscription to the general public is not made fully or is made partly, the latter party would take up the full or part of the shares, It is a sort of *Guarantee given by a party to another for a consideration*.

In the modern days, commercial banks and specialised Financial Institutions perform this function in the money market

These include the State Bank of India, public sector Banks, Industrial Financial Corporations, State Financial Corporations, Life Insurance Corporation of India, General Insurance Companies and others. Most of the Public companies give the contract of underwriting to these Institutions, particularly when the new companies are incorporated. The Promoters of the Company have to make necessary arrangements for the underwriting of shares as an important aspect of their contribution for setting up the company.

The *procedure for underwriting* shares of the Company may briefly be outlined as under :—

(i) First of all, the Promoters have to contact any of the Underwriters, especially commercial banks or any of the Financial Institutions, whosoever, is more convenient and is agreeable for the same.

(ii) The copies of Prospectus, Memorandum and Articles of Association along with the business plans of the company or the Project Report so that the Underwriter may find out the financial soundness and the viability of the underwriting. Whatever other papers or documents are required for the purpose, the same may be submitted by the company through its Secretary.

(iii) When the Underwriter is satisfied with the position or prospectus, an *Underwritten Agreement* is entered into between Company and the Underwriter Institution on a stamp paper. Generally, such Agreements are in printed form available with the concerned financial Institution and the same is executed on the stamp paper of the requisite amount.

(iv) On execution of the Agreement. the concerned financial institution may arrange to pay the amount of shares underwritten or in the alternative, the financial institution, on behalf of the Company, invite the public for subscription to shares through publication in newspapers etc,, and afterwards whatever gap is left, the same is filed in by the underwriting Institution.

(v) It is also necessary for the Company to inform the Registrar of Companies about the underwriting arrangements and file a copy of the underwriting agreement with the Registrar.

Mostly the Companies have to make underwriting arrangements before the Prospectus is issued and the name of the Underwriting Bank or Institution is mentioned in the Prospectus. However, the underwriting arrangement can be made strictly in accordance with the rules provided in the Articles of Association.

Secretarial Participation

Under the stage of subscription of share capital, the Company Secretary should, generally, perform the following duties :—

(i) He should, first of all, finalise the underwriting arrangements and prepare the draft of the Agreement in consonance with the underwriters and execute the same.

(ii) He should prepare the draft of the Prospectus or Statement in lieu of Prospectus in consultation with the experts.

(iii) Convene the first meeting of the Board of Directors and pass the Resolution approving the Prospectus as well as underwriting arrangements as per the Provisions laid down under the Articles of Association.

In this meeting, the company secretary should also get confirmation of the appointment of Bankers, Auditors, Solicitors, Secretary and the Underwriters.

(iv) After getting the Prospectus printed, a copy of the same should be filed with the Registrar of Companies immediately.

(v) Listing of Shares on the Stock Exchange, the application should be made with the Stock Exchange Authorities alongwith the copies of Memorandum, Articles, Prospectus etc. The Listing Agreement should also be executed.

(vi) Make necessary arrangements for opening a current account with the Bank after passing the requisite Resolution in the first Board's Meeting and submitting necessary documents to the Bank for the purpose.

(vii) Arrange for printing of various forms, and stationery like share certificates, application forms. allotment forms, transfer forms and other registered for the purpose.

(viii) Getting the Prospectus or Statement in lieu of Prospectus published within 90 days of filing the Prospectus with the Registrar.

(ix) All or any of the arrangements for raising the share capital of the Company.

SHARE CAPITAL

Generally speaking, the term 'Share Capital' is used to refer that amount which has been collected by a Company by issuing various classes of 'Shares' (documents, in writing, issued by a Company under its Common Seal acknowledging receipt of money on account of capital of the company). In Company Law, the term 'Share Capital' is used in many senses. It may mean the actual capital raised by a Company at a particular time to meet its long-term requirements or it may mean the ultimate amount raised through shares issued by a Company. The actual meaning is taken depending upon the class of capital or the actual requirements of the Company.

Requirements of Capital :

A Company may require capital at different times for different purposes. Generally, the capital requirements may be divided into the following :—

Long-term : The Company may require funds for a longer period for purchase of fixed assets like Building, Machinery etc. We may call it Long-term or Block or Fixed Capital. The fixed assets are acquired for productive purposes and these remain in business for 5 years, 10 years or even longer.

Medium-term : The Company may require funds for a period of 3 to 5 years for payment of interest on debentures or even for redemption of debentures etc. This may be classified under medium term capital requirements. The Company may raise such funds by way of public deposits or issuing the debentures etc.

Short-term : The funds may be required for purchase of raw-materials, processing them and the day-to-day working like payment of wages, salaries, water and electric charges etc. We may call it short-term or working capital requirement. The period for which short-term capital is required is maximum one-year.

Classification of 'Share Capital'

The capital raised by a limited or registered Company by issuing 'Shares' may be classified under the following heads :—

(i) **Authorised or Nominal Share Capital** : It represents the maximum amount which can be raised by a Company through issuing the shares. This amount is mentioned in the capital clause of the Memorandum of Association, and is shown in Company's Balance Sheet as the first amount under 'Share Capital'.

(ii) **Issued Capital** : Out of the authorised share capital, whatever amount is offered to the public for subscription, is called the Issued Capital.

(iii) **Subscribed Capital** : Out of the amount of share capital offered by a company to the public, the amount which is actually subscribed or paid by the public by way of purchasing the shares of the company, is called the 'Subscribed Capital'. It may be *fully subscribed*, when the amount is fully paid by the public whatever is issued by the company. It may be *over-subscribed,* when the amount paid by the public is more than whatever offered by the company. In such cases, the Company may adopt *pro-rata* allotment of shares, i.e. allotting the shares in proportion to applications received vis-a-vis the shares offered for subscription. It may be *under-subscribed* also, when the actual amount received is less than that offered. Under the circumstances, the company may request the underwriter to make good the gap remaining.

(iv) **Called-up Capital** : It represents the portion of subscribed capital which has actually been called or demanded by the company at a particular period of time, e.g. on a share of Rs. 10 issued by the company Rs. 5 may be called on application, Rs. 4 on allotment and Rs 1 on final call. If the applications are only invited, then the called up capital will be counted at Rs. 5 per share.

(v) **Paid-up Capital** : Out of the amount called up by the company it is not necessary that all the amount is paid by public at a particular time. So the amount which is actually paid by the public comes under the paid-up capital. For example, out of 1000 shareholders, only 990 pay the allotment money on shares.

(vi) **Unpaid Capital** : The amount which has been called by the company but not paid by the public, comes under the category of 'Unpaid Calls' or 'Unpaid Capital'. Generally, the shareholders who make default in payment of calls made by the company, are served with a notice and thereafter the amount is forfeited, i.e. forcibly retained by the company.

(vii) **Uncalled Capital** : It is that proportion of subscribed capital which has not been demanded by a Company at a particular time. Like on a share of Rs. 10, only Rs. 6 have been called, than Rs. 4 per share would be treated as uncalled capital.

(viii) **Reserved Capital** : It represents that part of the called-up capital which a company decided not to call for the time being and keep some part in reserve to meet the contingencies at a future date. Such an amount is kept separate and may be utilised only in emergent cases or at the time of winding up of the company.

(ix) **Working or Current or Floating Capital** : That amount which is kept liquid or ready cash to meet the day-to-day requirements of the company, may be called the working capital. It may be kept as cash in hand or bank balances.

'SHARES' AND THEIR CALSSIFICATION

In the ordinary language, the shares refer to those units of Capital of the Company in which it is divided. These are of the fixed amount and specific in quantity so as to form the 'Share Capital' of the Company. According to *Section 2(46)* of the Companies Act, 1956, it is 'a share in the capital of a Company and includes stock except when a distinction between stock and shares is expressed or implied.' As such, a share is a part of capital of the company which entitles a person to become the member of a Company and gives him a right to specific part of the capital of the Company. It may be evidenced by a document or certificate issued by the Company under its common seal acknowledging receipt of money on account of Share Capital, called the '*Share Certificate*.' It bears a distinctive number, fixed amount and may be easily transferred from one person to another.

According to *Section 86* of the Companies Act, 1956, a Company limited by shares is allowed to issue only *two types of Shares* viz. (i) Preference Shares and (ii) Equity or Ordinary Shares. Earlier to the Act, the *Deferred Shares* were also issued by the Companies, which represented those shares whose payment was deferred or postponed throughout the life-time of the company. Such shares used to be held by the promoters or directors of the Company. But, now the companies cannot issue these types of shares except by private companies who are exempted from the purview of provisions laid down under the aforesaid section of the Companies Act.

Preference Shares

These are the shares which are given preference for payment of dividend by the Company over the other classess of shares. The rate of dividend is generally fixed on these shares. However, the holders of preference shares do not enjoy the voting power in the company. These may be sub-classified into the following classes.

Cumulative Preference Shares—On these types of shares, the dividend is accumulated over the years. If the company is not able to make payment of the dividend on preference share during a particular year, the dividend can be accummulated for the furture years when it may be paid out of the profits of the company. If the Company goes into liquidation, no arrears of dividend may be payable unless actually declared or the Articles of Association provide for the same.

Non-Cumulative Preference Shares—The dividend is paid only when there is sufficient profit earned by the company during a particular year and no dividend is paid when there is no profit residue for payment of the dividend. The dividend on such preference shares cannot be accummulated over the years.

Redeemable Preference Shares—The Preference Shares which may be refunded or paid back after a specified period of time, may be called Redeemable Preference Shares. Normally, the principal amount of shares is never paid by the Company on any share except on liquidation but these are exceptions to it. A Public Company may issue such type of shares under the Act subject to a certain limit and on the terms and conditions like the Articles of Association must permit for issuing such shares, the shares are fully paid up, those shall be redeemed only out of the profits remaining after payment of dividend and an equivalent sum for redemption shall be transferred out of the profits of the Company to the Capital Redemption Reserve A/c or the redemption may be made out of the share premium account.

Participating Preference Shares—These shares are held by the Promoters or Directors of the Company. Besides the fixed rate of dividend as paid on Preference Shares, the holders of these Shares can also get the share out of the surplus remaining after payment of the regular dividend but the principal amount of these shares is not refunded at all throughout the life-time of the Company.

Equity or Ordinary Shares

These are the shares on which the dividend is paid by the Company out of profits remaining after payment of dividend to preference shareholders. No preferential right is allowed but the dividend is paid as per the rate depending upon the availability of profit. It may be more than preference shareholders or may be less also. These are really risk-bearing shares. The holders of these shares also enjoy the voting power in the Company.* On the liquidation of the Company, the amount of these shares is payable after the payment to preference shareholders is already made.

However, *Section 88* of the Companies Act, 1856 lays down the provisions prohibiting issue of shares, other than preference shares, with disproportionate voting rights. This means that a Company cannot issue some Equity Shares which carry more rights to dividend, capital or otherwise, than other Equity Shares. If there are excessive voting rights, the same may be terminated by passing a Resolution in a company meeting.

Difference between 'Share' and 'Stock'

'Shares'	*'Stock'*
1. The shares are generally issued by a new Company to raise its capital.	1. Stocks cannot be issued by a new company but the existing Company can issue the stocks by re-conversion of fully-paid shares.
2. Shares may or may not be fully paid.	2. The stocks are always fully paid.
3. Shares are freely transferable in round numbers but not in small fractions.	3. The stocks are not freely transferable in small fractions but may be transferred in multiples.
4. The shares of fixed amount and all shares are of equal denomination.	4. Stocks may be of different denominations.
5. Shares are having the nominal value which is printed on the share certificate.	5. Stocks do not have the nominal value.
6. Shares have a distinctive number printed on the share certificate.	6. Stocks do not have any distinctive number.

Actually speaking, 'Stock' represents the aggregate value of fully-paid shares of a Company. It is consolidated to facilitate division of capital of the company into fractions of various denominations, otherwise for all practical purposes, the stocks represent

* According to Section 87(1) of the Companies Act, 1956, every holder of Equity Shares shall have a right to vote on every resolution relating to that share capital, placed before the Company.

parts or fractions of capital of the Company and similar to the 'Shares'.

Procedure for Issuing Shares

Briefly, the procedure for issuing shares by a public company may be outlined as under:—

(i) Before actually issuing the Shares, the Company has to take certain preliminary decisions as to the amount of share capital, number of shares, nature of shares, amount to be called in fractions, listing of shares at the Stock Exchange and underwriting arrangements etc.

(ii) The proportion of Equity and Preference Shares has to be fixed up in accordance with the provisions laid down under the Companies Act so that no disproportionate rights to equity shares may be granted. Under the rules, the ratio between Equity and Preference Shares should be at least 3:1.

(iii) The formalities for listing of shares at the Stock Exchange have to be completed, as explained earlier in this chapter.

(iv) Obtaining Approval of the Controller of Capital Issues which is obligatory on all companies as per the provisions of Capital Issues (Control) Act, 1947. A limit of Rs. 50 lakhs in 12 months is fixed for all public companies registered under the Companies Act, 1956. Beyond that, the companies are exempted for taking a prior permission of the Controller of Capital Issues, otherwise the prior approval has to be obtained by making an application to the Authorities of Capital Issues and furnishing necessary information as required by them for the purpose of giving a written permission for issuing share to the public. The application has to be submitted on the prescribed form available from the Office of the Controller of Capital Issues and submitted with a treasury challan for the amount of prescribed fees and it must be accompanied by a copy of Industrial Licence obtained by the Company for doing business, Project Report giving the details of project cost and other financial highlights, a copy of letter from the financial institution agreeing to finance the company, details of subscriptions made by promoters, directors and others, underwriting arrangements made by the Company, a Certificate signed by the Secretary and/or Director stating that the information furnished in the application is complete and correct to the best of his knowledge and belief and a Certificate from the Auditors of the Company that the information given in the application has been verified by him and is found correct and true.

(v) Applications for Shares should be received from the subscribers on the printed form attached to the Prospectus within the prescribed time either at the company's registered office or at the office of Company's Bankers appointed for the purpose. Every application should be complete in information and signed by the applicant. The remittance of application money should be made by a crossed draft or cash deposited into Company's Bank. All the applications, on receipt, have to be scrutinised at the Company and only those may be accepted which are correct and complete. Applications not received within the stipulated time may be rejected. Normally the Bankers of the Company handle all the share applications as per the instructions given to them by the Company. After closing the subscription lists, the Bankers send the applications to the Company and the amounts received by them are credited to the Company's Account with the Bank.

(vi) Afterwards, the allotment of shares is made to the applicants keeping in view the various provisions laid down under the Companies Act, 1956. That is the stage where the Company Secretary and the Directors of the Company have to take utmost care and exercise proper precautions, otherwise heavy penalties may be imposed under the Act.

ALLOTMENT OF SHARES

The terms 'Allotment' is used to define the act or process through which the shares of a company are entrusted or distributed to the persons who have applied for the purchase of shares of the company. It is a very important aspect of raising share capital of the company and it has to be valid after fulfilling the provisions of Companies Act. Any allotment which is made in contravention to the rules is an 'Irregular Allotment' and may be challenged in the Court of Law by the applicant of shares. Hence, it is necessary that the allotment should be made keeping in mind the pre-requisites and the restrictions imposed at law.

Pre-requisites of Allotment

In order of the fact that the allotment is validly made, the following pre-conditions must be fulfilled:—

(i) The minimum subscription of share as mentioned in the Prospectus of the Company, must have been received i.e. the minimum required share applications must have been received by the Company.

(ii) A copy of the Prospectus or Statement in lieu of Prospectus must have been filed with the Registrar of Companies.

(iii) At least 5% of the nominal value of shares must have been received in cash on the applications for shares.

(iv) In case of a new Company, the money received on applications must have been deposited with any scheduled commerical bank and the same must be kept there until a certificate of commencement of business is obtained.

(v) A minimum time gap of four days must have been given between the date of issue of Prospectus and the allotment.

(vi) Within a period of at least four weeks of the close of subscription, the application for obtaining permission from the Stock Exchange to deal in shares must have been received. Such applications should have been made within 10 days of the issue of Prospectus.

The above conditions have been laid down under *Sections 69 and 70* of the Companies Act, 1956. It is further provided that if the aforesaid conditions are not satisfied within a period of 120 days of the first Issue of Prospectus, all moneys received on application must be refunded to the applicants without any interest. If the application money is not refunded within 130 days of the date of issue of the Prospectus, the Company Directors shall be liable to repay the money with interest at the rate of six per cent per annum.

Procedure for Allotment of Shares

On fulfilling the conditions of Company Law, the following

steps should generally be taken in respect of the allotment of shares:–

(i) If the number of applications received are the same or is less than shares for which the Prospectus was issued, then there is no problem because the directors may allot the same number of shares as applied for. If the Issue has been over-subscribed, the directors of the company may follow either the Chit or Lottery system or adopt the Pro-rata system in which the shares are allotted in proportion to the issued and the applied for. For example, if the Company has invited applications for 10,000 equity shares for which 15,000 applications are received, then the directors may allot 10 shares to a person who has applied for 15 shares. The exact system will depend upon what has been approved by the Board of Directors in the meeting.

(ii) A Resolution is passed at the meeting of Board of Directors of the Company confirming the allotment of shares and authorising the Company Secretary to issue Letter of Allotment to share-allottees and a 'Letter of Regret' to persons/applicants whom shares could not be allotted.

A Specimen of Resolution is given below:—

"Resolved that 10,000 Equity Shares of Rs. 100 each, numbering 0001 to 10000 (both inclusive) be and hereby allotted to the parties in proportion of 15 : 10 amongst the total number of share applications received by the Company. Further resolved that the Secretary be and hereby directed to issue forthwith the letters of allotment and the letters of regret to the concerned applicants of shares."

(iii) The Letters of Allotment are got prepared and communicated to the allottees signed by the Secretary. If no share has been allotted to any applicant, then a letter of regret has to be sent invariably. However, before issuing the Letter of Allotment, it must be ensured that in the application form the clause of consent of the applicant that he is agreeable to accept any number of shares as allotted by the Company, is duly signed by the applicant because allotment is a lawful contract made between the applicant and the Company and, hence, it should be complete and intact in all respects.

(iv) The excess money, if any, received on application, should afterwards be adjusted towards share allotment money after transferring the amount lying in Shares Application Account to Share Capital Account.

Secretarial Participation

As a Company Secretary, one should ensure that the abovesaid procedure has to be adopted and necessary conditions laid down for allotment of shares have been satisfied. The Secretary should also know the drafting of letters of allotment or regret for \ddressing to the respective applicant and arrange to get them printed, issued, signed and communicated immediately. The Secretary should also get the necessary Resolution passed in the Board Meeting file a copy with the Registrar.

Right Share

Wherever a Company wishes to increase its subscribed capital by isssue of fresh shares, as additional shares, in the existing Share Capital, it may be done by issuing the Shares to the existing Shareholders as they have the right to purchase such Shares. Such Shares are called the 'Right Shares'.

Section 81 of the Companies Act. 1956 deals with 'Right Shares' and it stipulates that where a public company decides to increase its subscribed capital by the issue of additional shares at any time after the expiry of two years of formation or of one year of the first allotment of Shares, whichever is earlier, such shares must be offered to the existing shareholders of the Company in proportion to the paid-up capital on those shares. If the offer is declined by the existing shareholders, then those shares may be offered to the public for subscription. For this purpose, the Company must first give a notice to the existing shareholders giving them a stipulated period within which they may accept the offer otherwise the Company would offer them to the others. The notice may contain 15 days period at the most. However, in case the existing shareholders accept the offer of 'Right Shares', the same must be allotted in proportion to the existing shareholding by each of the existing shareholders vis-a-vis the number of additional shares offered. The Right Shares may also be issued in fraction and a '*Fractional Share Certificate*' may be issued.

Under the Companies Act, the facility of renouncing the Right Shares is also provided to the shareholder. The *right of renunciation* consists of leaving the shares for oneself, rather giving the shares to others. That means, not exercising the right to take shares for which the shareholder is entitled to take but forgoing the right in favour of others.

However, the provisions regarding Right Shares shall be applicable only when the Articles of Association provides for it and a special Resolution is passed in the Company Meeting. The provisions also do not apply to private companies and to further offer of shares by the Company. A permission of the Central Government is also required to be obtained, after making an application on the prescribed proforma.

The Procedure for Issue of Right Shares must be followed by the Company Secretary and he must ensure that the Right Shares are well within the limit of Authorised Capital of the Company and a resolution is passed in the Board Meeting before moving the matter for permission from the Controller of Capital Issues (if the new issue involves capital of more than Rs. 50 lakhs limit). Thereafter the Resolution is to be passed at the General Meeting of the Shareholders. Proper notice has to be given to the existing shareholders for accepting the Right Shares. Thereafter the work of issuing share certificates has to be carried out by the Company Secretary.

Shares at a Premium

A Public Company may issue the shares to the public at a premium i.e. at a price higher than the face value of the shares. This can be done when there is huge demand of Company's shares in the market. The amount of premium may be realised on application of shares or an allotment on together with any of the share calls. The provisions for issuing the shares at a premium have been laid down under *Section 78* of the Companies Act, 1956. According to the provisions, the Shares at a premium may be issued and the premium amount must be credited to a separate account called the 'Share Premium Account' and the amount lying therein must be utilised for the following purposes:—

(i) Writing off the Preliminary Expenses ;

(ii) Writing off the discount allowed on any shares or debentures of the commission paid on shares ;

(iii) Allowing premium on redemption of shares or debentures;
(iv) Issuing Bonus Shares.

However, the Articles of Association of the Company must also contain a provision to this effect and a prior formal permission of the Registrar of Company may be obtained by the Company but the utilisation of premium amount has to be done strictly in accordance with the provisions laid down under the Act.

Shares at a Discount

Section 79 of the Companies Act, 1956 provides for issuing the shares at a discount i.e. at a price lower than the face value of share. But, for doing so, the following conditions, as laid down under the Act, must be fulfilled:—

(i) The issue of shares at a discount is duly sanctioned by the Company Law Board;
(ii) The shares at a discount are issued within a period of two months from the date of sanction of the Company Law Board ;
(iii) A Resolution to this effect is passed at the general meeting of the Company, stipulating the maximum rate of discount and the other terms on which the shares may be issued ;
(iv) A period of at least one year has elapsed from the date of commencement of business of the Company and the date of issue of shares at a discount ;
(v) The rate discount does not exceed 10% unless a special permission for a higher rate of discount is obtained from the company Law Board;
(vi) The Company must include the details of discount allowed on issue of shares in the Prospectus.
(vii) The share must be of the class already issued.

If any default is made in complying with the above rules, every defaulting company officer shall be liable to a fine upto Rs. 50.

Bonus Shares

These are special classes of Shares which a Company may issue out of the amount of premium received under those circumstances when the Company has ample surplus funds remaining after distribution of dividends to reference and equity shareholders.

Sometimes the Company does not pay excessive dividend on shares rather issues the Bonus Shares to the existing shareholders. The Bonus Shares may also be issued to the employees or directors of the Company.

The Company Law permits the Companies to issue Bonus Shares by following the prescribed procedure. For issuing the Bonus Shares, the Board Meeting has to be convened and a special Resolution has to be passed at the general meeting of Company's Shareholders. After the Special Resolution, the Company Secretary has to prepare a list of members entitled to receive the Bonus Shares. The Transfer Books are closed for some time. The list is then placed before the Board of Directors in the meeting for their approval. Thereafter the Bonus Shares are allotted by sending a circular explaining how and on what basis the allotment of Bonus Shares is made. Then the letters of allotment are issued by the Company Secretary.

However, it must be ensured that the Company's Articles of Association must provide for issuing the Bonus Shares and prior permission of the Registrar of Companies is obtained for the purpose.

Register of Members

Under the Companies Act, 1956, a member is any person who has subscribed to the Memorandum of Association of a Company or any other person who has agreed, in writing, to become the member of the Company and whose name appears in the Register of Members of the Company.

According to the provisions laid down under *Sections 150* of the Companies Act, 1956, every company has to maintain a Register of Members containing the name, address, occupation of each member ; number and class of shares held by each member; distinctive number of shares and the amount of shares held; date of ceasing of membership and the details of conversion of shares into stocks, etc. The name of a Trustee need not be entered into the Register of Members, but *Benami* share-holdings must be entered into the Register.

Generally, the Register of Members is kept as a Bound Book and names of shareholders are arranged alphabetically. An Index of Members is also provided. The rules require that the Register must be uptodate all the time and has to be kept at the Registered Office of the Company and it must remain open for inspection by any member during the working hours without charging any fees.

The Register of Members has to remain closed before the Annual General Meeting of the Company or when a call on shares is to be made or an interim dividend on shares is to be declared or it may be closed after giving 7 days notice in press.

During the period of closure of the Register of Members, no transfer of Shares or change of membership can take place.

In not complying with the above provisions of law, or as laid down under *Section 154* of the Act the Company and every officer of the Company, in default, shall be liable to a fine upto Rs. 500 per day during which the default continues.

Share Certificates

A Share Certificate is a document in writing issued by a Company under its, Common Seal certifying the number of shares and the amount of shares paid by each of the shareholders. It is in the form of a printed document and forms an evidence of entitlement of shares by a shareholder. The Share Certificate is issued after the allotment of shares is made by the Company and every shareholder is entitled to receive the share certificate. The Companies Act, 1956, provides that the share certificates should be prepared and issued to each of the shresholder within a period of 3 months from the date of allotment of shares or within 2 months of transfer of shares in favour of a particular shareholder. The Share Certificates must be issued accordingly.

SPECIMEN OF A SHARE CERTIFICATE

A.B.C. COMPANY LTD.

(Regd. Office : 1/1, Asaf Ali Road, New Delhi-110002)

This is to certify that the person/(s) named hereinbelow is/are the register holder(s) of the within mentioned Share(s) bearing the distinctive number(s) herein specified in the above Company, and that the amount endorsed herein has been paid up on each such share.

Shares, each of Rs. 100

Amount paid per share Rs............

Calls paid Rs.........on..................and No. 1.................(Date)

Regd. Folio No.................. Certificate No...

Name (s) of Holder(s)................

No. of Shares held.........................

Distinctive Number (s)................ To................

Given under the Common Seal of the Company this......day of.................1987.

Revenue Stamp	Common Seal of the Co.	Sd/- Director	Sd/- Director	For A.B.C. Co. Ltd. Sd/- Secretary

---

Though the Company Act does not specify any form of a Share Certificate, still the Share Certificate must contain the name of the Shareholder, number and amount of shares held and paid up, distinctive numbers etc. The form and contents of the share certificate are usually given in the Memorandum and Articles of Association of the Company. Normally the Company prepares the share certificate in that form and deliver to the registered shareholders.

The Shareholder is required to keep the Share Certificate safe with him all the time. In case, it is lost, defaced, mutilated or torn, then the Act provides for issuance of a duplicate share certificate in place of the original one. *Section 84* of the Companies Act, 1956 provides that a Share Certificate may be renewed of a duplicate certificate may be issued if the original Share Certificate is proved to have been lost or destroyed or if it is mutilated, defaced or torn and surrendered to the Company. Briefly, the procedure is that when the Share Certificate is defaced, mutilated or torn, the shareholder may surrender the same to the Company and a duplicate certificate may be issued in place thereof. It the original certificate is destroyed or lost, then the shareholder shall have to produce a statutory declaration on a stamp paper stating the fact that the original certificate has been lost or misplaced and requesting for issuance of a duplicate one. A letter of Indemnity and/or a Bank Guarantee may have to be furnished in favour of the Company for the purpose. The Company may give a Public Notice informing the general public of the loss of Share Certificate and afterwards the duplicate Share Certificate may be issued, on payment of Rs. 2 for the duplicate certificate.

However, for issuing the Share Certificates or the duplicate ones, a resolution in the Board Meeting has to be passed. Those must be duly signed, sealed under Company's Common Seal and entered in the Register of Members before actually delivering them to the holders. One member is issued only one Certificate for all the shares held by him.

Secretarial Practice

In respect of the Share Certificates, the duties of a Company Secretary may be outlined as under :—

(i) To arrange for printing of Share Certificates and keep them in safe custody under the Authority or Board of Directors.

(ii) To get the Register of Members prepared on the basis of allotment of shares to members as per the resolution passed by the Board of Directors.

(iii) To get the particulars written in the main certificate form as well as the counterfoil and check them.

(iv) To get the Resolution passed at the Board Meeting for signatures of Directors and affixing the Common Seal of the Company. He should countersign all the share certificates before taking the signatures of the Directors of the Company.

(v) To arrange to issue a notice to all the shareholders informing them that the share certificates are ready for delivery and requesting them to collect the same on production of allotment letters.

(vi) To ensure that duplicate share certificates are issued only after completion of formalities.

Share Warrants

A 'Share Warrant' is a document, issued by a Company under its Common Seal, stating therein that the bearer of the document is entitled to receive the number of shares mentioned and also the dividend declared on shares. In other words, Share Warrants are a sort of Coupons against which the shares of the company may be delivered to any person holding them. These are like negotiable instruments such as a bearer cheque, transferable by mere delivery.

Sections 114 and 115 of the Companies Act, 1956 provide that a public company limited by shares may issue share warrants in respect of the fully paid up shares subject to the conditions that it is authorised by its Articles of Association to do so and the permission of the Central Government is obtained prior to the issue of share warrants, the name of the member is struck off from the Register of Members and instead, the date of issue of share warrant is mentioned there, distinctive numbers of shares are mentioned in the share warrant and the bearer of the share warrant may be treated as a member of the company for all purposes defined in the Articles of Association.

SPECIMEN OF A SHARE WARRANT

A.B.C. COMPANY LTD.

(Incorporated under the Companies Act, 1956)

Regd. Office :.........

Share Warrant No. ....

This is to certify that the bearer of this Share Warrant is the Proprietor of............Shares fully paid-up of Rs.............. each, distinctively numbered from...........To..............(both inclusive), in this Company, subject to the Articles of Association of the Company.

Given under the Common Seal of the Co. on this day of.........1987.

Sd/- Sd/- Sd/-
Director Director Secretary

SEAL

....

No.........
The A.B.C. Co. Ltd.
(Regd office———)
Dividend Coupon

On Shares included in the Share Warrant numbered as above, payable according to advertisement to be released of the company.

Rs......... Sd-

....

The *procedure* for issuing the Share Warrants is that first of all, the applications are invited by the Company from the shareholders of the company who wish to convert their share certificates into warrants. The application has to be submitted on the prescribed printed form and must be accompanied with the share certificates as well as the necessary fees as per the rules of the Company. The application also carries the stamp duty. On receipt of the application, if the Company Secretary finds everything in order, he may send a '*Lodgment Ticket*' to the shareholder to acknowledge receipt of the documents. Afterwards the printed Share Warrant Forms are filled up and kept ready for signatures of one or more Directors and affixing the Common Seal of the Company thereon. Necessary

Resolution may also be passed at the Board Meeting for the purpose. At the end, Share Warrants are delivered against Lodgment Tickets.

Alongwith the Share warrants, the forms of '*dividend coupons*' are also printed. Whenever, the Company declares the dividend, it may advise the share warrant holders to present the dividend coupons to Company's Bankers for payment of the dividend. These dividend coupons are different than the 'dividend warrants' in as much as that for the dividend coupons the Bank has to make a thorough scrutiny and issue a cheque or cash there against whereas a dividend warrant itself is in the form of a cheque and is paid directly by the Bank.

The bearer of the Share Warrant may also get it converted into a Share Certificate by surrendering the share Warrant to the Company and his name may be re-entered in the Register of Members. If the Share Warrant is lost or misplaced, a duplicate in lieu there of may be got issued on payment of requisite fee and executing the indemnity bond or furnishing a bank guarantee. The Company may give a public notice and afterwards issue the duplicate Share Warrant. Since the Share Warrant is like any other negotiable instrument payable to bearer, proper precautions are required to be taken.

Difference between Share Certificate and a Share Warrant

The aforesaid two documents may be distinguished on the following points :—

Share Certificate	*Share Warrant*
1. It can be issued by the Public as well as Private Companies.	1. It can be issued by the public company limited by shares only.
2. Prior approval of the Central Government is not required for issuing the Share certificates.	2. Prior Approval of the Central Government is required for issuing Share Warrants.
3. Share Certificate may be issued for partly paid up shares.	3. Share Warrants are issued for fully paid-up shares.
4. A Share Certificate may be transferred in favour of other person by a separate Transfer Deed and its registration with the Co.	4. It may be transferred to any other person by a mere delivery.

5. The holder of Share Certificate is a registered member of the Co. as his name is recorded in the Register of Members with the Co.	5. The holder of Share Warrant is not the member of the Company as his name is struck off as soon as the S.W. is issued.
6. For payment of dividend on a share certificate, a separate dividend warrant is issued.	6. For payment of dividend on a Share Warrant, the dividend coupon is attached to the Warrant.
7. It involves nominal stamp duty.	7. It involves heavy stamp duty.
8. It is not a Negotiable Instrument as it does not have any power of negotiation but only a marketable title to the owner.	8. It is treated as Negotiable Instrument payable to bearer.
9. Share Certificates may be issued for qualification shares to Directors or Promoters.	9. No Share Warrant can be issued in respect of the Qualification Shares.

Annual Return

Sections 159 to 162 of the Companies Act, 1956 lay down that every public company must prepare and file with the Registrar of Companies a Return containing the particulars regarding the Registered Office of the Company, Register of Members and Debenture-holders (past and present), its Directors and Managing Director etc. Such a Return may be called the 'Annual Return' and the same must be filed within a period of 60 days from the close of the year of the Company, duly signed by a Director, Managing Director or Secretary of the Company.

In case the detailed particulars, as mentioned above, have been given in the two preceeding Annual Returns, the present Annual Return may contain only the changes incorporated in the particulars.

Where the Annual General Meeting is not held, a return as required under the above sections of the Act, has got to be filed with the Registrar of Companies within sixty days of the date on which the Annual General Meeting was to be held. Such a Return must also contain a statement of reasons as to why the A.G.M. was not held.

As per the provisions laid down under *Section 220* of the Act, a copy of the latest Balance Sheet and profit & Loss Account of the Company must also be filed with the Annual Return.

MAKING CALLS ON SHARES

After allotment of Shares, a public Company may make the first, second and final calls on the shares- Since the full face value of shares is recovered in various instalments like some amount on application, some on allotment, some at first call and the rest of the amount may be called as the second and final call on shares, it is necessary to make the call as per the provisions laid down under the Companies Act, 1956.

A 'Call on Shares' may be defined as the money demanded by the Company from the sharesholder as a part payment of the face value of the 'Share' or the balance amount due after allotment of share. In other words, a call may be defined as the instalment due and payable by the shareholders of a Company.

Generally, the rules regarding calls on shares are given in the Articles of Association and the Prospectus issued by the Company or the provisions laid down under the Companies Act, 1956. *Section 91* provides that a call on share must be made on a uniform basis on all the shares falling under the same class. It means that no discrimination should be made between the same class of shareholders for the purpose of making the calls. Under *Section 220* only the Board of Directors are empowered to make calls on shares. Similarly, Table, 'A' as given in the regulation 13 to 18 apply to making the calls on shares. Overall, the general provisions in this respect are as under:—

(i) At least 14 days notice is required to be given to the members for each call made on share.

(ii) In between the two calls, at least a gap of one month must be given.

(iii) Not more thn 25% of the face value of a 'share' can be called-up at a time.

(iv) The Board of Directors are empowered to make a call through the Resolution and /or postpone one revoke the call already made.

(v) In case of joint holders of a share, each one of them is jointly and severally liable to pay the call money.

(vi) If any member wishes to pay the money at call in advance, the Directors may accept the advance money and may pay interest at the prescribed rate on such money received in advance.

(vii) If any member fails to pay the call money within the stipulated time, he is liable to pay interest at the rate of 5% p.a. or any lower rate of interest as provided in the Articles of Association or as sanctioned by the Board of Directors.

(viii) If any member fails to pay the call money due to him, he will not have the voting power till such time he pays the money.

I Practice, either the Company may frame its own rules well within the ambit of the Companies Act or those given in 'Table A' of the second schedule given in the Act. It should be ensured that none of the provisions should be contravened.

Procedure and Secretarial Participation

For the purpose of making the Calls on Shares, the Company Secrctary has to take the following *steps*—

(i) Convening the meeting of the Board of Directors and passing the Resolution sepecifying the amount called and the date by which the 'Call' should be made.

SPECIMEN OF RESOLUTION

"Resolved that the first call of Rs. 5 per Share on 1,00,000 Equity Shares of Rs. 10 each be and hereby made on the members of the Company and that the same be made payable on or before the 31st day of August, 1987 at State Bank of India, the Bankers of the Company, and that all the calls unpaid by that date shall bear interest at the rate of, . .per cent per annum from the date mentioned here in above until payment.

Further resolved that the Secretary be and hereby authorised to take necessary steps in the matter."

With the passing of the aforesaid Resolution, the work of making the share calls would commence and the Company Secretary would take further steps in the matter.

(ii) Closing the Transfer Books of the Company for the period till the work of calls is completed.

(iii) Preparing the *'Call Lists'* in which the names, addresses, number of shares held by each member, call due, amount paid in advance, if any and the balance amount due, to each member-all these details are given.

(iv) Issuing the *'Call Notice'* or 'Call Letter' after the list is ready to all such members from whom call money is due. It may also be published in the newspapers simultaneously for the information of the members. In this, all the details of proposed call i.e. the amount called, number of shares, the date by which payment must be received etc., are given.

(v) Receiving the money by Company's Bankers is completed within the stipulated period. The Bankers send the copy of call slips to the Company on the basis of which a comparison is made with the Call List. The money received by the Bankers is credited to a special account opened for the purpose.

(vi) Notices are issued to the defaulting members who have not paid the call money within the stipulated period and the amount of interest chargeable on such amounts is also specified.

Calls Paid in Advance

Any member or Shareholder of the Company may pay the amount of call due on shares in advance i.e. earlier than the call made by the Company. Many people may them pay the entire face value of the shares purchased by them either on share application or on allotment as they do not wait the Company to demand further money from them. Such amounts received by the Company, are called 'Calls in Advance'. Any Public Company may receive the money on calls in advance as per the provisions made in Companies Act and also the rules laid down under the Articles of Association of the Company.

The money so received in advance for the call on shares may be adjusted for further calls towards the share capital. But, under any circumstance, such a money cannot be refunded by the Company, unless the Company is wound up.

However, the Company may pay interest on such moneys received in advance provided it is authorised by the Articles of Association of the Company. The rate of interest so paid shall not exceed 6 per cent per annum provided any higher rate of interest is sanctioned at the general meeting of the Company.

Calls in Arrears

When any of the member commits default in making payment of the call money due on shares. it may be called as 'Call in Arrear'. Whenever the call money is in arrear, a list of the defaulting members is prepared and placed before the Board of Directors in their meeting. Upon this, the Board of Directors may take further action into the matter either by ordering for issue of Reminder Notices to the defaulting members, calling upon them to pay the call due within a specified period, with or without interest, or adjusting the amount from the dividends payable on shares or proceeding against the defaulting members legally for recovery of money or giving the notice of warning that if the amount is not paid within a particular period of time, the directors may forfeit such amount as already paid by the defaulting member.

As per the decision taken at the Board meeting, the Company Secretary may proceed for further action in the matter.

Forfeiture of Shares

Whenever any Shareholder of the Company fails to pay the call money, as demanded by the Company, despite a notice to this effect, then the Company has the power to forfeit or retaining forcibly the amount already paid by such a Shareholder and we call it a 'Forfeiture of Shares'. Generally, a 14 days notice is served on the defaulting member asking him to pay the call money within a stipulated period. Despite it, if the money is not received, the Company may keep the already paid amount by such a defaulter member separately in a special account called the 'Forfeiture Account'. For example, if a Company has issued equity shares of the value of Rs. 10 and has taken Rs. 5 on application, Rs. 2 on allotment and Rs. 4 in two calls of Rs. 2 each. Now, if any member has paid Rs. 5 and Rs.2 per share but makes a default in making payment of calls each of Rs. 2, then the Company may forefeit the amount of Rs. 7 already paid by the defaulting member.

However, the forfeiture can only be made when the Articles of Association of the Company authorise them to do so or the provisions laid down in Table 'A' of the Companies Act are to be followed.

The legal procedure for forfeiture of shares is that first of all a reminder notice has to be served upon the defaulting member to pay the money within a stipulated period with or without interest, as per the resolution passed by the Board of Directors in their meeting.

If the money is still not received, a 14 days' Notice has to be served intimating the member that in case the money is still not received, the amount already paid by him on the shares held by him, will be forfeited. After expiry of the reasonable time from the last date of notice, a list of defaulters is prepared by the Secretary and placed before the Board of Directors in their meeting for necessary approval. Afterwards, the amount is forfeited and placed in a separate account. The necessary Resolution is passed at the meeting of the Board of Directors of the Company.

SPECIMEN OF RESOLUTION

"*Resolved* that 2 Equity Shares of Rs.10 each bearing distinctive numbers from...to...(both inclusive) on which Rs. 7 per Share having been paid and which were standing in the name of Mr.........of Delhi. be and hereby forfeited for non-payment of call money of Rs. 3/- per share having Call been made on......and for non-payment of interest thereon and that the said too shares be and hereby disposed of."

"Further Resolved that the name of Mr......who made default in payment of call on the aforesaid shares be removed from the Register of Members and that the said share certificate be and hereby got surrendered and cancelled. Any member whose shares have been forfeited by the company ceases to be the member of the Company but will still remain liable to pay the amount of unpaid calls unless the Company receives the full amount of shares. He also loses his claim for the paid up amount.

Re-issue of Forfeited Shares

The shares forfeited by a Company may be cancelled or re-issued to any other person at the discretion of the Board of Directors of the Company. Generally such shares are sold at a discount but the amount of discount should not exceed the amount already paid by the defaulter member on those shares. The re-issue of forfeited shares is also passed in the form of Resolution at the meeting of the the Board of Directors. The specimen of Resolution is given below :—

> "Resolved that .2 Shares of Rs. 10. each Rs. 7 already paid-up per share having been duly forfeited by a Board Resolution dated...bearing distinctive numbers from...to... be and hereby re-issued as fully paid-up to Mr.........of Delhi on his paying

Rs. 12 per share and such shares be and hereby passed for registration and that the share certificate for these Shares be signed and sealcd."

After the aforesaid Resolution, the forfeited shares may be re-issued to the other person on receiving the actual amount. The Share Certificate for the re-issue of forfeited shares can be issued only when the defaulted member has surrendered the earlier share certificate. If he fails to surrender the same, a public notice may be given and thereafter the share certificate for the forfeited shares may be cancelled.

The Company Secretary should, however, follow the procedure strictly in accordance with the legal provisions of the companies Act. If there is any lacuna in the procedure, the Company Secretary may be held liable for any default. Amongst the duties of the Company Secretary also include preparing the list of defaulter members, placing the same before the Board of Directors in their meeting, convening the meeting, drafting the necessary Resolutions, giving public notices or issuing the notice to the defaulter member etc.

Cancellation of Forfeitured Shares (or Reannulment)

The shares forfeited by a company may again be restored to the person from whom those have been taken forcibly for non-payment of the call money. We may call this process as 'Reannulment' or cancellation of forfeiture. When the shares are forfeited, the name of the member is struck off from the Register of Members but when it is restored on the defaulter member's paying the full amount due with interest, the name in the Register of Members is again written. However, the reannulment is done only when the defaulter member agrees to pay immediately the entire amount which was due to him in cash with interest as the Board or Directors may decide. A Resolution to this effect is also passed at the meeting of the Board of Directors, specifying the details of shares to be reannulled.

Surrender of Shares

By Surrender of Shares, we mean relinquishing the shares voluntarily by the shareholder on account of non-payment of the call money. Sometimes, the share-holder is not in a position to pay the call money to the Company and may call on the Company to pay the amount back (whatever he has already paid on the share) without waiting for the Company to commence the proceedings of forfeiture of shares. It is possible only when the Articles of Association of the Company permit to do so. Generally the provisions are made to this effect. On surrender of shares the Company may not refund the entire amount already paid by the shareholder but little less than that after deducting the amount of interest on the default amount plus other charges, if any. The name of the shareholder surrendering the share, may also be struck off from the Register of Members by cancelling the membership. The Company may also exempt the shareholder of the liability of the unpaid amount.

There is a *difference between the Forefeiture and Surrender* of Shares, based on the following points :—

Forfeiture	*Surrender*
1. It is a forced act on the part of the Company, when the shareholder makes a default in payment of any money on shares.	1. It is a voluntary act on the part of the Share-holder and not the Company.
2. The forfeiture takes place after giving a due notice to the Shareholder.	2. No notice is required in respect of surrender of shares.
3. The liability of the defaulter member on the shares for unpaid money always remains.	3. The liability comes to an end as soon as the shares are surrendered.
4. The forfeited shares are generally re-sold to others.	4. The surrendered shares may be cancelled or re-issued.
5. The money is not refunded on forfeited shares.	5. The money may be refunded on the surrendered shares.

Lien on Shares :

"Lien' is a form of creating charge on the securities and it may be defined as the right to retain the property belonging to others till such time when the claims of the person possessing the property is fully met. A Company limited by shares can also exercise the right of lien on the shares held by it on which the memebers are liable to pay their debts to the Company. The provisions are made in the Articles of Association in respect of exercising the right of Lien by the Company. 'Lien' is a technical word defined in the Indian

Contract Act, 1872 and used in respect of the security against a debt. In case of a Company, the rights of exercising lien on company's own shares are provided under the Articles of Association. If the debt is not repaid, the Company may be empowered to dispose of or sell the shares on which lien is kept by giving requisite notice to the debtor. In respect of the Issue of Shares, a Company may withhold the share certificates until all the moneys due by way of calls are not paid by the member or shareholder. The right of lien may also be exercised on the dividends payable on shares of the Company. Thus, a Company may exercise the right of lien not only on the fully paid up shares but also on partly paid shares in exceptional circumstances.

'Lien' and 'Forfeiture' may be distinguished on the following points :

Lien	*Forfeiture*
1. The Company may exercise the right of lien in respect of the debts due and unpaid calls.	1. Forfeiture may be done only in respect of those on which the calls are unpaid.
2. Lien is a form of creating charge on property kept as security against the debt.	2. Forfeiture is a form of penalty given by the Company for making a default in payment of calls on shares.
3. Lien does not deprive a member of his membership.	3. Forfeiture deprives a member of his membership.
4. In case of lien, if the property or shares are sold, then the balance remaining cut of proceeds after selling the debt is refunded.	4. There is no such thing in respect of the Forfeiture.
5. Lien does not result in reduction of capital of the Company in any way.	5. Forfeiture may result in reduction of capital if the forfeited shares are cancelled or not re-issued.
6. Lien is used in respect of security against the advance.	6. Forfeiture is not used in respect of any other security other than Company's own shares.

However, in both the cases, the shares may be sold or reissued in the same manner. If the debt is not paid back, the lien may be exercised and if the Calls on Shares are unpaid, forfeiture may be exercised by the Company.

TRANSFER AND TRANSMISSION OF SHARES

One of the special features of the 'Shares' of the Public Company is that the ownership is transferable from one person to another by negotiation and delivery. Although the shares of a Private Company cannot be freely transferred, yet the shares issued by a Public Company may be transferred from one person to another.

Section 82 of the Companies Act, 1956 stipulates that the shares or interests of any member in a Company shall be movable property, transferable in the manner prescribed in the Articles of Association of the Company. The Articles of Association may impose certain restrictions on the transfer of shares despite the fact that the Companies Act treats the 'Shares' as any other movable property.

In practice, the shares of a Company are transferred by executing a Transfer Deed executed by the holder of shares and the same is registered in the Books of the Company. However, the important provisions of the Company Law in respect of transfer of shares are given hereunder :—

(i) A Company cannot register the transfer of shares in its Book until a Transfer Deed on the requisite stamp paper is executed by the transferor and the actual share certificates together with the Transfer Deed are delivered.

(ii) The application for transfer of shares may either be given by the transferor or transferee but the company shall not register the transfer of partly paid up shares if the transferor gives an application without the consent of the transferee.

(iii) In respect of the deceased member, the application for transfer given by the legal representative shall be valid.

(iv) The Directors of the Company are empowered to refuse registration of transfer of any of the shares but they shall have to give a notice, in writing, of their intention to this effect to the persons concerned.

(v) Whenever a request for transfer of shares is made, the necessary transfer forms must be duly completed and delivery should be made within a period of two months from the date of request application.

Reasons for Refusing Registration of Transfer :

The following may be the reasons for the Board of Directors

refusing to register the transfer of Shares :—

(i) When any call on shares is unpaid and has become overdue for payment ;

(ii) When the transferor is a debtor of the company and the Company has kept a lien on shares to be transferred.

(iii) When the shares are partly paid up and are being transferred in the name of a minor who is incapable of making any contract.

(iv) When the shares are partly paid-up and are being transferred to a person whose financial position is considered to be so weak that he might be incapable for further calls on shares.

(v) When the Deed of Transfer is defective, incomplete or irregular.

(vi) When the Board of Directors feels that the transfer is not in general interest of the Company.

Appeal Against Refusal :

When the Board of Directors of a Public Company refuse to register any transfer of shares for any of the reasons whatsoever, the aggrieved party i.e. the transferor or the transferee has a right to appeal against such refusal. The provision has been made under *Section 111* of the Companies Act, 1956. According to that the Appeal shall lie with the Central Government and it should be made on the prescribed form and the required fees shall also have to be deposited for the purpose of hearing the Appeal.

On receipt of the Appeal, the Central Government may serve notices to the Company and other parties and give them the reasonable opportunity or hearing to explain and thereafter pass orders as deemed fit, and the orders shall be binding on the Company.

However, the Appeal shall be filed within two months of the date of refusing the transfer.

Restrictions on Transfer of Shares :

However, there are certain restrictions imposed by the Government on transfer of shares by the Public Company and, in the following, cases, a prior approval of the Central Government may be required :—

(i) When the amount of shares to be purchased from a publlc

company exceeds 25% of the total paid-up equity share capital of the Company ;

(ii) Where the Central Government, by a special Order, has put restrictions on transfer of specific companies ;

(iii) Where a company or companies under the same management, hold 10% of more of the subscribed capital of any other Company ;

(iv) Where a Company holds 10% or more of the nominal value of the equity share capital of a foreign company having business in India shall not transfer any share to any citizen of India or any other person without prior approval of the Central Government.

(v) Where the Central Government feels that transfer of any share will be prejudicial to the public interest or controlling power of the Company or may lead to concentration of economic power.

Procedure for Transfer

The following steps are generally taken for effecting transfer of Shares and a Company Secretary must adhere to them :—

(i) A Transfer Deed on the prescribed form has to be submitted to the Registrar of Companies after preparing or filing in the particulars in the from, obtaining signatures of transferor, affixing stamp duty and signatures of witnesses.

(ii) Details of the Transferee are to be filled in and his signatures obtained on the transfer deed.

(iii) The Transfer Deed has to be deposited with the Company together with the Share Certificates after depositing necessary registration fees.

(iv) Issuing the slip by the Company Secretary on receipt of Deed and Certificates. Thereafter a thorough scrutiny is made by the Secretary of the documents submitted for transfer.

(v) Finally, a formal Transfer Receipt is issued to the transferee, subject to the approval of Board of Directors of Company and a Lodgement of Transfer is issued to the transferor.

(vi) An entry is made in the Register of Transfer of the Company.

(vii) The old Share Certificate is cancelled and a new Share Certificate is issued.

(viii) A Resolution for cancelling the old share certificate and issuing a new one is passed at the meeting of the Board of Directors.

(ix) An intimation is sent to the transferor for taking delivery of the new share certificates.

Blank Transfer Deed

A Blank Transfer Deed is one which is a prescribed Form for transfer of shares from one person to another and it is duly signed, stamped and witnessed by the transferor but does not bear the particulars of the transferee i.e. the names and addresses of the transferee are not filled in except all other particulars. The effect of it is that the shares may easily be transfered from one person to another freely till such the transferee wants it to be registered with the Company and wants to become the member of the Company in the Register of Members.

Although, in practice, the Blank Transfer Deed or Form is a valid document, and serves the purposes, yet it should be restricted in order to prevent its misuses.

There are many uses and abuses of the Blank Transfer Deed. *The uses* are that the shares may be freely exchanged between the persons and the speculators may do speculation in shares and earn a lot of profit for themselves. The shares may be easily kept as a security for the loan and the lender, if necessary, can get the shares transferred in his name otherwise return the shares as it is when the debt is fully repaid. Particularly, in case a loan is raised against shares from the bank, the Blank Transfer Deed is required to be executed and it provides lot of a facilities both to the borrower and the lending bank as it saves them from frequent completing the formalities of registration. However, the *abuses* of Blank Transfer Deed are that it encourages speculation in shares and the chances of benami transactions are increased.

In order to prevent the abuses of the Blank Transfer Forms, certain *restrictions* have been imposed under the law. These are :

(i) When the Share Certificates alongwith the Transfer Forms are presented to the Registrar of Companies, it must be completed in all respects;

(ii) When the transferee does not want to re-sell the shares, he may fill in the Blank Transfer Forms and deliver to the Company along with Share Certificates for registrations;

(iii) After the Transfer Deed is duly completed and executed, it must be presented for registration with the Company within a period of two months from the date of its execution or completion.

(iv) When the shares are quoted and dealt with at the recognised Stock Exchange, then within six months of commencement of business by the Company, all shares must be given at the Stock Exchange with complete transfer deed.

(v) When the shares are deposited with any Government or its Undertaking or Statutory Corporation or State Bank of India or any other public sector Bank as a security for advance, the Transfer Deed must be completed in all respects.

However, the aforesaid restrictions do not apply to the transfer of shares by a Company to any other Company or Body Corporate or a Corporation owned and controlled by the Central Government or any of the State Governments.

However, before registration of transfer of shares, the Company must take proper precautions so that none of the *forged transfers may* take place. In respect of the forged transfer of shares by a Company, it shall have to indemnity the subsequent parties i.e. transferees of shares.

Transmission of Shares

'Transmission' is a technical legal word used for transfer of Shares issued by a Company. To define it more specifically, we may say that *when the title in the property of shares is transferred by the operation of law and not by sale, it is called 'Transmission of Shares'*. For example, when a person dies the shares owned by him are automatically pass on the legal heirs of the deceased. Similarly, when the Company is in liquidation, the shares are automatically transferred to the Official Liquidator appointed by the Government. In these cases, the shares are not sold but those come in possession with title of ownership by virtue of Law.

Difference between Transfer and Transmission

However, there is a difference between 'Transfer' and 'Transmission' inasmuch as :

Transfer	*Transmission*
1. It is a voluntary assignment by a person who owns the shares.	1. It is an automatic process and applies with the operation of law.
2. It is done in the presence of owner of property or when he is alive.	2. It may be done even in the absence of owner or even when he is not alive.
3. It is based on the conscious act of the owner.	3. It is based on happening of some event like death, bankruptcy etc.
4. It may be done through an Instrument in writing.	4. No instrument is required for effecting transmission.

However, the transmittee (i.e. a person to whom the shares have been transmitted) gets and enjoys all the rights and privileges as a transferee has like getting a title to the property of shares, getting the dividend on shares, getting a right to vote at the Company Meeting and others. But, it is necessary that the person on whom transmission of shares has been done, he must produce a satisfactory proof of the title to shares of the original owner and his legal status before the Board of Directors.

Procedure for Transmission

For the purpose of making transmission of shares, the following procedure has to be followed :

(i) First of all, a proof of the title of the original owner has to be produced before the Board of Directors of the Company and that can be done by production of copies of the allotment letters and/or the share certificates in original.

(ii) A proof of the legal status or his being the legal heir of the deceased owner has to be produced and that may be done by producing a succession certificate of the Court or a Will of the deceased or the Letter of Probate or an order appointing the Official Assignee of the deceased. In case of joint surviours, the actual rights in the property of the deceased have to be shown for the satisfaction of the Board of Directors of the Company transferring shares on transmission.

(iii) When the Board of Directors are satisfied, they may allow the registration of transfer of shares on getting a letter of request if the legal heir wants want to become the member of the Company. If he does not to remain a member of the Company any longer, the Directors may permit sale by transfer of shares.

(iv) Upon registration, the old share certificates are surrenderd and the new share certificates may be issued in the name of the legal heir and threafter he will be liable for payment of all future calls and will also be entitled to receive dividends and other benefits as to the original owner.

(v) On his failing to comply with the aforesaid, the Company may issue a notice to the legal heir requesting him to do so. If he fails, the company may refuse to register the transmission. In that case, he may file an appeal to the Central Government for registration of the transmission of shares.

It is the duty of a Company Secretary to ensure that the aforesaid steps are taken in respect of transmission, scrutinise letter of Request and other documents, a deed of transfer is executed on the basis of succession certificate or the letter of probate, an intimation is given to the Controller of Estate Duty, the particulars of the legal heir are recorded in the Register of Members and proper stamp duty and transfer fee is paid by the legal heir. However, if any person does not want to become the member of the Company and the Company gets an information of death, lunacy or insolvency of any member, it must send a notice within 90 days of getting such information to the legal heirs of the deceased requesting him/them to comply with the formalities and get the registration of shares in his/their names. That is also the duty of the Company Secretary.

Dividend on Shares

The word 'Dividend' is used to refer to that amount which is divided out of profits of Company amongst the Shareholders or Members. When the share capital is issued and subscribed from the public it is implied that the person who purchases the shares in a Company, will get an amount at a periodical interval as a fair return on the amount invested by him and that is called ihe 'Dividend' on Shares.

Generally speaking, all the shareholders of the Company are entitled to receive the dividend on shares. The holders of Preference shares are to receive a fixed rate of dividend decided at the time of issue of such shares, whereas the Equity Shareholders are entitled to receive the dividend only when the Company has earned sufficient profits during a particular year so as to pay tax on profits, provide for depreciation on its assest and transfer a portion to the Reserves. Whatever remains as a residue of profits, the payment of dividend to preference shareholders is first made and after that the payment of dividend on equity shares is made. The dividend may be paid as a specific amount per share or it may be paid as a percentage on amount paid up on shares.

The Articles of Association of a Company usually prescribe the method and the manner in which dividend may be declared and paid by the Company. In the absence of any specific provision in the Articles, the rules laid down under Table 'A' of Companies Act, 1956 shall apply in respect of the declaration and payment of dividend on shares.

The *procedure* is that first of all, the Directors of a Company in their Board Meeting decide whether the Company has earned sufficient profits during the previous year so as to pay the dividend on equity shares, after the provision for tax on profits is made, depreciation is provided and a specific amount is transferred to the Reserves of the Company. When it is felt that the Company may pay dividend on equity shares, the Board of Directors, as per the provisions of Articles recommend the rate at which dividend may be paid on Equity Shares of the Company and pass the necessary Resolution to this effect. After this, a Resolution is required to be passed at the Annual General Meeting of Shareholders of the Company. Upon this, the dividend is declared and necessary arrangements are made for its payment to the equity shareholders. The dividend on shares may be paid in cash or by issuing the Share Warrants which may be made collectable or payable at par through the Bankers of the Company.

It may not be out of place to mention here that the Directors are not empowered to declare any dividend on shares but they may recommend the same to the Shareholders in the Annual General Meeting. Similarly, the Shareholders have no power to ask payment of the dividend or to alter the rate or terms for payment of the dividend. Instead, they can simply demand that preference in payment of dividend may be given to the preference shareholders and thereafter the equity shareholders may get the dividend. It lies on the Directors of the Company as to how and when they make payment of the dividend. The Directors are not required to take permission of the shareholders for payment of *interim dividend* (i.e. the amount of dividend paid before the final decision on dividend is arrived at).

Legal Provisions

Given below are some of the important provisions made under the Companies Act, 1956 in respect of payment of dividend on shares :—

(i) *Section 205 (1)* lays down that a Company cannot declare or pay dividend on its shares except out of the current year's profits after charging depreciation as per rules or out of the undistributed profits for any previous financial year or out of the current year's profits and profits of the previous year or out of the moneys provided by the Central or State Government in pursuance of the guarantee provided by that Government. The aforesaid Section also provides that if depreciation has not been provided in any financial year in the past, it will have to be provided out of the current year's profits or any other financial year or years before the dividend is declared or paid.

(ii) If any loss is incurred by the Company in any previous year, or years, it shall be set-off against or made good for from the profits of the current year or any previous financial years to the extent of full amount of loss or an amount equal to depreciation provided in current or previous year, or previous year concerned, whichever is less.

(iii) The Central Government, if it thinks in public interest, may allow any Company to declare or pay dividend for any financial year out of the profits of the Company for that or any previous year without providing for depreciation.

(iv) *Section 205 (5)* lays down that the dividend may be paid in cash, by cheque or by Warrant sent through post to the registered member or through registered post to joint members.

(v) *Section 206* lays down that a company can only pay dividend to the registered holder of its shares or to his order to his bankers.

(vi) *Section 207* lays down that every director of the Company shall be punishable with imprisonment and fine where a dividend has been declared by the Company but has not been paid or the dividend warrant has not been posted to the shareholder entitled to the dividend within 42 days from the declaration of dividend.

(vii) *Section 211* read with Schedule VI of the Companies Act lays down that it is the statutory obligations on a Company to provide for the proposed dividend in the Company's Profit and Loss Account and show in the Balance Sheet under the head 'Current Liabilities and Provisions'.

Interim Dividend and Dividend

As stated earlier, an Interim Dividend is the amount which is paid to the shareholders in between, i.e. before the close of the financial year when finally the dividend for the full year is declared and paid. It is generally paid half-yearly and in anticipation of good profits to be earned by the Company by the end of financial year. When the final dividend is declared payable, the amount of interim dividend is deducted out of it and the balance is paid. The two may be distinguished on the following lines :—

Interim Dividend	*Dividend*
1. It is paid in the middle of financial year.	1. It is paid after the close of the financial year, of the Company.
2. It may be declared by the Board of Directors on passing a Resolution at the Board Meeting.	2. It is recommended by the Board of Directors and finally sanctioned by the Shareholders in the Annual General Meeting.
3. It is subject to adjustment out of the final dividend.	3. No adjustment is made in the final dividend declared.
4. It may be cancelled by passing another Resolution in Board Meeting once it is declared.	4. It cannot be withdrawn once it is declared and paid.
5. It does not come under the statutory obligations of a Company.	5. It is a statutory obligation on the part of the Company to pay or provide for dividend on shares.

6. It may be paid even when the assessment of Company's profits may not have been made.	6. It is paid only when the actual profits have been ascertained and other provisions have been made.
7. It is paid out of the current year's profits.	7. It may be paid out of current or previous year's profits.

Dividend Warrant

It is a piece of paper, in writing, containing an order to a Bank for payment of certain sum of money to a certain person towards dividend on shares owned by him. The Company Law provides that the dividend on shares may be paid either in cash or by cheque or by issuing the Warrant. Mostly the Companies pay the amount of dividend on shares by issuing the Dividend Warrant. It has two parts—one is an intimation letter addressed to the shareholder and the other part is the Dividend Warrant. It may be made payable to a specified Banker or Collectable at Part, whatever may be the arrangement with the Bank. It is a Quasi-Negotiable Instrument. Its amount may be collected through the Bank Account when it is crossed. Though not exactly a cheque but a special cheque.

SPECIMEN OF DIVIDEND WARRANT

A.B.C. Co, LTD.

Regd. Office :.................

Dated...........

No..............

Dividend Warrant

To

YOUNG BANK OF INDIA

....

Pay to..............or order the sum of Rs......... (Rupees.............. only).

For A.B.C. Co. Ltd.,
Sd/
Director/Secretary.

The above type of Dividend Warrants are got printed and signed by the officials of the Company under the Common Seal and passed on to the Shareholders by post, who receives the same, signs at the place meant for and deposits in his bank account, retaining the first part of the warrant for his personal record.

Loss or Misplacement of Dividend Warrant

Whenever a Dividend Warrant is lost, misplaced, stolen or mutilated, a duplicate dividend warrant in lieu of the original one may be issued. But, for this purpose, the concerned shareholder shall have to make an application to the Company informing the fact of loss or misplacement of the original share warrant and request the Company to issue a duplicate in lieu thereof. On receipt of such an application, it is the duty of the Company Secretary to verify from the list of dividend warrants whether the same has been paid or not. If the same has not been paid, the intimation to the Bank on which it was issued, has to be made and request the Bank to stop its payment. Afterwards, a fresh warrant is prepared and a Resolution to this effect is passed at the Board Meeting. On approval at the Board Meeting, the Shareholder shall have to execute an indemnity bond in favour of the Company on a stamped paper with witnesses. On receipt of the same, the duplicate share warrant may be issued by the Company Secretary after marking in the list of dividend warrants that a duplicate share warrant bearing No......... has been issued. The said notation is also marked on the duplicate warrant and then delivered to the Shareholder .

Unclaimed Dividend

When a shareholder fails to take delivery of the dividend warrants or fails to present the dividend warrants to the Banker or the Company for taking the payment thereof, it many be known as 'Unclaimed Dividend'. Although it is the statutory obligation of a Company to pay the dividend within 42 days of the declaration of dividend or the shareholder may claim its payment within six months from the date of declaration, otherwise penalties may be imposed, yet some amount of dividend remains outstanding with the Company.

Under the latest provisions of law, the amount of dividend for which warrants have not been delivered by the Company within 42 days of its declaration, the Company must open a separate account with the Bank in the name of 'Unpaid Dividend A/c' within seven days of the expiry of the said 42 days and transfer such unclaimed amount to that Account. If the Company fails to do so, it shall have to pay interest thereon @ 12% p.a. on such amounts to the shareholders. And, if the amount transferred to Unpaid Dividend A/c remains unclaimed for a further period of 3 years, the Company must arrange to transfer such amount to the Central Government under the head of General Revenues of the Government Account. A statement giving details of such amounts must also be submitted to the Government. Any claim for refund of unclaimed dividend amount shall have to be made to the Central Government thereafter. The Company Secretary must remember the provisions of law while dealing with the unclaimed dividends.

(IV) Commencement of Business

The Fourth Stage in formation of a Joint Stock Company is the '*Commencement of Business*'. A private limited Company may commence or start the business as soon as it is registered or Incorporated under the provisions of the Companies Act, 1956 but a Public Limited Company incorporated under the Act has to obtain a '*Certificate of Commencement of Business*' when it has to start the actual business. This Certificate is issued by the Registrar of Companies on fulfilling certain conditions by a public limited Company. Those conditions comprise of the legal provisions to be complied with in respect of issue of a Prospectus, Applications for Shares, Share Allotment, Listing of Shares, Underwriting Arrangements, Appointment of Bankers, Directors, Secretaries etc., and Minimum Subscription of Share Capital raised bv the Public Company.

Section 149 of the Companies Act, 1956, stipulated certain restrictions on the commencement of business by a public limited company and these may be explained as under :—

(i) A Public Company who has invited the public for subscribing to its share capital by issuing the Prospectus, it cannot commence business unless the shares have been allotted for an amount not less than the minimum subscription, every director of the Company has taken up the shares on payment of cash, for which the undertaking was given by him, no money is to be repaid to the applicants by the Company for default on the part of the Company in complying with the legal provisions and a duly signed and verified copy of the declaration has been filed with the Registrar to the effect that the aforesaid conditions have been complied with.

(ii) In respect of a company which has not issued the prospectus and is having the share capital, it cannot commence business unless a Statement in lieu of Prospectus has been filed with the Registrar of Companies, every Director of the Company has taken the shares by paying cash as per the undertaking and the declaration duly signed by the Company Secretary or a Director has been filed with the Registrar of Companies that the aforesaid conditions have been complied with.

Minimum Subscription

'Minimum Subscription' may be defined as that amount which, in the opinion of the Directors or Promoters of a Company, must be raised by issuing the shares so as to meet the expenditure on each of the following heads :—

(i) Purchase of any Property ;

(ii) Preliminary Expenses to be paid by the Company, including commission for subscription or underwriting subscription of Shares ;

(iii) Repayment of moneys borrowed by the Company for any of the aforesaid matters ;

(iv) Working Capital ;

(v) Any other expenditure incurred or to be incurred by a Company.

The 'Minimum Subscription' must be stated in Prospectus, giving the details of each of the head of expenditure. Thus, the amount of Minimum Subscription is not a fixed amount applicable in respect of all the public limited companies but it varies according to the nature of business and other requirements of the Company. The Directors or Promoters of the Company have to decide the Minimum Subscription and state the same in the Prospectus or Statement in Lieu of Prospectus.

Declaration of Compliance

When the conditions about the Minimum Subscription and other matters like allotment of shares, Directors' Shares etc. are complied, then a Declaration of Compliance is required to be made at the final stage which states that the requirements of *Section 149* of the Companies Act, 1956 have been complied with. This Certificate is submitted to the Registrar of Companies. However, the private limited companies are exempted from submission of the abovesaid Declaration of Compliance.

Certificate of Commencement of Business

On filing the Declaration of Compliance of the provisions as laid down under *Section 149* of the Compaines Act, 1956, the Registrar of Companies scrutinizes the Declaration and satisfies himself of completion of all the requirements by the public Company and thereafter issues a Certificate in the name of the Public Company called the 'Certificate of Commencement of Business'. This Certificate is essentially required for all public companies limited by shares or guarantee, but the private companies need not obtain such a Certificate as they may start business as soon as incorporation or registration is completed. A Public Company can also not exercise its borrowing powers without obtaining the above Certificate. If a public Company commences business or exercises its borrowing powers prior to obtaining this Certificate, or in any way contravenes the provisions of *Section 149* of the Companies Act, 1956, then every defaulting officer of the Company shall be liable to a fine to the extent of Rs. 500 per day till the default continues.

Debentures

The term 'Debenture' is derived from the foreign language and is used to refer to the 'debt' owed to others. In the context of Joint Stock Companies, the 'debenture' is used to refer to the debt raised by a Company from others through an instrument in writing. In other words, 'Debenture' is *an acknowledgment of debt, by a Company under its Common Seal, undertaking to pay back the same after a specified period to a particular person named therein with interest.*

Although the Companies Act, 1956 does not gave any specific definition of 'Debenture', yet *Section 2 (12)* of the Act lays down that the "Debenture includes Debenture Sotck, bonds and any other securities of a Company, whether constituting a charge on the assets of the Company or not."

It implies that the 'Debenture' may be a debt raised in the form of a Bond, Stock or any other security of a Company.

Whenever the financial requirements of a Joint Stock Company cannot be met by the issue of shares to the general public, the Puplic Limited Company may resort to Borrowings from the public and one of the important means for raising borrowings, is 'Issue of debentures' by the Company. A Debenture is a unit of the fixed amount payable after a specified period with interest. It may be secured against any of the assets of the Company or it may be unsecured. But the principal amount is subject to repayment and the interest is paid at periodical intervals.

Types of Debentures

The following are the various types of Debentures :—

Simple, Naked or Unsecured Debentures :

These are the debentures which are issued by a Company without keeping any security or without creating any charge on any of the assets of the Company. In case of winding up of the Company, the holders of this class of debentures are ordinary creditors of the Company and they have no right to claim any of the Company's securities.

Mortgaged Debentures :

These types of debentures are secured by creating a charge on the assets of the Company. The charge may be fixed on specific asset or general on all the assets of the Company. If the repayment is not made, the debenture-holders may ask for repayment by disposal of the assets which are mortgaged against these debentures. The Charge on assets is created by executing a Mortgage Deed between the Company and the Trustees (i.e. the representatives of debenture-holders). On liquidation of the Company, the Trustee may realise the security mortgaged and distribute the amount between the debenture-holders.

Registered and Bearer Debentures : When the Debentures are transferred through an entry in the Registers of the Company, those are called the 'Registered Debentures'. The repayment of the principal amount is made only to the person whose name appears in the register. These are not negotiable and the transfer can be made on the basis of Transfer Deed which has to be registered with the Company.

The *bearer debentures* are one which are payable to any person holding the instrument. The transfer of such debentures can be made by mere delivery. However, these may be converted into registered debentures on making an application to the Company by the holder.

Redeemable and Irredeemable Debentures : Those debentures, the principal amount of which is refunded or paid back after a fixed period, may be called 'Redeemable'. For redemption of debentures, the Company usually creates a special reserve or takes an insurance policy so that sufficient amount is accumulated at the time when debentures are to be redeemed. The Company has to make necessary arrangements for their timely repayment.

Irredeemable Debenture are those which are not paid off during the life-time of the Company. Normally such debentures are refunded on liquidation of the Company. However, the interest may be paid on these debentures at periodical intervals.

Convertible and Non-convertible Debentures : The convertible Debentures are those which may by converted into the Equity Share after a certain fixed period of time. An option is provided to such debenture-holders that if they wish, they could convert their debentures into Equity Shares of the Company. It may happen that the conditions of the money market may not be found favourable for the debentures and then the Company may offer an option to the investors to convert the debentures into Equity Shares. The investors may get the benefit of higher return on their investments, taking advantage of the fixed rate of interest and therafter the dividend on the same amount. By the time the debentures are convertible into shares, the company may achieve remarkable progress and the shares may fetch higher premium.

The non-convertible debentures are those which cannot be converted into shares any time. On such debentures, the holders may take interest on them but the option of conversion is not available. These debentures are useful for those investors who do not assume any risk and they are satisfied with the fixed interest received by them.

Difference between 'Debentures' and 'Shares'

The 'Debentures' are different than 'Shares' on the following points :—

'Debentures'	*'Shares'*
1. The Debentures represent the amount of borrowings by the Company.	1. The shares represent the owners' equity.
2. The principal amount has to be refunded after a fixed period of time.	2. The principal amount of shares is not refunded throughout the life-time of the Company.

3. The return on investment on debentures is called the 'Interest'.	3. The return on investment on shares is called the 'Dividend'.
4. The debenture-holder is treated as a simple creditor of the Company, may be secured or unsecured.	4. The shareholder is the member of the Company and is the joint owner of the Company.
5. On liquidation of the Company, the debentures are paid earlier than the shareholders.	5. On liquidation, the amount is paid at the end to the shareholders.
6. Generally, no conditions or restrictions are imposed while issuing the debentures.	6. Certain restrictions are imposed while issuing the shares and the provision of Companies Act are to be complied with.
7. The debenture-holders do not have the power of voting at the general company meetings.	7. The shareholders have the voting power in the general company meetings.

Debentures and Debenture Stock

The 'Debenture Stock' refers to the fraction of debentures issued by a Company and it differs from a 'Debenture' on the following points :—

Debenture Stock	*Debenture*
1. The debenture stock is a consolidated form of the loans raised by the Company.	1. The debenture is a distinct instrument of a fixed amount of debt raisd by a Company.
2. The debenture stock is divisible and can be transferred in fraction.	2. The debenture is indivisible and cannot be transferred as a fraction.
3. No stamp duty is payable on the debenture stock.	3. Stamp duty is required to be paid on each and every debentures.
4. The debenture stock is mostly accompanied by a Trust Deed evidencing the mortgage of assets of the Company.	4. In respect of unsecured or naked debentures, no Trust Deed is accompanied.

Issuing Debentures—Procedure

No restrictions have been imposed on the issue of debentures by limited companies under the Companies Act, 1956, just as on issue of Shares at a premium or at a discount. The debentures may be issued at par (i.e. at the face value) or at a premium (i.e. at a value higher than the face value) or at a discount (i.e. at a price less than the face value), depending upon the discretion of the Board of Directors of the Company. A private limited company may issue the debentures at any time as soon as it is registered but a public company shall have to obtain the certificate of commencement of business prior to the issue of debentures. The debentures can be issued for any amount as permitted by the Articles of Association of the Company. However, in case the amount of shares and debentures taken together exceeds the limit of Rs. 50 lakhs within 12 months then the prior consent of the Controller of Capital Issues will be necessary. And, no debentures can be issued carrying the rights of voting to the debenture-holders. The most important thing is that a Resolution must be passed at the duly constituted meeting of the Board of Directors of the Company before proceeding to issue the debentures whether privately or through a public invitation like shares.

The following *steps* are usually taken for issuing the debentures by a Company :—

(i) A Resolution is passed at the meeting of the Board of Directors of the Company after deciding the amount, number, nature, period and the rate of interest payable on debentures. The rates of interest payable on debentures will gear according to cost of living index over a period of time. However, the maximum ceiling on interest is fixed at 15 per cent p.a. under the amended rules.

(ii) In big Companies, a separate Committee may be set up to look after the work of issuing the debentures. However, in small companies, the Company Secretary may look after the entire work of preparing the Prospectus Debenture or Bond Instruments and the Trust Deeds to be executed by the Company. All these documents are got drafted and printed in consultation with the Legal Advisors or Solicitors.

(iii) Prior permission/approval of the Controller of Capital Issues has to be obtained if the amount of debentures to be issued plus the shares exceeds Rs. 50 lakhs within a period of 12 months. For this purpose, an application on the prescribed form is prepared and submitted to the Controller along with the necessary fees and his consent obtained in writing. Where the total amount of borrowing of a Company including debentures and loans exceed the aggregate of paid-up capital plus free reserves of the Company, a permission of the Shareholders—must be obtained by passing a Resolution at the general meeting of the Shareholders of the Company. However, if the bearer bonds or debentures are being issued, then the permission of the Reserve Bank of India must also be obtained by moving an application on the printed prescribed form.

(iv) The Trust Deed is then executed and necessary arrangements are made for creating a charge on the assets of the Company (in case the debentures are secured). The particulars of the charge created on the company assets are furnished to the Registrar of Companies, i.e. the charge is got registered and a certificate of registration of Charge is obtained.

(v) A Copy of the Prospectus or the Statement in Lieu of Prospectus is filed with the Registrar of Companies and also issued to the public by inserting publication in the daily newspapers. However, the filing of the abovesaid documents must be done at least 3 days earlier to the allotment of denbentures by the Company. An application to Stock Exchange must also be made if debentures are listed.

(vi) The applications for debentures are received and the allotment is made as per the decision taken by the Board of Directors at their meeting and after passing the Resolution at the meeting. All the money received with the debenture applications must be deposited in a separate account opened with any scheduled Bank.

(vii) Filing a Return of Allotment of Debentures is not obligatory under the law. Hence, the Return may be prepared after the allotment of debentures and filed with the Registrar of Companies, if necessary. Hewever, the allotment of debentures cannot be made until the beginning of the 5th day of issue of the Debentures Prospectus.

(viii) The Debenture Certificates should than be prepared with the list of debenture-holders and got signed by the Directors under the Common Seal of the Company by passing the necessary Resolution at the Board Meeting. However, it is necessary that the debenture certificates must be issued and delivered to the concerned debenture-holders within a period of three months of the allotment. The necessary entries must be made in the Register of Debenture-holders.

Rights Debentures

Like Rights Shares, the Rights Debentures may also be issued by a public company. The Rights Debentures are those classes of debentures which carry the right of voting with the debenture-holder. Generally, the debentures-holders do not enjoy the voting right at the company meeting but with these types of debentures, the holders of them get the voting right.

Although the provisions for issue of Rights Shares are laid down under *Section 81* of the Companies Act, 1956, yet the provisions of *Section 117* restrict the issue of Rights Debentures. *Section 117* of the Companies Act, 1956 states that debentures with voting Rights cannot be issued after April 1956. As per amendment in 1982, this section has been enacted to give effect to the recommendations of Company Law Committee. Still, the guidelines issued by the Central Government apply to the issue of Rights Debentures. The important points to note in respect of the Rights Debentures are: Such type of debentures must be issued for raising the long-term resources for meeting the capital requirements. The amount of such debentures should not exceed 20% of the gross current assets or the paid-up share capital plus free reserves. The debt-equity ratio including issue of debentures should not exceed 1 : 1. These debentures may be issued for periods of 7, 8 and 12 years and the rate of interest should not exceed the rates specified by the Government from time to time, though an additional interest or discount upto 1/2 p.c. may be allowed while issuing them. The face value of each debenture shall be Rs. 100.

The abovesaid guidelines should be adhered to while issuing the Rights Debentures and the details of position should be clarified under the provisions of Capital Issue (Control) Act, 1947.

Debenture Scrip Certificate

Like Shares, when the Debentures are issued in process viz. receiving a part of the face value of the debenture on application, some amount on allotment and the balance in instalments in the form of calls, then the debentures are said to have been issued in instalments and the full face value of the debenture is not received in lump sum. Under such circumstances, the Company issues to the debenture-holder a Certificate called the 'Debenture Scrip Certificate'. It is not the actual debenture instrument but simply a provisional certificate giving the details of debentures purchased and the actual number of instalments paid thereon. Whenever the next instalment is deposited with the Bank the debenture-holder takes the scrip with him to the Bank and deposits the money towards the instalment of the debenture. When the total number of instalments are complete, the regluar Debenture Certificate may be issued by the Company.

Trust Deed or Mortgage Deed

When a Company has to issue secured or mortgaged debentures before that the Company has to execute a document in favour of the representatives of the debenture-holders on a stamp paper, which is called the Trust Deed or Mortgage Deed. Since there are so many debenture-holders in number, it is not possible to execute individual Deed but all the debenture-holders usually appoint their representatives who are called the Trustees. The Trustees become a party to the Trust Deed, on one hand, and the Company on the other. On execution of the said Deed, a charge is created on the assets of the Company—either a general or floating charge over all the assets of the Company or a specific charge on any particular assets of the Company. But, it safeguards the interests of the debenture-holders.

The Trust Deed contains the number and nature of debentures, amount, particulars of property mortgaged, the nature and extent of charge created over the assets of the company, rights and powers of the Trustees, terms and conditions on which it may be enforced, arrangements for maintenance and insurance of the property mortgaged etc. The Trust Deed remains open for inspection by the member debenture-holders as per the rules and a true copy of the same may be supplied by the Company to every member on request and on payment of the requisite fees. *Section 118* lays down that such a copy on request may be supplied within seven days, otherwise the concerned company officer shall be liable for a fine. The Company and every Trustee is expected to go by the provisions made in the Deed. Thus, the Trust Deed is a useful document protecting the rights and interests of both the Company and the Debenture-holders and helps in enforcing the property mortgaged at the appropriate time.

Registration of Debentures

Section 128 of the Companies Act, 1956 lays down that where a series of debentures containing or giving any charge to the benefit of which the debenture-holders of that series are entitled *pari passu* created by a Company, it shall be sufficient if they are filed with the Registrar within *thirty* days after the execution of the deed containing the charge, or, if there is no such deed, after the execution of any debentures of the series, the following particulars :—

(a) the total amount secured by the whole series ;

(b) the dates of the resolutions authorising the issue of the series and the date of the convening deed, if any, by which the security is created or defined ;

(c) a general description of the property charged ; and

(d) the names of the trustees, if any, for the debenture-holders ;

together with the deed containing the charge, or a copy of the deed verified in the prescribed manner, or if there is no such deed, one of the debentures of the series.

It is clear from the above description that where a Company issues a series of debentures which are secured against the property of the Company and/or the Trust Deed has also been executed, it is essential that such series of debentures must be got registered with the Registrar of Companies by sending the aforesaid particulars. Where more than one series of debentures is issued, then particulars of dates of different issues and the copy of the Register of Debentures shall also be supplied to the Registrar of Companies. However, non-compliance of these provisions will not make the validity of debentures as ineffective.

Transfer of Debentures

Like Shares, the Debentures may also be transferred from one person to another. So far as Bearer Debentures are concerned, there is no problem in transferring them because the transfer may be effected by mere delivery of the instrument by the transferor to the transferee like a bearer cheque. The Company also does not keep any record in respect of the bearer debentures. But, in respect of the registered debentures the transferor has to make an endorsement on the back of the debenture instrument and deliver the instrument to the Company together with the transfer form duly stamped and signed by the transferor. The Company Secretary scrutinizes the documents and places the same before the Board of Directors in their meeting where a resolution is passed. Thereafter the particulars of the new debenture-holder are taken down in the Register of Debentures. An endorsement on the debenture is made and authorised by the Secretary or Manager of the Company and then delivered to the new transferee. The same must be delivered within two months from the date of application for transfer otherwise the defaulting official will be liable to a fine under the provisions of the Companies Act.

However, the procedure for transfer of Debenture Stock is almost the same as explained earlier except that the old certificate has to be cancelled and a fresh certificate is required to be issued in favour of the transferee. In case a Company refuses to transfer any debenture, an appeal may be filed by the transferor or transferee to the Central Government within a period of two months from the date of refusal by the Company.

Perpetual Debentures

Section 120 of the Companies Act, 1956 defines a 'Perpetual Debenture' as a condition contained in any debenture or in any need for securing any debentures, whether issued or executed before or after the commencement of this Act, shall not be invalid by reason only that thereby, the debentures are made irredeemable or redeemable only on happening of a contingency, however remote, or on the expiration of a period, however long. Accordingly, the Perpetual Debentures are those which are payable only in the event of winding up or payable at a remote period such as hundred years after issue or on some serious default by the Company. In other words, these may be called 'Irredeemable Debentures'.

Redemption of Debentures

The word meaning of 'Redemption' is refunding or paying back the money raised as a debt on issuing the debentures. Generally, when the debentures are issued as irredeemable by a Company, the principal amount in those debentures has to be repaid to the debentureholder after a certain fixed period or a fixed number of years. The interest may also be paid at the time of redemption. However, in most cases, the interest on debentures is paid at half-yearly or yearly periodical intervals. Anyhow, a large amount of cash may be needed at the time of redemption of debentures for which the Company has to make necessary arrangements either by creating regular reserves right from the time of their issue or by issuing shares or in any other way. The Company has to be governed by the terms and conditions of issue of debentures. The redemption may also be done by annual instalments of equal amount spread over a number of years. A separate account for the purpose of redemption of debentures is opened and the funds are created in that for payment to the debenture-holders.

Re-issue of Redeemable Debentures

Under *Section 121* of the Companies Act, 1956, a Company has a right to issue again those shares which have been redeemed or to keep the redeemed debentures alive. But, the Company can exercise this right of re-issue only when there is no manifestation of intention of cancelling them by passing a resolution at the company meeting or there is no provision in the Articles of Association to the contrary. This re-issue is a sort of replacement of the same debentures which have been paid-off and the holders of these debentures also enjoy the same rights and privileges as earlier. Even a transfer of debentures to a nominee of the Company for the purpose of keeping them alive will be treated as re-issue for the purpose of this Section of the Act.

Rights and Duties of Debenture-holders

A debenture-holder, as we have discussed earlier, is treated as a creditor of the Company whether he/she is the holder of secured or naked debentures. However, they have the right to claim payment of interest on debentures as well as the repayment of the principal where the debentures are redeemable after a period. Every debenture-holder has also the right to inspect the register of debenture-holders and the Trust Deed. He can also ask for a copy of the Trust Deed executed in connection with securing his interest in debenture, on payment of the requisite fees and the Company must supply the copy thereof within seven days of the date of request of the debenture-holder. Generally, the terms and conditions stipulated at the time of issue of debentures decide the scope of their rights and powers. They have their 'say' in the company meeting of the debenture-holders. But, they have no right to vote in the management of affairs of the Company as *Section 117* of the Companies Act, 1956 prohibits a Company to issue debentures with voting rights.

In case, however, a Company makes default in payment of interest or repayment of the principal amount, the unsecured debenture-holders may sue the Company through the Court of Law and the secured debenture-holders may enforce their rights in the property mortgaged against the debentures or they may apply to the Court to appoint the Official Receiver or for taking over the property mortgaged or for sale of the mortgaged property.

Interest on Debentures

'Interest' may be defined as the reward for waiting or a consideration to be paid by the borrower to the lender for using the money. In respect of issue of debentures by a Company, the borrowing of money in the form of debentures is made by the Comany and the debenture-holders must get the due consideration for investment of their money/s by allowing the use of money by the Company. The interest becomes due for payment after the expiry of a certain period from the date the money is borrowed and it has to be paid whether there is profit to the Company or not. The rate and the terms for payment of interest are decided by the Company and settled with the debenture-holders at the time of issue of the debentures. However, the Central Government has the power to fix up the ceiling of rate of interest payable on debentures. The present ceiling rate of interest payable on bonds or debentures has been fixed at 15 per cent per annum and the same goes with the cost of living. The interest on debentures may be paid half-yearly or annually as per the terms of issue of debentures.

Interest and Dividend

As we know, interest is the payment of money on a debt raised by a Company by issuing the debentures, whereas the 'Dividend' is the payament of money out of the profits earned by the Company, rather it is the division of Company's profits. However, the two terms may be distinguished on the following points :—

Interest	*Dividend*
1. Interest is the consideration	1. Dividend is the share of

for the debt payable to debenture-holders.	profits of the Company paid to shareholders.
2. Interest has to be paid whether there is profit or not to the company.	2. Dividend cannot be paid unless the profits remain after payment of tax, provision for depreciation and transfer to reserves.
3. Interest, being mandatory, it does not bear the recommendations of Directors and then approval of shareholders in the A.G.M.	3. Payment of Dividend to shareholders requires approval of shareholders in the A.G.M. vis-a-vis recommendations of the Directors.
4. The rate of interest payable on debentures is generally fixed as per the terms of issue.	4. The rate of dividend on Equity Shares always varies depending upon the quantum of profits and adjustments.
5. Interest cannot be paid as an 'Interim Interest' before the period when it becomes due.	5. Dividend may be paid as an 'Interim Dividend' before the close of year and adjusted out of final dividend.
6. Interest Warrants may be issued for payment of interest on debentures.	6. Dividend may be paid in cash or through the Dividend Warrants.
7. In case of winding up of the Company, interest may be given a preferential treatment than the dividend.	7. Dividend on equity shares may be paid at the last except the preference shareholders.
8. Interest on debentures is a fixed liability of the Company.	8. Dividend, unless declared, cannot become the liability of the Company.

BOOKS AND REGISTERS OF A COMPANY

The Books and Registers which a company, limited by shares or a registered company, is required to maintain, may be broadly classified under *three* heads :—

(a) *Accounts or Financial Books* : These are the books or registers in which the financial transactions made by the company during the financial year of the Company, are recorded. These may consist of Cash Book, Purchase Day Book, Sales Day Book, Returns Journals, Bills Receivable and Payable Books, Customers' Ledgers,

Stock Registers, etc. The Accounts or Finance Department of the Company maintains these books under the supervision and control of Company Secretary and/or a qualified Chartered Accountant or Cost Accountant appointed by the Company.

(b) *Statutory Books* : Under the provisions made in the Companies Act, 1956, every limited company must maintain the following books or records :—

1. Register of Members
2. Index of Members
3. Annual Return
4. Minute Books (Separate Books for the General Meetings as well as Board of Directors' Meetings)
5. Register of Directors and Managers
6. Register of Contracts in which Directors are interested
7. Register of Charges created by the Company
8. Register of Debenture-holders with Index of Debenture-holders.
9. Register of Directors' Share-holdings
10. Register of Investments not held in Company's name
11. Directors' Attendance Book

The above books serve the special purpose for which they are kept and are open to inspection by members or others as per the provisions laid down under the Act. However, these must be kept at the Registered Office of the Company or at any other place with the permission of the Registrar of Companies.

(c) *Statistical Books* : These are the books which give detailed information of the holding, transfer of shares and debentures, calls on shares and debentures, interest on debentures and dividend on shares etc. These are separate from the account or statutory books. Generally, a limited company may maintain the following statistical books :—

1. Share Application and Allotment Book
2. Share Calls Register
3. Debenture Application and Allotment Register
4. Debenture Calls Book
5. Shares Transfer Book
6. Debenture Transfer Book
7. Agenda Book
8. Registers of Share Warrants, Dividend Warrants, Coupons etc.
9. Registers of Share Certificates, Debentures, Bonds etc.

10. Safe Custody Register
11. Register of Power of Attorney etc.

These registers may be maintained, depending upon the requirements of a particular company.

However, the Books of Account and the Statutory Books must be open for inspection during business hours of the Company by the Registrar of Companies, authorised officers of the Government and the inspecting officer.

Statutory Books

Register of Members

In this Register, the particulars of shareholders are written down, who have subscribed to the share capital of the Company. The details are given elsewhere in this book.

Index of Members

Index may be defined as a list which points out or indicates. In reference to the limited company, a list giving the names of the members or shareholders is prepared to facilitate quick reference. Where the number of members exceeds 50, an Index of Members must be prepared so that it becomes easy to refer to the register of members. From the Index, the page number of the Register of Member is ascertained and then it becomes easy to refer to the concerned pages. Hence, the necessity of separate Index. The Index must also be kept at the registered office of the Company along with the Register of Members and must be made available to members on request during the business hours of the company.

Annual Return

It has been discussed elsewhere in this book.

Minutes Book or Register

'Minutes' are the records of the proceedings of a company meeting—whether the meeting of shareholders or Board of Directors or the Committee. Whenever any meeting is held, the point at the Agenda is taken up serially, brief of discussions held at the meeting and the resolution passed unanimously or by a vote of majority—all these details are recorded in a separate register called the 'Minute Book' or 'Minute Register'. This register is generally written in legible hand-writing and each of the Minute Book is initialled by the

Chairman and full signatures of the Chairman are obtained at the end of minutes of a particular meeting.

Section 196 of the Companies Act, 1956 lays down that the books containing the minutes of the proceedings of any general meeting of a company shall be (a) kept at the registered office of the company, and (b) open during business hours to the inspection of any member without charge, subject to such reasonable restrictions as the company may by its articles or in general meeting, impose so however that not less than two hours in each day are allowed for inspection.

Section 196(2) further lays down that any member shall be entitled to be furnished, within seven days after he has made a request in that behalf to the company, with a copy of any minutes referred to in sub-section(1), on payment of thirty-seven paise for every one hundred words or fractional part thereof required to be copied.

However, if in any case the company refuses to supply the copy of minutes to a member, or the company makes a default, the Court may, by order, compel an immediate inspection of the minute books or direct that the copy required shall forthwith be sent to the person requiring it.

Register of Directors and Manager etc.

Section 303 of the Companies Act, 1956 lays down that every company shall keep at its registered office a register of its directors, managing director, manager and secretary, containing with respect to each of them the particulars.

Under the provisions of the Act, the following particulars must be given in the register :—

(i) In case of individuals, the name and surname, in full, any former name, father's/husband's name and surname, residential address, nationality, business, occupation, if any, the office/s held in any other body corporate, date of birth etc.

(ii) In case of a body corporate, its name and registered office, nationality and other particulars.

(iii) In case of a Firm, the name of firm, address, nationality and particulars of partners

(iv) In case of nomination by other body corporate or firm, the name, address and other particulars.

Sub-section (2) of the abovesaid Section provides that the company must send to the Registrar a return, *in duplicate*, in the prescribed form pertaining to the particulars specified in the said register, within a period of 30 days of the first appointment of directors, manager or secretary etc. If there is any change, then the change must also be notified to the Registrar in duplicate, within 30 days of the change.

This register must be kept open for inspection during business hours of the Company for the outsiders and/or members of the Company. It must be kept uptodate all the time and the change, if any, be incorporated immediately.

Register of Directors' Share-holdings

Section 307 of the Companies Act, 1956 lays down that every company shall keep a Register showing, as respects each director of the company, the number, description, and amount of any shares in, or debentures of, the company or any other body corporate, being the company's subsidiary or holding company, or a subsidiary of the company's holding company, which are held by him, per in trust for him or of which he has any right to become the holder whether on payment or not.

The register shall be kept at the registered office of the company and shall be open to inspection during the business hours, subject to such reasonable restrictions as the articles or in general meeting, impose so as to allow inspection for not less than two hours in each day.

Register of Charges

Every company shall have to maintain a register containing the details of charges created by the company generally or on any specific asset or for mortgage of property in favour of the debenture-holders and others.

Section 143 of the Companies Act, 1956 provides for maintaining the register of charges and stipulate that such a register shall have to be maintained at the registered office of the company. It will contain all the particulars of all the charges and mortgages. It must be kept open for inspection for at least two hours per day during business hours. If the company refuses for its inspection, the Court may pass the order or compel the company to allow the inspection of the register. The Company Law Board may direct the rectification of any omission or mis-statement in the register.

Register and Index of Debenture-holders

Under the provisions of *Sections 152 to 154* of Companies Act, 1956, every company is required to maintain a register containing the particulars of debenture-holders of the company, giving the name, address, occupation, number and nature of debentures, amount etc. The register is required for the registered debentures only because no register is required for the bearer debentures. It must be kept at the registered office of the company and must be kept open for inspection by any of the debenture-holders of the company.

Certain restrictions are imposed in respect of the closing of this register like the Register of Members and those must be observed strictly.

A separate Index of Debenture-holders may be prepared giving alphabetically the names of the debenture-holders so as to facilitate reference to the register of debenture-holders.

Register of Contracts

Under the provisions of Companies Act, a separate register is required to be maintained by a company, giving the particulars of contracts entered into in which the company's directors' interests are involved. It must mention the date of contract/s, name of the party/parties with whom the contracts are arranged, terms and conditions of contract, name/s of directors interested in the contract and particulars of resolution passed at the meeting of the Board of Directors of the Company etc. The entries in the register must be made maximum within a period of seven days of the meeting of Directors in which the contract/s was/were approved. After entries, the register must be signed by all the directors of the Board in their next meeting. This register must also be kept at the registered office and kept open for inspection during business hours.

Statutory Report

Section 165(2) of the Companies Act, 1956 lays down that the Board of directors shall, at least twenty-one days before the day on which the meeting is held, forward a report (in this Act referred to as "the statutory report") to every member of the Company. It means that while holding the Statutory Meeting (i.e. the first lawful meeting of the members of a Company after its formation), the report which has to be prepared by the Board of Directors of the Company is known as the Statutory Report and it must invariably be forwarded to all the members of the Company before the Statutory Meeting is held.

Section 165(3) of the Act provides that the Statutory Report shall set out :—

(a) the total number of shares allotted, distinguishing shares allotted as fully or partly paid-up otherwise than in cash, and stating in the case of shares partly paid up, the extent to which they are so paid-up, and in either case, the consideration for which they have been allotted ;

(b) the total amount of cash received by the company in respect of all the shares allotted, distinguishing as aforesaid ;

(c) an abstract of the receipts of the company and of the payments made thereout ;

(d) the names, addresses and occupations of the directors of the company and of its auditors and also of the manager and secretary ;

(e) the particulars of any contract ;

(f) the extent to which each under-writing contract, if any, has not been carried out and the reasons therefor ;

(g) the arrears, if any, due on calls from every director and the manager ;

(h) the particulars of any commission or brokerage paid or to be paid in connection with the issue or sale of shares or debentures to any director or manager.

Thus, the Statutory Report shall have to be prepared on the above lines and certified as correct by not less than two directors of the Company. one of whom will be the Managing Director. The auditors also shall have to certify that the statutory report is true and correct to the best of their knowledge and belief.

Remuneration

Section 198 of the Companies Act, 1956 deals with the overall maximum remuneration payable to Directors and Managers of the Company. According to the provisions, a company may pay to its directors and manager in respect of any financial year remuneration not exceeding 11% of its net profits of that year. However, the Company may pay a minimum remuneration not exceeding Rs. 50,000 with the approval of the Central Government. The remuneration here includes any expenditure incurred by the company in providing rent-free accommodation and any other benefit/s or amenity free of charge or at a concessional rate or any obligation etc. The managing director or whole-time director may be paid monthly remuneration.

QUESTIONS

1. "Memorandum of Association is a fundamental and unalterable charter of a company." Comment.
(*B. Com. Pass, Delhi, 1986*)
2. (a) Describe briefly the procedure for the incorporation of a company.
(b) What do you mean by the 'Articles of Association' of a company ? State its important contents.
(*B. Com. Pass, Delhi, 1985*)
3. State the contents of the Memorandum of Association. Explain the procedure for the alteration of Registered Office of a Company ? (*B. Com. Pass, Delhi, 1984*)
4. What are Articles of Association ? What are their contents How can you alter the Articles ? (*B. Com. Pass, Delhi, 1983*)
5. Describe the duties of the company secretary in relation to the following :
(a) Issue of convertible debentures ;
(b) Payment of dividend on preference shares ; and
(c) Conversion of a private company into a public company
(*B. Com. Pass, Delhi, 1982*)
6. (a) Explain briefly the different steps involved in the formation of a public company.
(b) Discuss the secretarial procedure regarding alteration of objects clause in the Memorandum of Association of a company. (*B. Com. Pess, Delhi, 1981*)
7. (a) What is a Prospectus ? State its important contents.
(b) What are the statutory provisions regarding the issue of Share Warrants ? (*B. Com. Pass, Delhi, 1986*)
8. Describe the secretarial practice relating to the following :
(i) Making Call on Shares
(ii) Transfer of Shares (*B. Com. Pass, Delhi, 1986*)
9. Write short notes on any three of the following :
(a) Minimum Subscription
(b) Reserve Capital
(c) Special Resolution
(d) Forfeiture of Shares. (*B. Com. Pass, Delhi, 1985*)

10. (a) Outline the work of a Company Secretary in connection with the issue of shares at a discount.
    (b) State the Statutory conditions which must be satisfied before a public company can proceed with the work of allotment of shares. *(B. Com. Pass, Delhi, 1985)*
11. Write short notes on any three of the following :
    (a) Bonus Shares
    (b) Special Resolutions
    (c) Mis-statements in the Prospectus
    (d) Statutory Books. *(B. Com. Pass, Delhi, 1984)*
12. Explain the difference between transfer and transmission of shares. Outline the procedure for the transfer of shares. *(B. Com. Pass, Delhi, 1984)*
13. Write short notes on any three of the following :
    (a) Statutory Books
    (b) Legal provisions as to underwriting of shares
    (c) Legal provisions as to issue of Bonus Shares
    (d) Reports. *(B. Com. Pass, Delhi, 1983)*
14. Describe the duties of the Company Secretary in relation to the following :
    (a) Issue of convertible debentures
    (b) Payment of dividend on preference shares ; and
    (c) Conversion of a private company into a public company *(B. Com. Pass, Delhi, 1982)*
15. Explain the following :
    (a) Distinction between Interim Dividend and Final Dividend.
    (b) Legal Provisions regarding Annual Returns of a Company. *(B. Com. Pass, Delhi, 1981)*
16. What is minimum subscription ? Briefly state the provisions of the Companies Act with regard to raising of Minimum subscription *(B. Com. Pass, Delhi, 1987)*

4

COMPANY MEETINGS

As we know, a Joint Stock Company is that form of Business Organisation which is the creation of law. Its capital is contributed by many persons called the 'Shareholders' who may be treated like owners and the elected representatives of shareholders, called the 'Directors', who manage and control the affairs of the Company's business. Thus, we find that, in the Company Organisation, there is neither a single owner nor is there any single manager but they are many in number, depending upon the nature and volume of business of the Company. It is, therefore, difficult to pool the power of decision-making without a 'Meeting'.

A 'Meeting', therefore, is a gathering or get-together or congregation of persons, holding the power of decision-making, for the purpose of discussing certain matters and taking collective decisions. In other words, when the members or shareholders or the directors of a Company arrange to meet at a common place for the purpose of group discussion and taking decisions in the interest of company affairs, we may call it a 'Company Meeting'. Whatever decisions are taken at the meeting, the same form a part of official records of the company and the company working is governed accordingly.

Therefore, the work of holding meetings and conducting business therein, is one of the most important aspects of company's functioning. However, it should be kept in mind that the company meeting should be held strictly in accordance with the provisions laid down under the Companies Act, 1956. The company meetings are more formal in nature and the Company Secretary plays a major role or takes active participation in the sense that the requisitc documents or papers are prepared by him before the meeting is held, a proper record of the summary of discussions held, and the decisions taken at the meeting are maintained in accordance with the rules and regulations prescribed under the company laws.

Types of Meetings :

The Company Meetings may broadly be classified under the heads : (a) Shareholders' Meetings ; (b) Directors' Meetings ; and (c) Committee Meetings. The Shareholders' or Members' meetings may be sub-classified as Statutory Meeting, Annual General Meeting (popularly called the A.G.M.) and Extra-ordinary General Meeting. The details of various types of Meetings have been discussed in the following paragraphs.

Statutory Meetings : These are the meetings required to be conducted under a law, particularly for joint stock companies in India. According to the provisions laid down under the Indian Companies Act, 1956, every company formed under the Act has to hold a compulsory meeting of the shareholders of the company at least within a period of six months and not less than one month from the date of commencement of the company's business to consider a statutory report sent to the members containing the details of formation and commencement of business.

Annual General Meeting : It is a meeting of the shareholders of a joint stock company, required to be held every year under the law, to consider the annual appraisal of the affairs of a company and to approve the annual profit and loss account/Balance Sheet of the company. First of such a meeting is required to be held within a period of maximum 18 months of the date of incorporation and the next within six months after expiry of each financial year every time. However, the Registrar of companies may grant an extension for a maximum period of 3 months. The time between two annual general meetings should, in no case exceed 15 months.

The *legal provisions* in respect of the Annual General Meetings of Companies are as under :—

(i) Every Public and Private Company must hold the annual general meeting of the shareholders at least once in each calender year.

(ii) The first Annual General Meeting of the Shareholders or Members of the Company must be held within a maximum period of 18 months of its incorporation and thereafter within six months of the close of financial year of the Company. However, the Registrar of Companies may allow, as a special case, a further period of three months.

(iii) The Annual General Meeting is intended to enable the members of the company to discuss the affairs of the company and/or to make suggestions for improvement. However, the same should be based on the Auditors' Report and the report of the Directors of the Company.

(iv) A clear and explicit notice specifying the day, date, time and place of the meeting must invariably be communicated to all the members at least 21 days before the specified date of the meeting.

(v) The meeting may be held at the Registered Office of the Company or at any other place in the city where registered office of the company is situated.

(vi) A printed/audited copy of the Balance Sheet and Profit & Loss A/c., Auditors' Report and Directors' Report must be annexed to each notice sent to the shareholders.

(vii) The business transacted at the annual general meeting may be treated as *ordinary business* (viz. consideration and approval of annual accounts and auditors' report o consideration and approval of directors' report, declara tion of dividend, appointment of director/s in place c retiring ones o the appointment of auditors) and an other business may be treated as *special business* of tl A.G.M.

(viii) In case of default in any of the provisions laid down und the Act in holding the Annual General Meeting, t Central Government may, on application from a member, call the meeting or direct the company to h the meeting.

(ix) If the company fails to hold the meeting as per the di tions of the Central Government, the Company and e officer of the Company in default, shall be liable f fine upto Rs. 5,000 and a further fine for each d continuing default.

Secretarial Participation :

In respect of the Annual General Meeting, the Con Secrcetary has to perform the following duties :—

(i) He should arrange to get the annual accounts pr

and get them audited and obtain auditors' certificate.

(ii) Obtain or seek the permission of the Board of Directors and arrange for a Board Meeting preceeding the A.G.M.

(iii) Prepare the draft of Directors' Report and take signatures of all the directors thereupon.

(iv) Prepare the draft of notice and Agenda in consultation of the Chairman and get them all printed, after fixing the date of AGM.

(v) Prepare the Chairman's speech for the Annual General Meeting.

(vi) Arrange to despatch the notice, agenda together with the necessary papers to all the members or shareholders of Company.

(vii) Arrange to close all books of account, proxy form register, and keep all the records ready for the meeting.

(viii) Help the Chairman in the conduct of A.G.M. like ascertaining the 'Quorum' and making the required information readily available in the annual general meeting.

(ix) He should read the notice convening the meeting and the minutes of the last annual general meeting.

(x) Take the notes of the proceedings of the A.G.M. in serial order of the Agenda and get them noted in the Minutes Register.

(xi) Arrange to file necessary papers or documents with the Registrar of Companies, including the Annual Audited Balance Sheet, Profit & Loss Account, Directors' Report etc. and also furnish a copy of the Resolutions passed in the meeting.

(xii) Incorporate the additions or alterations suggested in the meeting and inform the Registrar accordingly.

The Annual Returns are also to be prepared and filed with the Registrar of Companies.

As such, we find that the Annual General Meeting of Shareholders or Members of the Company is an important aspect of company secretary's functioning.

Extra ordinary General Meeting : It is a special meeting called by the representatives of shareholders to consider any abnormal matter.

Board Meetings : The Board of Directors constitute a body consisting of elected representatives of the shareholders, to manage and control the affairs of a company. These are regular meetings held at periodical intervals to consider the matters of routine nature. These are formal and held under the chairmanship of a person who holds the post of a President or Chairman and Managing Director.

Committee Meetings : A committee is a group of persons appointed to carry out a particular function. The committee may be a 'Standing Committee' in which all the members are more or less permanent, or an 'Ad Hoc Committee' which may be formed for a particular purpose only. The members of a committee hold meetings for discussing and taking out certain decisions.

General Procedure

Briefly, the general procedure for conduct of a meeting is that, first of all, the members are sent a *notice* for a meeting to be held at a particular place, date and time. Alongwith the notice, an *Agenda* may be prepared which gives the details of business to be transacted at a meeting. On the appointed day, date and time, the members get together and sign an Attendance Register meant for the purpose of deciding the *Quorum*. A Quorum is 'the minimum number of members' who must be present at a meeting so that the proceedings may be carried out. In the absence of a Quorum, the meeting cannot be held and the same is automatically postponed to any future date. If the Quorum is complete, as per the rules laid down in the Articles of Association or standing orders, the proceedings of meeting may be carried on. Any person, amongst the members, acts as a chairman of the meeting who initiates the proceedings. A *Motion* is made by a member, called the proposer, who proposes any matter as per the agenda by putting it before all the members. Then it is seconded by any other member. Finally, the point is taken up at a meeting for discussion and decision. The same point is either unanimously agreed to by all or it may be put to *voting*. The voting is the process of giving assent or consent in favour or against the motion. It may be done by show of hands, standing, secret-ballets, proxy etc. After voting, the decision is arrived at and the chairman announces the decision. Like it, all the decisions are taken down on paper and called the 'Resolutions'. The brief of all discussions, in seriatum, is taken down in a book called the 'Minutes Book'. The Minutes are the records of proceedings of a meeting and the same are typed and cyclostyled for the information and approval of all the members as well as taking them on official records for necessary action.

Notice

A notice of meeting is an intimation, in writing, addressed to all the members respectively, advising them to attend the meeting to be held at a particular place and on a fixed day, date and time. It may be drafted, typed and cyclostyled by a private secretary. A specimen of the notice is given below :—

Date...........

Dear Shri Smt/Miss...........

....

This is to inform you that a meeting of the Board of Directors of A.B.C. Company (Regd, office.........) will be held on............(day).........(date) at.........P.M. (time) at.........(place). You are requested to be present.

A copy of the Agenda is enclosed.

Yours faithfully

Fnc : As above.
Shri..............

....

Secretary.

The following points must be remembered in connection with the 'Notice':—

(i) The Notice must notify the day, date, time and venue of the meeting specifically to the concerned member.

(ii) The notice must specify the nature of business to be transacted at the meeting, preferably enclosing a detailed Agenda as a part of the notice.

(iii) The notice must be drafted or prepared on a form so as to convey complete information and enabling the member to attend the meeting.

(iv) The notice must contain a reasonable time i.e. sufficient time be allowed to the member for preparing himself/herself for and enabling him/her to attend the meeting conveniently. The period of notice varies as per the rules laid down in the Articles of Association or the Companies Act.

(v) It must be served on all the members who are entitled to participate in the meeting.

(vi) It must be served on the last available address in India on the record of the Company. It may not be sent to a member whose whereabouts are not known or who is residing abroad.

(vii) The notice may be served verbally or on telephone or through a messenger or by dak, depending upon the rules of the company. However, it must necessarily be confirmed in writing.

(viii) Notice of Annual General Meeting must be accompanied by relevant documents, e.g. the annual accounts, report of Auditors and Directors, proxy forms etc.

(ix) The notice convening the Statutory Meeting must accompany the copy of Statutory Reports and other documents.

(x) The notice convening an Extra-ordinary General Meeting must contain the details of special business to be transacted at the meeting and also the terms of resolution.

(xi) Normally 21 days' notice is required to be given to the members for general meeting (Statutory, A.G.M. or xtra-ordinary General Meetings). A shorter notice may be given provided the members give their consent for it, particularly those holding at least 95 per cent of the paid-up share capital.

(xii) Where any member wishes to give a special notice to the company for any special resolution, 14 days' notice is necessary.

(xiii) The days in the notice period must be clear days i.e. excluding the day on which notice is issued, received and the postal transit period of one or two days.

Secretarial Practice

The Company Secretary should take the following *steps* in respect of the Notice for Company Meetings :—

(i) He should draft the notice by taking into account the instructions of Company's Board of Directors.

(ii) Depending upon the nature of company meeting, the secretary should inculcate the details of day, date, time, venue etc., in the notice.

(iii) The Notice may be got cyclostyled or printed taking into account the requisite number required.

(iv) Attach the necessary papers or documents including the Agenda.

(v) Communicate the Notice to all members within the period required under the rules.

(vi) If necessary, he should read the notice or Agenda in the meeting.

Notice

A notice of meeting is an intimation, in writing, addressed to all the members respectively, advising them to attend the meeting to be held at a particular place and on a fixed day, date and time. It may be drafted, typed and cyclostyled by a private secretary. A specimen of the Notice is given below :—

Dear Shri/Smt./Miss........... Date...........

....

This is to inform you that a meeting of the Board of Directors of A.B.C. Company Ltd. (Regd. Office.........) will be held on...... (day).........(date) at.........P.M. (time) at.........(place). You are requested to be present.

A copy of the Agenda is enclosed.

Yours faithfully,
Secretary

Enc : As above
Shri............
....

Agenda

An Agenda is a paper containing the list of business to be transacted at a meeting. In other words, it is the programme which gives the details of matters to be discussed and decided upon at a meeting as per the serial order. As we know, a meeting is a formal discussion on certain matters ; and therefore, whatever matters are to be put before the members of a meeting, those are serially arranged in the Agenda and taken up at the meeting in that particular serial order. Usually, no other matter is taken up at the meeting, except with the prior permission of the Chairman. All matters enlisted in the Agenda are taken up one by one at the meeting, discussed and decided upon.

The drafting of an Agenda is very easy. First of all, we have to give the heading as 'AGENDA' and then write the number and nature of meeting to be held. Thereafter the day, date and venue for the meeting are written. Then one by one all the matters to be taken up at the meeting, are listed in seriatum. Usually, the first item in the Agenda is "confirmation of the minutes of last meeting held on.........." It is necessary because a meeting cannot be held unless the 'minutes' i.e. the proceedings of the meeting held earlier are read over and confirmed by all the members of a meeting. Hence, the necessity for listing the same at serial number 1. The last item in the Agenda is usually "Any other matter with the permission of the Chair" i.e. the last item is always kept open. If there is any other matter which might arise during the course of meeting, the same may be taken up by seeking permission of the Chairman. As such, the first and the last items of the Agenda are always fixed. In between, we may list the items of business which may be taken up at a particular meeting.

The Agenda may be written/typed on a letter-head or a plain paper, rather it is cyclostyled so as to make available the required number of copies for all the members/participants of a meeting. It is always prepared in advance i.e. much before the date of a meeting and delivered by hand or by post, at the last available addresses of all the members. The idea behind sending the Agenda, much earlier to the date of meeting, is that each member should know, in advance, as to the business to be transacted at the meeting so that he prepares himself for thorough discussion and arriving at certain decision. The papers or supporting documents are enclosed with the Agenda so that complete information may be conveyed to each member.

Many times, the 'Notice' and 'Agenda' are made two-in-one i.e. the notice is not prepared separately as the Agenda itself serves the purpose of a notice.

Specimen of an Agenda

Date...............

AGENDA

Of the 4th meeting of Board of Directors of A.B.C. Company Ltd., Regd. Office : 5-Parliament street, New Delhi, will be held at Claridges Hotel, New Delhi, on Tuesday, the 12th July, 1987 at 4.00 p.m. to consider the following matters :—

1. Confirmation of the Minutes of last meeting held on 12th February, 1985.

2. Payment of Bonus to staff for the year ended 31st Dec. 1984.
3. Sanction of housing loans to staff.
4. Closure of Plant No. II.
5. Any other matter with the permission of the Chair.

New Delhi, 5th July, 1984

Sd/—
SECRETARY

So far as preliminary works of a meeting are concerned, the secretary should collect the necessary details and draw up the Agenda on the lines explained earlier. He/she must ensure that the Agenda is prepared without overlooking any important detail and that all the papers i.e. supporting documents are enclosed with the Agenda and despatched on time to each and every member/participant of meeting.

On the day of meeting, the secretary is usually expected to attend the meeting in order to take down the notes of proceedings. It must be remembered that only the relevant business details should be noted down. Since it is not possible to take down each and every detail of dicussion, the secretary should keep a copy of Agenda with him/her and go on noting down the relevant details of discussions held and the decisions taken. Later on, these are got typed out and got approved from the Chairman of the meeting.

Specimen of Notice for Annual General Meeting

A.B.C. COMPANY LTD.

Regd. Office : 10, Parliament Street,

New Delhi-110001.

NOTICE

Notice is hereby given that the 10th Annual General Meeting of the Shareholders of A.B.C. Company Ltd. (Regd. Office : 10, Parliament Street, New Delhi-110001 will be held at Ficci Auditorium, Barakhamba Road, New Delhi, on Wednesday, the 15th July,1987 at 11.00 A.M. to transact the business as listed in the Agenda enclosed herewith.

Secretary

Enc : As above

Specimen of Agenda for the Annual General Meeting

A.B.C. COMPANY LTD.

(Regd. Office : 10-Parliament Street, New Delhi.)

AGENDA

Of the 11th Annual General Meeting of the Company to be held on Sunday, the 10th July, 1987 at 9.30 A.M. at Hans Raj College Hall, Malka Ganj, Delhi-110007. The following matters will be taken up :—

1. Confirmation of the minutes of the last meeting of the last year.
2. Chairman's Report on the performance and progress of the last year.
3. Adoption of the Profit & Loss Account and Balance Sheet of the Company for the year 1986-87.
4. Audit Report for the year 1986-87.
5. Distribution of Profits for the year 1986-87.
6. Any other matter with the permission of the Chair.

Secretary

Attendance and Quorum :

Before the meeting commences, it is the practice to get the signatures of all the participants on a separate Attendance Register maintained to ascertain the 'Quorum' required for a valid meeting.

Derived from Latin, the word 'Quorum' refers to the minimum number of persons who must be present at the meeting. It is essential that the minimum number of members must be present at the commencement and throughout the meeting session, so that whatever business is transacted at the meeting, the same may be legally valid. Without a complete quorum at the meeting, the discussions held or decisions taken may be challenged and may be held null and void or the meeting may be postponed *sine die* i.e. automatically postponed without fixing up any future date.

Generally, the quorum is treated to be 1/3 of the total strength of members eligible to attend the meeting and vote. However, the quorum is decided as per the rules given in the Articles of Association of the Company or under the 'standing orders'. In the absence of any provision in any of the above, the rules given under the Companies Act, 1956 shall apply. The Act provides that the quorum for general meetings of shareholders shall be *two* for private companies and *five* for public companies.

According to *Sec. 287* of the Companies Act, 1956, the quorum of Board Meetings is one-third of the total strength of the Board of Directors or two directors, whichever is higher (any fraction being rounded-off as one). The Chairman of the meeting has to wait so long as the quorum is not complete. Once the meeting starts with the quorum and in between any member goes away, making the total number of present members falling short of the quorum, the business of the meeting must stop altogether because any business done in the absence of quorum is liable to be held invalid. The proxies cannot be counted while determining the quorum unless the Articles of Association of the Company concerned provides so specifically.

Though the deciding Authority in respect of the Quorum is the Chairman yet the Company Secretary should ascertain the quorum from the Articles of Association or the standing orders and inform the Chairman accordingly. He may count the number of members and verify the number from the Attendance Register. If the quorum is not present within half an hour of the appointed time of the meeting, he may advise the Chairman to adjourn the meeting. It may be adjourned for the same day and time in the next week or as per the decision of the Board of Directors (applicable to Board Meetings only). The General Meeting may be adjourned *sine die.*

The Chairman of a Meeting

A person presiding over or conducting the proceedings of a meeting, may be called the 'Chairman' of a company meeting. He is the sole authority for taking decisions in respect of the discussions, voting etc., held at the meeting and is responsible for maintaining proper decorum and discipline at the meeting.

The appointment of Chairman is generally made either by nomination or designation or by seniority amongst the members or as per the rules provided under the Articles of Association. The Chairman and Managing Director of an Organisation may be the ex-officio chairman of a meeting. However, it is necessary that the chairman is elected or designated beforehand. Under *Regulation 51* of Table 'A' of Companies Act, 1956 provides that in the absence of a regular Chairman or, if he is not present at the meeting within 15 minutes of the appointed time of a meeting any other member or director amongst those present for the meeting, may be elected as a Chairman.

Qualifications & Qualities

In view of the fact that the meeting is conducted successfully and legally valid, it is essential that the Chairman of a Meeting should possess the following qualifications and/or qualities :—

(i) He must have a sound educational background so that he is able to take decisions rightly and quickly.
(ii) He should have complete knowledge of the general rules or procedures for conducting the meeting as to how quorum is decided, how voting may be done, how the motions may be moved etc., etc.
(iii) He should have a command over the language/s.
(iv) He must have an impressive personality so that he may control the members at the meeting.
(v) He must have leadership qualities so that he can take a lead in commencing or winding up the proceedings of the meeting.
(vi) He should have tact, commonsense, even temper, patience, discretionary power and the firm determination so that he can control the affairs at the meeting well.
(vii) He must have a legal background for conducting the proceedings validly.
(viii) He must have the capacity to enforce discipline and decorum amongst the participants.

Duties and Powers

The Chairman, by virtue of his status or position, derives all the authority in respect of conduct of a meeting and he is duty bound to convene the meeting, conduct its business properly and informing all members fully well. His *main duties* are :—

(i) To attend the meeting at the appointed time and venue.
(ii) To ensure that the discussions are held in accordance with the serial order in the Agenda.
(iii) To maintain proper discipline and decorum during the meeting session.
(iv) To ensure that equal opportunity is given to all memebrs for discussion before taking a final decision.

(v) To ensure that the rules and regulations are observed properly.
(vi) To protect the interests of minority and giving preference to the majority.

For perfoımance of the above said duties, the Chairman has a right to exercise certain powers viz. :—

(i) The chairman can decide the order of priority for discussion by the members.
(ii) He may ask any member any point or stop him for doing anything which may be necessary for maintaining discipline or decorúm.
(iii) He can adjourn the meeting if the quorum is not complete or there is anything requiring him to do so in company's interest.
(iv) He may restrict any member to speak for a reasonable time.
(v) He may exercise his franchise by casting a vote for decision-making.
(vi) He can do anything so as to ensure that the meeting is well conducted within the rules.

Motion, Amendment and Resolution

A 'Motion' is a formal and definite proposal put before a meeting for consideration, discussion and taking decision thereupon. An 'Amendment' to the motion is any alteration in terms of the wordings of the main motion proposed by a member and seconded by another. An amendment may be made in the same way as a motion. The 'Resolution' is the formal decision taken at a meeting after discussing and voting upon by members. All the above three terms are different from each other on the following lines :—

A 'Motion'	*An 'Amendment'*	*A 'Resolution'*
1. It is an original proposal put before a meeting at first hand.	1. It is an alteration proposed in the wordings of the motion.	1. After the motion is discussed and voted upon, it is in the form of a decision arrived at the meeting.
2. It initiates the discussion at the	2. It interrupts the discussion at the	2. It is the end result of the discus-

meeting.	meeting.	sions at the meeting.
3. It may be altered.	3. It may be altered or substantiated.	3. It cannot be altered after passing at the meeting.
4. It should be in writing and signed by the mover.	4. It is also in writing and signed by the mover.	4. It is written in the minutes which are signed by the Chairman.
5. It is moved by one person and seconded by another.	5. It is moved by a person and seconded by another.	5. There is no such thing in a resolution.
6. It may be withdrawn before voting.	6. It may be withdrawn before voting.	6. It cannot be withdrawn if once passed.
7. No one can speak more than once on a motion.	7. No one can speak more than once on the same amendment.	7. There is no question of speaking after the resolution is passed.

Voting and Proxy

Voting is the process or basis of taking a decision at a company meeting. Whenever there is a difference of opinion amongst the members on a particular point, the voting is done in order to decide it by majority. There are several *methods* of voting. It may be done by poll i.e. casting a ballot paper into the box, by standing, by exclamation, by division, by show of hands or even by proxy. A 'proxy' is the person who is nominated by a member and is authorised to be present at a meeting in the absence of a member. Under the provisions of the Companies Act, every member of the company is authorised to appoint another person (a member or a non-member) to represent him at the meeting. There is an instrument, in writing, for appointing the proxy which should be deposited with the company within 48 hours of the commencement of the meeting. The proxy may be general or special. A general proxy may do all acts in general on behalf of the member, whereas a special proxy is appointed for a specific purpose only.

Board Meetings

The Directors are the persons who are the representatives of the shareholders of a Company. A body of directors formed for the purpose of management and control of affairs of the company, is called the 'Board of Directors.' According to the provisions laid down under the Companies Act, 1956, the meeting of the Board of Directors of any company may be held at least one in three months, and at least four such meetings must be held during one calendar year. The Board meetings may be held more frequently if the circumstances require and if provided for in the Articles of Association of the company. The notice of such meetings may be given in writing to every Director on the latest address in India available on company's record. The quorum for such a meeting is generally one-third of the total number of Directors or as provided in the standing orders or Articles of Association of the concerned company. The chairman, who has to preside over the meeting, may be named by the Directors themselves or the name may be given in the Articles of Association. The general procedure of conducting such meetings is the same as explained earlier. However, the Board of Directors may exercise all powers vested in them for managing the day-to-day affairs or policy matters.

Essentials of a Meeting :

All the provisions, as laid down under the Indian Companies Act 1956, are applicable throughout, right from formation, existence to the winding up of a company. *Sections 171 to 186* of the Companies Act, 1956 contain the various provisions for holding the general meetings by a public cempany and its subsidiaries. The Articles of Association of the respective private company may include the additional rules for the conduct of meetings but those private companies are free to make their own rules by including in the Articles of Association, in the absence of which, the provisions of the Companies Act are applicable.

However, for a Company, it is necessary that the meeting should be held validly so that the decisions taken at the meeting are legally binding.

For a legal and validly held meeting, the following things are necessary :—

(i) **Proper Convening** : The meeting should be covened properly in the sense that only the competent authority may call a meeting. For convening the Annual General Meeting, Statutory Meeting and the Extra-ordinary General Meeting, the Board of Directors of the respective company may call for such meetings by a duly passed resolution. The Company Board or the Central Government may also convene it. Moreover a due and proper notice may be given.

stating the exact details about the day, date, time and venue of the meeting and that the notice should be properly served/delivered at the latest available address in India of all the members called for the meeting.

(ii) **Properly Constituted** : The meeting is required to be held under the chairmanship of a duly elected and qualified Chairman who must have a thorough knowledge about the conduct of a meeting and, after completing the quorum, the meeting may be validly held. For an ideal Chairman of a meeting the *qualities and qualifications* should be that he must be able to address the meeting and co-ordinate the group activities like a good leader. He should know the general law and procedures of the meeting and be able to maintain orderly progress of the meeting. He should in five years' continuous service and/are on permanent rolls of the Company. Further resolved that the Secretary be and hereby authorised to complete all the formalities in this behalf.

Amongst the *duties* of a Chairman of a meeting, he must ensure that the meeting is properly convened by a duly served notice, the proceedings are conducted according to the law and rules in force, the discussions are made only on specific motions, proper decorum and discipline is maintained, equal opportunity is given to all for discussing and saying.

So far as the *powers* of the chairman are concerned, he is empowered to adjourn the meeting, maintain relevancy and order, decide the order and priority for discussions, decide the points to be discussed and exercise casting a vote.

It may not be out of place to mention here that in the absence of a permanent Chairman any one of the senior members nominated may take over as Chairman of the meeting.

For the Annual General Meeting, Extraordinary General Meeting and Statutory Meetings, minimum 21 days' clear notice is required but for Board Meetings, the length of notice may be decided as per rules given in the Articles of Association of the Company.

(iii) **Properly Conducted** : It is also necessary that the *proceedings* of a meeting should be lawfully carried on—strictly as per serial order given in the Agenda unless it is changed by the chairman with the consent of all members. For discussing any point, it should be brought on the 'Motion' duly proposed by one person and seconded by another. The members can speak only on a motion formally moved before the meeting. During discussions, all remarks should be addressed to the Chair. Only one person may speak at one time and not more than once on a motion. The Motions and the Amendments should be in writing and signed by the mover (proposer) and the seconder. The resolution may be passed with the consent of all the members or by a vote of majority.

(iv) **Proper Record of Proceedings** : When the decisions are taken at a meeting after a thorough discussion amongst all the members and or voting, the same should be properly recorded.

Minutes

Whatever has been discussed and decided upon at a meeting, the datails of all that may be called 'Minutes of a meeting'. In other words, Minutes are the records of the proceedings of a meeting. These form the part of discussions made by the members at a meeting and the final conclusions arrived at (technically called the 'Resolutions').

While drafting the 'Minutes', care should be taken that the points respective should be taken up in the same serial order as already listed in the Agenda. On each point, the discussions (in brief) be written and thereafter the resolutions passed unanimously or by a vote of majority be recorded. The minutes should be in seriatum, brief and to the point. These should be the same as recorded in the 'Minutes Book'.

The Minutes, again, are typed on a plain paper, rather cyclostyled so as to get as many copies as required for personal record of all members as well as for the official records. These should be got approved from the Chairman and signed by him. The rough draft may be prepared at first-hand and then got approved from the Chairman, before cyclostyling them.

SPECIMEN OF MINUTES

Minutes of the 4th meeting of Board of Directors of A.B.C. Company Ltd., Regd. Office : 5-Parliament Street, New Delhi, held at the Claridges Hotel, New Delhi on Tuesday, the 26 March, 1985 at 2.00 P.M.

The following were present : 15 members as per the Attendance Register. In Attendance : Shri B.S. Johsi, Chartered Accountant and Financial Consultant.

The following matters were taken up and the resolutions passed :—

1. The Minutes of the last meeting held on 12th February 1985 were read over by the Secretary and confirmed.

2. *Payments of Bonus* : The Chairman proposed to pay bonus to staff members of the Company at the same rate and terms as last year. It was seconded by the Treasurer.

Resolved that Bonus @8.33% (as of the last year) be and hereby paid to all the staff members of the company on the same terms and conditions. Further resolved that the Secretary be and hereby authorised to ensure immediate release of payment after completing necessary formalities in the matter.

3. *Housing Loan* : The matter was taken up at the meeting, moved by the Secretary and seconded by the Treasurer.

Resolved that housing loan upto a maximum of Rs. one lakh be and hereby granted to all such staff members who have put in five years' continuous service and are on permanent rolls of the Company. Further Resolved that the Secretary be and hereby authorised to complete all the formalities in this behalf.

4. *Closure of Plant No-II* : The matter was taken up at the meeting moved by the Chairman and seconded by the Treasurer. Resolved by a vote of majority that plant No. II be and hereby closed looking into the genuine difficulties. Further resolved that the Secretary be and hereby authorised to take up necessary action in the matter.

No other matter was discussed and the meeting ended with a vote of thanks to the Chair.

Sd/-
CHAIRMAN

New Delhi
26th March, 1985.

From the above specimen of 'Minutes' it may be noted that the language for recording the discussions and decisions (in the form of resolutions passed) is almost stereotype and the same may be used while drafting Minutes of any meeting. Another thing to note is that in 'Attendance' column, we may write the names of the members but in case the list of members is lengthy, it might not be possible to write the individual names. Hence, we may write 'as per Attendance Register'. In the column, 'In Attendance' we should write the name of any special guest or V.I.P. invited specially to attend the meeting. Besides it, if there is any condolence resolution to be passed at a meeting, the same is recorded as the first item in the Minutes.

However, the Secretary must ensure that the Minutes are properly drafted, and cyclostyled after getting the rough draft approved from the Chairman. A copy of it may be forwarded to each and every member for his personal record and information. A copy of Minutes may also be kept on official records for the purpose of guidance and taking up necessary action in the matter.

Specimen of Minutes of Annual General Meeting :

A.B.C. COMPANY LTD.

(Regd. Office : 10-Parliament Street, New Delhi-I)

MINUTES

of the 10th Annual General Meeting of A.B.C. Co. Ltd., Regd, Office at 10, Parliament Street, New Delhi-110 001 held on Wednesday, the 22nd July, 1987 at 10.30 A.M. at the registered office of the Company.

The following persons were present :

1. ....Chairman
2. ....Treasurer
3. ....Director
4, (Directors)
5. (Auditor)

and 50 shareholders of the Company.

1. The Secretary read over the notice convening the Annual General Meeting as well as the Minutes of the last Annual General Meeting held on 12th July 1986. at the request of the Chairman and the same were confirmed.

2. The Balance Sheet, Profit & Loss Account for the year ended 31st December, 1986 and the Directors Report were taken as read and adopted by all the members present.

3. The Auditor read over the Audit Report of accounts for the year ended 31st December, 1986.

4. The Chairman delivered the speech, highlighting the achievements made by the Company during the last year and apprised the members of the developmental plans for the year

1987-88. The copies of the speech were circulated and sent to the press.

5. *Payment of dividend* : The matter for payment of dividend on shares @12% p.a. was moved by the Chairman and recommended by the Directors.

Resolved that a dividend @12% p.a. on equity shares of the Company be declared and paid to the shareholders for the year ended 31st December, 1986.

6. *Appointment of Director* : The matter for appointing Mr. Intelligent as the New Director in place of Mr. Coward, retiring director was taken up and moved by the Chairman and seconded by the Treasurer.

Resolved that Mr. Intelligent be and hereby appointed as the new Director in rotation in place of Mr. Coward, who retires w. e. f. 31st July, 1987.

No other matter was taken up and the meeting ended with a vote of thanks to the Chair.

Sd/-
CHAIRMAN

Place : New Delhi
Dated : 22nd July, 1987.

SPECIAL RESOLUTIONS

A Special Resolution refers to the decision taken at the meeting of the company on a special policy or crucial matter or on a point which has a material effect on company's working. Generally, voting is done at the meeting for passing the special resolution and not less than 3/4 of the total votes should be cast in favour of the special resolution. In other words, we may say that the special resolution is the decision taken at the meeting on a matter that is supported by 3/4th majority.

The types of business or matters on which special resolutions are required may be enumerated as under :—

(i) Material Alteration in any of the Clauses of the Memorandum of Association of the Company;
(ii) Alteration in the Articles of Association of the Company;
(iii) Reduction in share capital of the company;
(iv) Payment of interest out of share capital of the company;
(v) Granting loans to companies under the same management;
(vi) Winding up the Company; and

(vii) Any other matter adversely affecting the interests of shareholders, debentureholders or the creditors of the company.

However, in respect of the Special Resolution, the duty of a Company Secretary is that he must take necessary permission of the Company's Directors by convening the Board Meeting, making necessary arrangements for convening the extra-ordinary general meeting of the shareholders in which the matter for special resolution is put on motion, the wording of the Resolution should be specific and clear, the copy of the special resolution is filed with the Registrar of Companies within the stipulated period as mentioned under the Companies Act, the required permission or order of the Company Law Board of the Competent Court should also be obtained and certified copies thereof should be invariably forwarded to the Registrar of Companies. Besides it, he must ensure to make necessary additions/alterations in the books and registers of the company after notifying the special resolution.

Specimen of Special Resolution

1. **For alteration in Company's Name :**

"Resolved that the approval of the Central Government having been obtained, the name of the Company being Jindal & Company Limited, be and hereby changed as Jindal Associates Limited.

Further resolved that the aforesaid alteration be and hereby made in the Memorandum, Articles of Association and all other documents of the Company."

2. **For Reduction in Share Capital :**

"Resolved that the share capital of the company be and hereby reduced from Rs. 12 lakhs divided into 12,000 equity shares of Rs. 100 each to Rs. 10 lakhs divided into 10,000. Equity shares of Rs. 100 each by reducing the liability of the company in respect of share capital by Rs. 2 lakhs.'

Difference between Ordinary and Special Resolution :

An ordinary resolution is one which is the decision taken, after discussion at a company meeting, in the ordinary course of company's business, may be unanimously or through voting. The special resolution is taken at the company meeting by a vote of 3/4th majority. However, the above two types of Resolutions may be distinguished on the following points :—

Ordinary Resolution	*Special Resolution*
1. It is passed in respect of the routine matters of the company.	1. It is passed in respect of special matters like material alterations in company documents or change in the policy.
2. The ordinary resolution is taken at the annual general meeting of shareholders.	2. It is taken at the extra-ordinary general meeting of the company.
3. Generally, there is no penalty imposed for default in ordinary resolution.	3. In case of default in the special resolution, the penalty imposed under the Act is heavy.
4. A copy of the ordinary resolution should not necessarily be sent to the Registrar of Companies.	4. A certified photo copy of the special resolution must necessarily be forwarded to the Registrar of Companies within the stipulated period of time.
5. An ordinary resolution may be taken with 2/3rd majority of votes.	5. The special resolution is taken with 3/4 majority of votes at the company meeting.
6. Not much care and caution in drafting the words of the ordinary resolution.	6. Much care and caution in giving the wording of the special resolution.

Legal Provisions in respect of 'Minutes'

The provisions relating to writing and maintaining the Minutes of a Company Meeting have been laid down under *Section 193* of the Companies Act, 1956. The important ones have been given below :

(i) Every Company shall have to keep minutes of proceedings of each and every general meeting in separate books maintained for the purpose i.e. the Minutes Book or Minutes Register.

(ii) The entries in the Minutes Book must be made within 30 days of the conclusion of the meeting.

(iii) The minutes of each meeting must contain a fair and correct summary of the proceedings.

(iv) Each page of the Minute Book must be initialled or refused and the last page must be dated and signed by the Chairman of the meeting.

(v) If any appointment of officers is made, the same should be included in the minutes.

(vi) The Chairman has an absolute discretionary power in regard to not including any matter which may be detrimental to the interests of the company or which may be defamatory.

(vii) The Minute Book must be kept at the Registered Office of the Company and kept open for inspection for at least two hours a day during business hours to any member without any charge.

(viii) Non-compliance of any of the provisions, shall make the Company and every officer, in default, be liable to a fine upto Rs. 50.

QUESTIONS

1. What is an Annual General Meeting of a Company? Outline the business usually transacted at this meeting. State the statutory rules governing the holding of annual general meeting. *(B. Com. Pass, Delhi, 1986)*

2. Write short notes on
   (i) Special Resolution
   (ii) Poll *(B. Com. Pass, Delhi, 1986)*

3(a) What is a 'Statutory meeting'? Discuss the duties of company secretary in connection with the holding of statutory meeting.

(b) Draft a notice, giving suitable agenda, for the meeting of Board of Directors of a public limited company. *(B. Com. Pass, Delhi, 1985)*

4. What is annual general meeting? What are the legal provisions as to this meeting? State the duties of the company secretary in relation to such a meeting. *(B. Com. Pass, Delhi, 1984)*

5(a) Draft Agenda for the Annual General Meeting of a company.

(b) Write a note on Quorum for the Annual Meeting. *(B. Com. Pass, Delhi, 1983)*

6. Explain any two of the following
   (a) Voting by Proxy
   (b) Minutes and Reports *(B. Com. Pass, Delhi, 1981)*

7. Write notes on :
   (a) Quorum
   (b) Statutory Meeting
   (c) Duties and Powers of the Chairman of a company meeting. (*B. Com. Pass, Delhi, 1980*)
8. Write notes on :
   (a) Motion and Amendment to Motion
   (b) Board Meetings
   (c) Essentials of a valid company meeting.

9(a) What is an 'Extraordinary General Meeting'?
(b) Who may convene Extraordinary General Meeting ?
(c) Draft an agenda of Annual General Meeting of a Public Limited Company. (*B. Com. 1987*)

5

PRIVATE SECRETARY : QUALITIES OF AN OUTSTANDING PRIVATE SECRETARY

All persons have got certain qualities. Some of these are innate or inborn whereas the others are to be developed by experience and exercise. Still, in most of the cases, the qualities are properly developed through constant practice, dedication and devotion. Particularly, for a private secretary, who has to maintain business relations with outsiders, cordial relations with superiors and friendly relations with colleagues. It is necessary that certain good qualities must be possessed by him/her so that the task may become interesting, fruitful and effective.

All the qualities to be possessed by a private secretary, in order to be outstanding and useful or indispensable in an office, may be broadly classified under the following heads :—

(*a*) Basic education and other qualifications :—

- (*i*) Universty Degree or its equivalent
- (*ii*) Secretarial Practice Course or Training
- (*iii*) Fluency in English-speaking and knowledge of other languages
- (*iv*) Knowledge of Business, Accounts and Finance
- (*v*) Knowledge of Office Procedures and Methods
- (*vi*) Knowledge of correspondence

(*b*) Proficiency of the job :—

(*c*) Capacity to handle confidential matters

(*d*) Personality Traits or personal qualities, which go to make the right standard and character.

Now, we shall discuss each one of the above qualities, in details, in the following paragraph :—

He is expected to be an all-rounder i.e. jack of all trades. He/she has to perform all sorts of works which facilitate the boss or executive in carrying out the details of his work. The private secretary is like an independent loyal right-hand of the boss. His/her activities may include right from typing and taking dictation to drafting routine official or business correspondence, reports, Agenda and Minutes of Meetings, etc. He/she may have to receive, sort out and record the incoming mail and then putting the same for the information and action to be taken. It is also his/her duty to attend the incoming telephone calls and receive the visitors, to fix appointments on behalf of the boss in consultation with him, dialling the telephone number for the boss and to put necessary communication between the boss and the outsiders. He/she is supposed to remind the boss to keep up the appointments or meetings/conferences. He/she has to supervise the work of the office where other staff members are also working. He/she has to ensure that all the records are maintained properly and to look after the stationery ond other supplies of office. He/she has also to attend the work connected with meetings/conferences and to fix up so many details about the programmes, including the tour/visit of the boss to any place within the country or outside the country. Not only this, when the boss is away from office, he/she has to keep the office running smoothly. In addition to the above, he/she has to handle many other works depending upon the exigencies. The objective is that he/she should make the boss free from all worries of routine works. Hence, he/she has to be an all-rounder i.e. competent to perform any work by maintaining the confidence of the boss. The task is really challenging but dignified and paying.

BASIC EDUCATION AND OHTER QUALIFICATIONS

Since a private secretary has to perform a number of important functions for his/her boss, it is primarily necessary that he/she should have a good educational background. He/she should preferably be a graduate, holding a university degree or its equivalent, with good percentage of marks or division in all the past examinations. Most of the Organisations prefer a convent-educated person. The idea behind it is that there should be a good base of english speaking, reading and writing. For an outstanding private secretary, it is necessary that he/she should be well-eductaed because the more the educaton, the greater is the awareness and better power of understanding, grasping and expressing thoughts. Hence, the importance of sound educational background for a private secretary. Particularly, for the senior secretary's position, holding of a university degree is essential but, for the post of a junior secretary, even 10+2 or first-class higher secondary would also do.

It may be noted here that the basic education may be in any field of study whether science, arts or commerce. Still, the knowledge of commerce is necessarily required for a good private secretary because most of the rountine office work is based on commercial practice.

Secretarial Course/Training

Now-a-days, there are facilities to undertake specialised course by way of obtaining a certificate or diploma in secretarial practice course conducted by the various institutions including those recognised by the Government. The duration of this course may be one year or two years. The prospective private secretary may successfully complete the course. There are various advantages of this course e.g. specialised knowledge in typing, shorthand, correspondence, office procedures, elementary book-keeping/accounts and also in business organisation. As this course is practice-oriented, the students may get basic training of working as a successful private secretary and he/she can become far better for working as compared to a fresh hand from school or college. After completion of the above course, the prospective candidate may successfully work as a junior private secretary and, after taking some practical experienee in the line, he/she may be absorbed as a Senior Private Secretary.

Fluency in English Speaking and Knowledge of other Languages

A private secretary must know his/her job well, including the dealings with in-person callers or visitors and over the telephone. For this purpose, it is necessary that he/she must be able to express well so that the outsiders may be easily tackled and dealt with sucessfully. The knowledge of languages, particulary English or Hindi (our national language) and one or two regional languages, would enable the private secretary to deal with visitors or callers effectively and successfully. Besides the above, it would be better for the private secretary to know any foreign language like German, French or Russian etc. because the same would be very useful in international trade dealings. As such, it would be better if more and more languages are known to the private secretary, particularly for reading or speaking purposes.

Knowledge of Business, Accounts and Finance

It is also necessary for a private secretary to have the elementary knowledge of business, commerce, accounts, and finance because he/she may have to perfom works connected with these faculties of knowledge. He/she may have to handle cash and backing transactions for the office of boss, write accounts and use the basic methods or procedures of the above subjects while discharging the duties as a private secretary.

Knowledge of office Procedures/Methods

For easy performance of the office routine duties, a private secretary is required to know the general procedures of office working. These may include the handling of inward mail, operating of various office machines and equipments, filing, indexing, communication systems etc. This would enable the private secretary to perform his/her duties efficiently.

Knowledge of Correspondence

As most of the office work involves writing of letters in office, the private secretary should have a thorough knowledge of the principles of good letter-writing, lay-out, styles of letter-writing and the drafting of routine business letters and official correspondence. Since the boss is very busy in his responsible and more important works, the private secretary must know the independent drafting of routine letters and correspondence.

Need for General Awareness and Knowledge

The General Knowledge consists of knowing the recent developments in political, economical and social fields as well as knowing the who's who at the national and international levels. It can be achieved by reading the daily newspapers, periodicals, magazines or Year Books. The private secretary should keep the up-to-date knowledge about these things as these are helpful in drafting speeches, reports etc. and also for utilising the information in the working of his/her organisation.

Proficiency of the Job

A private secretary must know his/her job well and, for this purpose, it is necessary that he/she should be efficient and proficient in typing and shorthand. He/she should be in a position to take dictation in shorthand and transcribe it accurately with a good speed in typing, There should be perfect knowledge of spellings of words, formation of sentences etc. The efficient handling of telephone, telex, intercom, dictaphone and other allied office machines and equipments like postal franking machine, cash register, adding and listing machine, calculator, cyclostyling machine etc. should be very well known to a private secretary.

Stenographic Skills

A private secretary has primarily to be a good steno-typist or a stenographer, possessing the skills of taking dictation in shorthand and transcribing the matter accurately and neatly. Though these may be the routine tasks, yet improving the skills in shorthand and typing add to the efficiency of a private secretary.

Firstly, he/she should keep the tools in sufficient quantity and ready for use. *A shorthand note book* with sufficient pages to take notes from the boss, the stale notes, which have been already transcribed, be crossed out and separated from current pages by using a rubberband around the used pages or folding a page of short-hand note book from where the current notes are to commence. It might also be a good idea using only one side of the short-hand notebook and leaving sufficient left-hand margin on each and every page in order to insert notations, corrections and instructions etc. Each page should be dated at the top to provide for future reference.

Two or more *pencils or spare pens* are indispensable. It is no use to look lost if the point of a pencil wears out and he/she does not have another one. That is why, a private secretary should always take two or more than one pencil/pen for emergencies.

Secondly, a private secretary should select a comfortable seat and the elbows have support during the dictation period because it helps in securing greater speed and taking dictation for longer durations.

A good private secretary should make it a practice to take dictation with interruptions. Many times, the interruptions are also helpful to a private secretary because if he/she is lagging behind, it is not good to ask the boss to wait for some time, rather take advantage of interruptions to catch up. Moreover, if anything is misheard or not heard properly, the private secretary may clarify the doubts or make a sense out of it.

During the course of dictation, the boss may appreciate *participation* of the private secretary. He/she should respond intelligently to what is dictated and may even participate by suggesting suitable words. If there is anything wrong, there is no harm in putting his/her own suggestion intelligently after listening carefully.

The private secretary has not to write non-stop as there are pauses often when the boss may receive a telephone call, a sudden visitor calling on or taking time to think. In these pauses, a good private secretary never wastes the time, rather uses it constructively by checking over the notes, filling in the omissions, clarifying the doubts and clearing the ill-formed symbols of short-hand.

It is useful to evolve special short-hand symbols or outlines for words, phrases and sentences which occur frequently in the boss's dictation. It helps in gaining good speed in short-hand.

The names, addresses and other remarks for carbon copies, mailing directions etc. should preferably be noted down in long-hand for future reference at any time.

CAPACITY TO HANDLE SECRET/CONFIDENTIAL MATTERS

A private secretary is a person on whom the boss/executive reposes full confidence. As such, all matter of office must be handled in such a way that no one else might know the information so long as it is not permitted to be disclosed. For this purpose, you should not enter into more and loose talks. If the information is leaked out untimely; it looses its importance, and many times, the results are horrible. The prtvate secretary should keep his/her mouth shut for all matters which are not required to be disclosed, rather use tact under such circumstances.

PERSONALITY TRAITS OR PERSONAL QUALITIES

In order to become outstanding and indispensable in office, a private secretary should possess certain personal qualities, which may be enumerated as under. These would help in making private secretary's standard and character.

Common Sense—Though common sense is not so common,

yet a private secretary should have the sense of knowing what is good, what is bad, what to do, what not to do etc. There are crtain things which nobody would tell him/her in the office. The private secretary should have the sense of finding them out and utilise them properly at the appropriate time.

Tact—It implies to act in a particular fashion at a particular time or under particular conditions. Every time the tact may be used so that you do not become bad to anyone and, at the same time, the purpose is served. It is the art of behaving differently under different circumstances. A boss is always interested in getting the work done. How you do it and what you should do about it—it all depends upon the tact you use.

Loyalty—A private secretary has to be loyal to the boss and his/her own organisation, watching and protecting the interests of both. One should always feel that his/her own existence depends upon the progress of the organisation. It would bring in devotion and faithfulness.

Courtesy—It consists of showing politeness in behaving with others as well as showing promptness in attending to all matters. Courtesy begets courtesy. The use of words 'Please' or 'Thanks' etc. should always be made, wherever necessary. It is an important part of behavioural pattern of a private secretary.

Punctuality—By punctuality, we mean reaching the office on time and also doing everything in time. For a private secretary, punctuality is necessary because of the importance of work. He/she should reach office in the morning even before time and ensure that before the boss reaches office, everything is set right. Punctuality also includes regularity.

Accuarcy—Everything should be done correctly because, the things done wrongly, might result in horrors. The accuracy may be brought in by constant practice.

Adaptability—The private secretary has to be adaptable to all circumstances. In practical life, it happens that one boss is transferred and the new boss takes over. All of them might not be having the same nature or temperament. The private secretaty should inclucate the habit of adjusting wiih all types of persons. There may be much more work at one time and there may not be any work at the other time. If the private secretary has got the quality of adaptability, he/she can adjust himself/herself under all the conditions, otherwise the thing may by difficult to pull on.

Attention and Concentration—We always say that the things done by halves, are never done right. Hence, the private secretary should do the work with full attention and concentration. If full fledged attention is not paid to any work, it might involve errors/ mistakes and also the quality in work does not come up.

Co-operativeness—The private secretary should always have an attitude of co-operating with the boss. The urgency of work may require the private secretary to sit late in the office or to attend the office during holidays or sundys. One should not mind it if the exigencies of work require it.

Even Temperament—The private secretary should neither be having the hot temperament nor too cool. In office, there may be occasions when the private secretary might be instigated to loose the temper but an outstanding secretary never does so. He/she should be cool minded when the weather is hot. Rather, the temperament should be well-balanced—neither too cool nor too hot. Extremes are bad in all cases.

Honesty—It is always good to be honest and hard-working. The private secretary should be honest, by forgoing all sorts of temptations. He/she should always watch and protect the interests of his/her boss and of the organisation.

Good Memory—The private secretary should not be forgetful. He/she must always remember the thing—whether paper, person or any other thing. If the memory is not good, other people may avail of undue advantage. Though everything should be written on paper, yet the memory should always be sharp in recognising any paper or person.

Impressive Personality—Last but not the least important is possessing a good personality in order to look smart and impressive. It may be done by having a neat appearance, by careful grooming, having good manners and etiquettes and by bringing a charm in voice.

If a private secretary adopts the above said personal qualities, he/she can become an outstanding person in the office and would be liked by all—the boss, colleagues and outsiders.

MANNERS, DRESS AND APPEARANCE

For the successful private secretary, it is necessary that he/she should have good manners or the right pattern of behaviour as well as a good and impressive look. Since the private secretary has to deal with all sorts of people in office, there is the greater importance of good manners and the look.

OFFICE MANNERS

In the ordinary language, 'Office Manners' involve the methods or ways in which a person should behave with superiors (including his/her own boss), colleagues or inmates, subordinates and the outsiders. In other words, 'Office Manners' imply the *behavioural pattern* or the *rules for proper behaviour in the office*. In short, the office manners include learning the ways of walking, talking and dealing with all sorts of persons in the office. It is rather the wisdom applying to one's own conduct in the office.

Generally speaking, 'Office Manners' involve the following :

(*i*) Good habits ;
(*ii*) Etiquettes ;
(*iii*) Achieving a charm in voice while talking over the telephone or dealing with the visitors/in-person callers ;
(*iv*) Personal grooming.

Good Habits

As the part of discipline and decorum in the office, a private secretary should learn and adopt good habits while talking, walking and working in the office. These good habits are liked by all and reflect in one's own personality. These also help in creating a good image of oneself as well as the organisation. At the same time, the dealings with others become effective and impressive.

There are few good habits which one must adopt e.g. keeping up one's own dignity, honour and self-respect by talking less but relevantly, sitting gracefully and comfortably, using courtesy titles for calling others, avoiding altogether the use of harsh and abusive language ; avoiding speaking loudly or doing anything untowardly on the desk, etc. All these good habits would help you in creating a cordial and the congenial working atmosphere.

On the other hand, there are some *bad habits* in which you, as a private secretary, should not indulge e.g. smoking cigarettes and chewing any thing while working on your desk, creating unnecessary noise by talking loudly over the phone or otherwise, telling vulgar jokes in the office, storing pencils behind your ears, keeping pins and clips in your mouth while talking with others, sitting ungraciously with your feet up on the table, biting nails, throwing papers or other items away from the right place, taking eatables on your desk beyond the lunch hours, combing hair or putting make-up on your desk, shirking chair and creating unnecessary noise in the office by whistling or shouting at others etc. All these are bad habits and are not liked by educated and cultured people. Moreover, these are the horrors of working in an office.

It may not be out of place to mention here that habits can be changed by self-restraint and self-control and all of us can do it, if necessary. For the successful working, it is necessary that one should adopt good and decent habits for working in the office.

Etiquettes

The dictionary meaning of the word 'Etiquette' is "*Customary rules of behaviour*". Actually speaking, etiquettes are the part and partial of our social customs. The etiquettes teach us as to how we should behave well while living in society. These become the set patterns of our behaviour towards others. For example, if a guest visits us, we should greet and welcome him warmly. Similarly, when we reach office in the morning, we should wish all our colleagues and co-workers a very good morning. When we depart, we should say, "good night" or we may say, "see you". When someone gives us something, we should say, "Thank you". When someone thanks us, we should say, "welcome" or "It's my pleasure" (Don't say O.K. because it does not sound well). Like the above, there may be several customary rules which we must all learn. These are useful and helpful in maintaining good human relations, in developing our own personality and in creating a good image of ourselves in the eyes of others. We become sophisticated and cultured citizens and the others are well-impressed.

Achieving a charm in voice

The next important aspect of 'office manners' is that we should speak or converse with a charm in our voice, over the telephone or while dealing with visitors. In other words, we may call them 'telephone manners' and 'manners while dealing with visitors/in-person callers'. Under all circumstances, a private secretary should learn to speak with a charm in voice and in a way that the others are impressed. At the same time, they do not offer you any resentment or resistance. Though it is not possible for a private secretary to favour every one every time, yet saying 'No' should also be done in such a way that others do not feel bad about it or that they do not become irritant. That is why, there is the necessity of achieving a special skill while speaking with others and that is to speak with a charm in your voice. The charming voice is such a big tool with the private secretary that even an angry visitor migh tbe pacified without doing any favour to him. Rather, it is the big art which all of us must learn to adopt and practise upon in practical business life.

Personal Grooming

Although it may sound common place, yet it is not incorrect to remember that 'first impression is the last impression'. In order to create this first imperssion, the chair of a secretary demands a 'well-groomed' person. The word 'grooming' implies 'shaping'—and shaping of certain qualities in personal and professional sphere.' 'Grooming' requires training regarding the appearance, mannerism and behaviour to tackle various situations in the office routine, with calm and professional competence. The appearance and mannerism go along with the grooming. As a secretary we must not undermine the importance of professional competence which inculcates self-confidence in tackling various problematic situations efficiently.

DRESS AND APPEARANCE

It is a fact that a well dressed person is to a great advantage. The same is the case with a private secretary. If he or she is well dressed and looks tidy, smart and impressive, it goes to greater advantages for himself/hereself, the boss and the organisation. Particularly in the modern days, more stress is laid on cosy and cut-to-size clothes which fit well in a person. The dealings with others become more effective and fruitful. Rather, the poorly dressed people have no place in the modern society. It does not mean that your clothes should be lavish and posh but those should be neat clean and fitwell to your personality. The same is the importance of your look and appearance. Both these things—the dress and appereance—go to make an effective and impressive personality of the private secretary.

Importance

We all know that there is the greater importance of dress and appearance. For a private secretary, the importance of both the things is due to the following *reasons* :—

1. The boss, colleagues and the outsiders like it and appreciate it.

2. The visitors form their opinion and impression about the organisation in which the private secretary is working. It is so

because, at first hand, they have to call on the private secretary and if he/she is wearing good clothes and having a good look, they are impressed.

3. It has the psychological effect on your working. When you are looking good, you feel happy and dignified. Hence, your morale is boosted upon.

4. It helps in setting a pattern for your fellow-workers and the juniors working in the same office.

5. The dealings become more effective and result-oriented.

It would not be out of place to mention here that out of the various *ingredients of appearance/look,* the dress is supermost. Next to it, comes the hair-style, make-up and maintaining a good physique by regular physical exercises and rich diet. Now, we shall discuss each of them in detail in the following paragraphs.

Type of Dress

It is necessary that, as a private secretary, you should put on neat, clean, sober, tidy and decent looking clothes of the most modern designs which should suit on you. Only those dresses should be put on which suit a person. These may not be very posh but suiting to your status, nor too cheap at the cost of variety, but the clothes should be of good quality to your requirements.

For maintaining proper dress, at all the times, a private secretary should make proper *planning* for *buying* the right type of clothes, in right quantity, at regular intervals and keeping in view the latest fashions/styles in mind. Much depends upon the right type of stitching and tailoring of clothes.

For office use, the dress should not be multi-coloured, too loose or too right but the dress should be simple, sober and should have the facility of work performance so that you can work well. It is adviseable that clothes of renowned standard textile mills be purchased and got stitched from a good Tailor and Draper. Ready-made garments hardly work for a longer period and also do not fit well always. While selecting you dress, care must be taken that these should suit to your own personality. People say 'Take food of your own choice, but put on clothes of others' choice," Keeping this thing in view, you should always select such type of clothes or dresses which would be liked by others very much. Also take into consideration that you yourself look good in that porticular dress.

Not only buying, but you should also take care about the

rotation of your dress while you go for your office. Howsoever possible, the same type of dress should not be repeatediy put on for days together. You should go on changing them every alternate day or as per your requirements and availability of number of dresses.

Also ensure that your clothes are neat and clean, by arranging for regular washing and press or drycleaning,

The different types of dresses are available for different weather —the summer dress, the winter dress and so on. For office purposes, for Gents, the dress suggested may contain a white or plain bushirt, shirt, pant and a combination suit or a warm cloth suit dark grey or brown or a combination pant and pullover, whatever suitable and available. However, for official use by ladies, the suggested combination of dress may be a saree of sobre colour and simple in design and the pullover or coat, matching the saree, or a ladies suit. It should always be noted that, for office purposes, the clothes and dresses should be plain, simple and sober both for gents as well as for ladies.

Physical Appearance

Not only clothes help in giving a good look or appearance, but also the other physical assets like your hair-style, make-up and maintenance/upkeeping of different parts of your body. For making and maintaining good physical outlook, one should keep a regular hair-dressing, careful grooming, cutting nails at regular intervals, cleaning the different parts of body regularly, taking regular normal diet, doing physical exercises and so on. All these things would certainly help a private secretary to maintain a good physique. One should always remember—'*A sound mind in a sound body*'. Hence, the importance of all these things for a private secretary.

It may be noted here that a combination of neat, tidy and sound physical appearance with the requisite personal quality would certainly help in making an impressive personality of the private secretary and these are certainly necessary for your success in life.

THE BOSS AND HIS PRIVATE SECRETARY

As we know, a private secretary is the loyal right-hand of a Boss or Executive in the office and he/she has to assist the boss in carrying out the details of his work. The Boss or Executive is a person who has to carry out the activities of an organisation and he is mainly concerned with the execution of the policies or programmes framed by the management, rather he is an important link in the hierarchy of management of an organisation.

The term 'Boss' is derived from the olden times, giving the idea of a person who gets the work done from his subordinates. In the present day world, this term has been replaced with the word 'Executive' which has been taken from the Latin word SEQUI SECUT, meaning thereby, carrying out the next activity needed. In a way, both the terms give the same meaning and denote a person, officer, manager, employer or a big personality/dignitary who holds some key post, shouldering the responsibilities and under whom a private secretary is directly working. Since a private secretary has to work directly under or for one and one person only, it would not be misleading if we call that person as 'Boss' or 'Executive' and the private secretary as a personal assistant, P.A. or P.S.

A private secretary has to assist or help a boss in carrying out his responsibilities and achieving the organisational goals. So, we may say that just as a Boss is an important personality in a Business Organisation, similarly the importance of a private secretary. If the private secretary is efficient and capable, the boss may get much relief and may devote more time to other important works but, in case a private secretary is not efficient or is incapable, the boss cannot carry out his important tasks with ease and efficiency. As such, we may say that the efficiency of a boss depends upon the efficiency of his private secretary.

THE RELATIONSHIP

The relationship between a boss and his private secretary is said to be that of a partner in business. Just as a partner is jointly and severally responsible/liable to the business of the firm of partnership, similarly the private secretary is, to a greater extent, responsible to the boss. That is why, a private secretary is treated as the loyal right-hand of the Boss. Hence, the boss has high expectations from his private secretary.

WHAT THE BOSS EXPECTS ?

The main expectations of a Boss from his private secretary are as under :

1. The private secretary should cope with the rush of routine office work by using his/her secretarial skills of typing, shorthand etc.

2. The private secretary should be able to deal with the outsiders either on telephone or in person successfully by screening them and using the techniques of discretion, tact and command in language.

3. The private secretary should organise the office of the boss very-well and in such a way that whenever anything is required, the same may be available without much wastage of time. The senior private secretaries are also expected to supervise and control the junior staff working in the office of the Boss.

4. The private secretary is expected to take utmost care of the decorum, dignity, honour of the boss and also watch and protect the interests, first of the boss and then of the organisation, because the boss only pays to the private secretary for the services rendered by him/her to the boss.

5. The boss also expects from his private secretary a co-operation on all matters and at all the times, in happiness and in grief too. The boss always keeps his private secretary in confidence and the same should not be shaken.

Ten Demands

Here are the ten points, which may give an idea to the reader as to what the Boss expects from his private secretary.

1. Don't lie. It wastes my time and yours. I'm sure to catch you in the end and that's is the wrong end.

2. Watch your work, not the clock. A long day's work makes a long day short, and a short day's work makes my face long.

3. Give me more than I expect and I will give you more than you expect. I can afford to increase your pay if you increase my profits.

4. You owe so much to yourself that you afford to owe anybody else. Keep cut of debt or keep out of my business.

5. Dishonesty is never an accident. Good man, like a good woman, never see temptation when they meet it.

6. Mind your own business and in time you'll have a business of your own to mind.

7. It is none of my business what you do at night. But if dissipation affects what you do the next day, and you do half as much as I demand, you'll last half as long as you hoped.

8. Don't do anything here that hurts your self-prospect. An employee who is willing to steal for me is willing to steal from you.

9. Don't tell me what I'd like to hear but what I ought to hear. I don't want a valet to my vanity, but one for my money.

10. Don't kick if I kick. If you're worthwhile correcting, you are worthwhile keeping.

WHAT A PRIVATE SECRETARY SHOULD DO ?

In accordance with the expectations of a boss, as explainec earlier, the privare secretary should play a major and important role in the Boss's business life. He/she should have an active participa tion on the following aspects :—

1. Relieving the boss of the monotony of routine office work like handling mail (both inward and outward), drafting routine business letters, taking dictation in shorthand and typing, handling the folders or files and assisting in all other routine matters of office so that the boss has much time for doing actual constructive work of greater importance.

2. Making available all the required information, data papers etc. readily so that the boss has not to waste time unnecessarily. For this purpose, the private secretary should organise the office of his/her boss so well that everything is visible at a glance.

3. Maintaining properly the diary of the Boss's appointments, engagements, tours, pragrammes, meetings etc. and also reminding the boss well in time so that he could prepare himself for all these. The necessary feedback may also be provided at a proper time.

4. Receiving warmly all the visitors, screening them and guiding them properly. So far as possible, the boss should not be disturbed unnecessarily for the sake of unwanted visitors. Even undesired/unwanted telephone calls may not be passed on to the boss, without his prior permission.

5. Acting as a mouthpiece of the boss in matters which the boss might not like to convey directly to others. Here, again, the private secretary should take utmost care of the decorum, dignity, honour and respect of the boss.

6. Making the things run smoothly even in the absence of the boss, when he is away from his desk or out of station. The problems, in his absence, may be solved by taking independent decisions in the interest or in the right earnest, or by seeking the co-operation of the next man to the boss in the organisation.

7. Doing creative things whenever the private secretary is free from routine office work, like useful readings, studying important files or preparing useful schedules etc.

The above guidelines would certainly help a private secretary in getting on good terms with the Boss and he would certainly take care his private secretary. The relations would be harmonious and cordial.

How a Private Secretary Can Become Indispensable in His/Her Organisation ?

It should be noted that as per the administrative policy, the office or boss is liable to be transferred from one place to another but, in offices, the private secretary has to remain whether Mr. A is the boss or Mr. B is the boss. As such, private secretary should adopt the habit of adjusting with all sorts of bosses in office life. Each boss is different from another in respect of nature and temperament. Some bosses usually loose their temper even on a trivial error committed by a private secretary whereas the others are such that they do not mind unless some serious mistake is commited by a private secretary. In order to be indispensable, the private secretary should be highly adjustible with all sorts of people, and by working hard, he/she should become indispensable to the Boss's office rather to the Boss's business life. For becoming indispensable in office and to the boss, the private secretary should remember the *following guidelines* :—

1. Give due respect and honour to your boss and also to all other superiors in the hierarchy.

2. Do not wait for your boss's instructions for doing each and every work. Once you have been explained the area of your work, start and do it yourself.

3. If you do not know anything, see what why it has been done in the past and start doing the same way. The past records of your office are the best guide to you. If necessary, do not hesitate in asking your boss but at the appropriate time when he is little free or in a good mood. You may also consult/refer to your office manual or procedure book, which every big organisation is having.

4. Remember—'Whatever you do, do it with your might, the things done by halves, are never done right.' This means that you should do everything in your office with full attention and concentration. If they are done half heartedly, then they may be wrong. This is the key to do everything right.

5. Whatever you do, keep its purpose in mind. Ensure as to what you are going to achieve by it. This will make efforts fruitful.

6. Never grumble when there is much work or when you are overloaded with the work. Fix up the priorities of work and continue doing it with cool mind. You have not to become impatient or nervous any time. Be confident that you would cope with everything, though it may be little late.

7. Always organise all things at your office in such a way that you have not to waste time in locating any paper, document etc.

8. You should not mind interruptions sincc those are bound to come especially when you have public dealing.

HANDLING TELEPHONE

Telephone is a means of oral or verbal means of communication in the offices. The telephone may either be obtained on rental basis from the Telephone Department or may be owned by a subscriber under the OYT (Own Your Telephone) Scheme. It may be used both for internal as well as external communication.

1. **Direct Main Line with Extensions**—Under it, the Telephone Exchange may allot a number on payment of amount and on one main line, 1, 2 or 3 extensions may also be allowed against payment of additional charges. Whenever an outside call come its, rings of all the extensions and whosoever wants may pick up the receiver and attend to the caller. The outgoing calls may also be made independently from each of such extensions. The talks may also be held from one extension to another extension by pushing a button for buzzer.

2. **Private Branch Exchange (P.B.X.)**—Where the Organisation is big, the extensions are not adequate to meet the needs. Hence a small private telephone exchange may be hired or owned from the Telephone Department. A separate switchboard is provided on one main line connected with the Telephone Exchange. The P.B.X. switchboard may be for 20, 50, 200 or more lines, depending upon the requirements of the subscriber. It is an independent complete system and is useful for bigger business organisations. It is operated with the help of a telephone operator who use the switches, cords etc. for connecting the incoming calls to required extension or for making of outgoing calls for and on behalf of any extension. The extension to extension talks may also be held with help of telephone operator who controls the entire P.B.X. switchboard. It is an old system and the disadvantage of it is that for every call the help or assistance of the operator is required.

3. **Private Automatic Branch Exchange (P.A.B.X)**—This system is an improvement over the P.B.X. Under this system, the calls may be made automatically by any person by dialling the number and without taking assistance from the operator. The operator receives the incoming calls and diverts them to the required extension. The outgoing telephone calls may be made by independently dialling the code number like 0 or 9 and then the required number. No help is required for making outside calls. The system is automatic, whereas in P.B.X. all the calls are through the operator. The P.A.B.X. Board is directly connected by a main line with the Telephone Exchange. The P.A.B.X. has got all the dvantages of P.B.X. plus the additional advantage that no help is equired of the Operator while making outgoing calls and, instead, the numbers may be dialled directly automatically from any of the xtensions.

For the purpose of handling telephone by a private secretary, ne/she should have a thorough knowledge about the various types of telephone systems used in offices.

About the P.B.X./P.A.B.X.

In conncetion with P.B.X. or P.A.B.X., the private secretary should remember the following points :—

1. In P.A.B.X. the operator receives the incoming calls only and for outgoing calls, these may be made directly from the respective telephone by dialling the code number like 0 or 9 and then dialling the required number automatically. In P.B.X. all calls are made through the operator—incoming, outgoing or even extension to extension.

2. The main parts of P.B.X./P.A.B.X. are :

Answering Cord—Which may be used to answer the calls.

Calling Cord—Which may be used to ring the telephone of a subscriber.

Jacks—Which are the holes on the switch board in which the plug is inserted to make the connections.

Dial—Which is the device to dial the numbers.

Dial Keys—These keys are used to dial the numbers by assisting the dial.

Speak and Ring Keys—These are used to ring the extension and speak to the subscribers.

Indicating Lamps—These are the lamps which glow when the call appears on the board, thus, indicating the calls.

Supervisory Lamps—These lamps indicate that the call is over and is to be disconnected.

Junction Test Switch—It may be used to check the busy and free lines on the board.

Re-set Switch—It may be used to cut the ring off.

Main Line or Junction Line—The **P.B.X./P.A.BX.** is connected to the main telephone exchange with the help of these lines, and on which the calls appear from outside.

3. For operating the P.B.X./P.A.B.X., the golden rules are—speed, accuracy and courtesy.

4. The procedure for operating **P.B.X./P.A.B.X.** is that whenever the calls appear on the board, the operator picks up the answering cord and inserts the same into the jack where the indication has appeared, pushes the speak and ring key to the speak position and speaks, the caller wishes to be connected to any extension the operator picks up the corresponding calling plug and inserts into the same extension jack and pushes the speak and ring key to the ring position. The called person's phone rings and he picks up the receiver and speaks. The call is through.

5. Whenever the operator receives the call for any extension, he/she asks the caller to whom he would like to speak in the particular room. When the name is given, the telephone operator has to check with the slide rack, confirms the name and then puts the call through. We call it as screening of calls.

6. For making outgoing calls from the P.B.X./P.A.B.X. the operator picks up the calling cord, presses the junction rest switch to pick a free line, inserts the plug in that jack, pushes dial key to the dial position, dials the number, restores the dial key and listens out, if the number is ringing and then connects it to the person who wanted the number and if it is busy, re-dials.

For making external communication over the telephone, the following facilities are available :

1. **Local Calls**—Which may be dialled from one's telephone instrument in accordance with the numbers given in the telephone directory. It has local jurisdiction, limited up the area of operation of local telephone exchange.

2. **Subscriber's Trunk Dialling (S.T.D.)**—Under it, the subscriber may dial directly any number at the other station. This facility can be availed of only to the cities which are connected on STD channels. For this purpose, different STD numbers are allotted to the respective city. First of all, the STD code number is dialled and when the line through, the number of the other person may be

dialled to get the line is through. This facility is very useful for quickly getting the number of a person at the outstation but advantageous only if the talks are for short durations like one minute or two minutes only. For more duration, STD proves costlier.

3. **International Subscriber's Dialling (I.S.D.)**—This facility is existing to UK where direct dialling may be made by any subscriber from India.

4. **Trunk Calls**—These are the outgoing telephone calls booked by a subscriber through the telephone exchange. They register the number to which the call is to be made and arrange to make the call through Telephone Exchange. The following are the various *kinds of trunk calls.*

(*a*) **Ordinary**—In which the number of the outstation caller is given by the Telephone Exchange in turn in the ordinary course. This call may be made for 3 minutes and if the talks are prolonged it may be further extended to another 3 minutes. The charges are also nominal.

(*b*) **Urgent**—The charges for such calls are just double than the ordinary call but the eall matures earlier than the ordinary call.

(*c*) **Demand**—Which can be connected on demand by the subscriber. The charges are heavy.

(*d*) **Lightening**—It is given topmost priority by the telephone exchange and the charges are about 8 times than the ordinary call.

TYPING DICTATION AND TRANSCRIBING

The letters, in an office, emanate from two sources—(i) Dictation by Boss to the private secretary and (ii) Preparing or Drafting of routine letters by the private secretary himself/herself. In this chapter, we shall discuss about the correspondence which may be dictated to a private secretary by his/her boss. There may be certain letters which may be written by a boss himself and the manuscript may be handed over to the secretary for typing. 'Manuscript' refers to the hand-written matter. For hand-written material, the private secretary should first read it over and clarify everything before starting typing of the same. In hand-written material, there may be a few words which may not be easily read and for them it is proper that the entire matter should be read out carefully. Whatever are the additions, deletions, over-writings or changes the same should be understood thoroughly and thereafter the typing should commence, otherwise there may be unnecessary cuttings or mistakes in the typed letter.

While typing the hand-written matter, called the 'Mauuscript', there may be certain corrections i.e. additions, deletions, punctuation-marks etc. in the rough draft, which may be clearly understood by you as a Typist.

Taking dictation in Short-hand :

Usually the important letters or those involving special skills or crucial decisions are dictated by the Boss. The dictation may be given face to face, when the stenographer and the boss—both of them are sitting together or over the Dictating Machine or Dictaphone. The details about Dictaphone have been given in the chapter 'Office Machines and Equipments' However, in both the cases, the dictation is taken in short-hand, a language of signs and symbols, which helps a writer to take notes at a faster speed. A private secretary is expected to be having the skills of stenography. We have already discussed about the 'Stenographic Skills' in the chapter 'Oualities of an outstanding private secretary'. However, while taking dictation in short-hand, a private secretary should remember the *following points* :—

1. The necessary tools like a shorthand note-book, pencial or pen or ball-pen and eraser etc. should be perfect and readily available so that whenever the Boss calls a private secretary for giving dictation, he/she may visit him for the purpose without wasting any time. If the necessary tools are not perfect or not readily available, it might waste the time of private secretary and also waste the time of the boss. Before going indside the Boss's chamber/cabin, the private secretary should ensure that sufficient blank pages are available in short-hand-note book. Two or more pencils, pen or ball-point pen should be always kept so that one should not look embarrassed if the point of a pencil wears out or the refil in ball-pen is exhausted.

2. Occupy a seat immediately after going inside, preferably in front of the boss. As a private secretary you need not wait for the boss to request you to occupy a seat because when he has called you for giving dictation, it automatically implies that you have to go immediately inside the chamber of boss and occupy a seat, where he/she can comfortably sit and take notes from the boss.

3. Always put the date on top corner of first and the other pages of the short-hand note-book. It is also advisable that the date should be written on each page of the short-hand note-book in order to facilitate reference at some latter date in future.

4. The name and address of the addressee and other names coming during the course of dictation should preferably be written in long-hand.

5. The private secretary may leave space for the words which may be either not heard properly or misheard and those remaining unclarified. At the end of dictation, the private secretary may ask for clarification from the boss.

6. You should make a note in your shorthand note-book about the letters which the boss may require to be typed on priority basis or those which are immediate or urgent. You should transcribe all such letters first.

7. During the course of dictation, try to obtain all the relevant papers, documents etc. from the boss. Mostly the boss himself passes on such papers to a private secretary at the time of giving dictation. If he does not give them to you of his own, there is no harm in asking the boss to deliver the same to you.

8. While the boss is giving dictation to you and some important guest comes inside the boss's cabin, and the boss also stops dictating, you may offer a seat to the guest and wait for a while to see whether the boss would continue dictation or not. Many times, the boss may tell you to come afterwards and in that case you must come.

9. Be calm and attentive when the boss is giving dictation to you so that no important fact is missed or left out.

10. If the boss asks you anything while giving dictation, give your independent opinion about it, if you know, otherwise you may say, "Sir, I'm not sure." It is of no use discussing unnecessarily with the boss. If you are sure about anything, you may say the same with confidence.

11. In case the Dictaphone or Dictating Machine is used for giving dictation, you may use the same skills as those of a good steno-typist. One may also directly type out the matter from the dictaphone.

12. When the entire dictation is over, you must come out quietly from the boss's chamber and start the typing work conveniently. Urgent letters should be typed first without wasting any time.

Transcription

After the dictation is over, the private secretary or a stenographer has to type out the matter written by him/her in short-hand.

For this purpose, one should always have the adequate supplies on the desk including the printed letter-heads in various sizes—big, medium or smaller ; the carbon papers, continuation-sheets and/or blank papers, eraser, stencil-papers, correcting fluid for use on stencil-papers, a standard dictionary to check the spellings, pins, clips etc. besides the Typewriter.

In the absence of any instructions to the contrary, it is necessary to make at least one extra carbon copy of everything which you type. If required, more copies may be taken out by inserting the required number of carbons. The carbons are also available in various sizes and separately for writing by hand es well as for typing. Select the suitable one for the type of work you are doing.

It should be remembered that all matter which is urgently required, the same should be done first and all the letters you type should be neat, correct and attractive in appearance. You must know the various styles and whichever is impressive and practical in your office, the same should be followed. You are also responsible for correct spellings, grammar and construction of sentences. Even though something is wrongly dictated, there is no harm in correcting it provided the sense remains all—right and it is not unliked by your boss.

The short-hand note book in which the material for transcription is inscribed by you, keep it to the right of your typewriter and also keep an eye on what you are typing. Go on cancelling the page by putting a line from top to the bottom of your short-hand note book when the matter is already transcribed. If there are any corrections, the same should be done before the paper is taken out of your typewriter. While erasing on a typewriter when you have inserted carbons also, take care that the impression does not come on the carbon copy. For this purpose, put a piece of rough paper below the carbon and then do erasing on the upper copy. It is good to verify the correctness of name and address from the original correspondence before you type it out. At the end of the day, check your shorthand note book whether all notes have been transcribed by you.

At many offices, there is a system of keeping a master copy of each and every letter typed out by a stengorapher. Every day, all such copies are kept in a master-file by arranging them datewise. Such a copy is an extra one and, as such, one more carbon and paper should be inserted while typing the material.

So far as Typewriter is concerned, we have given details in the chapter entitled Office Machines and equipments. However, a private secretary should also know the various parts of a typewriter by studying the Typewriter Manual. In case of any defect of minor nature occurred during the course of transcription, the same may be set right by himself/herself. The small works like changing ribbon, cleaning the letters of a Typewriter and using the various extra keys provided in the typewriter, must be all known to a typist. Your typewriter should be got serviced at regular intervals and you should cover it up before you leave office everyday in order to keep it perfect and free from dust etc. A bad worker always quarrels with hss tools whereas a good worker always loves his tools and cares for them.

TRAVEL ARRANGEMENTS AND HOTEL RESERVATIONS

Travel Arrangements

The modern bussiness has diversified and expanded to such an extent that no Manager, Boss or Executive can afford to limit his working to a local place. He has to travel far and wide to even the remotest parts of the world. For this purpose, a Private Secretary is expected to make necessary arrangements in order to make his/her Boss's tour comfortable and convenient. The arrangements may include booking tickets for a travel and getting the reservations in Hotels where the Boss may stay on.

The travellling by a Boss be either '*Domestic*' (i.e. to any place within the country) or '*Overseas*' (i.e. to a foreign country). However, the main objectives of travelling may be development of business-relations with outsiders, sales-promotion, purchases, periodical inspection or customer-service etc. For all practical purposes, the travelling is indispensable and very important from the organisational point of view and also for doing the things in the right earnest.

Usually, a private secretary is involved with many problems like finalising Tour Programme, furnishing details of information or documents required by Boss, making hotel reservations and carrying out the works in the absence of Boss etc. and an efficient secretary handles them successfully as a loyal right-hand of the Boss/Executive. Though the Boss has to proceed on business-tours at the cost and expenses of the Organisation, yet the Management of any Business Organisation is most cost-conscious and, therefore, the likely benefits are definitely more than the cost or expenses incurred on tour of the Boss/Executive.

Tour or Visit Programme

On the basis of information and details available, a private secretary has to chalk out and finalise the tour programme of Boss in consultation with him. The things to be decided are—the halting places the time, of stay required, making the necessary reservations for hotel accommodation and deciding to whom the Boss might visit and what is the purpose served.

The entire tour or visit programme should be properly typed out giving all the details datewise. A copy of the same may be handed over to the Boss and the other copy be kept on office record.

Booking Travel Tickets

After the programme is finalised, it is the duty of a private secretary to arrange for booking the seat or making reservations. The Executive mostly travel by Air so that they can reach to the place of destination without much wastage of time. If necessary and the facility of air-travel is not available, they may prefer going by train or any other mode of transport. However, for making the travel ticket availble immediately, the services rendered by various Travel Agents may be availed of. Mostly, in offices, the travel agents are already fixed and they provide the services of getting the reservations or seats booked for all officials. The Private Secretary should have the telephone number of the concerned Travel Agent. Efforts be made to contact thd office of the Travel Agent for necessary bookings. Such Travel Agents are usually having their offices well set-up and they have the arrangement for home-delivery of tickets after getting the seats reserved. The Travel Agents also charge nominal extra amount for the services rendered by them. In case of official trip, the entire charges are to be borne by the Organisation. Hence, they directly send the bill to the Boss's office which may be paid in the ordinary course. The private secretary should, however, ensure that the necessary travel-tickets are received from the Travel Agent in time and that those are handed over to the Boss or kept on his desk. In case of Air-ticket, the seat is required to be confirmed and the same should be got done.

In case of foreign visit or tour, there are other formalities also which may be completed e.g. Passport, Visa, Medical Certificate, foreign exchange etc. The private secretary should ensure that all the necessary formalities, in case of foreign travel of the Boss, are completed and the air-tickets are also duly confirmed for the date fixed for initiating the travel. If it is the first visit of Boss to any foreign country, the Passport has first to be obtained, for which the printed form is available from the Passport Office in India on payment of certain amount. The required from may, firstly, be obtained, completed with signatures of the Boss and submitted to the concerned office with necessary fees. Passport size photographs are affixed on the form and the particulars are identified and verified by any Gazetted Officer or a Member of Parliament. The Passport is received duly issued by the concerned government office after a period of about 3 to 4 weeks of submission of the application. All such procedural formalities should be got completed and passport be obtained. In case of an old Passport, it should be ensured that it is valid or got revalidated. In connection with the booking for foreign tour, the Travel Agent may also require the valid Passport and other papers which may be furnished before the seat by Air-travel is confirmed and okayed.

Travel Details and Documents

The Boss may require many travel details and documents for himself. All such details should be obtained or prepared by a private secretary and handed over to the Boss before time. These may include : Passport, International Driving Licence, Credit Card. Personal Insurance Cover, Foreign Exchange in the form of Foreign Traveller's Cheques, Health Aids or any other thing required during the course of journey by the boss. If required, the guide maps or road-maps of the place of visit may also be obtained and handed over to the boss.

Business information and details

While on a business tour, the Boss may require necessary information, details, files and folders containing the useful information. The same may be required for discussion with customers, suppliers, foreign agents etc. It is also the duty of a private secretary to prepare and keep ready all such information duly arranged as per the tour programme. It is advisable to prepare useful briefs of all the relevant details so that it is not bulky to carry. However, the important correspondence and other documents, in original, may be placed in a separate folder and given to boss for his personal custody and study. These may include the actual appointments with customers, calling of meetings/conferences, invitations, visiting cards of the Boss, contracts, sales literature, speech, addresses and telephone lists of friends, relatives and persons to be visited at the place of destination. All these details and documents are very useful and helpful to your Boss.

Final check-list

However, well before the day and time of departure to any outside place, within the country or outside the country, the private secretary should make a tally with the following check-lists :

Domestic Travel

1. Air-travel tickets
2. Adequate cash or travellers' cheques to meet journey expenses
3. Medical-aids
4. House keys
5. Car keys
6. Travel-kit
7. Visiting Cards
8. Tour Programme
9. Works to be completed in Boss's absence

Foreign Tour

1. Pass-port
2. Visa
3. Air-travel tickets
4. International Driving Licence
5. World Health Certificate
6. Foreign Travellers' Cheques
7. Credit Cards
8. Medical-aids
9. Travel-kit
10. Visiting Cards
11. Tour-programme
12. Addresses and Telephone lists of foreign agents etc.
13. Sales literature and other business material
14. Details of meetings and appointments with foreign agents, customers, suppliers etc.

Hotel Reservations

The private secretary should also ensure that necessary arrangements are made for hotel accommodation at the place of destination. For this purpose, if telephone facilities are available, the concerned hotels may be contacted on phone or by giving telex message or by sending telegram or writing a letter. The specimen of letter regarding booking hotel accommodation is given in chapter 'Social and Personal Correspondence' which may be perused for the purpose. If possible, a confirmation may be obtained in token of having booked the hotel accommodation. In case of a foreign visit of the Boss, the foreign Agents or other residents may be contacted for the purpose. At a new place, particularly in a foreign country, a lot of difficulties may have to be faced if proper hotel accommodation is not reserved well in advance. Hence, the necessary arrangements in this behalf must be made.

Hotel Reservations

For the outsiders who visit you in connection with some official work and are required to stay on for some time, it is necessary to book the hotel accommodation for them. This work is performed by a private secretary. Hotels are service-oriented organisations to take care and provide for all possible physical facilities/comforts to a tourist or visitor. There are different graues of Hotels like Class I, Deluxe, Three-star or Five-star. Most of the valued visitors always like to stay-in 'Five-star' Hotels.

Usually, the private secretary is expected to know the telephone numbers and addresses of the various three-star and five-star hotels at his/her place of work otherwise the local telephone directory may be referred to find out the telephone number of the hotel where the visitor would like to stay-in. As soon as the information reaches the private secretary about the arrival or date of arrival of the visitor, he/she should contact the concerned Hotel and get the accommodation reserved. It may be done by telephone or even by writing a letter. While requesting for hotel accommodation on telephone, always remember to tell your name, office's name and telephone number, name of Guest and place from where he is coming, the specific day/date on which the visitor would check-in and probable date of his checking-out as well as the mode of payment of hotel charges—whether to be paid by your office or by the visitor himself. All these details should invariably be conveyed to the concerned Hotel Manager or any one incharge over there. Exactly the same rules or principles, as stated above apply while writing a letter of request for hotel reservation. When the necessary booking has been done over the telephone, it is also necessary that a letter confirming the telepnonic conversation should also be prepared immediately and sent to the concerned Hotel. The choice of food of visitor, if known, whether vegetarian or non-vegetarian, may also be informed to the hotel authorities. The charges for hotel accommodation, boarding and lodging in a Five-star Hotel are almost identical and standardised. It is no fun to ask the same while booking the hotel accommodation. If necessary, there is no harm in asking about charges before getting the reservation made.

When the necessary reservation for a hotel accommodation has been done, it is the duty of a private secretary to bring out the fact to the knowledge of his/her boss and also to seek his further instructions for making any other arrangement for the visitor. How ever, all efforts be made to ensure that the visitor is not put to any inconvenience, particularly when he is our official guest.

Many times, the arrangements for excursion to places of tourists' interest are also to be made by taking prior reservations. If required, those arrangements may also be made by the private secretary on instructions of the boss.

However, all the necessary papers, literature or documents regarding the various arrangements made by you for the visitor may be handed over to him on his arrival to your station so that he feels relieved and comfortable.

Handling Works During Boss's Absence

When the Boss proceeds on tour, the Private Secretary has to ensure that all the works of office are carried on smoothly in his absence. For this purpose, there should be proper understanding between the Boss and the Secretary, particularly, on the following matters :—

1. How the routine letters would be disposed of in the Boss's absence ? Whether the private secretary may sign certain routine letters, not requiring policy-decisions, on behalf of the Boss ?

2. If there is any important or urgent matter, how the same would be dealt with ? Whether the co-operation of any other officer should be sought for ?

3. If the trip is lengthy, whether a periodic report of office be sent to him and how ?

4. Whether the private secretary may contact the Boss on tour and how, in emergent cases ?

5. If there is any substitute or leave reservist of Boss, in his absence, how and what information may be disclosed to him ?

In case there are no instructions to the contrary, the Private Secretary may himself/herself handle the works of routine nature and ensure that all works go on smoothly in his absence. The Mail or Dak received daily in office, should be received, opened, recorded, sorted out and placed in separate folders marked 'For immediate Action' or 'For information' respectively. If routine letters are replied by a private secretary, the typed replies together with the original letters may be placed under a separate folder marked 'For Signatures'.

It is also necessary that the private secretary should regularly and punctually attend the office in the absence of Boss and carry out the details of work as usual. Rather more responsibility is thwarted upon a private secretary in Boss's absence. If any matter cannot be decided upon in his absence, the same should be kept pending till he resumes duties in his office.

HANDLING FINANCIA AND ACCOUNTING MATTERS

An efficient private secretary has to handle cash transactions, bank transactions and maintain proper accounts for and on behalf of his/her employer. For this purpose, it is necessary that he/she must have a thorough knowledge about these aspects.

Petty Cash

It denotes the amount in cash available for incurring day-to-day small expenses like payments for postage, telegrams, entertainment, travelling etc. An advance sum is available from the cash section at periodical intervals and the secretary goes on making payments and maintaining an account of all the transactions. In practical life, any amount received or paid is entered into the proper books of account through a written piece of paper called the 'voucher'. There are 'receipt' vouchers in token of having received the amount and 'payment' vouchers as a documentary evidence of amounts paid to others. The basic rule of accounting is 'First write, then pay; if you forget anything, ask the paper.' Similarly, in business, all transactions are supported by some paper or document. The private secretary is expected to be expert in preparing the relevant vouchers and then to record them properly into the books of account. Now-a-days, the printed voucher forms are available from the stationery shops otherwise these are got printed by your Organisation. The format of a voucher is given below :—

Received with thanks from A.B.C. Company the sum of Rupees..............
on a/c of..........
Rs.........Signatures

Voucher No.............A.B.C. COMPANY
Date...........
DEBIT..
....

	Rs.	P.
....		
CREDIT..............................		
....		

Accountant..........................Manager.
....

The private secretary must ensure that the voucher is properly written and signed by the person entitled to take cash payment. At the end of day, all the vouchers may be recorded in the 'Petty Cash Book' maintained for the purpose of recording all small expenses incurred by a private secretary for and on behalf of his/her employer. The Petty Cash Book is of two types—(i) Simple Petty Cash Book ; & (ii) Imprest Petty Cash Book. The purpose of maintaining both types of cash books is the same but the formats are different. We are giving below a format of simple petty cash book :—

SIMPLE PETTY CASH BOOK

Receipts Rs. P.	Date	Particulars	Amount Rs. P.
200—00	1985	To Balance b/f	
	Mar 1	By Telegram Charges	10—00
	" 2	" Postage	50—50
	" 5	" Entertainment Exp.	20—00
	" 20		
		Balance c/f	80—50
			119—50
200—00	" 31	TOTAL	200—00

The transactions are recorded in the petty cash book datewise in the manner as shown in the above example. The petty cash book is balanced daily, weekly or as per the arrangement and the balance of petty cash in hand is taken out.

Under the 'Imprest' Cash Book, many columns are made for each head of expenditure and then the concerned expenditure is recorded in the relevant column, as per the example given below :—

IMPREST PETTY CASH BOOK

Receipt	Date	Particulars	LF	Total	Post-age	Tele-grams	Con-vey-ance	Enter-tain-ment
	1985							
200-00	Mar	To Bal. b/f						
	1	By convey-						
	6	ance		15-00			15-00	
	15	By Postage						
	25	&						
		" telegrams		50-00	30-00	20-00		
		Convey-ance & entertain-ment		45-00			25-00	20-00
				100-00				
	31	"Balance c/f		90-00				
200-00		TOTAL		20-000	30-00	20-00	40-00	20-00

In the manner like the above, a private secretary should maintain accurate and proper record of petty cash received and expenses incurred and finally take the initials of his/her boss.

Baning ransactions

The private secretary may also have to handle the transactions held with a Bank which may include depositing cash/cheques into the Bank for the employer, withdrawing cash by drawing a cheque, obtaining Bank Pass Book/Statement of Account and reconciling the bank transactions, etc. For proper handling of bank transactions, a private secretary must know and be able to fill in the prescribed pay-in slips of Bank for depositing cash/cheques. He/she must also know to write date, amount in words and figures, payee's name etc on the cheque and take signatures of boss for the purpose of withdrawing the amount from the Bank. At periodical intervals, the pass book may be sent to the bank for completion and return. The entries shown by bank in the pass book may be checked with our records and, if any mistake is located, the same be pointed out and got corrected from the Bank. A modern private secretary should be a 'pro' in all the above matters and ensure that his/her employer is not put to any problem at any time.

PLANNING AND ORGANISING THE OFFICE WORK

Planning the Work

By planning, we mean thinking before doing. In other words, it may be defined as the further course of action. For a private Secretary, planning is necessary as he/she should always do the work after carefully thinking about it, otherwise the works may not be done properly and, many times, the most important and urgent works remain unattended. While planning the work of office, the private secretary fixes up certain priorities, depending upon the nature and the degree of importance of work. Generally, a good private secretary formulates the programmes in the morning at the start of the day as to which works are to be done during the day and in what sequence ? Many people plan their work for tomorrow at the end of the previous day and then start the next day in the right earnest. Like planning the day's work, the planning may be done for a week, a month or a year. Without proper planning all the work may be done in a haphazard manner and, many times, it might result into a waste.

For proper planning, the total work is ascertained first and then it is arranged in a certain sequence by fixing up the priorities. The most important things may be done first and the rest afterwards and so on. The sequence in which the works are done, is set up automatically The performance of work becomes easy and result-oriented. The private secretary may take the help of a 'Reminder Diary' or 'Year Planning' in which, the works to be performed at a certain-time, are noted down and action taken accordingly. With the help of a reminder-diary, the letters/papers, on which some action is to be taken, are recorded datewise and proper action taken on the day for which it is recorded in the reminder diary.

In practical life, a certain pattern of office routine is set up through proper planning. Usually. at the start of the day, the inward mail is received and the work of opening, sorting and recording of dak is performed. The work of dak-distribution is completed. With the help of a reminder-diary, the relevant files and papers taken for issuing reminders or taking up any further action on them. After that the other works of the day, as per instructions of boss, are completed. Like this, at the end of the day, the entire letters, prepared today, are despatched and a list, of works for tomorrow is prepared by the private secretary. During the course of day, the private secretary may have to attend to a number of works like attending telephone calls, receiving visitors, taking appointments for the boss, arranging meetings, arranging travels and tours etc., besides the routine office work. Since there may not be any chaos or confusion to the private secretary, it is desirable that the planning of works may be done well in advance so that the performance of all the works may become interesting and nothing important remains to be unattended to.

The *practical hints* for proper planning or sequence of routine office works are given below :—

1. As a private secretary, you should reach office punctually rather before time so as to start the day's work in the right earnest.

2. Switch on all lights, cooler and other office machines/equipments after opening all doors and windows for proper ventilation and air-circulation.

3. Open the locks of your desk's drawers, filing cabinets and arrage your desk properly after proper dusting.

4. Ensure that the Boss's table is all-right and well-arranged.

Also check the desk-calendar for change of today's date and the clock whether it is running accurately.

5. Check the reminder-diary by referring to the date and take out all the files for today for the puprose of taking action.

6. Uncover all the office machines. Also clean up your own typewriter so as ensure that all the machines are ready for use at the point of need.

7. Get and collect all the dak received for your office. Open all envelopes, sort out letters and record them in the appropriate register. Mark letters for the purpose of distributing them to the appropriate or concerned officials.

8. Before the boss calls you for giving dictation or for an other work, try, to accomplish the works at your hand.

9. Prepare a list of today's appointments and engagements of your boss and put before him on his table. Also keep ready all the files or papers which the boss may require in connection with any meeting or conference etc.

10. Remind your boss well-before time about the meeting or appointment etc. so that he prepares himself for the same.

11 At the close of the day, ensure that all the letters prepared today and signed by your boss, are put into the letter-box or those are duly despatched.

12. Prepare a list of important visitors to your boss or any important meeting etc. for tomorrow and seek your boss's instructions.

13. Check the pending dak file and ensure that no important letter remains for disposal.

14. Before leving the office, ensure that all the office machines are duly covered and the main electric switch is off.

The above points would certainly help a private secretary in planning the works of his/her office.

Organising Office and the Work

Organising is the process of deciding the total work to be done, dividing and distributing the work, assignment of jobs and arranging for men, materials and machinery etc. in order to achieve the organisational objectives. Similary, by organising the office and the work, we mean arranging the things right and in such a way that you can see them at a glance and doing the things in the right earnest.

In light of this, the private secretary has to organise his/her office and the entire works in such a manner that it is useful in carrying out the details of Boss's work in the day to day office life. It involves properly arranging the desk, machines, equipments/appliances and other tools of work. Not only this, the general appearance of office should be good.

General Appearance of Office

The office should have a good look and neat appearance. The colouring of walls, ceiling and the flooring should be ideal combining light colours soothing to eyes and ideal for work performance. The lighting arrangement should be proper and the light should be in sufficient quantity and evenly spread over. The private secretary should ensure that there is proper arrangement of cleaning and sweeping of desks, chair, machines, equipments, racks, files etc. There should not be unnecessary dirt and filth in the office.

Here are some suggestions for keeping good the general appearance of office:—

1. Don't paste papers, posters, pictures, photographs or calendars on walls or on partitions. Only one calendar with bigger figures of date (but without any posture or photograph) and that too only one in the room should be hanged at a prominent place where the private secretary's attention should be directly attracted at the point of need.

2. The table desk and chair of the private secretary should be arranged and placed in such a way that there is no hindrance in movement and the accessibility to boss's cabin is easy and convenient.

3. The waste paper basket be provided (not too many in number) beneath the desk or on one side where the discarded papers etc. might be conveniently dropped into.

4. All windows and doors should have palmets and curtains and those should not be unnecessarily kept open always otherwise the outside dust might spoil the papers and carry them away with the winds.

5. The office machines, equipments and appliances should be placed adjacent to the private secretary's desk so that there is no unnecessary wastage of time for using them at the point of need.

6. The private secretary must ensure that every day the office is properly cleaned and sweeped. All the tables, chairs, equipments

and appliances are properly dusted and cleaned so that all the time, these are ready for use.

Table or Desk

The private secretary is provided with a separate desk or table preferably with 2 or 3 drawers which may be locked. The working tools of secretary like papers, pencils, eraser, clips, pins, stamp-pad and rubber stamps should be properly placed. For rubber-stamps the steel stands may be used. For papers, the wooden or steel trays or plastic trays may be used. The table should have a glass below which the necessary indices etc. may be placed for ready reference. There should be a small desk calendar of the current year fitted on a stand. This desk calendar may be used for noting down appointments, engagement, meeting etc. All the articles, being the tools of private secretary's work, should be kept and arranged in the respective drawers of the desk in such a manner that the private secretary may have an easy approach. One drawer should exclusively be allotted for retaining important documents or papers. It must be locked invariably whenever the private secretary leaves his/her chair or office. As for papers, letter-heads, carbon papers etc. the same should be arranged properly on a separate rack and the rack may be placed either on one side of private secretary's table or adjacent to typewriter so that there is no hindrance while working. The pin and clips should be inserted into the pin-cushions and need not be allowed to spread over everywhere.

Telephone

Proper care should be taken of the telephone instrument and accessories. The telephone instrument should be placed either on one corner of private secretary's table or at a place where there is not much hindrance and it is easily accessible to a private secretary because he/she has to use the same frequently either for attending the incoming calls or for dialling the outgoing calls. Care should be taken while placing the telephone instrument so that the receiver or the main instrument might not all down and broken. The telephone directory should be placed on the table top but kept separately on the rack or in drawer. However, the Telephone Directory should be kept inside the plastic cover available for the purpose and it safeguaurds from the sharp edges when new telephone directory is received. Besides it should be ensured that regular servicing and scenting of telephone instrument is done.

Newspapers, Periodicals Books etc.

The daily newspapers, periodicals, magazines and other books, which are received in the office, should be properly taken care of. These should not be allowed to pile up at various places. Only the current ones should be retained and the rest be arranged at a separate place or sent to store where these may be arranged and placed datewise. A proper record of them should be maintained by the private secretary in a separate register or notebook.

Machines, Equipments and other Suppliers

The private secretary is provided with various machines and equipments like a typewriter, adding-listing or calculating machine, filing cabinets, card-index cabinets, duplicating machine and photostat or electrostat machine. All these should be got properly dusted and kept in well-running condition all the time. These machines should be rapped with a cover while closing the office and all the switches should be got off. Proper servicing arrangements be made and a proper record of them be retained by the private secretary. The printed forms should be properly grouped and arranged separately on racks.

Reminder-diary

One should never rely on the memory, rather keep everything in black and white. A reminder diary is also called a due date diary in which separate pages are allotted for each respective date. Whenever follow-up action at a future date is desired, the same is diarised in this diary at the page of concerned date. Suppose some letter is written today, of which the reply is required within seven days. In the reminder-diary, on the seventh day, from the date hereof, the number of letter as well as file number is recorded. On that day, if reply is not received, a reminder may be issued for expediting reply. Suppose the reply is received, then we make a notation in the diary on that date that reply received. Everyday, this is referred to and the concerned files are taken out in order to ensure compliance. A reminder-diary is a usefeul tool for the private secretary for taking follow-up action.

Dak Distribution

The day of the private secretary starts with the mail or letters received in the office. It is one of the important tasks of a private secretary to ensure that all dak received during the day is properly opened, recorded, distributed and necessary action taken on each letter. When the dak or letters are received—whether through post office or messenger service or any other means—the following *process* be followed :—

1. The different types of letters like personal letters, registered letters and ordinary letters should be separately kept.

2. Except personal and or confidential envelopes, open all the envelopes, with the help of an office knife or by using the letter opening machine. Confidential envelopes should not be opened unless and until authorised by the employer. Generally, a senior private secretary is authorised to open confidential envelopes also While opening envelopes, care should be taken that the envelope should not be pierced in any manner but carefully from one corner so that the content remains safe and are not mutilated. In bigger offices, where the number of letters is large, the work of opening envelopes may be entrusted to a peon or messenger but the work should be got done in the presence of private secretary bimself/herself so that the contents are kept intact and safe.

3. Take out the letters, papers, documents etc. from the respective envelope and pin up together with the envelope. At first instance, the envelope covers should not be destroyed, unless and otherwise not required for verification.

4. Sort out the entire dak into main categories and arrange them on priority basis.

5. Affix the 'Dak Received' rubber-stamp on each and every letter received, but not on the documents like cheques, drafts, bills etc. Still, the care should be taken that the receipt stamp be put on on the letter either in the blank space available on top left corner in such a manner that the matter is not disfigured or distorted.

6. Record all the letters received in office in a separate register called the 'Inward Mail' or 'Dak Register.' In many organisations, only those letters which are received through registered post are recorded in this register and not the other letters. As a matter of principle and practice, all letters whether received by registered or ordinary mail, be recorded invariably.

7. Each letter received should be carefully read and contents scrutinized by the private secretary. If possible, helpful notes or markings may also be made in the margin or on a separate slip of paper annexed thereto. Some letters are for information only. Write the words 'seen and file' in the margin for taking boss's initials on them.

8. After recording in register, now keep all the letters in a separate cover or folder marked 'Dak Received'. The urgent or important letters be placed at top followed by others in sequence or priority. A slip may also be affixed on important letters, marking urgent etc. so that the boss's attention might be attracted toward them on priority basis.

9. Seek your boss's instructions for disposing of all the letters and record the action taken separately in the register.

Since much of the office work of a private secretary pertains dealing with the dak received, it is necessary that the private secretary should gain sufficient efficiency in it.

Filing and Indexing

A private seeretary has also to organise the filing and indexing systems, so that there is no problem while keeping the records and while locating any paper or document. In this connection, there are *two important aspects* : (i) The private secretary should familiarise herself/himself with the existing filing system and (ii) set up a new filing system for her secretarial work.

For knowing the existing filing system in the organisation, the private secretary should identify himself/herself with the system of classification and arrangement of files.

It may be noted here that particularly for the numerical classification, an index is required to be prepared and the private secretary should ensure that proper index is parpared and kept at a place easily accessible to him/her. Generally a copy of index of files duly typed is displayed at the desk of the private secretary below the table-glass so that the reference to it becomes easy and convenient.

So far as filing methods equipments are concerned, there are spike or wire files, box files, horizontal, vertical, suspended, open shelf or macrofilming. Depending upon the requirements of the organisation and the volume of work, a suitable filing method or equipment may be selected or the existing method be continued.

However, for organising the private secretary should take following steps :—

1. Take complete stock of all records, papers and documents etc. by noting the type of records, period of preservation and the equipment used.

2. Make an analysis of records by looking into the frequency with which the records are taken out and retrieved as well as the

practical use and legal requirements.

3. Arrange to keep away such records which are not workable and are obsolete.

4. Arrange the permanent records like Memorandum, Articles of Association, By-laws and Regulations, Lease Agreement etc. separately.

5. Prepare a list of dead files strictly in accordance with the instructions laid down in your Organisation's procedure book or manual and arrange to send them to records room or store.

6. Prepare a fresh list of all existing or live files in accordance with the convenience or as per procedure laid under procedure book.

As for setting up a new filing system for private secretary's own secretarial work, he/she should develop the right system. First of all, divide the entire secretarial work into the main catagories and then subdivide the main catagories into different sub-groups. The personal files of staff and others should be separated and may be arranged either namewise or numerically as convenient and practical. Other files, should be grouped as per any of the systems of classification as discussed earlier. Besides it, note down to keep some folders into your personal custody and for ready reference. These folders may consist of your who's who, information about your own organisation, collection of material and references useful for the office, form letters, copies of some important routine letters earlier dictated by your boss and frequently used in office. All these are helpful materials for efficiently discharging your routine official duties and necessary so that you could refer to them easily at the point of need without wasting your valuable time.

It is all the more necessary that a private secretary should know well as to what is contained in a particular file or folder. He/she should familiarise himself/herself with different files by handling them personally. Even he/she should be in a position to identify different files or folders by colour, bulk, design etc. All this can be done by handling files by self for sometime in the beginning, inserting papers, referring to them, retrieving them into the filing cabinets. An initial practice, and exercise would make the things smoother for himself/herself.

Here are some golden rules which a private secretary should observe :—

1. Don't allow your drawers or trays to overload with papers meant for filing. Make it a habit to file papers regularly either your-

self, if the office is small, or with the help of some messenger, peon or Daftri.

2. Never file the papers in a hochpoch manner. Arrange them datewise. Also keep the copy of reply with the original letter filed.

3. Punch the paper, to be filed, by taking a margin from the middle point of paper, rather make it two-fold to take the exact place of punching. Similar papers be punched together and filed together.

4. Do not allow more than enough papers to be retained in a single folder. The folder should not be bulky otherwise it is difficult to handle. Prepare another folder immediately as soon as the present folder is exhausted to its capacity. The number of the folder be mentioned on the second folder made in continuation to the eariler one. Always remember to put the date from which the seɔond folder of the same file number commences.

5. Follow the system of classification and arrangement of files which is already devised and the papers be filed strictly in accordance with it. Otherwise the papers may be misfiled.

6. Keep a check on the movement of file to and from your office. Make a proper note when the file moves out and take proper care when the file is received.

7. Before inserting any paper into the file, take care to look at the antecedents in order to ensure whether the present paper which you are filing, is relevant to this file or not.

8. While preparing a new file, do not forget to note it down in your index of files, otherwise it might create problem for you in future.

9. For cross references, i.e. one paper pertaining to two or more folders, do not forget to make a mention at both the places, otherwise it would be difficult for you to refer to such papers.

10. In many organisations, all the papers put in file, are serially numbered for the purpose of control and check. If so, do not forget to put the new serial number to a new paper filed. Do not leave it for another time.

11. Wherever necessary, put flaps or slips of different colours for important paper in the file. This factilitates drawing immediately the attention of your boss and reference becomes easy and quick.

However, in bigger Organisations, the private secretary rather a senior private secretary is provided with subordinate staff or assistants to cope with the work. The private secretary, at such places, may not do the work himself/herself but ensure that the work is carried out properly by guiding and instructing the subordinate staff on the abovementioned lines. In smaller offices, however, the private secretary may do the work himself/herself and/or take the help of messengers or peons. The objective should be to complete the work well within time and in a proper manner.

HOW TO SUCCEED AND GROW IN YOUR JOB

A steno-typist or a junior Private Secretary has got enormous chances of getting promotions and reaching to the new heights. There is no limit to which one can progress and grow in his/her job. There was a time when a typist, steno-typist or junior private secretary was not given any chance of promotion in the same or the other organisation but, of late, it has been realized that an outstanding steno-typist or secretary has got comparatively more knowledge of speaking, drafting, office procedures & methods, correspondence, filing and other aspects of office routine and he/she can successfully cope with it as an officer or executive. In the present-day world, there are living examples of secretaries or stenos getting quicker promotions inside the Organisation or elsewhere.

In order to achieve quick higher promotions, a private secretary should be on the path of progress in his/her own job and should try to learn and practice as much as possible. The knowledge and experience gained in practical business life—both are assets to a person for reaching to the newer heights. Primarily we should attain perfection in our existing job and then aspire for higher ones. As soon as one reaches at the upper level, the more is the need for general expertise and efficiency all-round which one can gain by more and more reading as well as by working hard and assuming more responsibilities. We should exercise getting along with other people on good terms in order to have smooth sailing and for getting favours from them.

For the purpose of achieving success and promotion your job, the following things should be remembered :—

Continue Your Studies

Generally the persons take up a job or service after passing ten plus two, matriculation, higher secondary or graduation. Many of them also undertake the courses in secretarial practice or stenography conducted by various Institutions. Still, for taking up promotion, it is necessary that one should be either a graduate or post-graduate or holding some recognised technical qualifications. It has been observed that persons, who aspire for higher promotions, continue their education in any field of their specialisation in order to make sound their educational background. It is advisable that you should continue your studies even during the course of your taking up job or service till such time that you reach to some higher level of education by taking up morning, evening or correspondence course etc.

Reading Daily Newspapers, Magazines and Periodicals

As some one has said, "Reading makes a perfect man and writing an exact man......", the same thing holds true in your case also. You should go on reading and reading to widen your horizon. The following materials for reading are suggested :—

1. Daily Newspapers—Hindi, English or in any other language.
2. Magazines & Periodicals e.g. Competition Success Review, Career & Competition; India To-day or others giving the latest developments in the nation and also at the international level.
3. Autobiographies—of great persons.
4. Year Books.
5. Entertaining Travel Books.
6. House Magazines, Journals etc.

By reading the above said materials, you can keep abreast with the latest economic & political developments & make your general knowledge uptodate. Whenever the time permits, as a private secretary, you should adopt the habit of reading. The Biographies and Autobiographies give you an inspiration to success in the career. Reading gives more and more knowledge. Knowledge is power.

Honesty and Hard Work

Work is worship. Always put your mind and heart into the work. Do not wait for others to tell you. Find out for yourself what has to be done. Do it with your might because the things done by halves are never done right. By working hard, you can develop a self-confidence which is very necessary for any assignment entrusted to you. You should not be a clock-watcher all the time, rather think that your work is very important for you, your boss, your organisation and the nation.

Put your Special Skills or Talents into Practice

Everyone is borne with some special talent which can further be developed by practising or exercising. Try to develop them according to the circumstances prevailing around you. Try to adjust yourself with the time and surroundings. Whatever you know, the one way of developing is that you should make suggestions to your boss or the Organisation. You should not feel shy in telling anything you know and which you feel would be useful in business at any stage. Do not mind about the criticism and do the things from your inner conscience or from the core of your heart and whatever appeals to you. If you know anything special and do not tell to your boss, you won't develop and you won't improve upon. See the things from the practical point of view and, wherever possible, use them in the practical life.

Know your Own Organisation

For getting success in your career, it is necessary that you should know fully-well about your own Organisation. Who's who, how the things are carried on and in what manner. Do not confine yourself to your own department or section—know something more of your organisation. Whenever time permits, visit others in the organisation and try to know more and more about your own Organisation. This would help you in getting the things done without any difficulty and your boss would also be happy. At the point of need, you can utilise the things for your own purpose also.

Assume Extra Responsibility

You should not be coward or fearful. Try to take up all sorts of works, particularly those which involve challenge or new dimensions. Whatever is given to you, do not restrict yourself to that. Try to take up more responsibility on your shoulders. Take lesson from your boss and see that he is assuming a greater responsibility and you can also do that. It would give more avenues and self-confidence. Just as we say, 'Risk is profit and profit is risk' similarly the more responsibility you assume, the more are the chances of your promotion and prosperity.

Get Along with People

It is also a key to success that you do not keep yourself aloof with the world, rather try to mix up with all sorts of people in all walks of life. This gives you an opportunity to learn from them. You must remember that all persons are not alike. They have different temperaments, habits and ways. While you are amongst people, you would try to learn tact and how to deal with them. Keep on good terms with all of them. You have not to loose your temper and maintain patience. Man is for man. You should be courteous and polite with all the people but, at the same time, you should be tactful and fair. Either in your own office, organisation or outside office. It is always advisable that you should get along with all sorts of people. Make them your good friends. It would help you in working and getting the things done through them.

Thoughtful Action

Whenever you are going to do anything, give a thought to it. Think before you do. In case anything is done without thoroughly thinking about, it would be a mere wastage of your energies and time and many a time the results may also be horrible. It is applicable to all things of life—whether you are typing, drafting, filing, talking to someone or doing anything for that matter. In case you adopt the habit of first thinking and then doing, it would save you from many troubles and at the same time bringing strength in you.

Though it is said that much depends upon your own luck, yet there are no two opinions about the fact that if you work hard with sincerity & honesty on the right lines, the success would come *to you some day* or the other. It might become late but not never. Therefore, a private secretary should go on working on the right lines with honesty, devotion, dignity & honour, the success is bound to be there. As the line of stenography or private secretaryship is the best now-a-days to get into some career, one should do this and do not become complacent with the existing job or work. Find out the new opportunities of progress and strive to achieve them. There is no end to what height one can reach in life. The best way is the right guidance and strong will.

QUESTIONS

1. Discuss the qualities of an outstanding private secretary ? What makes the personality of the private secretary ?
2. Describe the importance of dress, appearance, manners and etiquettes for an outstanding executive secretary.
3. Who is a 'Boss' ? What does he expect from his private secretary ? Discuss the secretarial participation in the Boss's business life .
4. What are telephone manners ? What important points